Uncertainty in Comparative Law and Legal History

Laws are imposed on facts. But what is the law to do when its rules for establishing facts do not—because they cannot—produce a satisfactory answer? Scenarios that raise this intractable uncertainty problem have been treated as isolated concerns, but are in fact endemic across legal systems. They can cross jurisdictional and doctrinal boundaries, have recurred throughout history, and demand creative thinking from those faced with them. This book explores the law's understandings of and responses to such situations from a comparative historical perspective. It investigates how the law has framed these most difficult problems of uncertainty; dealt with uncertainty's often unclear boundaries; and developed a broad range of different responses to solve or avoid it, across doctrine, time, and jurisdiction. The work examines a selection of key uncertainty problems across private law as elements of a singular uncertainty issue endemic in legal systems. This analysis will be of interest to historians and comparatists, but also to doctrinal, theoretical, and other scholars and practitioners. The analysis leaves us better informed and better equipped for dealing with future scenarios where uncertainty arises, including insights beyond national and doctrinal confines.

Andrew J. Bell is a Lecturer in Law at the University of Bristol, UK, and a Fellow of the European Centre of Tort and Insurance Law.

Joanna McCunn is a Senior Lecturer in Law at the University of Bristol, UK.

Transforming Legal Histories

This book series showcases work which takes a historical approach to question understandings about law. This approach places today's substantive law in its context, enabling an understanding of social and legal change and the complex relationship between change and continuity. It is designed to place the historical study of law at the heart of the law curriculum. The reach of the series is not limited in time or space, producing books that cover a wide range of jurisdictions and periods. The editorial board welcome proposals which engage with a general audience in relevant legal and non-legal fields including where appropriate, a student readership.

Series Editors
Russell Sandberg
Lydia Hayes
Katie Richards
Sharon Thompson

Titles in this series:

Subversive Legal History
A Manifesto for the Future of Legal Education
Russell Sandberg

Law and the Medieval Village Community
Reinvigorating Historical Jurisprudence
Lorren Eldridge

Uncertainty in Comparative Law and Legal History
Known Unknowns
Edited by Andrew J. Bell and Joanna McCunn

For more information about this series, please visit: https://www.routledge.com/Transforming-Legal-Histories/book-series/LAWHISTORY

Uncertainty in Comparative Law and Legal History

Known Unknowns

Edited by Andrew J. Bell and Joanna McCunn

Routledge
Taylor & Francis Group

LONDON AND NEW YORK

First published 2025
by Routledge
4 Park Square, Milton Park, Abingdon, Oxon OX14 4RN

and by Routledge
605 Third Avenue, New York, NY 10158

Routledge is an imprint of the Taylor & Francis Group, an informa business

British Library Cataloguing-in-Publication Data
A catalogue record for this book is available from the British Library

Library of Congress Cataloging-in-Publication Data
Names: Bell, Andrew J. (Lecturer in law), editor. | McCunn, Joanna, editor.
Title: Uncertainty in comparative law and legal history: known unknowns / edited by Andrew J. Bell and Joanna McCunn.
Description: Abingdon, Oxon [UK]; New York, NY : Routledge, 2025.
Series: Transforming legal histories | Includes bibliographical references and index. | Summary: "Laws are imposed on facts. But what is the law to do when its rules for establishing facts do not-because they cannot-produce a satisfactory answer? Scenarios that raise this intractable uncertainty problem have been treated as isolated concerns, but are in fact endemic across legal systems. They can cross jurisdictional and doctrinal boundaries, have recurred throughout history, and demand creative thinking from those faced with them. This book explores the law's understandings of and responses to such situations from a comparative historical perspective. It investigates how the law has framed these most difficult problems of uncertainty; dealt with uncertainty's often unclear boundaries; and developed a broad range of different responses to solve or avoid it, across doctrine, time and jurisdiction. The work examines a selection of key uncertainty problems across private law as elements of a singular uncertainty issue endemic in legal systems. This analysis will be of interest to historians and comparatists, but also to doctrinal, theoretical and other scholars and practitioners. The analysis leaves us better informed and better equipped for dealing with future scenarios where uncertainty arises, including insights beyond national and doctrinal confines"—Provided by publisher.
Identifiers: LCCN 2024033822 (print) | LCCN 2024033823 (ebook) | ISBN 9781032873756 (hardback) | ISBN 9781032883908 (paperback) | ISBN 9781003537526 (ebook)
Subjects: LCSH: Comparative law–Philosophy. | Uncertainty. | Intangible property. | Law–History. | Legal certainty.
Classification: LCC K552.U53 2025 (print) | LCC K552 (ebook) | DDC 340/.201–dc23/eng/20240724
LC record available at https://lccn.loc.gov/2024033822
LC ebook record available at https://lccn.loc.gov/2024033823

ISBN: 978-1-032-87375-6 (hbk)
ISBN: 978-1-032-88390-8 (pbk)
ISBN: 978-1-003-53752-6 (ebk)

DOI: 10.4324/9781003537526

Typeset in Galliard
by Deanta Global Publishing Services, Chennai, India

Contents

List of Contributors   *vii*
Preface   *viii*
List of Abbreviations   *x*

1   **Known unknowns: Uncharted waters**   1
ANDREW J. BELL AND JOANNA MCCUNN

PART 1
Life and death   23

2   **'In the beginning': Dealing with 'unknowns' at the start of life**   25
GWEN SEABOURNE

3   ***Commorientes*: Deaths, disasters, disappearances**   44
ANDREW J. BELL

4   **The subtle conclusion: Epistemic uncertainty and law at the end of life**   74
C.P. MCGRATH

PART 2
Causation and loss   101

5   **Causal uncertainty in tort law: The special case of mesothelioma**   103
KEN OLIPHANT

 6 Known unknowns: Loss of a chance and intractable
    connections   128
    SAMANTHA SCHNOBEL AND JUDITH SKILLEN

 7 Quantifying or avoiding the unknown? Damages for
    future lost earnings in tortious personal injury cases   153
    DAVID MESSNER-KREUZBAUER

PART 3
Meanings and intentions   183

 8 Contractual interpretation and *ad hominem*
    rules of construction   185
    JOANNA MCCUNN

 9 Unmixing intangible assets   206
    BENJAMIN DOUGLAS AND LORENZO MANISCALCO

PART 4
Broader perspectives on law and uncertainty   237

10 A spectrum of uncertainty   239
    MATTHEW DYSON

11 Known unknowns in Roman law: The second chapter
    of the *lex Aquilia*   259
    DAVID IBBETSON

PART 5
Conclusions   275

12 Known unknowns: Tracing a map   277
    ANDREW J. BELL AND JOANNA MCCUNN

    Index   *321*

Contributors

Andrew J. Bell, University of Bristol, UK

Benjamin Douglas, University College London, UK

Matthew Dyson, University of Oxford, UK

David Ibbetson, University of Cambridge, UK

Lorenzo Maniscalco, University of Bologna, Italy

Joanna McCunn, University of Bristol, UK

C.P. McGrath, King's College London, UK

David Messner-Kreuzbauer, Institute for European Tort Law of the Austrian Academy of Sciences and the University of Graz, Austria

Ken Oliphant, University of Bristol, UK

Gwen Seabourne, University of Bristol, UK

Samantha Schnobel, University of Birmingham, UK

Judith Skillen, University of Nottingham, UK

Preface

This collection is the product of a project first conceived in late 2018. It has since benefitted from the kindness and support of many.

We are grateful, firstly, for many opportunities to present a preliminary study and develop our ideas. These include the British Legal History Conference and the Society of Legal Scholars Annual Conference in 2019, and a *Juristenrunde* at ETL/ECTIL in Vienna. We thank attendees at those events for their interest and engagement.

The symposium that kickstarted the main project was hosted by the Centre for Law and History Research at the University of Bristol and funded by the Society of Legal Scholars' Small Projects and Events Fund. The discussions there proved immensely valuable in developing the project and bringing this collection together. We thank both organisations, as well as attendees and our session chairs: Paula Giliker, Chathuni Jayathilaka, Catherine Kelly, Andreas Televantos, and Jeffrey Thomson. We are also grateful to Katie McCay, who contributed invaluably as a research assistant, and to David Foster and Emily Gordon, who presented at our symposium and helped lay the foundations for the work. This volume would also not have resulted from that event without the kindness and advice of Ann-Christin Maak-Scherpe.

We are extremely grateful for the support and advice of our publisher, Routledge; the editors of the Transforming Legal Histories series; and their anonymous reviewers.

Our gratitude also belongs to the institutions that supported us along the way, and the inspiring communities of scholars they represent: the University of Bristol Law School and ETL/ECTIL in Vienna. Among our colleagues and friends, we would like in particular to thank Shreya Atrey, Alan Bogg, Peter Dunne, Paula Giliker, Chathuni Jayathilaka, Ernst Karner, Helmut Koziol, Yin Harn Lee, Kasia Ludwichowska-Redo, David Messner-Kreuzbauer, Ken Oliphant, Gwen Seabourne, Jeffrey Thomson, and Katherine Wade. Thanks are also due to the Max Planck Institute for Comparative and International Private Law, where Andrew spent a valuable research visit, supported by a scholarship.

A special note of thanks goes, finally, to Toby Boncey. His patient tolerance whilst coffee, cake, and anecdotes on the Electronic Communications

Code were inconsiderately paused to thrash out our study's early terms made everything possible.

The Editors
Bristol

Abbreviations

A –	Atlantic Reporter
ABGB[year] –	*Allgemeines bürgerliches Gesetzbuch*, General Civil Code (Austria)
AC –	Law Reports, Appeal Cases (3rd Series)
A.c.P. –	*Archiv für die civilistische Praxis*
AF –	Ames Foundation
All ER –	All England Law Reports
	(Comm.) – (Commercial Cases)
ALR[year] –	*Allgemeines Landrecht*, General State Law (Prussia)
ALRC –	Australian Law Reform Commission
App. Cas. –	Law Reports, Appeal Cases (Second Series)
App. Milano –	*Corte di Appello di Milano*, Milan Court of Appeal
B & Ad. –	Barnewall & Adolphus' King's Bench Reports
B & C –	Barnewall & Cresswell's King's Bench Reports
BCC –	British Company Cases
Beav. –	Beavan's Rolls Court Reports
Bell CC –	Bell's Crown Cases, Reserved
BGB[year] -	*Bürgerliches Gesetzbuch*, Civil Code (Germany)
BGH –	*Bundesgerichtshof*, Federal Supreme Court (Germany)
BGHZ –	*Entscheidungen des Bundesgerichtshofes in Zivilsachen*
BL Add. MS –	British Library Additional Manuscript
Bl. Comm. –	W. Blackstone, *Commentaries on the Laws of England*, Clarendon Press, Oxford 1765–1769
Bos. & P –	Bosanquet & Puller's Common Pleas Reports
Bro. PC –	Brown's Cases in Parliament
Broun –	Broun's Justiciary Reports
Bull. civ. –	*Bulletin civil de la Cour de Cassation*
Bulst. –	Bulstrode's King's Bench Reports
Burr. Rep. –	Burrow's King's Bench Reports
BW –	*Burgerlijk Wetboek*, Civil Code (Netherlands)
C & M –	Carrington & Marshman's Nisi Prius Reports
C & P –	Carrington & Payne's Nisi Prius Reports
Cal. 3d –	California Reports (3rd series)

Cal. Rptr. 2d –	California Reporter (2nd series)
Camp. –	Campbell's Nisi Prius Cases
Cass. civ. –	*Cour de cassation, chambre civile*, Court of Cassation, Civil Chamber (France)
Cass. com. –	*Cour de cassation, chambre commerciale, financière et économique*, Court of Cassation, Commercial, Financial and Economic Chamber (France)
Cass. req. –	*Cour de cassation, chambre des requêtes*, Court of Cassation, Chamber of Requests (France)
CC[year] –	*Code civil*, Civil Code (France)
CC (Greece) –	Civil Code (Greece)
CCGO[1797] –	*Codex civilis pro Galicia Orientali*, West Galician Code (Austrian West Galicia)
Ch. –	Law Reports, Chancery Division (3rd Series)
Ch. D –	Law Reports, Chancery Division (2nd Series)
CLJ –	*Cambridge Law Journal*
Cmnd. –	Command Paper, UK Parliament
Co. Litt. –	E. Coke, *The First Part of the Institutes of the Laws of England, or, A Commentary upon Littleton*, Societie of Stationers, London 1628
Colles –	Colles' Cases in Parliament
Conv. –	*Conveyancer and Property Lawyer*
CPR –	Civil Procedure Rules
Cr. App. R –	Criminal Appeal Reports
Crim. LR –	*Criminal Law Review*
Cro. –	Croke's King's Bench Reports
	Car. – (Charles I)
	Eliz. – (Elizabeth I)
	Jac. – (James I)
CUP –	Cambridge University Press
Curt. –	Curteis' Ecclesiatical Reports
D –	Dunlop, Bell & Murray's Reports, Second Series Session Cases
De GM & G –	De Gex, Macnaghten & Gordon's Chancery Reports
Den. CC –	Denison & Pearce's Crown Cases Reserved
Dick. –	Dicken's Chancery Reports
DJ –	*Deutsche Justiz*
Dods. –	Dodson's Admiralty Reports
East –	East's Term Reports, King's Bench
EEC –	European Economic Community
Env. LR –	Environmental Law Reports
EWCA –	Court of Appeal of England and Wales
	Civ. – (Civil Division)
	Crim. – (Criminal Division)
EWFC –	England and Wales Family Court

EWHC –	High Court of England and Wales
	(Ch.) – (Chancery Division)
	(Fam.) – (Family Court)
	(Pat.) – (Patents Court)
	(QB) – (Queen's Bench Division)
Ex. D –	Law Reports, Exchequer Division
F –	Federal Reporter
F 2d –	Federal Reporter (2nd series)
F & F –	Foster & Finlayson's Nisi Prius Reports
F Supp. –	Federal Supplement
Fam. –	Law Reports, Family Division
Gaz. Pal. –	*Gazette du Palais*
Giff. –	Giffard's Chancery Reports
GP –	*Gesetzgebungsperiode*, legislative session
H & C –	Hurlstone & Coltman's Exchequer Reports
H & N –	Hurlstone & Norman's Exchequer Reports
H Bl. –	Henry Blackstone's Common Pleas Reports
Hagg. Ecc. –	Haggard's Ecclesiatical Reports
HC Deb. –	House of Commons Official Report (Hansard)
HCA –	High Court of Australia
HKK/[section author] –	M. Schmoeckel, J. Rückert and R. Zimmermann (eds), *Historisch-kritischer Kommentar zum BGB*
HL Cas. –	Clark & Finnelly's House of Lords Reports New Series
HL Deb. –	House of Lords Official Report (Hansard)
HMSO –	Her Majesty's Stationery Office
Hunt. MS El. –	Huntington Library Ellesmere Manuscript
ICLQ –	*International & Comparative Law Quarterly*
IR –	Irish Reports
IX ZR –	*IX. Zivilsenat des Bundesgerichtshof*, Ninth Civil Senate of the Federal Supreme Court (Germany)
J & H –	Johnson & Hemming's Chancery Reports
J Eq. –	*Journal of Equity*
JCL –	*Journal of Comparative Law*
JCP –	*Juris-classeur périodique* (*La semaine juridique*)
JETL –	*Journal of European Tort Law*
JLH –	*Journal of Legal History*
JP –	Justice of the Peace Reports
JPIL –	*Journal of Personal Injury Law*
JZ –	*JuristenZeitung*
KB –	Law Reports, King's Bench
KBB[edition]/[section author] –	H. Koziol, P. Bydlinski, and R. Bollenberger (eds), *Kurzkommentar zum ABGB*
KIR –	Knight's Industrial Reports

Law Com. –	Law Commission of England and Wales
	CP No. – Consultation Paper
	No. – Report
Law Rep. Eq. –	Law Reports (1st series), Equity Cases
Lew. CC –	Lewin's Crown Cases Reserved
Litt. –	Littleton's Common Pleas Reports
Lloyd's Rep. –	Lloyd's Law Reports
	Med. – Medical
	IR – Insurance & Reinsurance
LMCLQ –	*Lloyd's Maritime and Commercial Law Quarterly*
LQR –	*Law Quarterly Review*
LR Ch. App. –	Law Reports (1st series), Chancery Appeal Cases
LR –	Law Reports
	CCR – Crown Cases Reserved
	CP – Common Pleas
	Eq. – Equity Cases
	PC – Privy Council Appeal Cases
	QB – Queen's Bench (1st Series)
M & S –	Maule & Selwyn's King's Bench Reports
M & W –	Meeson & Welsby's Exchequer Reports
Med. LR –	Medical Law Reports
Mer. –	Merivale's Chancery Reports
Misc. 2d –	Miscellaneous Reports (2nd series)
MLR –	*Modern Law Review*
Mood. CC –	Moody's Crown Cases Reserved
Mor. –	Morison's Dictionary of Decisions
MünchKomm[edition] / [section author] –	*Münchener Kommentar zum Bürgerlichen Gesetzbuch*
NE –	North Eastern Reporter
	2d – (2nd series)
NILQ –	*Northern Ireland Legal Quarterly*
NJW –	*Neue Juristische Wochenschrift*
NSWLR –	New South Wales Law Reports
NSWSC –	New South Wales Supreme Court
NW 2d –	North Western Reporter (2nd series)
OGH –	*Oberster Gerichtshof*, Supreme Court of Justice (Austria)
OHLE –	*The Oxford History of the Laws of England*, OUP, Oxford 2003–present
OJLS –	*Oxford Journal of Legal Studies*
OLG –	*Oberlandesgericht*, Higher Regional Court (Germany)
ONCA –	Court of Appeal for Ontario
ONSC –	Ontario Superior Court of Justice
OUP –	Oxford University Press

P –	Pacific Reporter
	2d– (2nd series)
P. Wms. –	Peere-Williams' Chancery & King's Bench Cases
Palandt[edition]/	*Palandt: Bürgerliches Gesetzbuch*
[section author] –	
PD –	Practice Direction
Peake –	Peake's Nisi Prius Reports
Phil. Ecc. –	Phillimore's Ecclesiastical Reports
PIQR –	Personal Injuries and Quantum Reports
Plow. –	Plowden's Reports
Prob. –	Law Reports (1st series), Probate
QB –	Law Reports, Queen's Bench (3rd Series)
QBD –	Law Reports, Queen's Bench Division
QCCA –	Court of Appeal of Quebec
R & R –	Russell & Ryan's Crown Cases Reserved
RD –	royal decree
Rev. jur. Ouest –	*Revue Juridique de l'Ouest*
RG –	*Reichsgericht*, Imperial Court of Justice (Germany)
RGZ –	*Entscheidungen des Reichsgerichts in Zivilsachen*
RJQ –	*Rapports Juridiques du Quebec*
RTR –	Road Traffic Reports
RvdW –	*Rechtspraak van de Week*
S. Ct. –	Supreme Court Reporter
Saxon BGB –	*Bürgerliches Gesetzbuch für das Königreich Sachsen*, Civil Code for the Kingdom of Saxony
Schwimann & Kodek	M. Schwimann & G. Kodek (eds), *ABGB*
ABGB[edition]/	*Praxiskommentar*
[section author] –	
SC –	Session Cases
	(HL) – House of Lords
SCC –	Supreme Court of Canada
Scot. Law Com. DP No. –	Scottish Law Commission, Discussion Paper
SCR –	Supreme Court Reports, Canada
SDNY –	United States District Court for the Southern District of New York
Seuff.A. –	*Seufferts Archiv*
SI –	Statutory Instrument
Sim. & St. –	Simons & Stuart's Vice Chancellor's Reports
SJ –	Solicitors' Journal
Staudinger BGB[edition]/	*J. von Staudinger's Kommentar zum BGB*
[section author] –	
Str. –	Strange's King's Bench Reports
STS –	*Sentencia Tribunal Supremo*, Supreme Court ruling (Spain)

Swin. –	Swinton's Justiciary Reports
T Raym. –	T Raymond's King's Bench and Common Pleas Reports
TFEU –	Treaty on the Functioning of the European Union
TLI –	*Trust Law International*
TLR –	Times Law Reports
TNA –	The National Archives (United Kingdom)
Torts LJ –	*Torts Law Journal*
TP[edition] / [section author] –	H. Thomas and H. Putzo (eds), *ZPO Kommentar*
Trib. civ. –	*Tribunal civil* (France)
UKPC –	United Kingdom Judicial Committee of the Privy Council
UKSC –	United Kingdom Supreme Court
Ves. –	Vesey Junior's Chancery Reports
VI ZR –	*VI. Zivilsenat des Bundesgerichtshof*, Sixth Civil Senate of the Federal Supreme Court (Germany)
West temp. Hard. –	West's Chancery Reports *tempore* Hardwicke
Wils. KB –	Wilson's King's Bench and Common Pleas Reports
WLR –	Weekly Law Reports
Y & CCC –	Younge & Collyer's Chancery Reports
YB [term] [regnal year] –	Year Books
ZEuP –	*Zeitschrift für Europäisches Privatrecht*
ZRG GA –	*Zeitschrift der Savigny-Stiftung für Rechtsgeschichte: Germanistische Abteilung*
ZRG RA –	*Zeitschrift der Savigny-Stiftung für Rechtsgeschichte: Romanistische Abteilung*

1 Known unknowns

Uncharted waters

Andrew J. Bell and Joanna McCunn

1.1 Introduction

For millennia, the law has been confronted with a fundamental problem:

> Do not facts, in their very nature, precede laws? Is it not to them the creation and necessity of laws are owing? ... If laws, therefore, were made for facts, and not facts for laws, upon what principle of nature or reason are laws to create, presume, or distinguish betwixt facts unknown...?[1]

Laws are imposed on facts,[2] and legal systems have evidential rules for ascertaining them. But what is the law to do when it must resolve a dispute, yet its ordinary rules for establishing the truth cannot produce a satisfactory answer? We refer to relevant facts here as 'known unknowns': we are ignorant of a key fact, but aware of that ignorance. This volume's aim is to investigate how private law has framed and responded to known unknowns across doctrine, time, and jurisdiction.

We deploy the term 'intractable uncertainty' to designate our primary interest. Our precise concern is discussed in Section 1.2 but, briefly, involves problems that, at least to some extent or in some situations, go beyond an ordinary evidential problem in the sense of a simple failure of a party to adduce some necessary evidence. Our known unknowns are thus, partly, *unknowable* and create a special kind of problem that the law must confront. Often, a special solution is devised to resolve the impasse, perhaps by providing a tiebreaking rule or default answer.[3] Scenarios that raise this intractable uncertainty prob-

---

1 T.M. Shadwell (ed.), *The Posthumous Works of Charles Fearne*, Butterworth 1797, 61–62.
2 Cf. J.A. Jolowicz, '*Da mihi factum dabo tibi ius*: a problem of demarcation in English and French Law', *On Civil Procedure*, CUP 2009; J.A. Jolowicz, 'Factfinding: A comparative perspective' in D.L. Carey Miller and P.R. Beaumont (eds), *The Option of Litigating in Europe*, UK National Committee of Comparative Law 1993, 136; H.L. Ho, *A Philosophy of Evidence Law*, OUP 2008, 1–6.
3 Contrast the generalisation that all uncertainty about past fact in England is resolved by a balance-of-probabilities, all-or-nothing test in A. Burrows, 'Uncertainty about uncertainty: damages for loss of a chance' [2008] *JPIL* 31, 33.

DOI: 10.4324/9781003537526-1

lem can cross jurisdictional and doctrinal boundaries, have recurred throughout history, and demand creative thinking from those faced with them. For
these reasons alone, they are prime targets for comparative and historical study
beyond private law's usual doctrinal boundaries, and present a field offering
enormous potential variation and inspiration.

A clear example is the *commorientes* problem, arising where a sequence of
deaths must be known (e.g. for inheritance) but is unclear—perhaps because
the sequence is scientifically impossible to unpick (e.g. 'instantaneous' bombing deaths), or equally because of a simple lack of evidence (e.g. with missing persons). Our 'intractable uncertainty' problem spans those instances; the
variably unknowable parts make up the singular, intractable difficulty. Work
on the problem has produced various framings and special solutions across eras
and jurisdictions, warranting comparative-historical analysis.

In this investigation, we are interested, firstly, in how the law comes to
frame the problem of uncertainty and deal with its often-unclear boundaries.
In particular, we wish to understand when, how, and why a special problem
comes to be recognised and a special solution adopted. We are equally interested in instances where such a problem is not recognised, or is reasoned away
or around by a legal system. Secondly, we are interested in the solutions developed for these problems: their forms; the underlying principles and policies
that drive them; and how they develop over time.

The work emerged from a pilot analysis of two problems. The first is *commorientes*, as just described. The second problem arises if the meaning or effect
of contractual language is ambiguous. The intractable problem spans cases,
ill-distinguished and under-theorised, where there is an uncertainty that might
conceivably be resolved by liberal application of ordinary interpretive rules
and those where the meaning is undeniably beyond their assistance. Roman
law provides a certain impetus to this combination; in the legal compilations
of the Emperor Justinian, *commorientes* decisions are discussed intermittently
alongside contractual and testamentary interpretive questions throughout a
title on 'doubtful cases' (Digest 34.5).

The uncertainty issues raised extend well beyond those confines, however,
to many interesting scenarios. In truth, the problem of intractable uncertainty
pervades legal systems. Unfortunately, though, in modern discussions, these
known unknowns are largely viewed as isolated problems in their respective
doctrinal fields, obscuring an exciting connective thread across them. This in
turn creates twin risks: the law may adopt inconsistent approaches to them,
and may not grasp the range of solutions available when faced with new concerns of this kind. There is a risk of uncritical path dependence for legal systems faced with (apparently) new problems.[4]

4 J. Bell, 'Path Dependence and Legal Development' (2012–13) 87 *Tulane Law Review* 787,
791–92.

These risks matter. In societies driven by ever-more varied and complex interactions, using new technologies and undergoing rapid socio-economic changes, new uncertainty problems will keep arising and with increasing frequency.[5] This is already evident, for example, from the causal disputes dogging toxic tort and environmental litigation.[6] Yet despite their extensive interest and significance, few efforts are made to interrogate known unknowns as such.

Our project makes this leap to see intractable factual uncertainty as a long-standing, undivided problem endemic to legal systems. It illuminates the functional problem of uncertainty by examining, alongside one another and across jurisdictions, the historical framing and resolution of numerous problem areas. This comparative-historical approach enables us to canvas a wide range of potential responses to the problem; consider the coherence of those chosen; and help equip us for future instances.

In the following discussion, we define our general target in uncertainty; indicate some frameworks that define its borders; and explain both our methodology and our selections for areas to analyse within that broad field.

1.2 Definitions and conceptual background

Studying the relationship between facts and law opens Pandora's box: 'all the endless concerns of the humanities with knowledge, reality and reason are threatening to break in'.[7] We must start by defining, cautiously, in outline, our investigation's core terms and conceptual background. Our enterprise sits, and should be understood, against a backdrop which features numerous related and more-or-less easily distinguishable concepts.

1.2.1 Uncertainty

The central element of our investigation is the notion of 'uncertainty'. Uncertainty comes in numerous forms, and the relevant terminology is not always clear or consistent. Commentators speak inter alia of 'scientific',[8] 'episte

---

5 L.A. Franzoni, 'Liability Law under Scientific Uncertainty' (2017) 19 *American Law and Economics Review* 327, 327–28.

6 See e.g. ibid.; G. Le Moli et al., 'Whither the Proof? The progressive reversal of the burden of proof in environmental cases before international courts and tribunals' (2017) 8 *Journal of International Dispute Settlement* 644. Our chapter selections are discussed below; we omitted environmental harms given e.g. the prominence of causal issues, otherwise covered elsewhere.

7 W. Twining, *Rethinking Evidence*, 2nd ed., CUP 2006, 28.

8 A. Milon and R. Bouvet, 'Scientific Uncertainty in Courts. A France-Germany Comparative Perspective on Litigation Surrounding Hepatitis B Vaccination' (2019) 26 *European Journal of Health Law* 5.

mic'/'epistemological',[9] 'factual',[10] 'extreme',[11] 'complete',[12] and 'aleatoric'[13] uncertainties and 'irresolvable doubt',[14] but these can be used in different, incompatible ways. Similar variation exists in other languages; German-language texts refer inter alia to a fact's *Ungewissheit/Unsicherheit* (uncertainty),[15] its objective and subjective *Beweislosigkeit* (unprovability/'unprovenness'), or to *Zweifel* (doubt) over it,[16] and whether it is *aufklärbar* (clarifiable)[17] or *feststellbar/bestimmbar* (ascertainable).[18] In France, one might inter alia speak of *incertitude* in science or law,[19] *aléa/aléatoire*,[20] or *doute* (*sans fin*).[21] Reference to *non liquet* situations is also common in continental Europe, recalling a Roman procedural background where a judge could avoid decision by asserting the facts' insolubility.[22] Like others, this term is insufficiently clear for our purposes.[23] Indeed, imprecision in the subject-matter might make vague terminology inevitable.[24] As noted, we have chosen to deploy the term 'intractable uncertainty' in this work.

The following definitional observations organise and limit our analysis.

9 G. Turton, *Evidential Uncertainty in Causation in Negligence*, Hart 2016, 155.
10 D.E. Phillips, 'Loosening the law's bite: law, fact, and expert evidence in *R v JA* and *R v NS*' (2017) 21 *International Journal of Evidence & Proof* 242.
11 D. Beyleveld and R. Brownsword, 'Emerging Technologies, Extreme Uncertainty, and the Principle of Rational Precautionary Reasoning' (2012) 4 *Law, Innovation and Technology* 35.
12 G. Treitel, 'The Presumption of Death' (1954) 17 *MLR* 530, 534.
13 Le Moli et al., n. 6, 649; (also ibid.: 'interpretive and normative ambiguity').
14 Beyleveld/Brownsword, n. 11.
15 H. Koziol, *Österreichisches Haftpflichtrecht*, vol. II, 3rd ed., Jan Sramek 2018, A.2 no. 309.
16 M. Neumayr and S. Webhofer, 'Beweislastregeln und Zweifelsregeln im Erbrecht' in F.A. Schurr and M. Umlauft (eds), *Festschrift für Bernhard Eccher*, Verlag Österreich 2017.
17 Ibid., 765; Koziol, n. 15, A.2. no. 305.
18 *KBB*[5]/Karner, §1302.
19 P. le Tourneau (ed.), *Droit de la responsabilité et des contrats. Régimes d'indemnisation*, 11th ed., Dalloz 2017, nos. 2132.10, 2131.52.
20 L. Williatte-Pellitteri, *Contribution à l'élaboration d'un droit civil de l'aléa*, Doctoral Thesis: Lille 2, 2003.
21 K. Bellis, 'La personnalité juridique et le cas de l'absent: Le principe de l'unicité du patrimoine n'a pas dit son dernier mot' [2015] *Rev. jur. Ouest* 9, 26.
22 Cf. below 1.2.3.3.
23 E.g. it can be ambivalent between unknown/unknowable facts, and can describe ordinary evidential problems uncontroversially resolved by burden-of-proof rules: I. Giesen, 'The Burden of Proof and Other Procedural Devices in Tort Law', nos. 4, 10, and E. Karner, 'The Function of the Burden of Proof in Tort Law', no. 2, both in H. Koziol and B.C. Steininger (eds), *European Tort Law 2008*, Springer 2009.
24 Bellis, n. 21, 23.

1.2.1.1 Factual uncertainty

Uncertainty in legal rules can have many causes: ambiguous language, conflicting norms, questionable statutory validity, or a principle's unclear ambit.[25] Such legal uncertainty is often tied to the rule of law in jurisprudential discussions.[26] This is not, however, the uncertainty with which we are primarily concerned. We are not interested in the uncertainty of substantive law, but of the facts to which it applies. It may be clear what the legal consequences of certain facts would be but remain unclear whether those facts obtain, given an absence of evidence or conflicting or incoherent indications.[27]

It is difficult, however, to identify the precise boundary between legal and factual uncertainties; the law/fact distinction is a longstanding concern seen to cut to the heart of law's existence as an independent science.[28] Treatises on evidence may say 'no satisfactory definition of the term "fact" has been or perhaps can be given'; fact may be distinguishable from law, but, even then, not consistently.[29] One might imply an association with a strong separation of 'is' and 'ought', but even this can be recognised as a permeable, if guarded, boundary.[30] The facts as established by the court represent a critical bridge point,[31] as do 'legal facts' or '*juristische Tatsachen*' such as ownership.[32] The boundary between law and fact is thus not always stable across or within jurisdictions and periods. One practical example of such difficulties is the pleading of foreign law, which may be treated as fact or law, without necessarily equating it with ordinary facts or domestic law.[33]

---

25 T. Endicott, *Vagueness in Law*, OUP 2000, 7; H. Kelsen, *Reine Rechtslehre*, 2nd ed., Verlag Österreich 1960, 346–48.

26 See e.g. L. Fuller, *The Morality of Law*, 2nd ed., Yale University Press 1969; G. Radbruch, 'Der Zweck des Rechts' in A. Kaufmann (ed.), *Gustav Radbruch Gesamtausgabe*, vol. 3, C.F. Müller 1990; N. Cornu Thénard, 'The Legal Construction of the Fact, between Rhetoric and Roman Law' in C. Ando and W.P. Sullivan (eds), *The Discovery of the Fact*, University of Michigan Press 2020.

27 The relationship between legal and factual uncertainty is discussed further in Part 4 of this volume: see 1.3.3 below.

28 C. Ando, 'Introduction' in Ando/Sullivan, n. 26.

29 H.M. Malek et al. (eds), *Phipson on Evidence*, 20th ed., Sweet & Maxwell 2021, no. 1.11. Cf. Cornu Thénard, n. 26, 39–40; Ho, n. 2, 7–10; Jolowicz, 'Factfinding', n. 2, 135. For a practical judicial perspective—legal argument and fact-finding being mutually influential—e.g. R. Ormrod, 'Judges and the Processes of Judging' in I.R. Scott (ed.), *Jubilee Lectures Celebrating the Foundation of the Faculty of Law, University of Birmingham*, Wildy & Sons 1981, 189.

30 M. Potacs, 'The Fact of Norms' in N. Bersier Ladavac et al. (eds), *The Normative Force of the Factual*, Springer 2019; Cornu Thénard, n. 26, 39, 43; C. Jabloner, 'Der Sachverhalt im Recht' (2016) 71 *Zeitschrift für Öffentliches Recht* 199, 202–3.

31 Jabloner, n. 30.

32 TP^{89}/Reichold, vor §284, no. 13; le Tourneau, n. 19, no. 415.04.

33 T. Hartley, 'Pleading and Proof of Foreign Law: The Major European Systems Compared' (1996) 45 *ICLQ* 271, 272.

Interpretive questions are another borderline example. Classical rhetoric treated all interpretation as a question of fact,[34] but medieval jurists parcelled off statutory interpretation as a matter of law.[35] Modern French contractual interpretation is still seen as a factual question, since it fundamentally concerns the parties' intentions.[36] But German law regards it as a legal question, albeit one dependent on matters of fact.[37] The focus of this question can also turn procedural. English judges were said to answer questions of law and juries those of fact,[38] but juries have never really been responsible for all factual questions.[39] English law assigns a written contract's interpretation to the judge, the interpretation of a (partly) oral contract to the jury;[40] the distinction arose by historical accident from rules of pleading.[41] Continental jurisdictions have seen comparable points arise in the criminal context, once lay participants become involved and issues arise over separating factual and legal questions.[42]

The precise borderline of factual uncertainty is thus difficult to trace and it would be perilous to be very prescriptive about it within this volume. We include issues of interpretive uncertainty, since, on some views, questions about the meaning of private documents are factual questions.[43] However, it must be remembered that understandings of what exactly constitutes a fact or factual uncertainty will vary across eras and systems.

1.2.1.2 *Intractable, objective uncertainty*

We are interested, then, in factual uncertainty. We are also interested in *objective* factual uncertainty, not mere subjective ignorance. Oftentimes, facts are known to actors who refuse or are unable to reveal that knowledge. For example, in court parties may exercise a privilege (e.g. against self-incrimination) or even conceal facts (spoliation of evidence, *Beweisvereitelung*), as where the

---

34 C. Humfress, *Orthodoxy and the Courts in Late Antiquity*, OUP 2007, 116–17.

35 A. Giuliani, 'From Presumption to Interpretation' in F. Treggiari (ed.), *Giuristi dell'Università di Perugia*, Aracne 2010, 451–54.

36 C. Valcke, 'On Comparing French and English Contract Law: Insights from Social Contract Theory' (2009) 4 *JCL* 69, 72–77.

37 *Palandt*[78]/Ellenberger, §133, no. 29.

38 *Isaack v Clark* (1613) 2 Bulst. 306, 314. Today, the distinction is more between the judge qua fact-finder/arbiter of law: Malek et al., n. 29, no. 1.27.

39 J.B. Thayer, *A Preliminary Treatise on Evidence at the Common Law*, Little, Brown 1898, 185.

40 K. Lewison, *The Interpretation of Contracts*, 7th ed., Sweet & Maxwell 2020, no. 4.05.

41 A.W.B. Simpson, *A History of the Common Law of Contract: The Rise of the Action of Assumpsit*, 1st ed., OUP 1975, 197. English law remains ambivalent on whether the question is of fact or law: Valcke, n. 36, 78–86. Canadian contractual interpretation is a mixed question of fact/law: *Sattva Capital v Creston Moly* [2014] 2 SCR 633.

42 W. Ernst, *Rechtserkenntnis durch Richtermehrheiten*, Mohr Siebeck 2016, 152–53, 184, 211–14; cf. Jabloner, n. 30, 209–13.

43 See e.g. L. Shmilovits, *Legal Fictions in Private Law*, CUP 2022, 96–97.

German BGH faced a tax adviser's refusal to deliver up documents.[44] Here, the court appreciates that it is ignorant of a fact, but that fact is not in itself uncertain in our sense. It is known, albeit not subjectively to the court or other parties.[45] In the BGH, this distinction came to bite: the lower court had treated the case as an objectively uncertain, insoluble (*non liquet*) scenario; the BGH emphasised the need to account for the defendant's knowledge and role in obscuring the facts.[46] Responses to such cases may create additional rules to encourage cooperation and alternative bases for establishing the necessary facts.[47]

In other cases, facts are objectively uncertain, unknown to all involved, but only because insufficient evidential trace is recovered. Where, for example, death or labour's strains mean a mother cannot disclose the sequence of her twins' births, the law confronts an uncertainty.[48] Other witnesses' evidence could resolve this easily. Uncertainty in this sense is still not our most-central focus, though it forms a critical penumbra around the very core.

We are primarily interested in problems of *intractable* uncertainty: a fact is not simply not-established on the evidence, but is, at least sometimes, understood to be *incapable* of being so established. This is seen with the aetiology of mesothelioma, for example, where courts have faced a complete scientific inability to identify which of multiple sources of asbestos exposure has provided a critical disease-causing fibre.[49] There is here what might be termed an epistemic uncertainty as to cause.[50]

Our focus on intractability does not mean, though, that we intend only to isolate such epistemic forms of uncertainty, as contrasted with a simpler lack of factual evidence. Dividing lines between these categories can be blurred, if not wholly elusive. Consequently, any strict separation at times produces arbitrariness or injustice, with some scenarios looking so similar in principle that different treatment appears problematic. It is often difficult to distinguish satisfactorily between a lack of evidence on the facts; a lack of present science to provide such facts; and the impossibility of ever, even with conceivable

---

44 BGH, 27 September 2001, IX ZR 281/00, see *NJW* 2002, 825.

45 Cf. the distinction between real-world facts and an established fact pattern: Jabloner, n. 30. Contrast a testator's first-hand knowledge of their intentions, unavailable to later courts; likewise, a common intention/meaning of contracting parties is a thing apart from their individual knowledge as litigants.

46 *NJW* 2002, 825, 827. Contrast also non-culpable generation of an uncertainty, or causing uncertainty through prior acts.

47 Like *Armory v Delamirie*'s *contra spoliatorem* presumption: (1721) Str. 505, 505.

48 Digest 34.5.10.1; I 1 §§14–16, ALR[1794].

49 K. Oliphant, 'Causal uncertainty in tort law: the special case of mesothelioma', this volume, 5.1.1.

50 A fact does not, though, need to be impenetrable to any existing science—merely perceived so by the decision-maker.

future science, being able to generate them.[51] For example, the increasing sophistication of forensic techniques allows deaths to be sequenced, where this was previously impossible.[52] As that scientific boundary moves, the boundary of the intractably uncertain moves too. This process is not predictable, however: improved scientific data may undermine previous certainties, and any individual case will still turn arbitrarily on matters such as the precise time of the bodies' discovery.[53]

In more extreme examples, the problems can stack up, with the circumstances that present an uncertainty obscuring the nature of the same. Suppose a ship disappears, presumed sunk, without our knowing the cause. We may have an evidential uncertainty about the cause, but also be unsure whether, were the cause known, the sequence of the crew's (presumed) deaths would be subject to evidential uncertainty (conceivably resolvable with physical/witness evidence) or epistemic uncertainty (irresolvable).

Given these sometimes blurred and unconvincing boundaries, many legal rules apply across any such divisions. Some *commorientes* rules, for example, apply across scenarios involving all of these forms of uncertainty—for instance, imposing a uniform default rule for deaths occurring within a given period, regardless of the (non-)availability of evidence or proof as to their sequence.[54] One key issue addressed by this volume is thus how the law recognises and circumscribes uncertainty problems. We are interested in cases where an uncertainty is singled out for special treatment by the law, and in how it relates to other, more-or-less intractable forms. Concomitantly, we are interested in cases where a potential intractable uncertainty is not recognised by the law at all.

1.2.1.3 Ex post uncertainty

Objective, intractable, factual uncertainty furthermore affects us from multiple temporal perspectives. We may be uncertain as to what *has* happened; *is* happening; *will* happen; or *would or might have* happened in a hypothetical alternative timeline. The law must generally be equipped to deal with all these variations, though only some are relevant presently.

Regulatory solutions are often provided for problems of *ex ante* uncertainty, with, for example, new technologies and environmental harms currently representing pressing issues for regulatory interventions. These seek to prevent and regulate potential future harms, frequently based on some version

---

51 Regarding the difficulty of predicting future advances, consider F. Pollock's prognosticating: *Principles of Contract at Law and in Equity*, 1st ed., Stevens and Sons 1876, 325.
52 A.J. Bell, '*Commorientes*: deaths, disasters, disappearances', this volume, 3.2.1.
53 Cf. e.g. *Scarle v Scarle* [2019] 4 WLR 119.
54 Bell, n. 52, 3.2.1.

of the 'precautionary principle'.[55] Various international instruments require, for example, that states take precautionary measures to prevent environmental degradation, even if there is a 'lack of full scientific certainty' about the harm.[56] By implementing such measures, the law responds to uncertain futures and unknown risks.

Again, however, our focus is elsewhere: we are primarily interested, not in regulatory rules responsive to *ex ante* concerns, but rules engaging after harm emerges. Regulatory responses are concerned with preventative action, but liability rules often seek to identify whether and how a harm has occurred, and what its legal consequences should be. Regulatory rules have squarely confronted problems of 'known unknowns', but they cannot hope to deal with every issue; when inevitably cases fall through the cracks, liability must pick up the pieces and cannot simply borrow the very different concepts of regulation.[57]

There are, though, borderline cases between past and future unknowns. Lord Hoffmann observed, in the context of loss of a chance,

> there is no inherent uncertainty about what caused something to happen in the past or about whether something which happened in the past will cause something to happen in the future. Everything is determined by causality. What we lack is knowledge.[58]

For example, the assessment of damages is an *ex post* problem at least insofar as it concerns the valuation of a loss already caused, even where the extent and value of that loss will ultimately manifest in the future. This seems clear enough under a once-and-for-all approach to damages awards. The situation looks different where provisional damages are awarded, or a Germanic *Feststellungsklage* brought—establishing liability in principle for damages then assessed at a future point, once relevant losses have actually manifested. Different approaches to this issue raise subtle variations, changing which side of a delicate boundary the concept falls on. Again, we steer towards inclusivity.[59]

55 See e.g. J. Spier, 'The Oslo Principles and the Enterprises Principles: Legal Strategies to Come to Grips with Climate Change' (2017) 8 *JETL* 218; D.A. Dana (ed.), *The Nanotechnology Challenge: Creating Legal Institutions for Uncertain Risks*, CUP 2011; M. Ambrus et al. (eds), *Risk and the Regulation of Uncertainty in International Law*, OUP 2017.

56 Principle 15, Rio Declaration on Environment and Development 1992; cf. art. 191(2), TFEU; for discussion, E. Fisher et al. (eds), *Implementing the Precautionary Principle*, Edward Elgar 2006.

57 See e.g. le Tourneau, n. 19, no. 2131.32; M. Spitzer and B. Burtscher, 'Liability for Climate Change: Cases, Challenges and Concepts' (2017) 8 *JETL* 137.

58 *Gregg v Scott* [2005] 2 AC 176, [79].

59 D. Messner-Kreuzbauer, 'Quantifying or avoiding the unknown? Damages for future lost earnings in tortious personal injury cases', this volume; S. Schnobel and J. Skillen, 'Known unknowns: loss of a chance and intractable connections', this volume; Oliphant, n. 49.

1.2.2 *The incidence of uncertainty*

Even in the above, circumscribed sense, known unknowns pose a problem that pervades the law. Some facts are inevitably unknown and uncertainty problems are accordingly well recognised in existing literature. For example, Papp Kamali's work demonstrates that doubts about death have plagued English law for at least a millennium;[60] there is an extensive, expanding European literature on causal uncertainty;[61] and the uncertainty inherent in language has generated a wide-ranging corpus.[62] Uncertainty is a perennial concern of legal discussions; the known unknowns analysed in this volume are individually much discussed. However, these debates rarely feed into one another. Beyond the ordinary law of evidence, instances of intractable uncertainty are generally viewed as the isolated concerns of their own fields, rather than symptoms of a broader problem that affects the whole law.[63]

We have chosen to confront the matter instead as exactly such a broad concern. However, we can feasibly only narrow in on limited instances. We thus focus on three particular foci of uncertainty that have confronted private law repeatedly and across its wide field of operation (the selection is discussed in Section 1.3, by reference to our methodology). These cover, firstly, problems relating to birth and death, where interrelating difficulties in scientific and witness evidence meet mysterious and morally charged natural processes. Secondly, there are problems with the interrelated areas of causation and loss; these play with connections and timelines, including inherently speculative, hypothetical alternative histories. Finally, there are problems that concern the intentions and meanings of parties and the words they use; whilst '[t]he state of a man's mind is as much a fact as the state of his digestion',[64] even the 'devil does not know the intent of a man'.[65]

---

60 E. Papp Kamali, 'Tales of the Living Dead: Dealing with Doubt in Medieval English Law' (2021) 96 *Speculum* 367.

61 E.g. Turton, n. 9; S. Steel, *Proof of Causation in Tort Law*, CUP 2015; C.B. Ehlgen, *Probabilistische Proportionalhaftung und Haftung für den Verlust von Chancen*, Mohr Siebeck 2013; C. Engel, 'Dogmatische Überlegungen zur Schadensteilung bei alternativer Kausalität mit Zufall' [2013] *Österreichische Juristen-Zeitung* 293; C. Quézel-Ambrunaz, 'La fiction de la causalité alternative. Fondement et perspectives de la jurisprudence Distilbène' [2010] *Recueil Dalloz* 1162; M. Lamoureux, 'La causalité juridique à l'épreuve des algorithmes' [2016] (25) *JCP* 1251.

62 E.g. G. Keil and R. Poscher (eds), *Vagueness and Law*, OUP 2016; M. Freeman and F. Smith (eds), *Law and Language*, OUP 2013; L. Solan and P. Tiersma (eds), *The Oxford Handbook of Language and Law*, OUP 2012.

63 The Justinianic Digest is an exception: Digest 34.5. Some modern scholars draw together uncertainty problems within limited bounds: e.g. Neumayr/Webhofer, n. 16; Burrows, n. 3; M. Del Mar, 'Legal Fictions and Legal Change in the Common Law Tradition' in M. Del Mar and W. Twining, *Legal Fictions in Theory and Practice*, Springer 2015, 237.

64 *Edgington v Fitzmaurice* (1885) 29 Ch. D 459, 483.

65 (1477) YB Pas. 17 Edw. IV pl. 2 fol. 1.

1.2.3 *Responding to uncertainty*

With this clearer picture of uncertainty and its incidence in view, we turn to the issue of where and how the law ordinarily addresses it.

1.2.3.1 *Evidential rules*

Primarily, unknown facts are ascertained using the law of evidence. As explained, our main interest is in uncertainty that goes beyond a simple evidential problem.[66] Nonetheless, the scope of our concern is shaped by the law of evidence in each system and period. Three elements in particular impact on known unknowns. These are the rules that regulate responsibility for establishing a fact (the burden of proof); how exacting the demand to establish the fact is (the standard of proof); and the acceptable forms of evidence and proof. The structure and content of these rules will shape the uncertainty problem, and may equally be engaged as means to resolve it (e.g. an exceptional reversal of the burden of proof).[67]

Without intervention, a known unknown will redound to the disadvantage of the party bearing the burden of proving it, who is inevitably unable to discharge that burden.[68] In modern law, it is axiomatic that the party who wishes the court to act generally bears the burden of proof.[69] However, the position has not always been clear-cut: in classical Roman law, a *iudex* enjoyed freedom in assigning the burden,[70] whilst in early medieval law it often fell on a defendant.[71]

Standards of proof are also relevant: the higher the standard adopted, the more facts will be incapable of proof. These standards vary across eras and systems. Under Romano canonical procedure, there was no real standard of proof: a judge was required to calculate whether sufficient evidence had been presented to amount to a 'full proof'.[72] In contrast, modern France has a system of 'free proof', whereby questions are left to the '*intime conviction*' of the judge;[73] Germanic systems rest on '*freie Beweiswürdigung*' leading to a very high probability or probability bordering on certainty.[74] Modern English law

---

66 Works on evidence might ignore the additional difficulties: Treitel, n. 12, 530.

67 Giesen, n. 23, 52.

68 R. Munday, *Cross & Tapper on Evidence*, 13th ed., OUP 2018, 124; V. Ulfbeck and M.-L. Holle, 'Tort Law and Burden of Proof—Comparative Aspects. A Special Case for Enterprise Liability?' in Koziol/Steininger, n. 23, 26.

69 Munday, n. 68, 133; J. Bell et al., *Principles of French Law*, OUP 2008, 86; Ulfbeck/Holle, n. 68, 30; Karner, n. 23, nos. 3–4.

70 M. Kaser, '*Beweislast und Vermutung im römischen Formularprozeß*' (1954) 71 *ZRG RA* 221.

71 R.C. van Caenegem, *Legal History: A European Perspective*, Hambledon 1991, 73.

72 R.H. Helmholz, *OHLE*, vol. I, 329.

73 M. Damaška, 'Free Proof and Its Detractors' (1995) 43 *American Journal of Comparative Law* 343, 344.

74 Ulfbeck/Holle, n. 68, nos 10–12; Karner, n. 23, no. 8.

only requires a civil case to be proven 'on the balance of probabilities', under-stood as a more than 50% likelihood of being true,[75] though it is controversial whether that differs practically from the continental line.[76] While the terminologies seem distinct, describing and comparing the internal decisional thinking of any judge is fraught and it is far from clear whether English and continental judges are looking for anything but the same level of satisfaction of personal doubts as to the truth.[77] These difficulties might then be reflected in the framing of special rules for uncertainty—across jurisdictions, these may engage by reference to differently framed standards and so in different instances, but we must be alive to whether any practical differences really emerge.

Finally, available forms of evidence will also affect the incidence and identification of known unknowns. Romano-canonical procedure strictly regulated the kinds of evidence that could be presented to establish a full proof.[78] This left significant room for uncertainty, since many cases turned on a fact that was not easily susceptible to full proof.[79] At common law, in contrast, the jury trial was long 'the principal criterion of truth'.[80] A jury verdict was 'essentially inscrutable'[81] with no specific kind of evidence needed to support it.[82] Any uncertainty could easily be buried in the verdict;[83] following the modern 'dethronement' of civil juries, courts have grappled with many uncertainty problems for the first time.[84] It is thus perhaps unsurprising that many legal responses to known unknowns emerge later in England than on the continent.

Across jurisdictions, meanwhile, developing forms of scientific analysis and evidence have the potential to shape the contours of the uncertainty problem over time. As more areas of knowledge and analysis are opened up, the sphere of uncertainty can shrink.[85] For example, modern science can increasingly unpick a classic 'two-hunter' causal scenario—two hunters fire towards a

75 Malek et al., n. 29, no. 6.56.
76 R.W. Wright, 'Proving Facts: Belief versus Probability' in Koziol/Steininger, n. 23.
77 Consider e.g. Ormrod's presentation of English judging, n. 29, 187–89. Philosophically distinct notions of probability might also engage, including objective and epistemic forms; cf. (re 'risk') e.g. S.R. Perry, 'Risk, Harm and Responsibility' in D. Owen, *Philosophical Foundations of Tort Law*, OUP 1995, 322–29.
78 Helmholz, n. 72, 328.
79 Ibid., 331.
80 Bl. Comm. III.348.
81 C. Donahue, 'Proof by Witnesses in the Church Courts of Medieval England: An Imperfect Reception of the Learned Law' in M.S. Arnold et al. (eds), *On the Laws and Customs of England*, University of North Carolina Press 1981, 137.
82 J. Baker, *OHLE*, vol. VI, 361.
83 J. Baker, *Introduction to English Legal History*, 5th ed., OUP 2019, 88; R.H. Helmholz and W.D.H. Sellar, 'Presumptions in Comparative Legal History' in R.H. Helmholz and W.D.H. Sellar (eds), *The Law of Presumptions: Essays in Comparative Legal History*, Duncker & Humblot 2009, 14.
84 A.W.B. Simpson, 'The Horwitz Thesis and the History of Contracts' (1979) 46 *University of Chicago Law Review* 533, 600.
85 Munday, n. 68, 137.

victim, who is hit and injured by only one of those bullets[86]—through ballistic analysis, limiting cases where uncertainty may emerge. Of course, additional data can also complicate the question as old conclusions and certainties are shaken, increasing uncertainty scenarios. Furthermore, if new analytical methods are later found to be unreliable, doubt may again resurface, as with the use of lung-float tests to determine a live or stillbirth.[87]

The law of evidence, then, cannot satisfactorily resolve all instances of known unknowns and is, *in extremis,* thrown back on deciding bluntly via the burden of proof. Yet the burden of proof itself 'is founded on a fundamental epistemological assumption that present knowledge about past facts is in principle possible', and fails when confronted with intractable uncertainty.[88] To avoid unsatisfactory outcomes in such cases, the law may resort to special solutions to the problem, in particular providing presumptions and legal fictions to bridge the gap that evidence cannot.[89]

1.2.3.2 Presumptions and fictions

Presumptions and fictions can establish a factual basis for the application of a legal rule, which is to some extent independent of that basis' truth in the world. Legal systems may institute such rules for various reasons, including expediting the resolution of disputes, ensuring just outcomes, and developing the law.[90] However, one key function or effect is to solve problems of intractable factual uncertainty.[91]

Presumptions were used like this in the Justinianic compilations,[92] which formed the basis for the law of presumptions elaborated by continental civil-law jurists between the twelfth and sixteenth centuries.[93] By the thirteenth century, presumptions were treated as partial proofs.[94] Depending on their

---

86 Oliphant, n. 49, 5.2.
87 G. Seabourne, '"In the beginning": dealing with "unknowns" at the start of life', this volume, 2.3.2. See e.g. Jabloner, n. 30; le Tourneau, n. 19, no. 2131.52.
88 H. Reece, 'Losses of Chances in the Law' (1996) 59 *MLR* 188, 205.
89 For further criticism of burden-of-proof decisions, see J.E. Coons, 'Approaches to Court-Imposed Compromise – the Uses of Doubt and Reason' (1963–4) 58 *Northwestern University Law Review* 750, 755–56.
90 M. Del Mar, 'Introducing Fictions: Examples, Functions, Definitions and Evaluations' in Del Mar/Twining, n. 63, xvi–xx; L.J. Cohen, 'Presumptions according to purpose: a functional approach' (1981) 4 *Albany Law Review* 1079.
91 Del Mar, 'Introducing Fictions', n. 90, ix; R. Gama, 'Presumptions and Fictions: A Collingwoodian Approach' in Del Mar/Twining, n. 63, 361.
92 Gama, n. 91, 350–51. Whether such presumptions featured in classical Roman law is controversial: Kaser, n. 70, 232; C. Willems, 'Coke, Collusion, and Conveyances. Unearthing the Roots of Twyne's Case' (2015) 36 *JLH* 129, 144–45.
93 Gama, n. 91, 350.
94 J.A. Brundage, 'Full and Partial Proof in Classical Canonical Procedure' (2007) 67 *The Jurist* 58, 63.

weight, they might shift the burden of proof or even establish a case.[95] Given the difficulties of establishing a full proof by evidence, they were vital to the legal system's functioning.[96] This law of presumptions also influenced the common law: English writers from the Middle Ages[97] to the nineteenth century[98] discussed presumptions in civilian terms.

Presumptive and fictitious rules take a number of forms, though, and there is little consensus on defining them or the boundaries between them.[99] An orthodox account is that a legal fiction requires a fact to be treated as true when it is known to be false, whereas a presumption requires a fact to be treated as true when there is insufficient evidence as to its truth or falsehood; only presumptions thus operate in situations of doubt.[100] Other writers draw the line differently, arguing that fictions do obtain in cases of doubt, and only differ from presumptions insofar as the latter 'take a stance on the likelihood' of the assumption being accurate.[101]

Moreover, though studied for centuries, the law of presumptions and fictions has a poor reputation.[102] Five centuries ago, Alciatus described the subject as '*confusa*' and '*inextricabilis*', and this judgement has resonated with later authors.[103] Studies can become mired in abstruse questions about classifications, or struggle with the disparate, often niche scenarios that presumptions cover.[104]

Such rules and analyses are not themselves the target of our work; we are interested in the functional problem of uncertainty. Whilst particular presumptions and fictions meet our project insofar as they are used to solve this problem, their relevance is limited to that extent. We take no stance on broader questions about presumptions and fictions themselves; our work actually demonstrates that these categories overlap in practice, with the same assumption

---

95 Helmholz, n. 72, 331–32.

96 Ibid., 331.

97 B. Shapiro, 'Classical Rhetoric and the English Law of Evidence' in V. Kahn and L. Hutson (eds), *Rhetoric and Law in Early Modern Europe*, Yale University Press 2001, 69.

98 Gama, n. 91, 354.

99 Helmholz/Sellar, n. 83, 11–13; Shmilovits, n. 43, ch. 2; M. Xifaras, 'Fictions juridiques. Remarques sur quelques procédés fictionnels en usage chez les juristes' in *Annuaire de l'Institut Michel Villey*, vol. 3, Dalloz 2012, 451.

100 Gama, n. 91, 352; W.M. Best, *A Treatise on Presumptions of Law and Fact*, Sweet 1844, 24; L. Fuller, *Legal Fictions*, Stanford University Press 1967, 9.

101 M. Del Mar, 'Legal Fictions and Legal Change in the Common Law Tradition' in Del Mar/Twining, n. 63, 226; J.R. Gulson, *The Philosophy of Proof in Its Relation to the English Law of Judicial Evidence*, Routledge 1905, 430.

102 Helmholz/Sellar, n. 83, 9.

103 Thayer, n. 39, 313; E.M. Morgan, 'Presumptions' (1937) 12 *Washington Law Review* 255, 255.

104 Helmholz/Sellar, n. 83, 10–13; Shmilovits, n. 43, 2–3. J. Menochius, *De Praesumptionibus*, Ziletti 1587–90, for example, included hundreds of specific presumptions.

applying for the same reasons in some cases where it is certainly false, and others where it is probably true.

Nevertheless, the issues we consider have often been discussed in the context of presumptions and fictions generally. Work in this area is thus highly relevant, and there have been some important recent contributions to the field. Prominent examples examine the influence of legal presumptions on the development of the law of evidence in the common- and civil-law traditions,[105] and explore the use of legal fictions from theoretical and historical perspectives.[106]

These enterprises evidence the importance of comparative-historical analysis in this area. However, in focusing on a specific form of legal rule, rather than an investigation of the underlying problem of uncertainty, they do not speak to the law's understanding of uncertainty itself, nor the range of solutions that might assist with future problems. They do, though, draw out the complex interplay of policy and principle underlying the creation and choice of different presumptions, helping us to understand how they have developed and reflect the changing priorities of societies and legal systems. This is key context for the appearance of such rules as responses to intractable uncertainty.

1.2.3.3 Decision-making rules

Finally, decision-making rules can significantly affect whether and how intractable uncertainties emerge and are resolved. This is an extensive separate field, also covered by recent comparative-historical contributions.[107] Its relevance will thus be noted here, but not systematically elaborated.

Rules for decision-making are, firstly, relevant insofar as they are bound up with the rules and mechanisms of evidence. For example, the discussion of juries above shows the significance for uncertainty of unregulated and unexplained decision-making. The availability to Scottish criminal juries of a third result, alongside 'guilty' and 'not guilty', of 'not proven' is also an interesting example.[108] Uncertainty problems may emerge more or less frequently or clearly as such conditions change.

Secondly, these rules can provide an explicit escape from intractable problems, as where decision-makers are freed from the need to provide an all-or-nothing decision and may, for example, make a proportionate determination

---

105 Helmholz/Sellar, n. 83, 5.
106 Del Mar/Twining, n. 63; Shmilovits, n. 43.
107 Ernst, n. 42; W. Ernst and B. Häcker (eds), *Collective Judging in Comparative Perspective*, Intersentia 2020.
108 Cf. J. Chalmers et al., 'Beyond Doubt: The Case Against "Not Proven"' (2022) 85 *MLR* 847.

instead,[109] or declare the case/its facts insoluble: *non liquet*.[110] We might also mention the non-decision of a hung jury.[111]

Such mechanisms can dispose of disputes without openly confronting the substance of uncertainty. Conceptual pressure on the problem of intractable uncertainty is thereby reduced, and the substantive law is less likely to be impacted. The existence of such outlets must therefore be borne in mind, especially if intractable uncertainty does not emerge in the substantive law where one might expect it.

1.3 Project methodology and structure

1.3.1 Methodology

Our analysis combines doctrinal, historical, and comparative methods to achieve a rounded understanding of intractable uncertainty across private law. This produces insights across three axes: jurisdiction, time, and problem area. While methodological remarks are indispensable, we heed the warning that '[c]omparative legal historians should find a middle road between elaborating a potentially overly sophisticated comparative methodology and simply getting on with the research'.[112]

The majority of the papers are what we term 'specific area papers' (SAPs); each interrogates one example area of intractable uncertainty in private law. These have been guided by the methodological framework discussed in Sections 1.3.1–1.3.2. Appended to these are two contextualising chapters intended to offer broader perspectives on the core discussions (see Section 1.3.3).

1.3.1.1 Comparative approach

In terms of comparative method, a form of functional investigation suggests itself immediately. Our core concern does not lie in any 'legally predicated, abstract subject matter', but an inevitable 'fact of life'[113] arising from the social resort to law: disjuncture between the factual knowledge which can be established under evidential rules, and the factual knowledge needed to operate relevant substantive legal rules.[114] This problem transcends the conceptual and

---

109 Ernst, n. 42, 137–42.
110 Ibid., 22–23, 60, 121, 130.
111 Ibid., 143.
112 M. Dyson, 'Comparative legal history: methodology for morphology' in O. Moréteau et al. (eds), *Comparative Legal History*, Edward Elgar 2019, 112–13.
113 E. Rabel, *The Conflict of Laws. A Comparative Study*, vol. 1, 2nd ed., University of Michigan Press 1958, 51–52; cf. M. Graziadei, 'The Functionalist Heritage' in P. Legrand and R. Munday (eds), *Comparative Legal Studies: Traditions and Transitions*, CUP 2003, 104–6.
114 Cf. Ando, n. 28, 1–2.

doctrinal frameworks applied within, and the boundaries between, individual systems.

The exact areas where such disjuncture emerges cannot be presupposed across all systems but, in given instances, limited natural-scientific knowledge will guarantee the emergence of the problem. We have therefore looked to ill-understood natural phenomena like birth, death, and disease.[115] Inherently uncertain hypothetical or future timelines provide a second area;[116] the nature of communication and notions such as meanings and intentions a third.[117]

In adopting this 'functional' position, no claim is made to any essentialist or universalist solution to the problem of intractable uncertainty.[118] We see no necessary reason to suppose that acceptable understandings of and solutions to the problem must be identical across private law, still less across national and cultural boundaries. A claim that local preference is irrelevant to the proper resolution of *commorientes* problems, for example, seems less credible now than perhaps in the 1960s.[119] However, even in areas touching critical socio-political and moral-ethical values, comparative research can still provide useful data.[120]

Likewise, no evaluative claim will be made that any rule is 'better' simply by virtue of its capacity to overcome intractable uncertainty, except in relation to that very function.[121] In such varied areas of the law as are being analysed, the delicate balance of myriad purposes and principles must be considered together.[122] Our present method is chosen rather to ensure comparability of our objects (those elements of the legal systems that deal with intractable uncertainty) across the papers, thereby achieving a broader understanding of uncertainty and approaches to it. This will enable others to engage in further analysis of particular areas raising the uncertainty problem, in light of this and other functions and concerns.

In terms of jurisdictional selections, we focused on Western European thought in line with expected historical influences. Contributors were asked to consider England and Wales and to supplement this, with a preference for France and Germany to maximise some common jurisdictional coverage without overextending the work. However, given the varied areas under discussion and the potential for enlightening comparisons elsewhere, contributors were

---

115 See Part 1 and Oliphant, n. 49.
116 See Schnobel/Skillen, n. 59; Messner-Kreuzbauer, n. 59.
117 See Part 3 and cf. V.G. Curran, 'Comparative Law and Language' in M. Reimann and R. Zimmermann (eds), *Oxford Handbook of Comparative Law*, 2nd ed., OUP 2019, 685.
118 R. Michaels, 'The Functional Method of Comparative Law' in Reimann/Zimmermann, n. 117, 350–52; J. Gordley, 'The universalist heritage' in Legrand/Munday, n. 113.
119 J.D.M. Derrett, 'Commorientes' (1962) 20 *University of Ceylon Review* 55, 56.
120 M.J. de Waal, 'Comparative Succession Law' in Reimann/Zimmermann, n. 117, 1059–61; Graziadei, n. 113, 109.
121 Cf. Michaels, n. 118, 379–81.
122 Ibid., 375.

free to adapt jurisdictional selections, including to non- and transnational legal frameworks.

1.3.1.2 *Historical approach*

This comparative perspective supplements historical analysis of the legal developments. Combining comparative and historical methods is in many respects natural.[123] Failing to integrate the disciplines invites the historian's error of assuming that development in one place can be understood in isolation, and the comparatist's of assuming systemic coherence, ignoring the piecemeal development of solutions.[124] Comparatists can be saved from mistaken assumptions as to (non-)common needs or the basis for similarities and differences between systems with the benefit of history's insight.[125] Historical scholarship also raises awareness of common ground between (European) legal systems born of a common tradition; of independent, parallel developments; and of intellectual stimulation and reception occurring, whilst aiding explanations of divergences in approach, doctrine, and result.[126] These considerations demand the combination of both methods.

Our historical interests span both 'internal' and 'external' legal history: we are interested in understanding how legal rules have developed over time, and the relationship between the law and wider socio-economic and technological changes.[127] We explore the ways in which the law has framed and responded to instances of intractable uncertainty, and examine the pressures and policies influencing choices and changes.

Given our Western European focus, we set the year 1100 as a default historical cut-off point: contributions could focus mainly on the revived legal tradition from the medieval rediscovery of Roman law to the present. Contributors were not, however, required to provide a full account of this broad historical span. Some instances of the uncertainty problem have reached critical developmental points earlier than others or have arisen at all only much later. Contributors have therefore focused on periods which best evidence and inform an analysis of their particular known unknown. Nevertheless, to aid

---

123 The two might present as twin disciplines or as forms of the other: H. Kötz, 'Was erwartet die Rechtsvergleichung von der Rechtsgeschichte' [1992] *JZ* 20; W. Ewald, 'Legal History and Comparative Law' (1999) 7 *ZEuP* 553.

124 J. Gordley, 'Comparative Law and Legal History' in Reimann/Zimmermann, n. 117, 762; D. Ibbetson, 'Comparative Legal History: A Methodology' in A. Musson and C. Stebbings (eds), *Making Legal History: Approaches and Methodologies*, CUP 2012, 132–33.

125 Gordley, n. 124, 768–72; K. Luig, 'Was bietet die Rechtsgeschichte der Rechtsvergleichung' (1999) 7 *ZEuP* 521; Dyson, n. 112, 110.

126 R. Zimmermann, 'Comparative Law and the Europeanization of Private Law' in Reimann/Zimmermann, n. 117, 595; cf. D. Johnston, 'Roman Law, Comparative Law and Legal History' (1999) 7 *ZEuP* 560.

127 D. Ibbetson, 'Historical Research in Law' in M. Tushnet and P. Cane (eds), *The Oxford Handbook of Legal Studies*, OUP 2005, 864.

comparison, all chapters first provide an historical overview of the area considered, sketching overall lines of development in the area, and situating those within the relevant historical context.

1.3.2 Specific area papers

Above, we observed that the problem of known unknowns is endemic in legal systems. For this project, we concentrated on its manifestation within private relationships. This provides a sufficiently limited field of analysis to enable coherent discussion and meaningful comparison. It also grants access to a rich historical tradition of relevant scholarship, and to some clear areas of movement and controversy in recent practice.[128] The SAP topics have been selected to secure a broad range of discussion within private law, collectively ranging across contract, tort, property, succession, equity, and remedies.

As noted, our analysis also focuses on three prominent uncertainty foci, and this volume is arranged to reflect those thematic relationships. This feeds into a comparison across the wider spectrum of private law. Part 1 thus deals with birth and death; Part 2 takes us to causation and loss; and Part 3 shifts to meanings and intentions. The two contextualising papers follow in Part 4, before our overall comparative conclusions are presented in Part 5.

The pilot study noted above identified key lines of investigation for the SAPs, later formulated as a series of questions for contributors as follows.

The Scope of the Uncertainty Problem

- How is the relevant element of uncertainty defined and circumscribed in the chosen systems (across the period of its development)? Does the definition or do the limits of the concept change?
- Are there multiple levels or regions of uncertainty and how do they relate to one another?
- At what point is an intractable uncertainty requiring some form of special rule recognised to exist? Are attempts made to reason the problem out of existence?
- Is there variation in the incidence or frequency of scenarios giving rise to the relevant uncertainty, and in what ways do these bear on the understanding of the problem?
- What social or historical trends accompany changes in the uncertainty problem?
- Does uncertainty remain central to understandings?
- Is the relevant uncertainty explicitly related to others dealt with by the law?

---

128 E.g. Oliphant, n. 49; Schnobel/Skillen, n. 59.

Solutions and Policy Goals

- What solutions are in fact selected in the relevant jurisdictions and in what periods? Are those solutions consistent across eras and jurisdictions?
- Do the solutions prefer all-or-nothing or compromised results?
- How significant (if at all) are concerns over a particular result imposed by default/presumption being (un)likely to be factually accurate?
- Are policy ideas brought to bear in resolving the uncertainty problem and, if so, what are they?
- Are those policy ideas used to justify the creation of a rule per se, a particular rule, or both?
- Do the policy choices involved change in kind/content and/or in form/ extent? What guides these changes?
- Are ideas of fault or responsibility for the creation of the uncertainty involved?

Again, given the extensive potential for variation across the papers, this framework was not imposed as a formal questionnaire. Contributors were instead asked to consider its elements and frame their responses under the two-part division of scope and solutions. These two points of analysis are bookended in each chapter with the aforementioned historical overview and the author's conclusions.

1.3.3 Broader perspectives

Two broader contextualising papers feature in our Part 4. These are intended to give further context by exploring the nature and boundaries of uncertainty beyond the confines of any individual private-law instantiation. They confront parallel issues and so could not be constrained by the same structural framing as the SAPs. The authors of these papers received copies of the above guidance and drafts of the other papers during their development, however; the papers have thus been prepared in light of the same common goals and with an eye to what context might best illuminate uncertainty within the project as a whole. They are not, though, formal responses or additions to the other papers.

Chapter 10 explores the nature of factual uncertainty by examining its interaction with legal uncertainty, comparing the ways in which these two uncertainties interrelate and are understood, tolerated, and resolved by legal systems. Criminal law has been used for this, to allow broad analysis across an entire area of the law. It reveals inter alia that the divisions between the mechanisms for resolving uncertainty in these two forms are less pronounced than we might assume, concordantly with the blurred fact-law boundary already mentioned.

Chapter 11 confronts another interrelation of legal and factual uncertainty, using Roman law and so accessing a historical tradition important for all of the systems under comparison. It considers the legal-historical uncertainty of the proper understanding and content of the *lex Aquilia*, examining the process by which lawyers rationalise their way out of a historical unknown and seek to overcome a lack of clarity through broken evidence.

1.4 Final thoughts

This completes the outline of our project, its aims, content, and method, as well as its broader context. The fruits of the individual chapters will be harvested and sorted into analytical baskets in our comparative conclusions (Chapter 12).

It remains only to confirm the temporal boundaries of the process. Initial outlines and comparative observations were exchanged among the contributors before revised versions were presented publicly in April 2021. Finalised papers were submitted or updated for publication in summer 2023, at which point the analysis rests.

Part 1
Life and death

2 'In the beginning'

Dealing with 'unknowns' at the start of life

Gwen Seabourne

From an early period in the development of western European legal systems, it was clear that difficulties might be caused by significant 'unknowns' at the start of life. Making a determination as to the presence of life in the foetus or newborn child, or as to the parentage (and especially the paternity) of a child, was sometimes necessary, but could be very challenging. Two medieval English examples will serve to show consciousness of, and concern with, a particular lack of certainty here (though similar views can certainly be found in the *ius commune*). An entry in the rolls of Parliament relating to an early four-teenth-century dispute over succession to the estates of Gilbert de Clare, Earl of Gloucester, which turned upon the claimed pregnancy of his widow, said that the question of what to do in the face of uncertainty as to the presence of a potential heir was 'difficult'. And, in the following century, an English lawyer commented, in relation to a question concerning legitimacy, that there were matters in this area of which '[n]o one [could] have cognisance ... but God'.[1] Part of the difficulty might now be labelled 'scientific uncertainty': these statements were made long before the availability of reliable tests for particular physical changes during pregnancy and the early stages of human development, or blood and DNA testing to determine biological parentage.[2] As the second example suggests, however, the area was also long seen as being affected by other barriers to fact-finding: events surrounding concep-tion, pregnancy, and birth were inherently mysterious, since they were matters within the special cognisance of God. The mystery was intensified by the fact that answering questions in this area involved engaging with what men in the

---

1 C. Given-Wilson et al. (eds), *The Parliament Rolls of Medieval England, 1275–1504*, vol. I, Boydell Press 2005, 354 (I am grateful to Rhiannon Cox for this reference); (1422) YB Mich. 1 Hen. VI pl. 8. See also R. Helmholz, *OHLE*, vol. I, 560.

2 See e.g. D. Haarburger and T.S. Pillay, 'Historical Perspectives in Clinical Pathology: Develop-ment of the Pregnancy Test' (2011) 64 *Journal of Clinical Pathology* 546; E. Saling and M. Dräger, 'Fetal heart activity and measurements of labor activities' in E. Saling, M. Dräger, and J.H. Stupin (eds), *The Beginnings of Perinatal Medicine*, De Gruyter 2014, ch. 2, 6; K. Albre-cht and D. Schultheiss, 'Proof of Paternity: Historical Reflections on an Andrological–Forensic Challenge' (2004) 36 *Andrologia* 31.

DOI: 10.4324/9781003537526-3

medieval period in particular thought of as the 'secrets of women'.[3] Despite such difficulties and mysteries, for several centuries legal systems had to find ways to deal with these 'unknowns' at the start of life, since significant rights and liabilities might turn on whether or not life was found to be present, and whether or not a particular individual was found to be the legitimate child of particular parents. While a number of the contexts have now altered in fundamental ways, due to scientific and social developments, changes in society, science, and technology also have a tendency to raise new areas of debate about 'start of life' issues, and the history of legal responses to uncertainties at the start of life remains instructive in responding to these.

2.1 Historical overview

From the medieval period onwards, developing western European legal systems produced multiple situations in which some decision had to be made as to the presence of life and the value assigned to it. Throughout Europe, rules of property transmission on death, and the transmission of status, depended on a combination of biological facts of human reproduction and rules chosen by those in authority to delimit the path of succession, increasingly including favouring those deemed 'legitimate'. It should be noted that those born outside marriage were not always treated as unworthy of inheritance in the earlier medieval period, even in relation to succession to thrones, and even in 'core' western European lands such as those areas making up modern France and Germany. This lesser concern with illegitimacy continued in some systems, such as the 'native' laws of Wales and Ireland, but, by the thirteenth century, legitimacy or illegitimacy, deriving from the presence or absence of the parents' marriage, generally made a significant difference to a person's legal position,[4] and so it was troubling that the identity of a child's father, in particular, might be a matter of uncertainty. In addition, the structure of homicide offences required a victim who had once been 'alive', and the punishment of women required a determination as to whether they were, or were not, pregnant with a foetus, the life of which was to be protected by the law.

Medieval legal systems had a 'primeval soup' of ideas relating to human reproduction and to the birth, value, and legal rights of the foetus/infant from

---

3 See e.g. M.H. Green, 'From "Diseases of Women" to "Secrets of Women": The Transformation of Gynecological Literature in the Latter Middle Ages' (2000) 30 *Journal of Medieval and Early Modern Studies* 5; M.H. Green, *Making Women's Medicine Masculine: The Use of Male Authority in Pre-Modern Gynaecology*, OUP 2008; K. Park, *The Secrets of Women: Gender, Generation, and the Origins of Human Dissection*, Zone Books 2010; I. Davis, 'The Experimental Conception Hospital: Dating Pregnancy and the Gothic Imagination' (2019) 32 *Social History of Medicine* 773, 779.

4 See e.g. S. McDougall, *Royal Bastards: The Birth of Illegitimacy 800–1230*, OUP 2017; T.G. Watkin, *The Legal History of Wales*, 2nd ed., University of Wales Press 2012, 57; C.T. Hickey, 'Bastardy: the Stain of Illegitimacy in Medieval Ireland' (2020) 28 *History Ireland* 14.

which to draw. These ranged from Greek philosophy through Roman law to Christian theology and contemporary medical ideas about pregnancy and foetal development. These sources might emphasise the importance of conception, 'animation', 'formation', birth, or viability, pointing to different possible thresholds for legal rights or protection.[5] With regard to legitimacy, canon law also had an impact, with secular systems often following the line of ecclesiastical courts or decisions, though there was some notable divergence between the canon law rules relating to legitimacy and those of the English common law, in particular, with regard to legitimation by subsequent marriage of the parents. In contrast to other European systems, and canon law, the English common law rejected this into the twentieth century.[6]

Clearly, there was movement in scientific understanding of the early stages of human life over many centuries, but the changes which were of most significance in terms of detecting pre-birth development and parentage came only in the nineteenth and twentieth centuries; so, for a considerable period of time, the law had to work in a situation of intractable uncertainty in relation to these important matters.

2.2 Scope of the uncertainty problem

There has been some variation in the exact scenarios in which it has been necessary to conclude as to the existence of (legitimate) life prior to, or at, birth. As far as the pre-twentieth-century common law of England (and Wales) was concerned, such determinations needed to be made in the following contexts in particular:

(i) the rights of the foetus/child in relation to succession to land or status;
(ii) applicability to the foetus/child of the law of homicide or abortion, and the deferral of execution of pregnant felons;[7]
(iii) the rights of others which depended on the existence or legitimacy of a foetus/child, such as a widower's qualification to hold his deceased wife's

---

5 A. Lefebvre-Teillard, *Autour de l'Enfant: du droit canonique et romain medieval au Code Civil de 1804*, Brill 2008, ch. 4; W. Müller, *The Criminalization of Abortion in the Medieval West*, Cornell University Press 2012, ch. 1, 3; M. Van Der Lugt, 'L'animation de l'embryon humain et le statut de l'enfant à naître dans la pensée médiévale' in L. Brisson et al. (eds), *Formation et animation de l'embryon dans l'Antiquité et au Moyen Âge*, Vrin 2008, 233–54; D. Albert Jones, *The Soul of the Embryo: An Enquiry into the Status of the Human Embryo in the Christian Tradition*, Continuum 2004, ch. 8.

6 See R.H. Helmholz, 'Bastardy Litigation in Medieval England' (1969) 13 *American Journal of Legal History* 360, 367; J.H. Baker, *Introduction to English Legal History*, 5th ed., OUP 2019, 528; Legitimacy Act 1926; J. Brundage, *Law, Sex and Christian Society in Medieval Europe*, University of Chicago Press 1988, 155.

7 On abortion, see Müller, n. 5. Canon law also needed to ascertain the presence of life before a child might be baptised.

land for life by the 'curtesy of England', which was made to depend upon his having produced legitimate issue with her.

All systems dealt with the 'criminal law' aspects. There was greater diversity in the situations relating to succession which required courts to deal with 'unknowns' at the start of life. Thus, for example, in systems which, unlike the common law of England, did not require a widower to have produced live, legitimate issue before he could hold land which his wife brought to the marriage, there would not need to be a finding relating to the fleeting presence of life, or its absence, in a now-dead child.[8] Another question with applicability only in some systems was that of the *viability* of a newborn, which has been part of the law of succession in other jurisdictions (notably France),[9] but has not been an explicit part of the law of succession in English common law.

2.3 Solutions and policy goals

Uncertainty on these matters of life and paternity was a human problem: God, of course, could be expected to know the truth. If it was possible to elicit divine judgment of the matter, then the difficulty was surmounted. There are some early instances of the use of an appeal to God, via the judicial ordeal, for a solution to knotty problems relating to the start of life,[10] and one notable case from fourteenth-century Scotland of the use of a judicial duel to decide whether or not a particular child had been born alive.[11] On the whole, however, these decisions were left to be made by fallible humans in the knowledge

---

8 On curtesy, see G. Seabourne, '"It is Necessary that the Issue be Heard to Cry or Squall Within the Four [Walls]": Qualifying for Tenancy by the Curtesy of England in the Reign of Edward I' (2019) 40 *JLH* 44. For examples from other legal systems of rights depending on the birth of live, legitimate issue, see H. Brunner, 'Die Geburt eines lebenden Kindes und das eheliche Vermögensrecht' (1895) 16 *ZRG GA* 63, 65; M. Dobozy (ed.), *The Saxon Mirror: A "Sachsenspiegel" of the Fourteenth Century*, University of Pennsylvania Press 2014, 79, 149.

9 E.C. Romanis, 'Is "Viability" Viable? Abortion, Conceptual Confusion and the Law in England and Wales and the United States' (2020) *Journal of Law and the Biosciences* 5; sec. 1(1), Infant Life (Preservation) Act 1929 (destruction of a child 'capable of being born alive'), and note the influence of ideas about viability on sec. 1(1)(a), Abortion Act 1967, as amended by sec. 37, Human Fertilisation and Embryology Act 1990. For viability in relation to succession in the 'learned law' and in France and Castile, from the sixteenth and seventeenth centuries onwards, see Müller, n. 5, 116–17; Lefebvre-Teillard, n. 5, 67, 69, 70; arts. 725 and 906 CC; F. Diesse, 'La situation juridique de l'enfant à naître en droit français: entre pile et face' (1999–2000) 30 *Revue générale de droit* 607, 648. For the Roman law basis, see Y. Thomas, 'L'enfant à naître et "l'héritier sien": Sujet de pouvoir et sujet de vie en droit romain' (2007) 61 *Annales* 29.

10 See e.g. R. Bartlett, *Trial by Fire and Water: The Medieval Judicial Ordeal*, Clarendon Press 1986, 19–20, including examples from early medieval Irish laws, eleventh-century Normandy, and thirteenth-century Norway.

11 W.D.H. Sellar, 'Courtesy, Battle and the Brieve of Right, 1368: A Story Continued' in W.D.H. Sellar (ed.), *Miscellany II*, Stair Society 1984, 1–12.

that they could not get at the absolute truth. While some thirteenth-century common-law treatise statements, surely influenced by contemporary scholastic theology, which was focusing on foetal humanity and potential, held pre-birth killing to be a form of homicide, the common law had, in practice, retreated from this position by the mid-fourteenth century. Whatever common lawyers, and their counterparts in other western European jurisdictions, might believe in relation to the truth of foetal formation and ensoulment, they were aware of the impossibility of making determinations as to the presence of foetal life, and foetal development, which would allow these beliefs to be translated into practice in a comprehensive way.[12] Live birth was generally treated as the point from which the law of homicide applied.[13]

Aware of the limitations of human knowledge, legal systems had to make choices as to the most desirable strategy to adopt to arrive at a result which was not unacceptable. In doing so, it is inevitable that they gave effect to policy goals, though these are often left unexpressed.

It is easiest to discern clear policy goals in relation to bastardy/legitimacy determinations in the property context. The desire for certainty as to succession to property, and for social stability (perhaps particularly in a world which did not accept full divorce with the possibility of remarriage, on grounds of adultery), can be seen in barriers different systems put up against 'bastardising' apparently legitimate children.[14] These barriers also reflected a lack of willingness to help the 'cuckolded' husband who had not 'kept his wife in order': it was not to be made too easy for him to disclaim paternity of a child which might 'contaminate' his bloodline.[15] In relation to 'presence of (counting) life' questions with regard to land, policy goals are less obvious. In some cases, at least, the impulse seems to have been to maximise the chances of land remaining within a particular line of descent, making it relatively difficult for it to pass outside this line, whilst accepting that people outside the line of descent (such as widowers, or other relatives) had some claim on family land. In relation to

---

12 Lefebvre-Teillard, n. 5, 62.
13 G.E. Woodbine and S.E. Thorne (eds), *Bracton on the Laws and Customs of England*, Harvard University Press 1968–77 (hereafter *Bracton*) II.341; G.O. Sayles (ed.), *Fleta*, Selden Society 1955–84 (hereafter *Fleta*), I.23; though see W. Whittaker (ed.), *The Mirror of Justices*, Selden Society 1893, IV.16; Müller, n. 5, ch. 5, 12; S.M. Butler, 'Abortion by Assault: Violence against Pregnant Women in Thirteenth- and Fourteenth-Century England' (2005) 17 *Journal of Women's History* 9; (1348) YB Mich. 22 Edw. III Lib. Ass. 94; J.H. Baker, *OHLE*, vol. VI, 555; J.H. Baker (ed.), *The Reports of Sir John Spelman*, vol. II, Selden Society 1978, 306; TNA KB 27/974 Rex m. 4 (1504), KB 9/513 m. 23 (1530).
14 See e.g. a petition of 1348, objecting to upsetting expectations and titles by legitimation: TNA SC 8/166/8625; M. Gerber, 'Illegitimacy, Natural Law, and Legal Culture on the Eve of the French Revolution' (2005) 33 *Journal of the Western Society for French History* 240, 243.
15 Lefebvre-Teillard, n. 5, 204; N. Harris Nicolas, *A Treatise on the Law of Adulterine Bastardy*, Pickering 1836, 44, 154, 255; J. Brydall, *Lex Spuriorum or the Law Relating to Bastardy*, Osborne 1703, 86.

the claimed pregnancy of a convicted felon, there was a balance to be struck between carrying out the prescribed sentence in a timely fashion, to shore up the authority of the law, and avoiding killing a valuable and innocent 'counting' foetus for its mother's transgression.

Lawyers and courts used a range of strategies to come to an acceptable outcome in these cases. It might sometimes have been possible to avoid an 'all or nothing' solution, e.g. by sharing lands in the case of disputed legitimacy, and no doubt individuals did sometimes come to private arrangements which involved some sharing of family land, but the idea of admitting the intractability of uncertainty, and splitting things down the middle between different contenders, was not favoured as a formal legal strategy.[16]

It was sometimes feasible to overcome uncertainty with a 'wait and see' procedure. In relation to claims of pregnancy, the thirteenth-century English treatise *Bracton* recommended delay as the way to deal with widows claiming to be pregnant by their deceased husbands, for example.[17] It was not possible simply to defer all decisions in such contexts, however, since there was still a need to make an interim choice as to who should be in possession, how profit and responsibility for any deterioration to the land should be allocated, until the waiting was over. Opinions might differ as to whether it was better to keep out the maturer claimant until it was clear that there was no better-entitled baby, as in the Clare case at the beginning of the chapter, or whether the maturer claimant should be given control of the land, unless and until a baby with a better claim should appear, as was prescribed in an influential medieval German work.[18] Another strategy which could help to get over the uncertainty of pregnancy in the context of the allegedly pregnant widow and her child's inheritance was the commonly accepted rule treating a foetus which would inherit, if born alive, as if it had already been born at the critical date, if it was later born alive, and if this deeming was to the benefit of the child.[19] This strategy accorded well with the value placed upon potential human life by medieval scholars, noted above. However, there was no need to embrace a particular theological position on the start of life to see the utility, on the assumption of the wish to keep property within the immediate family and the line of direct, preferably male, succession, of a rule which avoided the possibility of a live-born and undoubtedly legitimate child being passed over for more remote relations because of the timing of a father's death.

16   The Biblical example of Solomon's initial judgment, 1 Kings 3:16-28, was not, apparently, persuasive.
17   *Bracton* IV.227.
18   Dobozy, n. 8, 174.
19   Lefebvre-Teillard, n. 5, ch. 4, 53; R. Paisley, 'The Succession Rights of the Unborn Child' (2006) 10 *Edinburgh Law Review* 28; K. Reid et al., *Comparative Succession Law*, vol. 2, OUP 2015, 488; *Elliot v Joicey* 1935 SC (HL) 57; Digest 1.5.96, 50.16.231; art. 725 CC; §22 ABGB; §1923(2) BGB; *Trower v Butts* (1823) 1 Simons & Stuart 181; sec. 55(2), Administration of Estates Act 1925.

Where it was not thought feasible to 'wait and see', or to use time-warping deeming strategies, legal systems generally attempted to come to an answer through the use, alone or in combination, of:

(i) non-standard fact-finding mechanisms;
   (a) official criteria for answering the necessary question;
   (b) delegation of the choice of criteria to experts or others; and
(ii) presumptions.

2.3.1 Use of non-standard fact-finders or innovation in fact-finding/expertise

In many systems, the strategy adopted for answering these questions involved the use as fact-finders of those who would not usually be given such a role: women. In addition, and with some variations in chronology between jurisdictions, increasing use was made of 'medical experts', taking unknowns somewhat out of the hands of 'lay' decision-makers and the ordinary trial process.

The common law of England, and other western European jurisdictions, made regular use of women as sources of information as to whether or not a woman was pregnant, as she claimed, and whether or not a child had been born alive, although the involvement of women in legal process was usually very restricted.[20] The use of women in such contexts had antecedents in Roman law and was seen as a necessary expedient, given the regular involvement of women in childbirth. There are examples of the use of women as approved sources of information in relation to claims of pregnancy and as to whether or not a child had been born alive from at least the thirteenth century. The use of women to inspect and report on the presence of a foetus continued into the twentieth century in England and Wales, though this was something of an outlier in western Europe: generally, increasing respect for (male) medical professionals as the proper authority on pregnancy led to a move away from inspection by 'juries of matrons' or similar groups rather earlier.[21] In relation

20 See e.g. pt. VI, tít. VI, ley XVII, *Las Siete Partidas*; K. Watson, *Forensic Medicine in Western Society: A History*, Routledge 2010, 20, 37, 41; art. 35, *Constitutio Criminalis Carolina* (1532); tit. 25, art. 23, *Ordonnance Criminelle du Mois d'Août 1670*; C. Ekholst, *A Punishment for Each Criminal: Gender and Crime in Swedish Medieval Law*, Brill 2014, 67; K. Crosby, 'Abolishing the Jury of Matrons' (2019) 39 *OJLS* 259; S.M. Butler, 'Pleading the Belly: A Sparing Plea? Pregnant Convicts and the Courts in Medieval England' in S.M. Butler and K.J. Kesselring (eds), *Crossing Borders: Boundaries and Margins in Medieval and Early Modern Britain—Essays in Honour of Cynthia J Neville*, Brill 2018, 138.

21 Crosby, n. 20, 263, 281; Sentence of Death (Expectant Mothers) Act 1931. Although J. Oldham, *Trial by Jury: The Seventh Amendment and Anglo-American Special Juries*, New York University Press 2006, 80–114, 93–96, suggests that it was unusual by the nineteenth century, the *de ventre inspiciendo* procedure with regard to 'civil' cases was still mentioned in *Halsbury's Laws of England*, vol. VI, 2nd ed., 1932, 606. Note the earlier change in Ireland, at least in capital punishment cases: N. Howlin, 'Land Valuations, Market Practices, Pregnancy, Insanity: There's a Jury for That', *UCD Working Papers in Law, Criminology & Socio-Legal*

to the use of 'medical experts' in legal proceedings, a distinction between England and Wales, on the one hand, and much of the rest of Europe, on the other hand, is an accepted feature of the history of forensic medicine. In the Holy Roman Empire, for example, legislation from the 1530s required medical experts to be used in some circumstances, and use of 'public' medical experts was also a feature of trials in France, formalised in early modern legislation.[22] Medical expertise was drawn on in England in relation to disputes involving reproduction, but not in the same systematic way, with an official view being commissioned from a single medical source.[23]

2.3.2 *Provision of assessment criteria or delegation of the choice of criteria to experts or others*

There has been variation over time and jurisdiction with regard to the extent to which criteria have been provided for those given the task of determining the presence of life or legitimacy in the legal context, as opposed either to leaving ordinary triers of fact to make a determination on the big question as they saw fit, or regarding criteria as well as assessment as a matter best left to experts.

Some early legal sources did advise on how investigations should be conducted. *Bracton*, for example, sets out a (non-exhaustive) list of factors for an examination in the *de ventre inspiciendo* procedure for determination as to the existence of a pregnancy: the examiners were to feel the woman's breasts and abdomen, as well as 'doing anything else they need to do'.[24] With regard to the confirmation of a claimed pregnancy in the context of a felony conviction, and request for deferral of execution, some guidance might be given to the 'jury of matrons', but generally the common-law courts left it to the women to look for what were designated 'certain secret signs' of pregnancy (or, more specifically, 'quickened' pregnancy).[25]

Studies Research Paper No.22/2017 <https://researchrepository.ucd.ie/bitstream/10197 /9932/1/SSRN-id3082208.pdf> accessed 27.01.2022, 7; sec. 13, Juries Procedure (Ireland) Act 1876 (39 & 40 Vic. c. 78). See also Watson, n. 20, 41; Lefebvre-Teillard, n. 5, 67.

22 Watson, n. 20, 36. See C. McClive, 'Blood and Expertise: The Trials of the Female Medical Expert in the Ancien-Régime Courtroom' (2008) 82 *Bulletin of the History of Medicine* 86, 90.

23 See e.g. Watson, n. 20, ch. 1; D.M. Dwyer, 'Expert Evidence in the English Civil Courts 1550–1800' (2007) 28 *JLH* 93; C. Crawford, 'Legalising Medicine: Early Modern Legal Systems and the Growth of Medico-Legal Knowledge' in M. Clark and C. Crawford (eds), *Legal Medicine in History*, CUP 1994, 89.

24 *Bracton* II.202; F. Maitland (ed.), *Bracton's Note Book: A Collection of Cases Decided in the King's Courts During the Reign of Henry III*, vol. 3, C.J. Clay 1887, 417–18. See also Watson, n. 20, 20; art. 36, *Constitutio Criminalis Carolina* (1532).

25 *Machon v Holt* (1422) YB Mich. 1 Hen VI pl. 8. On quickening, see e.g. S. Gavigan, 'The Criminal Sanction as It Relates to Human Reproduction: The Genesis of the Statutory Prohibition of Abortion' (1984) 5 *JLH* 20, 21, 34; *R v Philips* (1811) 3 Camp. 75, 111; J. Chitty,

There are statements in medieval common-law cases which were taken to set out a strict sound criterion for a finding of life in curtesy disputes.[26] The classic twelfth- and thirteenth-century common-law expression of the test of live birth in this context involved the newborn's cry being heard 'within four walls', and some statements from cases in the late thirteenth century show an insistence on this as the test.[27] There was, however, from (at least) the later fifteenth century, a shift away from insistence on one prescribed criterion and towards accepting that movement or other signs of life could suffice. In broadly similar contexts of property rights for a parent depending on the child's live birth, other medieval legal systems also included some specification of criteria,[28] but this was not a dominant tendency in any jurisdiction.

As (professional, male) medical expertise was given a recognised role, assessment criteria and methods of assessment were increasingly delegated to medical men. Such criteria as were given explicit mention then paid less attention to proxies, such as making a sound or movement, and placed more emphasis on the underlying question of whether breathing and heartbeat had been detected.[29] Systems differed in the timing and nature of the delegation to medical professionals of criteria-setting, in line with the general differences with regard to the role of medical expertise within the legal process noted above, and with regard to the relative importance of women's expertise and that of medical men (as can be seen in the longevity of the jury of matrons, and the 'quickening' criterion associated with this institution in the English common law, in contrast to other systems).[30] There might also be variation in the way in which medical expertise was to be incorporated, whether by entrenching medically agreed criteria in general rules, or by allowing a new appeal to contemporary medical opinion in each case. An example of this last sort of contrast can be seen through comparisons of the way in which systems set (or did not set) a

---

A Practical Treatise on Medical Jurisprudence, pt. I, Roworth 1834, 4; *R v Whycherley* (1838) 8 C & P 262, 487; Bl. Comm. IV, ch. 31, 1.

26 For hints of the relevance of naming, or baptism, in older 'Germanic' systems, see Lefebvre-Teillard, n. 5, 62, 63; *Bracton* IV.360ff.; *Fleta* VI.55.

27 *Glanvill* VII, 18; *Bracton* IV.360–61. G. Seabourne, n. 8.

28 Lefebvre-Teillard, n. 5, 67; Brunner, n. 8, 65ff.; A. Salmon (ed.), *Philippe de Beaumanoir, Coutume de Beauvaisis*, Picard 1899, no. 618; Ekholst, n. 20, 129.

29 *R v Enoch* (1833) 5 C & P 539; *R v Crutchely* (1837) 7 C & P 814, 816; *R v Poulton* (1832) 5 C & P 328; *R v Trilloe* (1842) C & M 650, 651; *R v Reeves* (1839) 9 C & P 25, 26. For concentration on respiration in nineteenth-century French infanticide cases, for example, see A. Tillier, *Des Criminelles au village: femmes infanticides en Bretagne 1825–1865*, Presses Universitaires de Rennes 2001, 27. Adversarial common-law procedure was, perhaps, more likely than civilian systems to highlight disagreements. See also the succession case *Brock v Kellock* (1861) 3 Giff. 58, which shows a range of different opinions as to indicia of life. See also D. Seaborne Davies, 'Child-Killing in English Law – Part I' (1937) 1 *MLR* 203, 206-08; S.B. Atkinson, 'Life, Birth and Live-Birth' (1904) 20 *LQR* 134.

30 In late eighteenth-century Scotland, for example, a more general question as to the presence of pregnancy was put, leaving criteria and method of enquiry to medical men: Crosby, n. 20, 273.

maximum period of human gestation for the purposes of legitimacy decisions. There was never a legislative setting of this period in England and Wales: the matter was one for the reception of evidence in individual cases, from 'medical men' and sometimes midwives, and triers of fact might have to choose between conflicting views.[31] Other western European systems, including French and German jurisdictions, were less reluctant to set out effective, or deemed, maximum limits,[32] but there might still be movement between a strategy of setting general time limits with regard to human development and one of delegating the matter to medical opinion at the time a decision had to be made, building in somewhat greater flexibility. In relation to determinations of the viability of a newborn, French succession law moved from attempts to draw lines based on numbers of weeks of gestation to a delegation strategy: the Code Civil of 1804 opted to leave the meaning of 'viability' to be defined by current expert opinion.[33] A wish to leave tests open for development in medical thought is evident in modern statutes in England and Wales relating to the definition of live birth, in which, for example, a child is to be regarded as having been born alive if it breathes or demonstrates 'any other signs of life'.[34] A slightly different balance exists in the politically controversial area of abortion, which takes into account both medical opinion and also wider opinion on how to set different levels of permissibility for termination of pregnancies, depending on gestational stage.[35]

From the medieval period onwards, it is clear that evidence of the relevant indicia of life might be given by witnesses at a birth, but post mortem examination of the body was also part of legal procedure in all jurisdictions in doubtful cases, becoming the preserve of increasingly professionalised medicine from the early modern period onwards, and involving more invasive procedures.[36] Lest we see the move towards 'medicalisation' of determination of whether or not criteria had been met as an unqualifiedly 'progressive' step, however, it should be borne in mind that conclusions as to the quality of medical expertise

---

31 For an instance of a judge simply asking the opinion of a medical man present in court, though not necessarily giving it decisive weight, see D. Le Marchant, *Report of the Proceedings on the Claim to the Barony of Gardner*, Butterworth 1828, lvii; *Report of the Trial of Waterhouse v Colonel Berkeley for Crim. Con.*, 5th ed., Turner and Hadley 1821, 20.

32 See further below.

33 Lefebvre-Teillard, n. 5, 67; arts. 725, 906 CC.

34 Sec. 1(1), Births and Deaths Registration Act 1953, as amended by sec. 41, Still-Birth Definition Act 1992.

35 Abortion Act 1967; see also F. De Meyer, 'Abortion Law Reform in Europe: The 2018 Belgian and Irish Acts on Termination of Pregnancy' (2020) 20 *Medical Law International* 3.

36 See e.g. K. Dekoster, 'The Legal Foundations of Post-Mortem Examinations in Early Modern Flanders: Princely Legislation, Custom, Doctrine and Judicial Practice' (2019) 1 *Tijdschrift voor Rechtsgeschiedenis* 128, 151; Tillier, n. 29, 27–41; G. Haessler and F. Haessler, 'Infanticide in Mecklenburg and Western Pomerania: Documents from Four Centuries (1570–1842)' (2011) 22 *History of Psychiatry* 75, 86, 87.

in earlier periods are not necessarily positive.[37] This can be seen in the rise and (incomplete) fall of one of the methods which found support in several legal systems for testing whether a deceased newborn had ever breathed: the 'hydrostatic' or 'lung-float' test. This test rose to prominence in the eighteenth century, as a result of support by academic and practical medicine. It came to be doubted 'in learned medical circles', by 1750, on the ground that causes other than the infant having taken a breath might result in the floating of the lung and a positive finding, and modern medical research does not recommend relying on it. Before falling out of favour in England, it led to convictions and executions, which must now be regarded as highly questionable.[38]

2.3.3 Presumptions

Presumptions have been used in both 'criminal' and 'civil' contexts with regard to selected 'unknowns' at the start of life. In the criminal context, jurisdictions across western Europe in the early modern period made strikingly similar legislative, presumption-based, responses to the problem of determining whether or not the now-dead child of an unmarried woman had been born alive and then killed (as opposed to having been stillborn). In England and Wales, an Act of 1624 obliged the woman to show that a child she had borne and disposed of had been born dead.[39] This resembled quite closely the pattern of the French 'Edict against the Concealment of Pregnancy' of 1556, and provisions of the *Constitutio Criminalis Carolina* in the Holy Roman Empire, which likewise presumed murder if there was concealment and infant death.[40] Similar

---

37 See e.g. Tillier, n. 29, 27–41.

38 M. Gaskill, 'The Displacement of Providence. Policing and Prosecution in Seventeenth and Eighteenth Century England' (1996) 11 *Continuity and Change* 341, 359; M. Clayton, 'Changes in Old Bailey Trials for the Murder of Newborn Babies, 1674–1803' (2009) 24 *Continuity and Change* 337, 344, 348, 349. For continued use of, and controversy over, the lung-float test in other jurisdictions, see A. Ahmed, 'Floating Lungs: Forensic Science in Self-Induced Abortion Prosecutions' (2020) 100 *Boston University Law Review* 111.

39 Act to Prevent the Murthering of Bastard Children 1623 (21 Jac. I c. 27). See Seaborne Davies, n. 29, pt. I, 203; A-M. Kilday, '"Monsters of the Vilest Kind": Infanticidal Women and Attitudes to Their Criminality in Eighteenth-century Scotland' (2008) 11 *Family & Community History* 100, 104; P.C. Hoffer and N.E.H. Hull, *Murdering Mothers: Infanticide in England and New England 1558–1803*, New York University Press 1984, 7, 22.

40 F-A. Isambert et al. (eds), *Recueil général des anciennes lois françaises depuis l'an 420 jusqu'à la révolution de 1789*, Belin-Leprieur, Paris 1821–33, (1556) 13:469–71, 471–73; see also (1708) 20:527–29; J. Hardwick, *Sex in an Old Regime City: Young People, Production, and Reproduction in France, 1660–1789*, OUP 2020, 25; K. Wrightson, 'Infanticide in European History' (1982) 3 *Criminal Justice History* 1, 5. Similar laws existed in Ireland, Sweden, and Denmark: D.L. Kertzer, *Sacrificed for Honor: Italian infant abandonment and the politics of reproductive control*, Beacon Press 1993; Bl. Comm. IV, ch. 14, 198. It was not, however, a universal strategy: see J.M. Ferraro, *Nefarious Crimes, Contested Justice: Illicit Sex and Infanticide in the Republic of Venice, 1557–1789*, Johns Hopkins University Press 2008, 118.

statutes would be enacted in Scotland in 1690,[41] and the English 1624 Act, or its scheme, was also, for example, accepted in some American colonies in the late seventeenth and eighteenth centuries.[42] The striking similarity of the laws has been noted by historians, and explained by the similarity of (adverse) circumstances for the mothers of illegitimate children, precipitating desperate action, and the advantage seen by rulers in reaffirming 'commitment to traditional values' in times of change and stress by being seen to act against immorality and the perceived unruliness of sexually active women.[43] In the English context, the implications of the Elizabethan Poor Law, as well as concern about women's sexual deviance, are sometimes emphasised as prompting this action, and a rise in prosecutions for infanticide from the 1580s onwards noted.[44]

These provisions, differentiating unmarried from married women, or others,[45] may be read as condemnatory of the 'sinful' sexual behaviour which gave rise to the situation and the uncertainty, or as a product of a belief that single women were likely to kill their babies, or both. Although the additional burden on unmarried mothers seems considerable, there are narratives on the Jacobean Act which seek to minimise its impact.[46] One, found in some Victorian law books, argues that this change in the law was never meant to be permanent, and was renewed 'almost by accident' under Charles I. The idea that this was in some way accidental is worth questioning: there is nothing particularly odd about 'sunset clauses' and renewals at this time, certainly nothing to suggest that it was not seriously meant.[47] There is more evidence to back up the narrative which emphasises the ways found to avoid convictions and executions, through interpretation of the law in favour of the accused, thus reducing the impact of the presumption. From a relatively early time, there are signs of a limitation of the circumstances in which the presumption operated (requiring some initial evidence that there had been a live birth), and also the construction of routes to rebuttal of the presumption, through evidence of preparations such as the readying of linen, or else unsuccessful attempts to seek help for the birth.[48] In the eighteenth century, the idea that concealment

---

41 Kilday, n. 39, 105; Act Anent Murthering of Children 1690 (2 W&M c. 50).
42 Hoffer/Hull, n. 39, 59–63.
43 Wrightson, n. 40, 11; Kilday, n. 39, 104.
44 See Kilday, n. 39, 104. Hoffer/Hull, n. 39, 7, 22.
45 Gavigan, n. 25, 24.
46 Act to Prevent the Murthering of Bastard Children 1623 (21 Jac. I c. 27).
47 Act to Prevent the Murthering of Bastard Children 1623 (21 Jac. I c. 27); Act for Continuance and Repeal of Diverse Statutes 1627 (3 Car. I c. 5); sec. 31, Act for the Further Release of His Majesty's Army 1640 (16 Car. I c. 4); J.F. Stephen, *History of the Criminal Law of England*, Macmillan 1883, ch. 27, 118. Contrast W. Cobbett, *Parliamentary History of England from the Earliest Period to 1803*, vol. 17, T.C. Hansard 1806–1820, 451–52: observation in a 1772 Commons debate that the law had been considered at length.
48 M. Hale, *Historia Placitorum Coronae*, Nutt and Gosling 1736, ch. 39, no. 289; Gavigan, n. 25, 25; Bl. Comm. IV, ch. 14, 198; A. Loughran, *Manifest Madness: mental incapacity in the*

of birth should give rise to a presumption of murder seems not to have been accepted widely, as explanations of 'infanticide' based on ideas of the likelihood of mental disturbance in new mothers gained ground.[49] Repeal of the 1624 Act was called for in the later eighteenth century, and occurred in 1803, leaving the prosecution to prove a live birth, in line with the general law of homicide.[50] Nevertheless, the fact that the Act was softened in the eighteenth century, and later repealed, should not be seen as support for the idea that it was not seriously intended, nor that it had no effect, nor that it was somehow unthinkable to the generous common-law mind to have such a presumption. Although ways were found to save some young women who might have been hanged,[51] there were convictions and executions as a result of this legislation,[52] and, even in the nineteenth century, when it had been repealed in England and Wales, the idea of adjusting the requirement of proof of live birth before anyone could be found guilty of a child's homicide did not entirely disappear. It can be seen as a strategy in the Indian Penal Code of 1860, under which the prosecution 'did not have to prove that a child had been born alive ... before proceeding with a charge of murder'.[53]

The other commonly used presumption in western European legal systems from the medieval period onwards (and which still has some relevance) is that usually expressed as *pater est quem nuptiae demonstrant*, or, in earthier English paraphrase, 'Whoso bulleth my cow, the calf is mine', presuming legitimacy of children born within, or immediately after, a valid marriage.[54] In the common

criminal law, OUP 2012, 204; Hoffer/Hull, n. 39, 69, 75; Clayton, n. 38, 339; M. Jackson, *New-Born Child Murder: women, illegitimacy and the courts in eighteenth-century England*, Manchester University Press 1996, 151.

49 Lougran, n. 48. Montesquieu criticised the French presumption: *Esprit des Lois*, Bk. 26, ch. 3.

50 Loughran, n. 48, 206; Jackson, n. 48, 158–68; Act for the Further Prevention of Malicious Shooting 1803 (43 Geo. III c. 58). Repeal attempts: Hoffer/Hull, n. 39, 85; Cobbett, n. 47, vol. 17, 452–53 (1772). K.M. Brennan, 'A Fine Mixture of Pity and Justice, the Criminal Justice Response to Infanticide in Ireland, 1922–1949' (2013) 31 *Law and History Review* 793, 798. See also Seaborne Davies, n. 29, 213–16. The lesser concealment offence: sec. 3, 43 Geo. III c. 58; sec. 14, Offences against the Person Act 1828 (9 Geo. IV c. 31); and sec. 60, Offences against the Person Act 1861 (24 & 25 Vic. c. 100).

51 Hale, n. 48, ch. 39, no. 289; Gavigan, n. 25, 25; Bl. Comm. IV, ch. 14, 198; Hoffer/Hull, n. 39, 69, 75; Clayton, n. 38, 339; Jackson, n. 48, 151. Repeal in England and Wales: 43 Geo. III c. 58.

52 See e.g. the cases of Margaret Spicer (1677), Mary Bucknal (1680); *Old Bailey Proceedings Online*, www.oldbaileyonline.org, version 8.0, accessed 02.03.2021, *Ordinary of Newgate's Account*, May 1677 (OA16770504 and OA16770504).

53 D.J.R. Grey, 'Gender, Religion, and Infanticide in Colonial India, 1870–1906' (2011) 37 *Victorian Review* 107, 108–9; D.J.R. Grey, '"It is impossible to judge the extent to which the crime is prevalent": Infanticide and the Law in India, 1870–1926' (2020) 30 *Women's History Review* 1028, 1038.

54 Digest 2.4.5; A. Lefebvre Teillard, '« Pater is est quem nuptiae demonstrant »: jalons pour une histoire de la présomption de paternité' (1991) 69 *Revue historique de droit français et étranger* 331; M. Gerber, *Bastards, Politics, Family and Law in Early Modern France*, OUP

law, reluctance to 'bastardise' a child which seemed to be legitimate was initially expressed through the language of pleading and procedural rules, but by the early modern period, this was being discussed in the language of presumption, as had been the case in continental European jurisdictions for much longer. Sir Edward Coke's interpretation of medieval authorities as embodying a clear rule that, as long as the husband was 'within the four seas', a child born to his wife was presumed legitimate, unless he was shown to be incapable of fathering a child, probably over-simplifies the position. However, the early modern period in England did see a strengthening of this presumption,[55] with its weight beginning to be reduced in the eighteenth and nineteenth centuries, allowing a wider set of arguments and evidence to be acceptable as rebutting it.[56] There certainly was movement towards allowing evidence of the lack of probability of a husband being the father of a child conceived by his wife, from the eighteenth century onwards. Some impetus towards more ready acceptance of evidence in rebuttal of the presumption may also be ascribed to the context in which many of the later discussions took place. In England and Wales, these were often not the 'standard' family property dispute, but, rather, disputes at the poles of the social spectrum: 'pauper' settlement cases and peerage cases. It may be that there was a greater desire to find the 'right answer', as opposed to a 'workable answer' in these cases, or more belief in sexual misbehaviour amongst the licentious rich and the feckless poor.[57] In the case of the determination of succession to peerages, there may also have been some

---

2012, 7; Nicolas, n. 15; R. Helmholz, *OHLE*, vol. I, 560, 787–96; (1304) YB Hil. 32 Edw. I pl. 27; (1406) YB Hil. 7 Hen. IV pl. 13; (1440) YB Hil. 18 Hen. VI pl. 3.

55 Co. Litt. 244a: see e.g. (1304) YB Hil. 32 Edw. I pl. 27; F. Pollock and F.W. Maitland, *The History of English Law before the Time of Edward I*, vol. II, CUP 1895, 396; *Bracton* IV.299; *Britton* Bk. III, ch. 2, no. 15; (1359) YB 33 Edw. III, Lib. Ass. 8; *Calendar of the Patent Rolls 1461–1467*, HMSO, London 1893, 539–40. Nicolas argued that the presumption was becoming stronger until the eighteenth century: Nicolas, n. 15, 24.

56 Nicolas, n. 15, ix, 24, 121; *Pendrell v Pendrell* (1731) 2 Str. 925. See also e.g. Lord Redesdale in the *Banbury Peerage Case* (1811) 1 Sim. & St. 153; E. Guttmann, 'Presumptions of Legitimacy and Paternity Arising Out of Birth in Lawful Wedlock' (1956) 5 *ICLQ* 218. In making comparisons between jurisdictions in this area, it should be noted that the overall likelihood of a finding of bastardy was influenced not only by this presumption, but also by the existence of rules on legitimation by subsequent marriage, and limitation of the occasions on which the matter could be raised, and these differed in different systems: see e.g. Guttman, 'Presumptions', 220, 228. For common-law rules against posthumous bastardising, see e.g. (1276) YB Mich. 4 Edw. I pl. 3; (1281) YB Edw. I Weyland Assize 1; (1283) YB Hil. 11 Edw. I pl. 6. Canon law, more concerned with finding truth and upholding purity and chastity, as opposed to avoiding upsetting property holding or established social relationships, was always more prepared to receive evidence that a child born in a marriage was in fact the child of an adulterer, and this difference in rules caused some tension with the common law: Helmholz, n. 6. Common lawyers emphasised that this strong presumption of legitimacy was a difference from canon law. See e.g. (1479) YB Hil. 18 Edw IV pl. 28; Co. Litt. 244a; M. McGlynn (ed.), *The Rights and Liberties of the English Church: Readings from the Pre-Reformation Inns of Court*, Selden Society 2012, 165.

57 E.g. Le Marchant, n. 31; *R v Inhabitants of Mansfield* (1841) 1 QB 444.

influence from the existence of the procedure of bastardising children by Act of Parliament, independently and in association with parliamentary divorces.[58]

The strength of the presumption has sometimes been overstated. Caricatured accounts of older law may claim that, if the husband was 'within the four seas' at relevant times, matters tending to make access to the wife highly unlikely (such as the fact that the husband was in prison) were not to be taken into account, though this is not supported by evidence, and early sources suggest quite the opposite.[59] It was seen as sometimes producing unreasonable outcomes in the individual case, however,[60] and did possess considerable weight. The desire not to find 'adulterine bastardy' remained a factor even after the relaxation of inhibitions on allowing in evidence to rebut a presumption of legitimacy. 'Adulterine bastardisation' was a matter on which a higher-than-usual standard of proof was demanded, into the twentieth century.[61] Although the scope of its operation narrowed, the common-law presumption against the illegitimacy of a child born during, or shortly after, marriage continued, if in an attenuated form, into the twentieth century, and beyond.[62]

Other western European secular systems also operated a relatively strong presumption in this area, and, likewise, some form of presumption remains.[63] There were differences between systems in terms of just how strong the presumption was and what evidence was allowed to rebut it. This can be seen, for example, if one compares the freedom with which evidence intended to show a husband's impotence could be included in the nineteenth century. While the common law would allow evidence of impotence to be used in rebuttal, whatever the cause of that impotence and whenever it had arisen, the French Code Civil allowed only evidence of 'accidental impotency', and not 'natural impotency [*impuissance naturelle*]' to be used in this way.[64] This difference probably has less to do with profound 'national' variation in ideas about masculinity, and more to do with the unsatisfactory experiences of the early modern French system with the detection of 'natural impotency' in the divorce context, via the *procédure du congrès*.[65]

---

58 See e.g. TNA C 89/3/50, for William Lord Parr (1543).

59 See e.g. T. Reeve, *Law of Baron & Femme; of Parent & Child*, Oliver Steele 1816, 270. For statements to the opposite effect, see e.g. *Britton*, Bk. III, ch. 2, no. 15 and McGlynn, n. 56, 165.

60 Nicolas, n. 15, 162, 247; Le Marchant, n. 31, lviii; Helmholz, n. 6, 361; J.D. Stair. *Institutions of the Law of Scotland*, Anderson 1693, Bk. III, tit. III.

61 Guttmann, n. 56, 217, 219, 228; *In re Bromage* [1935] Ch. 605; sec. 32, Matrimonial Causes Act 1950.

62 For extension of the presumption to encompass assisted reproduction, see e.g. sec. 27, Family Law Reform Act 1987.

63 See e.g. France: art. 312 CC; Germany: §1592 BGB.

64 Nicolas, n. 15, 187–202; M.-L. Engelhard-Grosjean, 'The French Law of Filiation' (1976–77) 37 *Louisiana Law Review* 701, 702. Guttmann, n. 56, 228; arts. 312, 313 CC[1804].

65 Lefebvre-Teillard, n. 5, ch. 2, 11; M.P. Breen, '"An Uncertain, Useless, and Disgraceful Means of Proof": Marriage, Law, and Authority in the Épreuve Du Congrès' (2015) 87

In cases in which a child was born shortly after the death of a woman's husband, the *pater est* presumption encountered another factual unknown—the maximum length of human gestation, which was a matter of some dispute into and beyond the nineteenth century. Coke stated as unquestionably justified by medieval cases a simple rule as to when the child would cease to be covered by the presumption of legitimacy following the death of the mother's husband. He set a 'cliff edge' at 40 weeks.[66] Later cases and writers, however, did not clearly accept this. An early eighteenth-century 'popular' law book, for example, stated that a child born 40 weeks and 8 days after the death of its mother's husband would be legitimate, because the law has 'appointed no exact certain time for the birth of legitimate issues',[67] and there was some willingness to believe that the normal period of gestation might be lengthened in certain circumstances.[68] In the nineteenth century, despite the increasing respect for medical practice, and despite a tendency in other jurisdictions to pin down a definite legal extent for pregnancy, in terms of ending the presumption in favour of a husband's paternity at a set point,[69] the common law seemed to play up the possibility of doubt and dispute.[70] The combination of doubt and an adversarial system seems to have prolonged into the twentieth-century readiness to accept extremely long gestation periods, favouring the legitimacy of a child of married parents.[71] As noted above, other western European systems were less reluctant to set maximum periods for gestation in relation to disputes about legitimacy.

A possible situation which exercised lawyers in different jurisdictions was the relatively rare (but, should it occur, intractable) set of circumstances designated '*turbatio sanguinis*'. This would occur if a woman was widowed, and remarried quickly, then had a child. Was this to be presumed to be the child of her first or her second husband? This problem produced some different responses, favouring the first husband, or the second, and even floating the idea of allowing the child to choose between the two candidates.[72] Recognising

---

Journal of Modern History 771.
66 Co. Litt. 123b.
67 G. Jacob, *Every Man His Own Lawyer: Or, a Summary of the Laws of England*, Nutt and Gosling 1736, 336.
68 Nicolas, n. 15, 70ff.; *Thecar's case* (1628) Litt. 177; *Alsop v Bowtrell* (1619) Cro. Jac. 541.
69 Le Marchant, n. 31, lx, lxi; France: art. 315 CC[1804], now art. 313. For earlier statements of a certain end-point, see Salmon, n. 28, vol. 1, ch. 18, no. 582 (39 weeks and a day).
70 See the emphasis on differing views in Le Marchant, n. 31.
71 See Le Marchant, n. 31; Davis, n. 3; *Gaskill v Gaskill* [1921] Prob. 425, 434; *Preston Jones v Preston Jones* [1951] AC 391, 402.
72 The possibility of choice was floated, rather vaguely, in (1347) YB Mich. 21 Edw. III pl. 40, and occasionally stated thereafter in common-law sources: Co. Litt. 8a. Shared paternity is mentioned in an obiter statement in *Re Heath* [1945] Ch. 417 (Cohen J), see Guttmann, n. 56, 228, but has not otherwise found favour, until the recasting of family relationships in more recent times: A. Ruffini, 'Who's Your Daddy?: The Marital Presumption of Legitimacy in the Modern World and Its Application to Same-Sex Couples' (2017) 55 *Family Court*

the intractable uncertainty of this issue, some systems took steps to avoid the possibility of doubt in this area by restraining early remarriage.[73] We may see such restraints as something of an admission that the *turbatio sanguinis* problem could be impossible to solve (though it certainly also had antecedents in Roman law rules of proper mourning behaviour).[74]

2.3.4 *Avoiding the occurrence of doubt, or legislating it out of existence*

As an alternative to waiting and seeing, or employing the strategies noted above, for dealing with doubt, legal systems might respond to uncertainties before birth by legislating them out of existence. Thus, in England and Wales, the problem of knowing whether or not a live foetus was ever present, when somebody appeared to have made an attempt at abortion, was avoided by the way in which statutory abortion offences were structured. Statutes of 1803 and 1861 did not require it to be shown that there had in fact been a pregnancy before a person could be convicted, focusing instead on the fact that actions had been done in an attempt, or with the intent, to procure miscarriage or abortion.[75] Much twentieth-century and twenty-first-century law relating to abortion removes the need to ask 'is there life?' in a slightly different way, by asking, instead, whether specific criteria are met regarding stage of gestation and the state and circumstances of the foetus and woman.[76]

2.4 Conclusions

It is one of the odder aspects of this history that, in significant areas, increased scientific certainty has come only once the legal issue has lost much of its relevance. This can be seen, for example, with regard to the need to determine foetal life in order to defer capital punishment. Capital punishment was in decline through the nineteenth and early twentieth centuries, and is now no more in western Europe, these developments mostly pre-dating the period over which it became possible to detect early pregnancy with a very high degree of reliability. Likewise, before it became possible to determine paternity with a very high level of certainty, in the twentieth century, the once-extensive limitations on the rights of the 'bastard' were removed to a great extent. It is true that

---

Review 307. In twentieth-century Germany, the BGB favoured the presumption that the child was that of H2: see §1593 BGB. Guttmann, n. 56, 227 suggests French law would favour H1, though this is not specified in the CC.

73 Arts. 228, 296 CC[1804]; Guttmann, n. 56, 217, 227.

74 J. Evans Grubbs, *Women and the Law in the Roman Empire: A Sourcebook on Marriage, Divorce and Widowhood*, Routledge 2002, 220–23. For pre-Conquest English laws penalising the widow's remarriage within a year, see T.J. Rivers, 'Women's Rights in Anglo-Saxon Law' (1975) 19 *American Journal of Legal History* 208, 213; J. Hudson, *OHLE,* vol. II, 234, 444.

75 Sec. 2, 43 Geo. III c. 58; Offences Against the Person Act 1861; Gavigan, n. 25, 35.

76 See n. 36.

there is an exception, in relation to the survival of the importance of biological heredity in relation to the conferring of 'noble' titles based on descent from a particular ancestor alone, as was seen recently in a peerage case, suggesting that the law on 'unknowns at the start of life' retains some faint connection to its ancient bloodlines, but, for the most part, 'bastardy' is an irrelevance.[77] There are, however, certainly 'live issues' in this area.[78] Science alone cannot determine which waymarks in human development, or which indicia, should be regarded as legally significant,[79] since these matters also have important social and political ramifications. In addition, reproductive technology has, in some ways, brought with its new possibilities more uncertainty, which must be dealt with against a background of polarised claims to knowledge, rather than acceptance of lack of knowledge.[80] In forming law for these new areas, it may be instructive to bear in mind that, in the past, the common law, like most secular legal systems, generally restricted itself to trying to find workable, 'good enough' answers to particular practical problems relating to 'unknowns' at the start of life which arose in legal disputes, rather than claiming infallibility, or omniscience, or ambitious and unified theories as to the meaning of 'life'. Given some of the odd formulations and tests which were the products of attempted distillations of even limited areas of legal practice with regard to these 'unknowns', that seems to have been wise, and the modern incarnation of legal response to unknowns at the start of life, with laws and regulations framed according to generalised rules about development timescales, and according to what is politically acceptable,[81] essentially follows a

---

77 *In the matter of the Baronetcy of Pringle of Stichill* [2016] UKPC 16; G. Black, 'Identifying the Legal Parent/Child Relationship and the Biological Prerogative: Who Then is My Parent?' (2018) 1 *Juridical Review* 22; B. Häcker, 'Honour Runs in the Blood' (2017) 133 *LQR* 36.

78 There remains contention over the definition of 'live birth', and disagreement whether it is possible or desirable to have a specific legal definition in this area: see e.g. E.C. Romanis, 'Challenging the "Born Alive" Threshold: Fetal Surgery, Artificial Wombs and the English Approach to Legal Personhood' (2020) 28 *Medical Law Review* 93, 107, 108, 110; *C v S* [1988] QB 135, 145 (Heilbron J); *Re A (Children) (Conjoined Twins: Surgical Separation)* [2001] Fam. 147, 241–42 (Walker LJ); Nuffield Council on Bioethics, *Critical Care Decisions in Fetal and Neonatal Medicine: Ethical Issues* (2006), para. 8.13; J. Hammack, 'Imagining a Brave New World: Towards a Nuanced Discourse of Fetal Personhood' (2013) 35 *Women's Rights Law Reporter* 357, 370.

79 See n. 3, and G.T. Laurie et al., *Mason and McCall Smith's Law and Medical Ethics*, 11th ed., OUP 2019, 9.05.

80 For twentieth-century scientific developments in relation to detection of pregnancy, foetal/neonate life and parentage, see references n. 2.

81 Romanis, n. 78, 120; sec. 1(1)(a), Abortion Act 1967; sec. 37, Human Fertilisation and Embryology Act 1990. For rules on legal parenthood in the case of assisted reproduction, see e.g. R. Kerridge and A.H.R. Brierley, *Parry and Kerridge, The Law of Succession*, Sweet and Maxwell 2016, 19, para. 2.41; sec. 27, Family Law Reform Act 1987; secs. 27, 28(2)(b), Human Fertilisation and Embryology Act 1990; K. O'Sullivan, 'Posthumously Conceived Children and Succession Law: A View from Ireland' (2019) 33 *International Journal of Law, Policy, and the Family* 380; Reid et al., n. 19, 486–88.

similarly 'disaggregated' approach. Not even deference to the achievements of science has effaced the feeling that the 'true answer' to the big questions may always be beyond law's remit or capacity, and the comparative history of legal responses to 'unknowns at the start of life' may be of some use in highlighting the different balances which may be struck between prescription of rules and procedures, scientific expertise, and 'inexpert' lay fact-finding.

3 Commorientes

Deaths, disasters, disappearances

Andrew J. Bell

This chapter confronts an uncertainty problem related to death; one bringing fluid boundaries, deep-seated difficulties, and unintuitive results.[1] '*Commorientes*' captures its gist, referring to parties who die together (in some sense), while also serving as a label for the various legal problems and rules that result from such co-incidence.[2] The critical uncertainty is the deaths' sequence. This sequence matters, in particular, where surviving another (even momentarily[3]) is a requirement in order to inherit from them, and the particular *commorientes* have interrelated succession arrangements.[4] Cases thrown up by this, superficially simple, setup have 'embarrassed the jurists of every country'[5] and have often involved shipwrecks, wars, fires, and floods;[6] outliers include murders[7] and domestic tragedies.[8]

Though the core issues are long known, in support of this book's broader investigation, the present chapter will offer a fresh and more detailed perspective by focusing not on particular '*commorientes* rules/problems' per se, but on the conceptualisation, boundaries, and resolution of the uncertainty problem buried within them and adjacent areas. By analysing commonalities, divergences, and developmental trends across jurisdictions with this broader focus, we can begin to appreciate, better than existing analyses allow, how

---

1 Cf. M. Albrey, 'Coincidence and the Construction of Wills' (1963) 26 *MLR* 353, 353.

2 J. Mee, 'Commorientes, Joint Tenancies and the Law of Succession' (2005) 56 *NILQ* 171, 171.

3 E.g. *MünchKomm*[8]/Leipold, §1923 no. 6.

4 E.g. W. Burge, *Commentaries on Colonial and Foreign Laws*, vol. 4, Saunders & Benning 1838, 11; E. Créteau, 'Un éclairage historique sur l'abandon de la théorie des comourants par la loi du 3 décembre 2001' (2019) 200 *Revue internationale d'histoire du notariat* 45, 45.

5 W.M. Best, *A Treatise on Presumptions of Law and Fact*, Johnson 1845, §141.

6 E.g. P. Zacchias, *Quaestiones medico-legales*, vol. 1, Posuel 1701, 396; S. Stryck, *Tractatus de successione ab intestate*, Schrey & Hartmann 1697, 1232.

7 E.g. *In re Green's Settlement* (1865) LR 1 Eq. 288; Cass. req., 06.11.1895, Gaz. Pal. 1895. II, 628.

8 E.g. childbed deaths: P.J. Pelletan, *Clinique Chirurgicale*, vol. 1, Dentu 1810, 324–41; L.J.C. Mende, *Ausführliches Handbuch der gerichtlichen Medizin*, pt. 1, Dyk 1819, 438–39; Obertribunal Stuttgart, 11.05.1847, (1848) 2 Seuff.A. No. 125.

DOI: 10.4324/9781003537526-4

these rules fit together and sit with close cognates and broader socio-legal circumstances. A clearer and deeper picture thus emerges than before for the surprising variety of means of conceptualising and responding to, and the basic place of, uncertainty of this kind.

After an overview of historical dealings with such cases, the piece analyses the scope of the uncertainty entailed, demonstrating inconsistent tracing of its boundaries across systems and significant factual blurring between this and other problems. The chapter then analyses the range of solutions deployed and the different mechanisms of their engagement with the uncertainty. A conclusion draws out the overarching developmental trends and preferred frameworks discernible. We will see that the problem, freshly viewed in terms of the underlying uncertainty, is broader and more complex than many treatments suggest; that more solutions are practically workable and conceptually defensible than generally assumed; but that, in particular, modern demands for clarity and expediency drive a convergent trend for fewer, simpler, and broader statutory mechanisms of default resolution.

3.1 Historical overview

Roman jurists provided some treatment of *commorientes*,[9] and later European discourse picked up that thread intermittently.[10] For *litigation* to arise, though, events must produce multiple, proximate deaths with insufficient evidence as to sequence/timing, with parties also having access to law, property worth the fight, and no better resolution available. This combination will have been relatively rare.[11] For example, richer families can better minimise, and acquire evidence concerning, deaths from flood, plague, etc. Modern incidence rates are driven by technological and socio-economic developments: mass, motorised travel increased occurrences, for instance; increasing safety measures reduce

---

9 See especially Digest 34.5.

10 E.g. G. Menochio, *De praesumptionibus, coniecturis, signis, et indiciis commentaria*, Gymnich 1595, lib. 6, praesumptio 50; Zacchias, n. 6, 396–406; T.H.F. Gaedcke, *De iure commorientium*, Oeberg 1830.

11 Cf. E. Créteau and N. Rostovtseva, 'The Concept of Commorientes in French and Russian Inheritance Law' (2020) 8 *Russian Law Journal* 4, 17 n. 31, 21. An eighteenth-century English case generated 'attention, as well as surprise': T.M. Shadwell (ed.), *The Posthumous Works of Charles Fearne*, Butterworth 1797, 37, 58; per H.F. Jolowicz, 'Some Curiosities in the History of the Commorientes Rules', in *Festschrift Fritz Schulz*, vol. 2, Hermann Böhlau's Nachfolger 1951, 293–94, prior cases must have occurred and heightened interest is likely attributable to these victims' status and a long dry spell.

them.[12] Mass-destructive military technologies (and industrialised atrocities) have produced many cases.[13]

Correspondingly, case-dependent common-law discussions of the issue arrived late, though juries likely resolved some earlier disputes.[14] Early reports reveal: one case resolved by witness evidence;[15] two apparently settled;[16] and one cryptic judgment involving co-owners dead 'by one blow'.[17] Litigation increased in the early nineteenth century, however, alongside far-flung imperial activities,[18] and World War II triggered another wave.[19] (However, Scotland still lacked precedents in 1944.[20]) Twentieth-century legislation then introduced broad new presumptive rules.[21]

Terminologically, '*commorientes*' is imported and, with one exception,[22] only features in twentieth-century reports, though some commentators adopted it earlier.[23] Lawyers were thus drawing on civilian material, though the courts were rejecting its answers.[24] Comparative references to civilian systems nevertheless remained common.[25]

---

12 *In re Rowland* [1963] 1 Ch. 1, 17–18; W. Nagel, *Das Versterben untereinander erbberechtigter Personen auf Grund derselben Ursache*, Thesis: Göttingen 1983, 2; L. Schoeman-Malan, 'Comparative analysis of commorientes —a South African perspective: Part 1' [2017] *De Jure* 36, 37; cf. travel and communications in disappearance cases, e.g. K. Bellis, 'La personnalité juridique et le cas de l'absent: Le principe de l'unicité du patrimoine n'a pas dit son dernier mot' [2015] *Rev. jur. Ouest* 9, 24–25; *Palandt⁵*/Danckelmann, VerschG Einleitung, no. 2.

13 E.g. *Hickman v Peacey* [1945] AC 304; Cass. civ., 21.01.1960, Bull. civ. I No. 47, 37; BGH, 07.02.1974, IX ZR 64/72.

14 *Mason v Mason* (1816) 1 Mer. 308 went to a jury; *Doe d. George v Jesson* (1805) 6 East 80, 82 n. a)¹ suggests a lost case; J. Pitt Taylor, *A treatise on the law of evidence, as administered in England and Ireland*, Maxwell & Son 1848, §128. Cf. Jolowicz, n. 11, 293–95; T.P. Gallanis, 'Death by Disaster: Anglo-American Presumptions, 1766–2006' in R.H. Helmholz and W.D.H. Sellar (eds), *The Law of Presumptions: Essays in Comparative Legal History*, Duncker & Humblot 2009, 199.

15 *Broughton v Randall* (1596) Cro. Eliz. 502.

16 *Hitchcock v Beardsley* (1738) West temp. Hard. 445; *General Stanwix's case*, in Shadwell, n. 11, 37–72, though cf. Jolowicz, n. 11.

17 *Bradshaw v Toulmin* (1784) Dick. 633.

18 E.g. *Wright v Sarmuda* (1815) 2 Phil. Ecc. 266 n. c); *Taylor v Diplock* (1815) 2 Phil. Ecc. 261.

19 Cf. O. Kahn-Freund, [Untitled note] (1942) 6 *MLR* 89, 89.

20 *Drummond's Judicial Factor v HM Advocate* 1944 SC 298, 301, 304–5.

21 Beginning with sec. 184, Law of Property Act 1925 (hereafter LPA) (from sec. 107(3) Law of Property Act 1922); sec. 31, Succession (Scotland) Act 1964. One niche English rule for cases involving trustees of land was provided as early as 1830: sec. 8, Executors Act 1830.

22 *Re Phené's Trusts* (1869–70) LR 5 Ch. App. 139.

23 E.g. Best, n. 5; H.C. Coote, *The common form practice of the Court of Probate*, Butterworths 1858, 101–9.

24 Cf. Jolowicz, n. 11, 289–90, 295–97.

25 E.g. William Teeling, HC Deb. (24.01.1958), vol. 580, col. 1444; *Hickman v Peacey* [1945] AC 304, *passim*.

In that civilian tradition, meanwhile, scattered discussions featured in Justinian's Digest as concise responses to concrete scenarios.[26] Their interpretive reasoning developed into presumptions (perhaps post-classically[27]) and remained influential;[28] key constellations resurfaced repeatedly.[29] The age of codification then brought new rules, roughly contemporaneously with English developments: Germany codified a presumptive rule in 1900,[30] though it had Germanic predecessors;[31] France codified rules in 1804.[32] Again, cases included examples of travel and wartime destruction.[33]

The analysis below thus primarily considers developments after around 1800, when the existence of discussions either side of the English Channel facilitates comparison.

3.2 Scope of the uncertainty problem

3.2.1 Factual scenarios

Defining *commorientes* problems is tricky, not least because, factually, the concept is widely expandable. The clearest starting point is multiple deaths in one disaster.[34] Where the Roman texts indicate any scenario, these include shipwrecks,[35] wars,[36] building collapses,[37] and fires.[38] Some later writers thought such a scenario critical; others disagreed.[39] However, a 'common

---

26 E.g. Digest 34.5.9.1; Digest 34.5.16.pr. (imperial decisions).
27 M. Kaser, 'Beweislast und Vermutung im römischen Formularprozeß' (1954) 71 *ZRG RA* 221, 239.
28 Cf. R. Zimmermann and J. Gleim, 'Überlebens- oder Kommorientenvermutung bei „gemeinsamer Kalamität"? Schottland, England und die kontinentaleuropäische Rechtsentwicklung' (2018) 135 *ZRG RA* 526, 542–47.
29 Like shipwrecked fathers and sons: e.g. Menochio, n. 10, 693; Zacchias, n. 6, 398; P. Gane (tr.), *The Selective Voet*, vol. 5, Butterworth 1956, 264–65; R.J. Pothier, *Traité des Successions*, ch. 3, sec. 1, § 1; K.L. Arndts von Arnesberg, *Lehrbuch der Pandekten*, 6th ed., Cotta 1868, §27 n. 1.
30 §20 BGB[1900].
31 E.g. I 1 §39 ALR[1794]; §25 ABGB[1811].
32 Arts. 720–22 CC[1804].
33 E.g. Cass. civ., 06.03.1928, Bull. civ. No. 43, 86; Cass. civ., 21.01.1960, Bull. civ. I No. 47, 37.
34 Cf. F. Chapman, 'The Presumption of Survivorship' (1914) 62 *University of Pennsylvania Law Review* 585, 586.
35 Digest 34.5.9.pr., 22, 23; Digest 23.4.26.pr.; Digest 24.1.32.14.
36 Digest 34.5.9.1; cf. Digest 24.1.32.14.
37 Ibid.
38 Ibid.
39 Cf. Zimmermann/Gleim, n. 28, 542–43. Against a common-event requirement were e.g. C.F. Mühlenbruch, 'Ueber die Priorität des Todes' (1821) 4 *A.c.P.* 391, 397–99; Arndts von Arnesberg, n. 29, §27 n. 1. For one, e.g. B. Windscheid, *Lehrbuch des Pandektenrechts*, vol. 1, 2nd ed., Buddeus 1867, 122 n. 5. Cf. medico-legal texts naturally focusing on common accidents, e.g. Zacchias, n. 6, 396; F.-E. Fodéré, *Traité de médecine légale et d'hygiène publique*, 2nd ed., Mame 1813, 215.

calamity' is definitely not necessary in principle,[40] insofar as uncertainty can pertain regardless: deaths occur whose temporal relationship is important, but unclear. This is reflected in systems tending in modern times to frame the problem more broadly.

For example, the rule in Germany's §20, BGB[1900] applied only to victims facing a 'common danger'. Only here was there said to be a factual foundation for the particular simultaneous-death result imposed by the provision, which, in line with popular understandings, ignored the existence of a short interval between the deaths and also reflected the inability of any *commoriens* to enjoy any property inherited during that interval.[41] The scope given to the problem thus followed from the solution given to it. However, 'common danger' did itself then generate interpretive controversy, confusing the problem's boundary. Did it mean the absence of a more specific cause of death than a common dangerous event,[42] or death from the typical risks of a common dangerous event?[43] Was 'danger' necessarily something beyond a victim's control,[44] and when was control lost?[45] Such conflicts obscured the overarching uncertainty problem.[46] Meanwhile, application of the provision by analogy could anyway serve in practice for non-common danger cases.[47]

Replacement legislation introduced in 1939 (§11, *Verschollenheitsgesetz* [VerschG]–Disappearances Act) went on instead to generalise the rule to all cases where it could not be proven that one deceased survived another: the much-criticised, narrower scope of §20 had reduced the rule's practical value.[48] Certainly its implications had defied 'popular understandings' where the 'common-ness' of deaths by infectious diseases, simultaneous fires set by one arsonist, or mass killings fuelled intricate debate.[49] The older rule had also conflicted with other systems,[50] including Germanic codes: Prussia's rule supplemented common dangers (which thus represented a non-exhaustive focal

---

40 Nor implied linguistically by '*commorientes*'; cf. the usages in M.F.G. Sturz, *Dissertatio de consuetudine commoriendi*, Roth 1790.

41 B. Mugdan, *Die gesammten Materialien zum Bürgerlichen Gesetzbuch für das Deutsche Reich*, vol. I, Decker 1899, Protokolle 69.

42 E. Hölder, *Kommentar zum Bürgerlichen Gesetzbuch*, vol. I, Beck 1900, §20 no. 1.

43 F. Böckel, 'Kommorienten' (1902) 93 *A.c.P.* 478, 485.

44 Fromm, 'Zum Begriff der gemeinsamen Gefahr in §20 BGB' (1909) 12 *Juristische Monatsschrift für Posen, West- und Ostpreussen und Pommern* 18.

45 W. Kluckhohn, 'Ueber den Begriff der gemeinsamen Gefahr in §20, zugleich der Lebensgefahr in §17 des Bürgerlichen Gesetzbuches' (1911) 107 *A.c.P.* 354, 371–72.

46 Though see Hölder, n. 42, §20 no. 2 criticising the narrowness of §20 given the uncertainty problem's breadth, an argument somewhat swamped in the debate.

47 *Palandt²*/Danckelmann, §20 no. 1; *Palandt⁵*/Danckelmann, VerschG 11 no. 1.

48 (1939) 101 *DJ* 1311, 1314.

49 Cf. Kluckhohn, n. 45, 365–69, 371–72.

50 (1939) 101 *DJ* 1311, 1314.

point) with deaths 'otherwise at the same time';[51] Austria targeted multiple deaths regardless of their cause.[52]

In England, common calamities are frequently mentioned in *commorientes* contexts, but statutory rules have been broader and never specifically limited to common events.[53] Such rules arrived relatively late in general, though, and single tragedies did have a role both as a point of focus for associated legislative debates[54] and in particular cases.[55] The terminology of 'common calamity' also only arrived later to case reports, but had featured earlier in the literature.[56] In any event, the issue was framed as 'proof of survivorship' and this (inter alia) suggests the problem could always have been seen more generally.[57] For all the relevance of singular disasters within it, modern lawyers saw a wider uncertainty issue.

France is somewhat different, however. Its original codified provisions targeted deaths 'in the same event' (arts. 720–22 CC[1804]), raising tortured questions over 'sameness' rather like the BGB's. Was a double-suicide one event or two?[58] Did three murders around a house[59] or two in one bedroom[60] constitute single events? The approach taken could be very narrow and attracted controversy.[61] The courts interpreted other elements of the provisions strictly, too; they only applied to intestate succession and parties respectively called to

---

51 I 1 §39 ALR[1794].
52 §25, ABGB[1812]; cf. §48, CCGO[1797]; F.E. von Zeiller, *Commentar über das allgemeine bürger-liche Gesetzbuch für die gesammten Deutschen Erbländer der Oesterreichischen Monarchie*, Geistinger 1811, 127–28.
53 See e.g. sec. 184, LPA; sec. 46(2A), Administration of Estates Act 1925 (hereafter AEA); sec. 8, Executors Act 1830. Cf. J.E. Tracy and J.J. Adams, 'Evidence of Survivorship in Common Disaster Cases' (1940) 38 *Michigan Law Review* 801, 802–3 defining 'common disaster' artificially broadly for similar results.
54 E.g. HC Deb. (24.01.1958), vol. 580, cols 1441–68; (19.02.1964), vol. 689, cols 1308–13.
55 See the examples in nn. 14–18.
56 E.g. Best, n. 5, §141. Cf. 'same calamity/accident': e.g. Pitt Taylor, n. 14, §127.
57 Cf. *Hickman v Peacey* [1945] AC 304, 314–15, 337–38; J. Hubback, *A Treatise on the Evidence of Succession*, Johnson 1845, 144. Suggesting a non-exhaustive focal point, W. Dunlop (ed.), *Beck's Elements of Medical Jurisprudence*, 2nd ed., Anderson 1825, 208–9 gave 'common accident' as but one category of survivorship case.
58 Trib. civ. Die, 27.03.1933, Gaz. Pal. 1933.II, 39 (two).
59 Trib. civ. Seine, 02.08.1889, Gaz. Pal. 1889.II, 268 (no).
60 Cass. req., 06.11.1895, Gaz. Pal. 1895.II, 628 (yes). On multiple murders and common danger in Germany, cf. Bayerisches Oberstes Landesgericht, 29.07.1922, (1922) 42 OLG 250.
61 See Cass. req., 06.11.1895, Gaz. Pal. 1895.II, 628, *Note*. For later examples, cf. Cass. civ., 25.01.1956, Bull. civ. 1956.I No. 46, 35 (bombing waves); Cass. civ., 22.10.1957, Bull. civ. 1957.I No. 389, 313 (death camp deportation).

succeed one another.[62] Beyond the provisions' core scope, even any analogical application was also problematic.[63]

Despite any controversy, the 'same event' limiter is still retained today, even following reform (art. 725-1), and even despite the stipulated result (equivalent to simultaneity) now matching in effect that reached in cases beyond the articles' scope.[64] The earlier rules had especially suited the narrower target of common calamities, insofar as they relied on relative capacity for resisting mortal threats to justify certain sequenced results.[65] Among the other reasons given for a narrow application were the exceptional and subsidiary nature of the legal presumptive rules and the questionable necessity of broader application, given the ordinary operation of evidential rules, including generous factual presumptions.[66] The unitary nature of the broader underlying uncertainty problem has thus seemed to matter less here, with ordinary evidence trusted to limit the problem field in practice to a manageable outlier.

Elsewhere, however, the problem has actually expanded yet further, especially to the unproven deaths of missing persons: the uncertain sequencing of merely presumed deaths is often linked to the narrower problem of uncertainly sequenced proven deaths. Such expansions further undermine the significance of any common disastrous cause of death.

England's *Wing v Angrave* shipwreck decision, for example, treated disappearances as indistinguishable from disasters insofar as a sequence of deaths was left unclear by (at least) one's uncertain timing.[67] Meanwhile, in *Re Phené's Trusts*, the estate of a missing man, presumed dead, could inherit if he had survived the testator and, referring to proven-death cases, the court held that 'those who found a right upon a person having survived a particular period must establish that fact affirmatively'.[68] This mirrored the rule in the

---

62 E.g. Trib. civ. Seine, 02.08.1889, Gaz. Pal. 1889.II, 268; Y. Ould Aklouche, *La qualité d'héritier*, Defrénois, Issy-Les-Moulineaux 2017, 136. On 'sameness', other limitations and successor regimes, e.g. H. McCall, 'Presumptions of survivorship among commorientes' (1937–38) 12 *Tulane Law Review* 623, 625–26; Chapman, n. 34, 589.

63 Trib. civ. Die, 27.03.1933, Gaz. Pal. 1933.II, 39.

64 For examples, see e.g. McCall, n. 62, 627.

65 See below 3.3.2.3. A 1950s proposal favoured a simple presumption of simultaneous death; the 'same event' limit was predictably questioned then: *Travaux de la Commission de Réforme du Code Civil. Années 1953–1954 et 1954–1955*, Recueil Sirey 1957, 13, 20, 43.

66 E.g. C. Demolombe, *Cours de Code Napoléon*, vol. 13, Lahure 1879, 126–40. That author thought it anyway sometimes more certain and equitable for each succession to run its course separately (ibid., §110); both this and the narrow approach to intervening rules show solutions again influencing scope.

67 *Wing v Angrave* (1860) 8 HL Cas. 183, 208–9, 218. Cf. the case categories in C.M. Tidy, *Legal Medicine*, William Wood 1882, 25 (common accident; presumptive death).

68 (1869–70) LR 5 Ch. App. 139, 145–52; the court also cited (ibid.) single-death disappearance cases, which in turn referenced calamities, e.g. *Doe d. Knight v Nepean* (1833) 5 B & Ad. 86, 91–92.

Wing litigation.[69] If no specific *time* of death is set by a presumption of death for missing persons, disappearances do produce essentially the same uncertainty problem. Modern legislation sidesteps sequencing issues precisely here: a missing person's time of death is now determined conclusively, reducing resort to *commorientes* rules.[70]

In Germany, the BGB[1900] similarly aligned calamities (§20) systematically with presumed deaths (§§13–19); now, the special VerschG covers both. However, a presumptively established time of death under the VerschG has previously been held not to be determinative of sequencing.[71] Thus, unlike in England, the *commorientes* presumption might still apply in the absence of ordinary proof of sequence.[72] (Such a conflict of presumptions offers broader potential application and increased conceptual pressure for the *commorientes* rule and the overlap in the problems becomes clear.) The same pairing also features earlier in the Germanic tradition.[73] Steinberger, for example, approached disappearances precisely from the perspective of (Roman) *commorientes* rules: the latter required a supplement for cases where it was also uncertain whether the deaths had even occurred.[74]

Systematically, the issues feature as general personhood questions,[75] in contrast to English statutes' predictably more piecemeal collection of individual rules (though English literature sometimes produced broader discussions drawing on civilian work[76]).[77]

French law, by contrast, regulates disappearances separately.[78] This is unsurprising given the continued presence of a 'same event' criterion for *commorientes*, but where a disappeared person was never strictly speaking dead (nor yet alive) under the *Code Civil*'s original *absence* provisions,[79] comparison

---

69 See *Underwood v Wing* (1855) 4 De GM & G 633, 659–60. Cf. generally G. Treitel, 'The Presumption of Death' (1954) 17 *MLR* 530. Disappearances and confirmed, uncertainly sequenced deaths also both featured in sec. 8, Executors Act 1830.

70 Secs. 2, 3, Presumption of Death Act 2013; on the earlier law, cf. Treitel, n. 69, 539.

71 BGH, 07.02.1974, IX ZR 64/72, see [1974] *NJW* 699.

72 This is controversial; e.g. ibid.; *MünchKomm*[8]/Leipold, §1923 no. 18; (1939) 101 *DJ* 1311, 1314. Pre-1939, cf. Hölder, n. 42, §20 no. 3; Böckel, n. 43, 486–88; Kluckhohn, n. 45, 354.

73 See e.g. Arndts von Arnesberg, n. 29, §§26–27; Windscheid, n. 39, §53; I 1 §§35–39 ALR[1794]; §§45–48, CCGO[1797]; §§24–25 ABGB[1812].

74 F.R. Steinberger, 'Verschollenheit', in J. Weiske et al. (eds), *Rechtslexikon für Juristen aller teutschen Staaten enthaltend die gesammte Rechtswissenschaft*, Wiegand 1858, 693–94.

75 Though contrast e.g. *Schwimann & Kodek ABGB*[4]/Posch, §11 nos 1, 3.

76 E.g. Best, n. 5, §§139–41; contrast Dunlop, n. 57, 208–18, using civilian learning but pulled under survivorship.

77 E.g. sec. 184, LPA (proprietary title); secs. 4(2), 54(4), Inheritance Tax Act 1984 (hereafter IHTA) (inheritance tax). Cf. Ontario Commissioners on Uniformity of Legislation, 'Commorientes' (1938) 16 *Canadian Bar Review* 43, 51.

78 Art. 725-1 (succession; formerly arts. 720–22) vs. arts. 112–32 for absentees (personhood; formerly arts. 133–43).

79 Cf. Bellis, n. 12, 27–30. Introducing presumed death was a key aim for later reform efforts: *Travaux de la Commission de Réforme du Code Civil. Année 1945–1946*, Recueil Sirey 1947,

would anyway have been less simple. Moreover, the *Code*'s then *commorientes* solutions, rooted in age- and sex-based survival assumptions, were credible only with common, deadly threats.[80] *Commorientes* thus naturally stood apart, showing once more that the solutions applied have had an influence on the scope of the uncertainty problem recognised.

Overall, the '*commorientes* problem' therefore has a deceptive boundary as an intractable uncertainty. Beyond classic disasters, the same uncertainty and principles can be, but are not invariably, understood to encompass temporally problematic, proven, or presumed deaths in separate incidents. There is feedback, in particular, between favoured solutions and the scope of the problem admitted.

More recent, 'third-generation'[81] statutes go even further in this direction. For example, the US Uniform Law Commission's Uniform Simultaneous Deaths Act (USDA) 1993[82] provides for a person not proven to have survived another by 120 hours to be regarded as having predeceased them (secs 2–4), even where the sequence is otherwise certain. The solution to a problem emerging classically in uncertainty is thus recentred; the broader ('new') problems identified are (cost and administrative) inefficiency, injustice, and arbitrary variation resulting from momentary survivorship, where one deceased represents a mere conduit for title.[83] The new solution avoids precise time-of-death problems, which can only still emerge around the 120-hour boundary. The rule thus bypasses any uncertainty within the period surrounding death, rather than targeting it directly, and sweeps up some otherwise certainly sequenced cases along the way.

England's Law Reform (Succession) Act 1995 preferred a longer time-frame: a deceased intestate's spouse who dies within 28 days is treated as having not survived them.[84] Again, even absent uncertainty, sequences regarded as problematic expand the field: expense, inefficiency, unclarity, and potential departure from the deceased's intentions (if all assets descend to one spouse's heirs) prompt the incorporation of the expanded survivorship requirement.[85] Uncertainty within a wider timespan is made irrelevant and the practical importance of evidential problems is reduced to those around the 28-day boundary point. (In the related context of testamentary survivorship clauses, sec. 11, Succession (Scotland) Act 2016 even provides a rule for residual uncertainty, i.e. as to whether the second death occurred within the boundary of

---

476, 488.
80   See below 3.3.1; 3.3.2.3.
81   Mee, n. 2, 197.
82   The original USDA was promulgated in 1940; see generally Gallanis, n. 14, 196–98.
83   See USDA 1993, Prefatory Note; Tracy/Adams, n. 53, 805, 830–31.
84   Sec. 1(1), amending AEA.
85   Law Commission, *Family law: distribution on intestacy*, Law Com. No. 187, HMSO 1989, paras 56–57.

the survivorship period.) Short-lasting survivors are covered regardless of (un) certain sequencing.

These rules stray beyond '*commorientes*' issues narrowly understood,[86] but recognise an extended field: deaths in a problematic temporal relationship. The problem expands around a broader-seated dissatisfaction and a seamless rule applies uniformly; the solution's usefulness is not constrained by *uncertainty*'s boundaries.

Elsewhere, however, such ideas are ill-favoured. In Germany, for example, a 1940 proposal suggested that common calamity victims should not inherit from one another, even when their deaths' sequence is clear.[87] It was thought unjust that, where the VerschG's uncertainty rule did not apply, succession depended on the survival of one or other party by minutes.[88] Relevant scenarios also produced unhappy disputes over survival, requiring the close investigation of the deceased's lives and corpses.[89] Applying a default rule even in cases where sequencing is possible doubtless relieves such litigation pressures and public dispute over potentially grisly evidence, and at least one later German author sought a similar result, albeit by rejecting an extension of *commorientes* rules and instead reading a qualification of minimum conscious survival time into succession's survival requirement in the context of common accidents.[90] This similarly removes some of the practical sting from an uncertain time of death. However, the solution is rejected by others given, inter alia, the clear statutory provisions currently in place, the perceived difficulty of drawing clear new boundaries, and the legal uncertainty which expansion could produce.[91]

This is, though, to dismiss some of the wider imperatives guiding expansionary approaches, which pertain beyond any artificially restricted boundaries, and to ignore inevitable blurring at the *commorientes* concept's limits. Clear and just boundaries are always hard to place on the scenarios involved. Comparable car accidents might see parties dying: instantly (sequence unknowable); chronologically apart whilst trapped at the scene (knowability depends on discovery, forensics, interferences, etc.); or close in time later in hospital (depends on monitoring, formal death verification procedures, etc.). The potential collapse of *commorientes* scenarios into endless variations in this sort of way is actually well known to German discourse; past discussions of expansion beyond common calamities often took similar form.[92] Equally, it

---

86 Cf. Mee, n. 2, 197.

87 H. Lange et al., *Erwerb, Sicherung und Abwicklung der Ebschaft: 4. Denkschrift des Erbrechtsausschusses der Akademie für Deutsches Recht*, Mohr 1940, 4–6.

88 Ibid., 5.

89 Ibid.

90 Nagel, n. 12, 155–250.

91 See *MünchKomm*[8]/Leipold, §1922 no. 12 n. 3 with references. Criticising Nagel's concept specifically, see A. Ruscher, *Die Bestimmung des Todeszeitpunktes aus erbrechtlicher Sicht*, Lit 1989, 173–83.

92 E.g. Böckel, n. 43, 484; see generally Zimmermann/Gleim, n. 28, 552–53.

remains clear that the effects of momentary survivorship among victims can lead to highly and arbitrarily divergent practical results.[93] The boundaries here can never be perfectly crisp, even where sequences are ultimately identified by some means; the results never wholly predictable and the area suffering from ill-definition and arbitrariness. Seamless regions bleed together, and deliberate 'overinclusion' through expansionary rule-framing neatly sidesteps problems.

It must also be remembered, though, that the injustices caused by momentary survivorship pertain less often where a *commorientes* rule's solution separates, as Germany's simultaneous-death rule does, deceased's successions.[94] The impetus to expand will then be weaker. In this context, again, then, solutions can clearly feed constructions and reconstructions of the uncertainty problem. Still, as Nagel notes, *commorientes* rules framed specifically around 'uncertainty' will only function within the still-awkward boundaries of such 'uncertainty'.

3.2.2 Uncertainty

Thus, alongside bleeding fact patterns run varying levels of uncertainty. Cases arise for (appellate) decision relatively rarely, though, and in part because witnesses and scientific evidence carry us increasingly far towards sufficient certainty for a factual determination.[95] Nevertheless, capricious boundaries can again obtain here. Several, sometimes ill-distinct, levels of uncertainty can be engaged.

Roman sources describe their uncertainties vaguely; they refer in different ways to parties dying 'with' or 'at the same time' as one another with limited context.[96] The basis or extent of not knowing seems unexplored, beyond, perhaps, careful investigation not helping.[97] Whether there were, for example, no witnesses (do not know), or a lack of knowledge and understanding to infer an answer (could not know) does not emerge. This doubtless relates, inter alia, to the absence of modern science, which renders that difference acute.[98] Later, even Pothier could still discuss parties dying at 'nearly the same time' without unpacking uncertainty's nature or depth: public battles and covert murders, domestic infernos and distant shipwrecks all raised their various

---

93 Nagel, n. 12, 2–10.

94 Cf. below 3.3.2.2.

95 Cf. P. Orji, 'Simultaneity of death and survivorship—law of uncertainty and improbability' [2013] *Conv.* 501, 505–7.

96 Cf. G. Hamza, 'Réflexions sur les présomptions relatives aux comourants (*commorientes*) en droit romain' (2008) 1 *Revista Internacional de Derecho Romano* 42, 44; *Hickman v Peacey* [1945] AC 304, 333, 342–43.

97 Cf. Digest 34.5.10.1.

98 Cf. Mende, n. 8, 436–37.

presumptive inferences apparently regardless of the facts being 'unknown' or 'unknowable'.[99]

This ambivalence is also understandable where the boundary between these ideas is necessarily ugly. Suppose witnesses see two drowning victims being (only) submerged together.[100] The respective lengths of time actually taken to drown are unknowable,[101] but do have a vague outer limit: maximum conceivable survival time. Knowable submersion times might therefore still permit a sufficiently firm conclusion on sequence: parties submerged an hour apart will certainly die in corresponding order. However, that boundary of sufficient knowability will be fraught, and further complicated with different proxies, like mere entry into the water,[102] or personal characteristics, like swimming ability.[103]

With increasing capacity to investigate events, levels of uncertainty become more evident. By the nineteenth century, medico-legal experts could offer more useful forensic-pathological evidence, if also defensively in the face of criticism of their discipline.[104] Some writers could then dismiss (the heart-breakingly common) instances involving childbed deaths, for example, as issues for science, not law;[105] for expert interpretation of whatever evidence did exist. Thus, where French witnesses stated that a deceased newborn's heart had beaten after its mother's death, experts were simply relied on for interpretation of this.[106] Unsurprisingly, medico-legal texts offer amongst the earliest discussions of the late-emerging *commorientes* issue in England[107] and prominent, relatively extensive continental treatments.[108] Science expands the realm of the (known or unknown) knowable; inaccessible unknowables shrink.

Scientific progress is perfidious, however. A double-hanging scenario, resolved in *Broughton v Randall* by witnesses' testimony as to movement on the gallows, could hardly be so decided today given more complex,

---

99 Pothier, n. 29.

100 Cf. *Underwood v Wing* (1855) 4 De GM & G 633, 640, 654.

101 Ibid., 657, 660.

102 Ibid., 640–41, 660; Cass. req., 21.04.1874, S.1874.I.349.

103 Cf. Cass. civ., 06.03.1928, Bull. civ. No. 43, 86; *Sillick v Booth* (1841) 1 Y & CCC 117, 124–26.

104 See e.g. F.C.K. Krügelstein, 'Analecten über die Lehre von der Erstheit des Todes' in C.F.L. Wildberg (ed.), *Jahrbuch des gesammten Staatsarzneikunde*, vol. 6, Weber 1840, 301–5 (also providing an overview of existing works); Fodéré, n. 39, 226–28. For contemporary scepticism about the clarity and reliability of the scientific data, e.g. Mühlenbruch, n. 39, 392–94; von Zeiller, n. 52, 128.

105 See e.g. Best, n. 5, §144 n. (a); Nagel, n. 12, 57–59; cf. Mende, n. 8, 439–40 (though German cases might have involved no 'common danger': e.g. Obertribunal Stuttgart, 11.5.1847, (1848) 2 Seuff.A. No. 125).

106 Pelletan, n. 8; cf. I. Offer-Stark, 'When halakhah, science, technology, and ethics converge' in H. Fox and T. Meacham (eds), *Jewish Law Association Studies XXVIII*, Lieberman 2020, 200–2.

107 E.g. Dunlop, n. 57, 208–18.

108 E.g. Zacchias, n. 6; Fodéré, n. 39; Mende, n. 8.

process-oriented understandings of dying.[109] Experts could also hardly now rely on considering the impact of mammary buoyancy or menstruation on drowning victims' survival.[110] Falsification resets apparent 'progress'.[111]

As well as the limits of the unknowable, science has also touched uncertainty's innermost core by creating novel situations where evidence cannot hope to produce a sequence; in particular, instantaneous, mass death by aerial bombing. Jurisdictions like Germany will be less affected here, however, insofar as a default statutory result of simultaneous death means a novel chance of *proving* simultaneity will hardly have altered litigation pressures.

Nevertheless, a very core difficulty might be seen here in concepts of 'simultaneous' or 'instantaneous' death. True simultaneous death may not be physically possible; statutory drafting also sometimes appears not to countenance it.[112] English judgments attempting to confront it show tortured discussions raising (meta-)physical spectres like time and matter's infinite divisibility, double-guillotines, and the distinction between being killed and dying.[113] Judges may keep their footing by establishing uncertainty even for instantaneous deaths in terms of *proof of* simultaneity being less-controversially impossible:[114] thus, the uncertainty condition for applying the English Law of Property Act's (LPA) *commorientes* rule was still met where bombing victims seemingly died together instantaneously.[115]

In earlier English *commorientes* cases, however, simultaneity was often expressly discussed without any qualms.[116] This reduced later, but simultaneity could still arise for discussion where it was enormously improbable. Reporting one case in 1901, for example, the key problem was framed as there being 'no means of ascertaining which, if either, [deceased] survived the other, or whether both perished at the same moment'.[117] Simultaneity was vanishingly unlikely, however, for that case's killings during the Boxer Rebellion. In that sense, the lurking idea of simultaneous death could serve to increase a sense of

---

109 (1596) Cro. Eliz. 502. Cf. Nagel, n. 12, 20–44; Trib. civ. Die, 27.03.1933, Gaz. Pal. 1933. II, 39. Contrast though, perhaps, reliance on timings produced by formal, knowable verification/certification procedures (cf. OGH, 17.12.2019, 2 Ob. 62/19k), if reliable (cf. *Y.N. Kulkarni v Laxmibai Kesho Gopal* (1922) 24 *Bombay Law Reporter* 836, para. [4]).

110 Tidy, n. 67, 30; Tracy/Adams, n. 53, 819 n. 116. Cf. also ibid., 829–30 (guinea pig data); Fodéré, n. 39, 237–39 (gender stereotypes).

111 Potentially producing systemic distrust: cf. Offer-Stark, n. 106, 181–83.

112 E.g. sec. 184, LPA; art. 720 CC[1804]; §25 ABGB[1811]. Contrast unusual, explicit inclusion in secs. 9–10, Succession (Scotland) Act 2016.

113 E.g. *In re Lindop* [1942] 1 Ch. 377, 383; *Wing v Angrave* (1860) 8 HL Cas. 183, 199; *Hickman v Peacey* [1945] AC 304, 317–18, 323, 327–28, 333–35, 338–340, 345.

114 Ibid., 337–40, 345.

115 Ibid.

116 E.g. *Wright v Sarmuda* (1815) 2 Phil. Ecc. 266 n. c); *Mason v Mason* (1816) 1 Mer. 308; *In the Goods of Selwyn* (1831) 3 Hagg. Ecc. 748; still somewhat visible in *Wing v Angrave* (1860) 8 HL Cas. 183, 199, 204, 213.

117 *In the Goods of Beynon* [1901] Prob. 141, 141–42.

uncertainty, even though ordinary concepts had long meant it was no serious possibility: 'whoever presumes it... does little less than confess... belief of a miracle'.[118] Lawyers have thus sometimes appeared to promote default answers by emphasising the uncertain possibilities.[119]

The issue can also impact testamentary interpretation and produce discrepancies. In *Pringle*, three sisters died in a bomb shelter; two (including the testator) were deemed under the terms of a will to have died 'simultaneously', the third to have died after the testator under the LPA rule, which was applicable because the sequence was 'uncertain'.[120] The deaths were uncertainly timed, sequenced, and simultaneous, insofar as the meaning of 'simultaneity' read into the will differed from the accepted understanding for instantaneous bombing deaths. The bizarre-looking result maintained a broad application of the default rule whilst trying to meet testamentary intentions.[121]

'Simultaneity' is thus slippery; an uncertain core for the *commorientes* uncertainty problem, useful for preserving or manipulating the latter's scope.

Procedurally, a related feature of uncertainty is that it can be moulded by the standard of proof applied. Proof on the balance of probabilities can reduce recognised uncertainty by allowing scantier evidence to win out, whilst higher standards can increase the number of instances deemed uncertain—favouring, and further necessitating, gap-filling default rules. This also goes again to a shifting boundary between the knowable and unknowable: if even a slight imbalance in probabilities can establish a conclusion, minimal new scientific input may shift results; more decisive scientific shifts might be needed to generate impact where the proof burden is higher. In both respects, the (at least theoretically[122]) higher civilian standard of proof might thus matter; likewise, any higher standard imposed for common-law *commorientes*.[123] This is discussed with solutions below (Section 3.3.1), where it is otherwise generally clear that civilian systems accepted presumptive and default rules whilst the common law preferred holding to the burden of proof (before shifting, given time and some unsatisfactory results, to a comparable position later).

Finally, forms of *commorientes* uncertainty can clearly stack up. If a ship with explosive cargo disappears, presumed sunk, there can be uncertainty

118 Shadwell, n. 11, 41–48, 42.
119 Cf. Ontario Commissioners, n. 77, 43–44 (however improbable, simultaneity is possible); Tracy/Adams, n. 53, 803 (in any uncertainty, desirable to apply any rule).
120 *In re Pringle* [1946] 1 Ch. 124.
121 Cf. Demolombe, n. 66, 148–49 on limiting any presumptive answer and accepting disparate answers to the same sequencing question for different purposes. Cf. 'coincident' in *In re Rowland* [1963] 1 Ch. 1, and the logically difficult Digest 34.5.9.pr. (each *commoriens* dying both first and second). Generous approaches to interpretation may also avoid such issues: Zimmermann/Gleim, n. 28, 571–72; cf. e.g. sec. 9(2), Succession (Scotland) Act 2016.
122 Cf. R.W. Wright, 'Proving Facts: Belief versus Probability' in H. Koziol and B.C. Steininger (eds), *European Tort Law 2008*, Springer 2009.
123 E.g. New Zealand's sec. 3, Simultaneous Deaths Act 1958 (reasonable doubt).

over whether the passengers' deaths are subject to resolvable uncertainty. It is unknown, because of their uncertain cause, whether their sequence could have been disentangled (unlikely if caused by explosion; perhaps if by shipwreck).[124]

Simple known-unknown and knowable-unknowable divisions repeatedly prove deceptive.

3.2.3 Comparable questions

Variable facts meet variable levels of uncertainty, then, without necessarily producing clean, clearly justifiable boundaries (as opposed to practically and politically advantageous results). It should also be noted that simultaneity and concurrence have elsewhere generated comparable questions.

For example, incompatible, apparently simultaneous incidents needed sequencing in England's *Hales v Petit*.[125] Sir James Hales had drowned himself; at issue was when he committed that felony (forfeiting a co-owned lease) and died (the lease accruing by survivorship). The court held the property forfeit before death, when Hales jumped into the water:

> The felony is attributed to the act; which act is always done by a living man… Sir James Hales being alive caused Sir James Hales to die; and the act of the living man was the death of the dead man.[126]

As awkward as any tortured *commorientes* discussion, this did not hold. Avoiding logical convolutions and unconvincing factual dissections, incompatible simultaneous events were instead reconciled by acknowledging their instantaneous occurrence and prioritising one regardless.[127] Policy-based priorities were a preferable mechanism.[128] No analogy was later drawn in *commorientes* cases, despite similarly problematic chronologies, logical insolubility, and the solution's pragmatic advantage, although one argument proposed understanding the entire timespan touched by uncertainty as one 'instant'.[129]

In the Roman Digest, meanwhile, *commorientes* were interspersed with other instances of uncertain sequencing (births,[130] meeting qualifications

---

124 Cf. Hubback, n. 57, 144: calamities can destroy the critical evidence for deaths they cause.
125 (1561) 1 Plow. 253.
126 Ibid., 262.
127 C. Viner, *A General Abridgment of Law and Equity*, vol. 14, 2nd ed., London 1793, 'Instant', B.1; Co. Litt. 185b.
128 Cf. survivorship's operating before wills: K. Gray and S. Gray, *Elements of Land Law*, 5th ed., OUP 2009, 7.4.16.
129 Shadwell, n. 11, 44–47.
130 Digest 34.5.10.1. Cf., proximate to *commorientes*, I 1 §§14–16 ALR[1794]; Mugdan, n. 41, Motiven 30.

for legacies[131]) and concurrence (equal qualification to receive legacies[132]). The thinking for these doubtful cases was thus to some extent paired/cross-informed.

3.2.4 Summary

In sum, the *commorientes* idea has no well-delimited factual bedrock and can expand broadly depending on the utility of associated solutions. A range of uncertainties emerge from simultaneous events, sequences that (present) science cannot separate, separable sequences insufficiently evidenced, and even certain sequences. Beyond any broadened sense of the parameters, though, comparisons to other doubtful situations are limited. Variation in the underlying scenarios and their scientific-technological circumstances also allow apparent boundaries to move and blur. Actors sometimes willingly shift them; uncertainty can be emphasised to favour applying standard rules. The fluid regions of fact and uncertainty interact, moreover, and doctrinal dividing lines risk making difficult, arbitrary distinctions. More extensive understandings partly avoid this, though, by sidestepping 'uncertainty' to focus on short-lived survivorship.

3.3 Solutions and policy goals

Turning from the *commorientes* problem's structure to its resolution, three categories of response require discussion:[133] establishing a basis for proceeding under other rules by either 1) relying on the ordinary burden of proof or 2) creating a presumptive or fictitious sequence, or else 3) imposing an entirely novel solution sharing or reallocating property.

3.3.1 Ordinary burden of proof

We begin with systems that reject any special solution in favour of ordinary proof. Systems have, at least formally, always reserved the possibility of ordinary fact-finding, regardless of any specific *commorientes* rules,[134] and this evidences the uncertainty problem's blurred scope and core of unknowability.

Beyond this foundational point, courts in England declined to produce any special solution for *commorientes*.[135] Novel suggestions were eschewed and

---

131 Digest 34.5.10.pr.
132 Ibid.
133 Cf. L. Schoeman-Malan, 'When disaster strikes—a case law analysis of simultaneous deaths' (2017) 38 *Obiter* 275, 283.
134 Cf. Fodéré, n. 39, 223–24; Mende, n. 8, 437, 440; B.B. Benas, 'Commorientes' (1942) 6 *MLR* 88, 88; Tracy/Adams, n. 53, 801, 807.
135 Seminally in *Underwood v Wing* (1855) 4 De GM & G 633; *Wing v Angrave* (1860) 8 HL Cas. 183.

there was a refusal to recognise any doctrinal, as opposed to merely practical difficulty.[136] Very early decisions did toy with 'presumptions', but courts overwhelmingly emphasised the need for positive proof of survivorship; absent this, they proceeded on the basis that neither deceased was proven to have survived the other, without going so far as to find simultaneous death.[137]

This rejection of presumptive rules focused on their limited logical foundations and insufficiently accurate conclusions about the true course of events; emphasis lay on the likelihood of a result being incorrect, with references to Romano-French rules.[138] With the same problem and principles understood in England to extend beyond disasters, especially to disappearances, this scepticism about general factual suppositions was perhaps inevitable. Survival turned on each individual's separate (themselves potentially uncertain) circumstances. Fact-based scepticism about the conclusions of French rules for single disasters was thus natural. With disappearances, English courts likewise stressed factual truth: the end-point of the period of absence required to presume death could not serve as a presumed *time* of death, because the absent person's *already* being dead became *increasingly* likely over that period.[139]

Nevertheless, especially earlier in the nineteenth century, courts could at least consider generous inferences of fact in individual cases.[140] Examples included assuming that (military) men were more resilient facing mortal dangers, and women inherently weaker;[141] ideas equally evident in continental discussions.[142] *Ommaney v Stilwell* offers a more unusual approach.[143] Edward Couch sailed to the Arctic in 1845 and his fate was unknown when his father, James, died in 1850. The Chief Clerk thought a presumption based on youth and strength favoured Edward's having survived James. Facing an 'extreme inability to come to a satisfactory conclusion' and 'relying on the chances in favour of the youth and strength of the son', the Master of Rolls saw 'no reason to differ' from this.[144] However, a generalised legal presumption of relative strength is an unconvincing tool where parties faced different circumstances. Meanwhile, as a concrete factual finding favouring the son, this would still only hold if he was especially capable among the Arctic sailors and so likely

---

136 Tracy/Adams, n. 53, 806; McCall, n. 62, 624.

137 *Wing v Angrave* (1860) 8 HL Cas. 183. For earlier decisions stating the rule but adding limited references to an 'assumption'/'presumption' of simultaneous death, see *Satterthwaite v Powell* (1838) 1 Curt. 705; *Taylor v Diplock* (1815) 2 Phil. Ecc. 261; cf. below 3.3.2.2.

138 E.g. Hubback, n. 57, 145; cf. 'The Uniform Simultaneous Death Act' [Notes and Legislation] (1953) *Iowa Law Review* 750, 751.

139 *Doe d. Knight v Nepean* (1837) M & W 894, 913; *Re Phené's Trusts* (1869–70) LR 5 Ch. App. 139, 151–52. Contrast Germany, e.g. Windscheid, n. 39, 121 n. 1.

140 Cf. Tracy/Adams, n. 53, 810–13.

141 E.g. *Taylor v Diplock* (1815) 2 Phil. Ecc. 261, 278–79; *Colvin v Procurator-General* (1827) 1 Hagg. Ecc. 92.

142 E.g. Fodéré, n. 39, 237–39, 249.

143 (1856) 23 Beav. 328.

144 Ibid., 331–33.

among the longer-surviving of them (seen alive after James' death). Whether this was the decision's intended basis is unclear, but the judgment does not, for example, make much of the fact that only around 30% of the sailors saw 1850.[145] The case and its suppositions are thus difficult. It is an unusually late and blatant instance of such adventurous decision-making, however. The ordinary-proof approach concretised around a tendency to dismiss such extrapolations; cases might be criticised for 'guessing at facts', 'such… as would be reached by applying the civil law rule' with 'little or no evidence to support a conclusion'.[146]

As discussed above, the possibility of simultaneous deaths could also be suggested to increase perceived uncertainty and promote default answers/disfavour an adventurous factual finding. A similar trend to this can still be seen in the law, now in relation to statutory presumptive rules, and shows continued use (or manipulation) of the burden and standard of proof. Stressing uncertainty can help discourage moves away from the statutorily determined results. In *Re Beare*, for example, even uncontradicted medical evidence as to sequence could not displace the LPA's default answer.[147] A similar reticence with even leading experts' medical opinions has sometimes also served across the Channel and earlier to promote available default rules at the expense of less definite assessments of concrete facts. When a Seine ferryboat sank in 1751, for example, a merchant family were drowned; although the facts could lead celebrated doctors to the opposite conclusion, a presumption was applied that the adult daughter survived her parents.[148] This contrasts with the optimism of contemporary medical men themselves about their ability to help make accurate determinations.[149]

Returning to twentieth-century England, when Jenkins J felt unable to reach a conclusion in *Re Bate*, given discordant medical testimony, the suggestion is almost that any discord will mean insurmountable uncertainty. Required is 'a conclusion of fact on grounds which so far outweigh any grounds for a contrary conclusion that [you] can ignore the latter'.[150] Based on a review of House of Lords dicta, this was framed as the *minimum* possible standard for proof here.[151] As noted, such stances on the burden and standard of proof increase recognised instances of uncertainty, limiting departures from any default rule. In Ireland, a statutory interpretation that produces a higher

---

145 A fact in evidence, but not emphasised in judgment: ibid., 329–30.
146 Chapman, n. 34, 592–94.
147 *The Times*, 04.10.1957, 5; cf. *In re Lindop* [1942] 1 Ch. 377, 379–83.
148 *Parlement de Paris*, 07.09.1752, in Fodéré, n. 39, 220–21. Cf. Trib. civ. Die, 27.03.1933, Gaz. Pal. 1933.II, 39, but also e.g. Cass. civ., 06.03.1928, Bull. civ. No. 43, 86 (*Code* rules ousted by extensive general evidence of personal characteristics); Cass. civ. 1, 21.01.1960, Bull. civ. I No. 47, 37 (particularly clear contrast between injured and uninjured bodies).
149 E.g. Mende, n. 8, 442; Fodéré, n. 39, 226–28.
150 [1947] 2 All ER 418, 421.
151 Ibid.

standard of proof is similarly favoured, inter alia for better avoiding (familial) litigation.[152]

Accordingly, though, there is also now less temptation to emphasise the breadth of the range of scenarios that are conceivable on the facts. In *Bate*, for example, *Hickman* was distinguished 'because no question of simultaneous deaths' arose.[153] If simultaneous death is possible at all, it was *possible* with the Bates' deaths, as with those in *Hickman*. This possibility could have been admitted. That it was dismissed suggests that the need to establish a sense of uncertainty sufficient to justify a default answer was already, and more credibly, satisfied by the stricter position on proof. (Limited recent dicta buck the trend and favour a normal 'balance-of-probabilities' standard of proof;[154] this could accordingly reduce the modern sec. 184 *commorientes* rule's suppressive effect on litigation.)

Early arguments also sometimes interrogated the *proportion* of the potentially true scenarios that favoured one or other litigant winning, though these fell flat. In *Wing*, for example, it was stressed that Wing would receive the estate under any scenario;[155] he would take in different capacities, however, so the argument failed.[156] It could thus apparently only have succeeded where recipient and capacity of receipt were already certain and dispute anyway unlikely. The case report gives no sense that Wing's succeeding in the wrong capacity might be preferable to his not succeeding at all. Similarly, in *Mason* the Master of the Rolls understood the 'stress of the argument' in the early *General Stanwix's Case* as favouring the deceased General's representatives, because two out of the three potentially true scenarios would have seen them succeed.[157] Such thinking was not conclusive and *Mason* went to trial. (A similar style of argument was made in a contemporary Swiss case.[158])

The shift from potentially generous inferences to more constant emphasis of uncertainty (using first 'simultaneity', then the statutory 'certainty' idea), manipulating burden and standard of proof, can be viewed against contemporary trends. The early background is the novelty and extreme difficulty of the problem, which combined with expanding medical-forensic analysis and produced some more adventurous conclusions before the case-law stabilised matters. Scientific advances risk increasing litigation, but equally thus increasing the force of the general policy demands of clarity and certainty which support default positions.[159]

---

152 *Re Kennedy* [2000] 2 IR 571.
153 [1947] 2 All ER 418, 420.
154 *Scarle v Scarle* [2019] EWHC 2224, paras [16]–[25].
155 *Wing v Angrave* (1860) 8 HL Cas. 183, 204–5.
156 Ibid., 210–12. Cf. *Ross's Judicial Factor v Martin* 1955 SC 56.
157 *Mason v Mason* (1816) 1 Mer. 308, 312–13.
158 See J.H. Kopp, 'Beitrag zur Lehre von der Priorität des Todes', in J.H. Kopp (ed.), *Jahrbuch der Staatsarzneikunde*, J.C. Hermann 1814, 181–88, 186–87.
159 See below 3.3.2.

Nineteenth-century English lawyers even ultimately showed scepticism about continental analysis where the latter did engage more concrete case facts, as where the French approach encouraged dissecting the deceased's health, temperament, etc.; for English courts this involved mere guesswork. Even medico-legal works, naturally more inclined than others to promote factual investigation, might look on the French general approach and default framework only as a highly flawed best attempt.[160] Criticisms perhaps, though, underplayed both the advantages of having a clear, positive default answer available and French courts' willingness to default to one.

However, the common-law approach did bring positive benefits, too, and did not just avoid other options. To an extent, it appeared to operate as an equaliser: 'inability to ascertain the truth no more assisted the claim of [one party] than that of [the other]'[161] (if most obviously where, absent proof, estates fell into intestacy/vacant[162]). The approach ultimately advantaged parties not required to prove survivorship, however, favouring legal successors to property's pre-deaths owners.[163] (And, unlike in Germany, for example, England's succession rules did not mean that this advantage would lead to an arbitrary result based on first possession following death.[164]) The effective result compared to a presumption of simultaneity,[165] which might have been a more direct and reliable mechanism to achieve the desired results, but was ruled out by concern for true facts: simultaneity was impossible, improbable, and/or unprovable. For disappearances, similarly, policy featured in argument, but could not produce a decisive, radical new form of rule, despite a purely factual approach's potential to generate some unfortunate results.[166]

In Germany, no rule was initially planned for inclusion in the BGB, either, in preference to Romano-French presumptions. German lawyers' criticisms of the latter as to factual truth were similar to their English counterparts' in relation to, for example, the insufficient basis for the sorts of conclusions imposed and the potential for complex rules to generate only more uncertainty, unpredictability, and litigation.[167] As discussed below, the solution actually reached

---

160 E.g. Dunlop, n. 57, 207, 217–18.
161 *Wing v Angrave* (1860) 8 HL Cas. 183, 207–8.
162 As in Wing's cases; cf. in Scotland *Ross's Judicial Factor v Martin* 1955 SC 56; *Drummond's Judicial Factor v HM Advocate* 1944 SC 298.
163 *Taylor v Diplock* (1815) 2 Phil. Ecc. 261, 278; cf. Hubback, n. 57, 146, 149–52.
164 See Jolowicz, n. 11, 296–97; Mugdan, n. 41, Protokolle 68.
165 A fact recognised: e.g. Hubback, n. 57, 150.
166 See *Doe d. Knight v Nepean* (1833) 5 B & Ad. 86, 95–96; (1837) M & W 894, 913–14. Cf. Demolombe's arguments in France—n. 66, 119, 128–32—on the serviceability of evidential rules (in arguments for restrictively applying legal presumptions) and the inevitability of untruthful decisions.
167 See e.g. Mugdan, n. 41, Motiven 32; Böckel, n. 43, 480. Again, even medico-legal texts might focus on *expediency* more than *accuracy*: cf. A. Henke, *Lehrbuch der gerichtlichen Medizin*, 4th ed., Dümmler 1824, §505.

for in Germany was a different presumption (simultaneity), not English-style factual puritanism rooted in ordinary proof.

Meanwhile, though, beyond the scope of arts. 720–22 and in the absence of factual hooks, the French courts did actually produce results similar to German and English courts; they could proceed as if neither party survived the other and administer the successions of each as if the other had not existed.[168]

3.3.2 Presumptive bases

3.3.2.1 Number of rules

Turning to default presumptive rules, a preliminary issue is how many are used, and thus how much conceptual and epistemological weight bears on each.

Roman *commorientes* discussions were casuistic, with isolated treatment of separate fact patterns (father/adult son; father/minor son; etc.), understood as experience-based opinions on the better inference for those facts.[169] Later interpretations disagreed on generalising these decisions.[170]

The *Code Civil* reflects this background and a modern shift, with an original framework of multiple (non-comprehensive[171]) presumptive rules based on age and sex now replaced by a single rule that common calamity *commorientes* cannot succeed one another.[172] Many authors had recognised the problematic complexity (and incompleteness) of the earlier rules.[173] As von Zeiller earlier suggested in Austria, intricate discussions could be left to individual cases to avoid complicating statutory rules and exceptions, which would themselves then generate unreliability and uncertainty.[174] Beyond regional codifications, the position was also more complex and controversial than now in nineteenth-century German states; a prominent opinion accepted Romanist presumptions for the survivorship of parents and children, alongside a general default of simultaneous death.[175] The BGB's first draft included no rule (one being thought unnecessary given the rules on proof, or else certain to impose a different, insufficiently supported result[176]); the second did, but now as a clear, singular presumption (simultaneous death).

---

168 E.g. Trib. civ. Die, 27.03.1933, Gaz. Pal. 1933.II, 39
169 Kaser, n. 27, 235–38, 239.
170 Cf. above 3.2.1.
171 E.g. Cass. civ., 08.02.2005, Bull. civ. 2005 I No. 79, 69, though early opinion supplemented the stated rules through general principles of strength of age or natural order; see generally Créteau, n. 4, 48–50.
172 Arts. 720–22 CC[1804]; art. 725-1 CC.
173 See *Travaux* (1957), n. 65, 13.
174 von Zeiller, n. 52, 128.
175 Arndts von Arnesberg, n. 29, §27; Windscheid, n. 39, 122. A French-style force-of-age concept was preferred by e.g. Gaedcke, n. 10.
176 Mugdan, n. 41, Motiven 32.

The English trend is somewhat different, with judicial distaste for any specific presumptions (discussed above) eventually giving way to several statutory provisions.[177] However, the distinctions now drawn—unlike the older continental tradition—do not endorse different factual survival suppositions, but limited responses to policy issues. (Correspondingly, 'common calamities' have not been separated from other instances.) A specific concern over married *commorientes* spawned an exception for intestate spouses to the LPA's general survivorship rule, for example, now further expanded by such concerns.[178] Factually driven presumptive approaches require more (complex) rules to be defensible; policy-driven positions can, depending on their content, rely on fewer rules.

Various such policies bear on the provision and content of rules. Many militate only towards the creation of *any* default solution, including clarity, certainty, and reducing expensive and burdensome litigation.[179] Avoiding the potential for an arbitrary result based on first post-death possession, as a consequence of the operation of successions generally, also fell into this category for civil lawyers.[180] Many such general concerns also promote fewer, simpler rules. In England, whether sec. 184, LPA actually covers 'simultaneous' death was thus a question arguably resolvable by the need for a more complete single response to the mischief being targeted by the rule.[181] Factually driven presumptive frameworks like the 1804 French rules fail against such criteria.[182]

Other policies favour particular solutions and piecemeal frameworks, rather than broader uniform rules. Such an approach can respond to difficult and blurred boundaries, but may produce little more predictability or clarity than squarely factual approaches, albeit whilst providing opportunities to promote other goals, like privileging certain categories of beneficiary.[183] This contrasts most strongly with solutions at the other end of the spectrum, which, whilst the simplest, offer random results. Prussia's *Allgemeines Landrecht* (ALR), for example, comparably determined the sequence of twin births by lots,[184] eschewing even broad priorities (like males first[185]) and fictional simultaneity.

---

177 E.g. sec. 184, LPA; sec. 46(2A), AEA; sec. 4(2), IHTA. (Sec. 8, Executors Act 1830 is a very niche exception in the early period.) Cf. secs. 9–11, Succession (Scotland) Act 2016; secs. 2–4, 6 USDA 1993; and New Zealand's sec. 3, Simultaneous Deaths Act 1958.

178 See former sec. 46(3), now sec. 46(2A), AEA. This has been said to show disdain for an LPA rule that requires complex replacement: J.D.M. Derrett, 'The Hindu Succession Act, 1956: An Experiment in Social Legislation' (1959) 8 *American Journal of Comparative Law* 485, 500; J.D.M. Derrett, '*Commorientes*' (1962) 20 *University of Ceylon Review* 55, 82–83. In defence of simplicity, see e.g. Ontario Commissioners, n. 77, 47–49.

179 See e.g. ibid., 44, 47, 49; Treitel, n. 69, 536, 538–39.

180 See the references in n. 164.

181 See *Hickman v Peacey* [1945] AC 304, 338, 343.

182 Cf. 'The Uniform Simultaneous Death Act', n. 138, 751; Treitel, n. 69, 538–39.

183 E.g. Roman patrons: Digest 34.5.9.2.

184 I 1 §16 ALR[1794].

185 Cf. Gane, n. 29, 264.

(The rule's limited practical significance likely offset the artificiality involved, given that it only applied if a sequence was particularly necessary.[186])

Thus, even the number and generality of *commorientes* rules reflect competing tensions between respecting truth and both general and particular policy imperatives.[187] Systems nowadays tend to prefer fewer and simpler general rules.

3.3.2.2 Presumptions of simultaneity

Substantively, a common presumptive answer to *commorientes* questions is simultaneous death. This answer is inevitably difficult, insofar as it likely never corresponds with truth, though the extent to which such correspondence is demanded can vary (inter alia with the perceived form of the rule).[188] Some rules, like art. 725-1 CC, do not strictly impose simultaneous death, but stipulate the consequence that neither of the deceased will be called to the succession of the other (leapfrogging sequencing to reach the same results).[189] Concerns over the theoretical or practical possibility of 'simultaneity', if not over the policy or acceptability of its results, are avoided when a system in this way does not explicitly find simultaneity. In any event, rules stipulating simultaneity or its equivalent have been accepted often and since ancient times.[190] Such rules represent a solution that has for some time been the direction of travel for European thought.[191] Simultaneity is now provided for in, for example, Germany, Austria, and the Netherlands.

Policy bases used to support simultaneity rules include their effect in reducing complexity and arbitrariness.[192] For von Zeiller, a statutory simultaneity rule could avoid complex layered frameworks leading to exceptions and uncertain and unreliable results; more intricate probabilistic thinking about the likely course of events could be given over to free proof in individual cases.[193] Necessity has also driven presumptive rules and 'simultaneity' results—without a provision, the uncertainty of the fact would otherwise create a gap

---

186 See I 1 §§14–15 ALR[1794]; cf. Henke, n. 167, §§112–13 (also noting that answers to the birth-sequence question can be more political than medical).

187 Cf. Treitel, n. 69, 530, 535–36, 545–46.

188 Consider Mühlenbruch, n. 39, 400; Ruscher, n. 91, 166: the rule must concern the burden of proof, because it cannot produce a real presumption of fact; contrast Mugdan, n. 41, Protokolle 69, implying a necessary factual foundation for the rule originally (matching a common-calamity restriction on its scope).

189 Contrast earlier reform proposals—*Travaux* (1957), n. 65, 20—and the paraphrasing of commentators like Créteau, n. 4, 45 ('*parfaitement simultanée*').

190 E.g. Digest 34.5.9.pr.; Digest 34.5.18.

191 Cf. Zimmermann/Gleim, n. 28, 566–67, 557–61.

192 E.g. *Travaux* (1957), n. 65, 13, 20; Nagel, n. 12, 7, 146, 183; cf. Demolombe, n. 66, 127–40.

193 von Zeiller, n. 52, 128.

in regulation.[194] (Not everyone, though, has recognised a clear-cut need.[195]) Statutory presumptions of simultaneity are also defended as an equitable means to meet practical demands insofar as they can end doubt.[196] Like an ordinary-proof solution, the approach frees a system from needing intricate rules to coordinate a response, where such rules might themselves produce fresh complexity and uncertainty.[197]

Though England resisted presumed simultaneity, some earlier cases did edge that way. In *Wright v Sarmuda*, assuming simultaneous death was said to be fair and reasonable.[198] The court in *Satterthwaite v Powell* was similarly content to discuss the default burden-of-proof-driven result as a presumption of death at the same moment.[199] Often used,[200] this framing is false: it was simply that nothing could conclusively be said of survival or predecease; the solution accepted insolubility. Several statutory rules do, though, now join the trend favouring presumed simultaneity or an equivalent, including the Inheritance Tax Act 1984 (presume death at the same instant) and the amended Administration of Estates Act 1925 (treat parties as not having survived each other).[201] The latter rule is bolstered by further policy aims, including avoiding inefficient estate administrations; effects also achievable with an ordinary simultaneous-death rule for cases involving uncertainty. All such rules can avoid undue preferences.

3.3.2.3 Presumed sequences

Though less common today, systems have also often used rules that sequence victims' deaths. This, too, raises questions of historical truth and policy impact. Much turns on the framework's nuance.

For example, several Roman texts took parents to die before adult sons and, factually, these assumptions certainly sometimes hold good as factually more likely.[202] Consider the shipwreck of a frail father and strong adult son. In policy terms, the conclusion also preserves the ordinary line of succession and so, often, favours deliberate succession arrangements.[203] The same applies

---

194 E.g. Hölder, n. 42, §20 no. 2.
195 See e.g. Mugdan, n. 41, Motiven 32; Demolombe, n. 66, 127–140.
196 Mugdan, n. 41, Protokolle 68.
197 Cf. Böckel, n. 43, 484 and again e.g. von Zeiller, n. 52, 128.
198 (1815) 2 Phil. Ecc. 266 n. c), 277.
199 (1838) 1 Curt. 705, 707.
200 See e.g. Chapman, n. 34, 594; 'The Uniform Simultaneous Death Act', n. 138, 751; L. Schoeman-Malan, 'Comparative analysis of commorientes', n. 12, 43; cf. also Tracy/Adams, n. 53, 807.
201 Sec. 46(2A); see also sec. 9(1), Succession (Scotland) Act 2016; cf. mutual survival; 'The Uniform Simultaneous Death Act', n. 138, 750.
202 See e.g. Digest 34.5.9.1, 4; Digest 34.5.22; Digest 23.4.26.pr (*verisimilius*). Cf. Tacitus' account of Lucius Vetus and his family dying in appropriate order: *Annales*, 16.11.
203 Cf. Digest 34.5.9.4 stressing the son's inclusion in the father's will as heir.

for the equivalent rules for minor children (child dies first).[204] Factually, such assumptions cannot always hold, though; some scholars suggest that a (policy-based) secondary reason for a decision was added where the factual reasoning was weakest.[205] Sequences have also often been seen as special exceptions (to simultaneity),[206] though 'simultaneity' could also be formally constructed as an impossible, fictious sequence: dying both first and second.[207]

Later continental writers also imposed sequences using factual and policy bases. Sometimes, factual presumptions could be applied regardless of policy implications, though at best as plausible speculations. For example, vanguard soldiers would die before the rearguard in battle, and murderers kill adults before less threatening children.[208] Similarly, where a father and son died in a battle begun at midday, when their daughter/sister became a nun, the latter's civil death, being deliberate, concluded first.[209] France's 1804 provisions set a framework based on age and sex as an ultimate legal default position—old age and childhood were periods of relative weakness; women were weaker.[210]

In rarer instances, factual assumptions were completely departed from and external goals alone drove decisions. For example, a Roman freedman was deemed to outlive even his adult son out of respect for his patron, who could then inherit.[211] Comparably, a humane impulse to maximise freedom could determine the sequence of a slave's twin births.[212] In France and Germany, the (equivalent to) simultaneity now preferred exemplifies the triumph of factually improbable, practically convenient results. General policy arguments and concerns to best match deceased's intentions have won out over factual inferences, and thus sequenced results; they often attack sequenced solutions' propensity to let estates devolve to unexpected or undesired collateral relatives.[213]

The same is not quite true for England. Sequencing from experiential assumptions did emerge in some earlier case law; a flagrant example is *Sillick v Booth*, where the court was (controversially[214]) willing to draw presumptions of survival from general characteristics, like health and experience.[215] The developing, stabilised burden-of-proof approach put paid to this. Thereafter, legislative interventions, albeit late-coming, did not tend as continental experience

---

204 E.g. Digest 34.5.9.4; Digest 34.5.23. Pupillary testaments might complicate matters.
205 See e.g. Mühlenbruch, n. 39, 406; Hamza, n. 96, 52.
206 E.g. Windscheid, n. 39, 122; cf. Derrett, n. 178, 62–66.
207 Digest 34.5.9.pr.
208 Pothier, n. 29; Burge, n. 4, 14.
209 Fodéré, n. 39, 219–20.
210 See generally Créteau, n. 4, with further references and e.g. Fodéré, n. 39, 222–26. See e.g. Cass. civ., 06.03.1928, Bull. civ. No. 43, 86 for the statutory defaults overturned on other circumstantial evidence.
211 Digest 34.5.9.2. Cf. also Digest 36.1.35.
212 Digest 34.5.10.1.
213 E.g. Zimmermann/Gleim, n. 28, *passim*; Nagel, n. 12, 4–7.
214 See Chapman, n. 34, 591.
215 (1841) 1 Y & CCC 117.

might have suggested: the LPA's *commorientes* rule has favoured a younger party's survivorship. The legislature's reasoning for this particular rule is unclear—while cost-efficiency seemingly prompted the creation of a rule, the thinking on sequence is obscure.[216] However, it presumes death in the natural, expected line, and so will promote deliberate arrangements. The thinking must have been detached from assumptions about a likely sequence of deaths on the facts, regardless: given its application beyond common events, the rule cannot function in that way.[217]

In passing the rule, one policy concern was briefly revealed: the rule could send land in unanticipated directions, because wives were often younger than their husbands.[218] Such concerns have contributed to the departure from the general rule made for spouses, noted already. This specifically targeted spouses' estates descending on intestacy, though, rather than a general uncertainty or *commorientes* analysis.[219] The general, sequenced rule thus remains in place, though its policy basis is neither clear nor firm compared to a presumption of simultaneity—and in truth it requires a stronger support—because it favours one side.

Further policy reasons supporting specific sequencing decisions include respecting the presumed intent of an insured for an insurance policy's benefit to be felt,[220] and, somewhat differently, the policy of the forfeiture rule. Forfeiture entails a party's loss of inheritance interests so that they cannot benefit from their wrongdoing; since 2011, English murderers (including murderer-suicides) barred from succeeding by the forfeiture rule on intestacy or to a gift under a will are 'to be treated… as having died immediately before' their victims for these purposes.[221] This mechanism followed Law Commission criticism of forfeiture's implications for descendants: formerly, the rule simply excluded killers, and thus their descendants, from inheriting; the latter suffered for another's wrongdoing arbitrarily, and inconsistently with the deceased's likely wishes.[222] The convenience of a deemed/fictional predecease now outweighs the imperative of truth. Improbable or impossible policy-driven death

---

216 See Gallanis, n. 14, 192. Cynics might see an attempt to increase death duty revenues—e.g. 'Current Topics' (1927) 71 *SJ* 549, 550; cf. Parliamentary responses to the *Re Beare* decision: HC Deb. (24.01.1958), vol. 580, cols 1441–68 (Double Death Duties Bill).

217 Though sometimes treated otherwise: Ontario Commissioners, n. 77, 47–48; Derrett, '*Commorientes*', n. 178, 66 (assuming derivation from French rules, themselves actually limited to common events).

218 Thomas Bramsdon, HC Deb. (15.05.1922), vol. 154, col. 136.

219 Law Commission, *Family law: Distribution on Intestacy*, n. 85, paras 56–57.

220 See e.g. 'The Uniform Simultaneous Death Act', n. 138, 759.

221 Secs. 1(2), 2(2), Estates of Deceased Persons (Forfeiture Rule and Law of Succession) Act 2011. Cf. J.J. Olenn, 'Til Death Do Us Part: New York's Slayer Rule and *In re Estates of Covert*' (2001) 49 *Buffalo Law Review* 1341; Tracy/Adams, n. 53, 803.

222 Law Commission, *The Forfeiture Rule and the Law of Succession*, Law Com. No. 295, HMSO 2005, paras 1.2, 1.6–1.9, 3.2–13. On the former rule, see ibid., paras 2.1–31; R. Kerridge, 'Visiting the sins of the fathers on their children' (2001) 117 *LQR* 371.

sequences thus again emerge, including far beyond uncertainty. The accepted arguments against allowing discretionary departures from this blunt rule also reveal familiar concerns: unpredictability, potential family acrimony, and the generation of litigation, expense, and delay.[223] Again, blunt simplicity and responsive complexity stand in tension where a rule needs to be chosen.

3.3.3 Sharing and reallocating

Finally, we come to more daring solutions to sequencing difficulties, involving reallocating or sharing (total) disputed assets. Here, voluntary settlements must be mentioned first. Two of England's earliest known cases were reportedly resolved only through settlement;[224] one reputedly at Lord Mansfield's instigation.[225] Settlement is often a promising option, able to achieve nuanced resolution without expensive litigation.[226] The default framework in place will still affect the likelihood and content of a negotiated agreement.

Beyond this, one early, cryptic common-law example of 'sharing' is *Bradshaw v Toulmin*—the heirs of joint tenants 'dead by one blow' took the property in joint tenancy.[227] This was a pragmatic result not otherwise achievable; it bypassed the uncertainty of survivorship and maintained the co-ownership status quo by putting the deceased's heirs in the deceased's places. The approach is not without difficulties—in particular insofar as it kicks the uncertainty can down the road, subjecting the ultimate result to the caprice of future events affecting the heirs. More modern solutions for these and similar, specific situations have relied instead on division into equal/proportionate shares.[228] Similar scenarios include, for example, a testamentary disposition that designates beneficiaries who are to take successively: under the USDA 1940, a co-decease of such beneficiaries meant that their estates took proportionately (sec. 2).[229] This was also applied where the *commorientes* included the testator themselves.[230]

---

223 Law Commission, *The Forfeiture Rule*, n. 222, paras 3.25–27.
224 *Hitchcock v Beardsley* (1738) West temp. Hard. 445; *General Stanwix's case*, in Shadwell, n. 11, 38–39.
225 Ibid.; *Wright v Sarmuda* (1815) 2 Phil. Ecc. 266 n. c), 268; but contrast Jolowicz, n. 11.
226 *Scarle v Scarle* [2019] EWHC 2224 was 'crying out' for it per counsel: P. Southworth, 'Daughter beats stepsister in £300,000 inheritance battle hinging on which parent died first', *The Telegraph*, 13.08.2019, <https://www.telegraph.co.uk/news/2019/08/13/woman -beats-stepsister-300000-high-court-inheritance-battle/>.
227 (1784) Dick. 633.
228 E.g. sec. 10, Succession (Scotland) Act 2016; sec. 3 USDA 1940; sec. 4 USDA 1993; cf. 'The Uniform Simultaneous Death Act', n. 138, 758–59. On *Bradshaw* and its difficulties, see Mee, n. 2, 185–91.
229 Cf. 'The Uniform Simultaneous Death Act', n. 138, 756–57.
230 Ibid., 757.

'Common calamity' also deserves mention here. The phrase featured in nineteenth-century UK *commorientes* literature,[231] but no *commorientes* case reports until 1944.[232] This has been the phrase's main use since, but reports previously employed it only in the different situation where various, related interests of multiple parties were touched by one source of harm and an argument was made that a loss should be borne proportionately. Cases involved disputes over land rents after reduced harvests[233] and, later, financial interests and chattels.[234] In these and *commorientes* scenarios, there was an equality between the parties: uncertainty touched all of the *commorientes*' successors just as common-threat victims faced the same source of loss. It is therefore curious that the usage of 'common calamity' shifted so decisively without analogous arguments for proportional total asset division following.[235] The *commorientes* issue's late arrival in judges' hands, and the temptations of modern evidence, perhaps ruled this out.

Finally, there is at least one instance where uncertainty might be dodged entirely and property simply reallocated. Under sec. 8, Executors Act 1830, a person could be appointed to convey, in a trustee's stead, land held on trust where, inter alia, it was unknown which of several trustees was the last-surviving or whether the last was alive. The current equivalent rule lurks in sec. 44, Trustee Act 1925.[236] Here, an uncertainty over survival is left untouched and its effect dodged with a discretion to make necessary appointments to convey land to any appropriate owner. This is an unusually radical response. It does, though, resolve only a niche, technical problem in the management of trust property; unlike other instances, uncertainty here only directly affects control of property (subject to trust), not its ultimate enjoyment.

Thus, some moves towards more daring solutions to uncertainty in the sequencing of deaths emerge at relatively limited points, but do not find broad traction. With *commorientes* cases increasing into the modern era, jurists were perhaps too sceptical of departures from ordinary rules or too wedded to Romanist positions, which at least bore the authority of age, to consider radical shifts. Fictions were also under critical discussion in the key period.[237]

---

231 E.g. Best, n. 5, §141.
232 *Drummond's Judicial Factor v H.M. Advocate* 1944 SC 298, 301. 'Same calamity' does feature earlier, but is somewhat different.
233 *Dunipace v Lawrieston* (1636) Mor. 16581; *Kirby v Ormsby* (1701) Colles 134.
234 *Bank of England v Morice* (1737) 2 Bro. PC 465; *In the Matter of The Royal Bank of Australia* (1852) 2 De GM & G 517.
235 There are even factual (near-)crossovers: shipwrecks (*The Elizabeth* (1819) 2 Dods. 403; *Barras v Aberdeen Steam Trawling* [1933] AC 402; *Beale v Thompson* (1803) 3 Bos. & P 405) and bombings (*In re Orbit Trust's Lease* [1943] Ch. 144; *MacFarlane's Trustees v Neill's Trustee* 1949 SC 384).
236 This is perhaps the reason for the sec. 184, LPA rule's qualification 'subject to any order of the court', words otherwise obscure: *Hickman v Peacey* [1945] AC 304, 316, 346–47.
237 See D. Lind, 'The Pragmatic Value of Legal Fictions', 5.2, 5.5; M. Lobban, 'Legal Fictions before the Age of Reform', 10.5; M. Del Mar, 'Legal Fictions and Legal Change in the

To this extent, it was perhaps difficult to innovate with *commorientes* precisely when they became more common. Later, certainty and simplicity seem to have been much too important to disrupt core paradigms in the name of more radical decisions.

3.3.4 Summary

In sum, experiential inferences initially supported the presumptive sequencing of multiple deaths in continental Europe. This has increasingly been ousted by policy-driven simultaneity. By the time a common-law response to the problem started settling, meanwhile, standardised factual inferences were too weak and such rules were rejected; reliance on ordinary proof later gave way to various discrete, policy-driven presumptions. Policy concerns can and do support even factually impossible results, and cover more or fewer scenarios in the framings used by all of the systems considered.

It might be added that good inheritance planning avoids many difficulties regardless of the applicable rules.[238] Many older cases involved non-ideal drafting[239] and difficult wills remain prominent.[240] Ancient disputes also sprang from drafting choices, like the appointment of a substitute heir for 'whichever [party] died second'.[241] In setting rules, systems must therefore account for parties adapting and, with time and awareness of *commorientes* problems, themselves combatting them. Testamentary survivorship clauses, for example, achieve results comparable to third-generation statutes—indeed, they inspire them[242]—though ill-planned versions can compound difficulties.[243] Criticisms of solutions (for oversimplification, arbitrariness, etc.) must consider this:[244] they may need only to highlight the problem to serve their purpose.

3.4 Conclusion

The legal systems discussed have all faced difficulties with deaths touched by uncertainty and concurrence and, whilst there is extensive convergence in approaches presently, they have produced and accepted a wider and more complex range of rules and responses than has generally been appreciated.

Common Law Tradition', 11.1.2, all published in M. Del Mar and W. Twining (eds), *Legal Fictions in Theory and Practice*, Springer 2015.

238 Cf. Zimmermann/Gleim, n. 28, 569, 571–72 (noting also the effect of more generous interpretations of wills); Ontario Commissioners, n. 77, 44–45, 50.

239 E.g. *Underwood v Wing* (1855) 4 De GM & G 633; *Wing v Angrave* (1860) 8 HL Cas. 183.

240 E.g. *In re Rowland* [1963] 1 Ch. 1; *Jump v Lister* [2016] EWHC 2160.

241 Digest 34.5.9.pr. Cf. Digest 34.5.16.pr.

242 See Law Commission, *Family law: distribution on intestacy*, n. 85; cf. also Zimmermann/Gleim, n. 28, 562–66.

243 E.g. *Jump v Lister* [2016] EWHC 2160. Legislation can anticipate this, e.g. sec. 6, USDA 1993.

244 Cf. e.g. Del Mar, n. 237, 243–50 on the developmental functioning of fictions.

The rules and uncertainty at issue emerge most clearly with disaster cases, but arise comparably from separate deaths, presumed deaths, and even merely temporally close, certainly sequenced deaths. Recognition of the comparability and expandability of the scenarios involved has varied, as has recognition of the problems that underpin the area, including costs and litigation pressures, and especially different levels of uncertainty. Uncertainty is an initial driver of rules and analyses, but is not itself entirely decisive; rules are sometimes crafted to be both under- and over-inclusive from that perspective, as other concerns and advantages are accounted for. Variability here is also tied to the *solutions* available and their practical usefulness, and to incidence rates for the problem and related practical pressures. Scientific and technological developments have also played a part in changing the boundaries of uncertainty. Modern opinion has tended towards understanding the problem more broadly.

This pairs correspondingly with simpler solutions. The Romano-French tradition's wider menus of answers have fallen away;[245] singular presumptions of the modern Germanic ilk are common. Even common-law systems have established relatively simple statutory default rules. Among the solutions used, (more-or-less unconvincing) generalised inferences and (more-or-less impossible) attempts to find or approximate truth have given way to policy-driven responses, generally favouring broad aims like achieving certainty, and considered to produce socially acceptable answers.

The overall result, despite significant uniformity in the results currently preferred—something like presumptive simultaneity—is significant divergence in the conceptual frameworks and concrete answers that have appeared acceptable to different systems at different times. It is a hard thing to overcome the urge for 'truth', but 'good' results of many kinds, driven by contemporary local priorities and understandings, can still be found when a 'factually correct' result is hopelessly elusive. 'Good' results can also then be exploited and applied even more broadly, and even where the 'correct' result is actually clear.

---

245 Cf. Zimmermann/Gleim, n. 28, 566–67.

4   The subtle conclusion

Epistemic uncertainty and law at the end of life

C.P. McGrath *

4.1 Historical overview

Death can induce a form of judicial fatalism. As Lord Mustill once conceded, 'of death we know nothing'.[1] Yet it is not intuitively obvious that death can be treated as an uncertainty as this volume presumes.[2] Whether a person is dead has been, for much of human civilisation, a question that, given time, straightforwardly presents its own answer; nature wins out, the human body is reclaimed,[3] even if there may be confusion or uncertainty over *how* that situation has arisen.[4] The importance for the legal system of clarity here is, however, obvious; much hangs on death. Ideally, and indeed usually, death is once and final; such a decision is not expected to be unwound, albeit mistakes here in past centuries have driven the search for greater certainty and further possible upheavals may lurk on the far horizon.[5] Beyond the law's own internal interest, the law's treatment of death speaks directly to how we conceive the human person.[6]

  The factual uncertainty considered in this chapter is simply stated: how do we determine whether someone is dead? Answering this customarily depends on how one defines death in the first place, whether for legal purposes or

* The author is grateful to the School of Law and the relevant sponsors for the award of a PC Woo Fellowship that supported this work, and to Shouyu Chong for very helpful research assistance in relation to this chapter. I am also grateful to the Hillway Foundation for their support.

1 *Airedale NHS Trust v Bland* [1993] AC 789, 897.
2 See President's Commission for the Study of Ethical Problems in Medicine and Biomedical and Behavioral Research, *Defining Death: A Report on the Medical, Legal and Ethical Issues in the Determination of Death* (1981) which pithily opens, 'Death is the one great certainty' (3).
3 Winslow's 1740 suggestion to rely on putrefaction was characterised as raising 'notable logistic and public health disadvantages': President's Commission, ibid., 13; D. Gardiner and A. McGee, 'Diagnosing Death' in C. Danbury et al. (eds), *Law and Ethics of Intensive Care*, 2nd ed., OUP 2020, 141, describing 'the ancient, and externally obvious, signs of death-for example, rigor mortis, decapitation and decomposition'.
4 P-L. Chau and J. Herring, 'The Meaning of Death' in B. Brooks-Gordon et al. (eds), *Death Rites and Rights*, Hart 2007, 14.
5 Developments in cryogenics may become relevant here: ibid., 13.
6 Gardiner/McGee, n. 3, 144–46.

DOI: 10.4324/9781003537526-5

otherwise. Whilst in many situations this has been straightforward to answer, advances in medical technology have created previously unconsidered situations where (re-)definition of death has been required. This is not the only reason why one might define death in law, but in practice it has driven legal developments here, and retains power to do so.[7] In what follows, we interrogate the tensions inherent in the uncertainty of death and the values engaged in the law responding to that.

The following rough pattern emerges. Initially there is little if any legal intervention. This raises an obvious curiosity: if there is no legal definition, how do you know whether, for the law's purposes, someone is dead? As factual uncertainty over death persists regardless of legal intervention—death is not a legal concept per se—and elicits responses from numerous extra-legal frameworks, it has been possible to remain in this initial stage for a substantial period.[8] The legal system may simply outsource resolving the uncertainty here, acting as an evidential gatekeeper.[9] It is challenging to characterise such a resolution as the product of internal, legal, conceptual analysis. Rather, it appears legal only in the sense that the legal system will certify as authoritative the decision of external actors. Beyond this initial stage, a maturity of sorts sees a legal definition emerge, whether as a means of selecting between competing extra-legal frameworks or breaking from them. Such definition need not be comprehensive within a legal system. It may be constrained to a given context. Such a context may provide an inflection point around which pressure for a general legal response coalesces. Likewise it may prompt a shift in the relevant legal stakeholder from courts to legislatures. Maturity in this sense identifies the point at which a given legal system codifies a definition rather than simply looks to proof of extrinsic definitions, even if the selected definition originated beyond the law.

4.2 Scope of the uncertainty problem

Uncertainty as to whether someone is dead is grounded in fundamentally inscrutable biological processes that prompt a metaphysical question as to what it means to say a person is dead. Indeed, such is the uncertainty here that some have suggested we die not once, but twice, distinguishing the human self from the human organism.[10] It is a question from which legal (and other) consequences flow but which requires both conceptual and practical responses to resolve: how do we conceive somatic death, and how do we prove any

---

7 Ibid., 141.
8 T. Kaan, 'The End of Life: Defining Death in Singapore' (1992) 4 *Singapore Academy of Law Journal* 310, suggesting that, historically, the law may have assumed that death was so 'patent' that no internal legal conception was needed: 310.
9 Ibid., 310.
10 J. McMahan, 'An Alternative to Brain Death' (2006) 34 *Journal of Law, Medicine & Ethics* 44.

conception?[11] This unavoidably biological quality, which will ground and bound any concept of somatic death,[12] means it is ultimately impossible to identify the moment the agonal period ends.[13] Likewise, attempts to determine death, whether in law or otherwise, are exercises in retrospectivity, identifying a given state recognised as death.[14] Such epistemic uncertainty means the date and time at which death was *certified* might be clear, but only on the basis that death has already taken place.[15]

Given the importance of the related consequences, the law cannot avoid some response to this uncertainty. Whether the law is incentivised to identify the relevant state as early as possible is a central aspect of any solution here. The focus of what follows lies in exploring how the English law has responded to this uncertainty, but the broader context of that response requires developments in other systems, particularly in the United States, to be mapped. Similarly, other legal systems may be drawn on to provide examples of alternative options that have been adopted, but the goal here is not to provide a fully comparative account of legal responses generally. The next section explores the tensions, values, and choices that a legal system is faced with in responding to the uncertainty here, before the following section considers how systems have responded in practice.

4.2.1 *The importance of death for law*

Inherent uncertainty over death is compounded by the undeniable importance of death for the operation of any legal system. Fundamental legal questions hinge on clearly identifying death: When was the deceased killed? When do rights or other legal responsibilities begin? A properly functioning legal system cannot allow uncertainty around death to abound.[16] Even if it may be straightforward in some situations, death instantiates too many fundamental consequences, whether personal or proprietary, in a mature legal system to rely on a purely biological timeline, not least as natural biology may now, in some cases, be supplanted by technology. Any response on the part of the law cannot be said to represent a *special* rule, or, in that sense, act as an exception

---

11 Tension between death as a biological process and as a social practice is not unique to any legal response: contrast J. Bernat, 'The Whole-Brain Concept of Death Remains Optimum Public Policy' (2006) 34 *Journal of Law, Medicine & Ethics* 35 with B. Sarbey, 'Definitions of death: brain death and what matters in a person' (2016) 3 *Journal of Law and the Biosciences* 743.

12 Although as Kaan notes, even then, the transplantation context drives home the fact that somatic death allows for the person to have died whilst their organs remain alive, otherwise there would be no point in transplanting dead organs: Kaan, n. 8, 316.

13 Gardiner/McGee, n. 3, 148.

14 G. Laurie et al., *Mason and McCall Smith's Law and Medical Ethics,* 11th ed., OUP 2019, 17.25.

15 Ibid.

16 Sarbey, n. 11, 745, noting the emphasis on the need for a legal solution present in the US developments discussed below.

to any *existing* legal doctrine; rather it represents the good functioning of the system itself. Legal systems often require a 'sharp distinction' between life and death to allow sensible operation of the relevant legal rules; there is seldom, if ever, any suggestion that the law can recognise any 'intermediate state'.[17]

Timely and rational resolution has understandably often been required for broader religious and cultural reasons,[18] likely preceding any need for legal resolution and creating frameworks on which law can draw. Reliance on extra-legal framework(s) may resolve any uncertainty out of *legal* existence, but risks leaving law heavily reliant on such frameworks. Whether legal resolution is grounded directly in legal doctrine or not emerges as a key distinction between such resolutions. Whatever the law's response, there is scope for tension between cultural and legal practice,[19] not least over the fact that cultural practice may find it easier to generate scalar responses rather than deal in binaries. Conversely, however, it is open to law to treat death as a legal fiction, potentially rejecting other frameworks,[20] a concern that may be particularly powerful in the transplantation context.[21]

By whatever route, however, the law's primary concern is to establish a certainty upon which legal consequences can hinge,[22] even if that certainty is the product of a largely arbitrary preference for one framework over another.[23] Indeed, given the metaphysical question of what state constitutes human death, assuming that can be measured, it may be the case that any such legal resolution involves 'an element of choice' such that it represents some degree

---

17 P.D.G. Skegg, *Law, Ethics and Medicine,* Clarendon Press 1984, 186–87.

18 Laurie, n. 14, 17.02, noting that for both medical and social reasons we often need to know the earliest point at which we can say a person is dead.

19 Sarbey, n. 11, 744; J.R. McConnell, 'The ambiguity about death in Japan: An Ethical Implication for Organ Procurement' (1999) 25 *Journal of Medical Ethics* 322.

20 S.K. Shah et al., 'Death and Legal Fictions' (2011) 37 *Journal of Medical Ethics* 719. Elsewhere, Truog suggests that one important counter to such a route is the usual necessity that such legal fictions are transparent to society in their fiction: see R.D. Truog, 'Defining Death: Getting it Wrong for all the Right Reasons' (2015) 93 *Texas Law Review* 1885, 1909–10; D. Price, *Legal and Ethical Aspects of Organ Transplantation,* CUP 2000, 41–43; R.A. Charo, 'Dusk, Dawn and Defining Death' in S.J. Youngner et al., *The Definition of Death: Contemporary Controversies,* Johns Hopkins University Press 1999, 290, suggesting that resort to fiction is one plausible option where the law seeks to treat death purely as a social construct, rather than relating it to the underlying biological phenomena.

21 M. Earle, 'Death', in J. Laing and J. McHale (eds), *Principles of Medical Law,* 4th ed., OUP 2017, 22.32, n. 64.

22 As Hedley puts it, 'Death neither increases nor reduces one's liabilities, it simply draws a convenient line under them'. Clarity is needed to assess 'how things stood at the instant before death': S. Hedley, 'Death and Tort' in Brooks-Gordon et al., n. 4, 243.

23 See I. Goold and J. Herring, *Medical Law and Ethics,* Palgrave 2014, 209, suggesting that in some ways the choice here is analogous to other situations where there is a 'degree of artificiality' in how the law selects the relevant point on which to act; D.W. Elliott, 'When is the Moment of Death?' (1964) 4 *Medicine, Science And The Law* 77, 79, suggesting that what mattered most was simply, 'having the question settled one way or the other'.

of fiction.[24] The further that fiction lies from dominant narratives around death in a given system, the more challenging—and obviously fictional—that legal resolution will be.

4.2.2 The role of medical progress

Two developments within modern medicine have plausibly generated a particular need for the law to respond and resolve uncertainty here.

The first is the reality that bodily processes can now be medically sustained, often through ventilation; death can now be delayed,[25] dying has become 'a fragmented occasion'.[26] When assessing whether care should be continued, constructing the counterfactual of what will happen if it is not provided hinges in part on how death is defined. The law could focus on the appropriate care required at a given point rather than seek to define the patient as being in a given state,[27] but this would risk fragmenting the legal consequences of death. Allocation of finite life-saving resources might also generate pressure towards a legal definition. A focus on one patient's wellbeing may be easily overlain with collective wellbeing and pressure towards timely resolution;[28] death in law is not simply an individual matter.[29]

The second is organ transplantation. Given the entwined relationship between death and potential organ availability it cannot be discounted as generating pressure towards clarifying the legal position. Indeed, the statutes underpinning transplantation regimes often provide a context to specify or otherwise settle or codify what death means, whether only in that context,[30] or as a means of providing a solution that can be used more broadly as well.[31]

---

24 Skegg, n. 17, 185–86; as Kaan puts it, we must select a point in the process where the person is 'deemed' to be dead, Kaan, n. 8, 314.
25 Laurie, n. 14, 17.03, noting that, here, the actions of the medical team essentially determine at what point death will take over.
26 Chau/Herring, n. 4, 13.
27 Ibid., 25–26.
28 C. Foster, *Medical Law*, OUP 2013, 99, noting, beyond the individual themselves, the interests of family members, the efficacy of any transplant regime, and the need to manage resources.
29 Chau/Herring, n. 4, 13. They also draw a parallel here with the position in relation to identifying the status of embryos.
30 H.N. Joo, 'The Organ Transplantation Act and Recent Trends in Korea' (2013) 25 *Asia-Pacific Journal of Public Health* 209, noting that brain death was approved only in relation to transplants, in parallel with the classical cardiopulmonary criteria operating outside that context.
31 The UK position is discussed below, but other examples are easily found: see sec. 41, Victorian Human Tissue Act 1982; the Japanese Organ Transplant Law 1997; the German Transplantation Act 1997; sec. 3, Singaporean Human Organ Transplant Act 1998; and art. 3(4), Korean Organ Transplantation Act 2000. Likewise, statutory intervention might specify particular procedures in relation to ascertaining death in the transplantation context: see sec. 2A (5), (6), Singapore Interpretation Act 1965, as amended (c. 1, 2002 Rev. Ed.); and arts. 14–17,

The familiar concern here is that decision-making has been reversed and either some different or special definition of death will be deployed to improperly justify transplantation.[32] A general legal approach to death, one not specific to transplantation, may be one effective response, but there is still scope for tension with relevant extra-legal frameworks.[33] Transplantation can also clearly plausibly generate pressure towards timely resolution of uncertainty over death given this impacts the efficacy of any transplant programme; again, relevant interests go beyond the individual. Yet transplantation has likely only added pressure given that the root uncertainty creates challenges beyond this narrow, fraught context.[34] A technology-driven inflection point would have arisen for law regardless,[35] even if transplantation can act as an important context here.[36] Likewise, if putative advances like xeno-transplantation disentangle death's relevance here, pressure would remain nevertheless given the capacity to now sustain life artificially.[37] There is, then, no *particular* point at which a special legal rule has been required, although some systems have indeed adopted a particular rule or rules in response to a particular problem. Rather, the increasing power of medical science has, in modern times, sharpened the need for a legal response to uncertainty over death.

4.3 Solutions and policy goals

4.3.1 The unavoidable context of extra-legal frameworks

Law is not the only conceptual framework that responds to epistemic uncertainty over death; the ultimately philosophical question of what it means to say a person is dead remains vibrant and contested.[38] Likewise, whilst the focus here is human death, that is only one category of death amongst many.[39] The relationship between law and any extra-legal frameworks may define whether the law's response embraces a monolithic or plural approach and any legal

---

Korean Organ Transplantation Act 2000. In Singapore, for a period a distinct definition pertained within the transplantation regime; as Kaan fairly suggests, if a standard is acceptable in one context, it is hard to see why it should not be accepted in another: Kaan, n. 8, 322.

32 Laurie, n. 14, 17.18–17.19.

33 Truog suggests that the transplantation context creates a stark choice if the legal and medical definitions diverge: revisit the legal definition (and the values of the transplantation regime) or enforce the dead donor rule: Truog, n. 20, 1904ff.

34 Laurie, n. 14, 17.18

35 C. Machado et al., 'The concept of brain death did not evolve to benefit organ transplants' (2007) 33 *Journal of Medical Ethics* 197. Speculatively, the possibility of head or brain transplants may further drive definitional responses here: see Chau/Herring, n. 4, 15–16.

36 Laurie, n. 14, 17.09.

37 Earle, n. 21, 22.31.

38 Laurie, n. 14, 17.01: it is a question which 'borders on the metaphysical'.

39 Sarbey, n. 11, 748, drawing on Veatch's arguments.

resolution may generate tension with these narratives.[40] The extra-legal frameworks that can claim authority here are manifold and often deeply culturally embedded,[41] albeit they cannot, of themselves, trigger legal consequences.[42] Law must invite—or concede—their relevance in its own sphere, but there may be compelling reasons to do so. One such obvious extra-legal framework is, of course, medical science,[43] but such definitional claims might also be grounded in theological, philosophical, or social frameworks from culturally accepted lay practice, to that of an individual themselves.[44] Any legal resolution may be only and exactly that, but it needs to cohere with relevant internal legal values, speak into relevant cultural understandings, and remain 'useable' in practice.[45] The potential then for multiple competing means of determining death, whether at law or between the law and lay practice, creates an inherent risk of controversy and confusion.[46]

The scope of a given extra-legal framework may also be relevant here. Whilst there are outliers, such as Japan, where—in the transplantation context—individual choice over the use of a given criterion may be relevant in defining death,[47] legal responses commonly operate collectively, emphasising legal certainty. Death in law tends not to mean different things to different people.[48] Even where rights to religious freedom can be used to object to a

40 Chau/Herring, n. 4, 14; albeit as Bernat notes, humans may share a 'univocal' phenomenon of death with other higher vertebrate species: see Bernat, n. 11, 37.

41 Q. Yang and G. Miller, 'East-West Differences in Perception of Brain Death' (2015) 12 *Bioethical Inquiry* 211.

42 As Kaan notes, this is one reason to emphasise the importance of the separate—even potentially concurring— judgments that law and relevant extra-legal frameworks might make. Whilst the latter can flexibly evolve or differ as part of broader, pluralist social discourse, whatever choice is made by the law acts as the crucial boundary that others, particularly clinicians, will have to observe: Kaan, n. 8, 315–16.

43 Although that is not to suggest that the matter is, normatively, best solved by treating death as a medical issue: Chau/Herring, n. 4, 17. As Gardiner suggests, '[i]t was societal forces that established a duty upon doctors to diagnose death': Gardiner/McGee, n. 3, 154.

44 A. Bagheri, 'Individual Choice in the Definition of Death' (2007) 33 *Journal of Medical Ethics* 146. Bagheri suggests individual choice can be resolved with collective definition by allowing objection to the use of a given criterion. See the efforts to accommodate religious beliefs in the New Jersey Declaration of Death Act 1991; R. Veatch and L.F. Ross, *Defining Death: The Case for Choice*, Georgetown University Press 2016, ch. 6; S. Weyrauch, 'Acceptance of Whole-Brain Death Criteria for Determination of Death: A Comparative Analysis of the United States and Japan' (1999) 17 *Pacific Basin Law Journal* 91.

45 Chau/Herring, n. 4, 28.

46 Ibid., 21, discussing the decision by a Danish Council of Ethics, in advance of legislation settling brain death criteria, to back cessation of cardiac function in order to respect common lay opinion; B. Andreassen Rix, 'Brain Death, Ethics and Politics in Denmark' in Youngner et al., n. 20, 229.

47 M. Morioka, 'Reconsidering Brain Death: A Lesson from Japan's Fifteen Years of Experience' (2001) 31 *Hastings Centre Report* 41.

48 Bagheri, n. 44, 147, noting the dissonance that the usual respect for individual autonomy in healthcare is, by necessity, often absent here.

given definition of death, such claims are moderated through court process.[49] Collective acceptance of an extra-legal definition supplies a plausible incentive to draw on it legally, but this incentive is reciprocal, given that any collective legal resolution will hold both *broadest* authority and inescapable jurisdiction. The obvious communitarian interests that are engaged in these scenarios also incentivise general—even if contextualised—legal resolutions.

The agreed diagnostic markers for death used in medical practice represent a crucial, generalised, extra-legal framework here. Medical science provides a normative basis for a general solution structured within an authoritative institutional framework where decisions can be validated and healthcare resources practically managed. Indeed, the drive to practicality in resolving uncertainty around somatic death is generally visible in that definitions commonly seek to identify some earlier point to 'pre-empt' complete cellular death.[50] But merely stating accepted medical facts no *more* resolves uncertainty than any other framework. Extra-legal frameworks primarily operate here to identify a range of values and definitional resolutions upon which the law might draw, or in contrast to which it might develop.[51] The emergence of diagnostic medical criteria for determining death has been highly influential here, but is only one such framework.

4.3.2 The plurality of legal response

When US President Jimmy Carter established the President's Commission for the Study of Ethical Problems in Medicine and Biomedical and Behavioral Research in the late 1970s, death was amongst the topics ripe for consideration given medical advances. The Commission's seminal 1981 report, *Defining Death*, was a focal point for readdressing national practice, proposing the model statute Uniform Determination of Death Act (UDDA).[52] Traditional medical praxis of determining death was now acknowledged as 'neither clear nor fully satisfactory'.[53] Whilst advances in medical technology had created some novel legal challenges, the basic need for legal certainty around death had likewise become problematised.[54] The very fact that medical science drove the need for reassessing practice undermined the extent to which it alone could 'meet the

---

49 Gardiner/McGee, n. 3, 152–53. Reflecting on the Canadian case of *McKitty v Hayani* (2018) ONSC 4015; [2019] ONCA 805, they suggest it is, at least ethically, open to argue that non-religious objections to criteria fixed by medical practice or law ought to be respected here as well.

50 Ibid. See also ibid., 139, 148, noting earlier similar pressures given putrefaction was 'a very safe diagnostic criterion, but not a very timely one'; Goold/Herring, n. 23, 213.

51 The challenge of the relationship between legal and biological categories, and the potential for tension where the law diverges from the underlying biological phenomena, is not limited to death: see R.A. Charo, 'Dusk, Dawn and Defining Death' in Youngner et al., n. 20, 277.

52 President's Commission, n. 2.

53 Ibid., 7.

54 Sarbey, n. 11, 745.

public concern'; instead a *legal* framework would both supply reassurance and scaffold these medical developments.[55]

An accompanying survey of ten international legal systems revealed legal practice that was uniform in neither content nor legal basis.[56] Some systems possessed a statutory framework,[57] albeit in some federal systems a partial local framework had only been recently superseded by federal statute.[58] In some there was simply no *legal* rule in place at all;[59] in others the statutory framework had ended a preceding silence. Formal law reform bodies often acted as institutional drivers. Some systems identified a legally prescribed series of tests for determining death;[60] others, again, left this to medical guidance.[61] Finally, in some the transplantation context had explicitly driven developments—even where the resulting legal framework was intended for general use[62]—whilst in others this was less obvious.[63] Medicine had driven reassessment, but was also supplying novel responses in answer, with the law increasingly turning to this framework to clarify its own resolution.

4.3.3 The neurological turn

The medical response to the developing need for new criteria in relation to death would prove crucial to many legal systems, including the United Kingdom.

Determining death for legal purposes was a role long held by the medical profession,[64] often to ensure certainty and quell fears of an accidental, Lazarene experience.[65] This role was well embedded by the nineteenth century, helped

---

55 President's Commission, n. 2, 45.
56 President's Commission, n. 2, 147ff. Skegg suggested that this range itself highlighted the extent to which a system could choose what death means for itself: Skegg, n. 17, 186.
57 Argentina, Norway, Greece, Spain.
58 Canada.
59 France and the United Kingdom. In the former, the rule simply clarified the procedural role of medical decision-making.
60 Argentina, Finland, France, Greece, Norway.
61 United Kingdom.
62 The Argentinian, Czechoslovakian, Finnish, and Greek statutes were concerned with donation and transplantation and, likewise, the Australian rules had been generated in response to an ALRC report on 'Human Tissue Transplants' (ALRC Report 7, 1977).
63 France and the United Kingdom.
64 D. Tankard, 'Defining Death in Early Tudor England' (2006) 3 *Cultural and Social History* 1. As even the Pope acknowledged in 1957, 'Where the verification ... is concerned, the answer cannot be deduced from any religious and moral principle': Pius XII, 'The Prolongation of Life' (2009) *National Catholics Bioethical Quarterly* 332.
65 A.C. Breu and A. Rodman, 'The Last Breath: Historical Controversies Surrounding Determination of Cardiopulmonary Death' (2022) 161 *Chest* 514; J.D. Arnold et al., 'Public Attitudes and the Diagnosis of Death' (1968) 206 *Journal of the American Medical Association* 1949. Certainty was often captured in the language of the diagnosis being 'safe': Gardiner/McGee, n. 3, 139.

by improvements in resuscitation.[66] Medical debate over determining death had settled on cardiopulmonary or cardiorespiratory death,[67] mapping closely onto commonly accepted lay notions of what constituted death.[68] When the French Academy offered a prize for safer, prompt, and easy diagnosis of death, Eugène Bouchut's winning response in 1846 focused on cessation of the heartbeat for five minutes, aided by use of a stethoscope.[69] Confidence in certainty improved whilst reliance on this cardiopulmonary model coalesced medical and common lay ideas of somatic death.[70]

Once patients could be maintained despite previously fatal injury, reassessment was clearly needed.[71] As the President's Commission pondered, were patients in a state beyond coma (*coma dépassé*)—whose hearts and cardiopulmonary function could be kept functioning artificially—in fact, actually dead?[72] Although the interlinked nature of the three relevant systems was always a biological reality—a 'cycle of life'[73]— replacing the function of the heart and lungs served to highlight the role of the brain in understanding death,[74] whether or not potential transplantation was a relevant consideration.[75]

Medical developments here are well documented. The near simultaneous (if apparently unrelated)[76] arrival, in August 1968, of the seminal report of Harvard Medical School's Ad Hoc Committee on the definition of brain death,[77] and the Declaration of Sydney issued by the 22nd World Medical Assembly, provided some professional and ethical stability. The 'Harvard Criteria' provided a framework for patients in a state of 'irreversible coma', for whom death was diagnosed as a permanently non-functioning brain.[78] Whilst debate over the precise criteria and confirmatory procedures would continue,

---

66 Gardiner/McGee, n. 3, 137–38.

67 Chau/Herring, n. 4, 16.

68 Kaan, n. 8, 311.

69 Breu/Rodman, n. 65. This is, of course, a continued and widespread method for declaring death in the majority of non-critical, intensive cases: Gardiner/McGee, n. 3, 147.

70 President's Commission, n. 2, 13.

71 Death can then be viewed as marking the futility of resuscitation (see Gardiner/McGee, n. 3, 137) but doing so simply highlights the persistent nature of the factual uncertainty here: how do we identify such futility?

72 President's Commission, n. 2, 22; Gardiner/McGee, n. 3, 139.

73 Laurie, n. 14, 17.09.

74 C. Pallis, 'Return to Elsinore' (1990) 16 *Journal of Medical Ethics* 10.

75 President's Commission, n. 2, 23.

76 Gardiner/McGee, n. 3, 139.

77 Ad Hoc Committee of the Harvard Medical School to Examine the Definition of Brain Death, 'A Definition of Irreversible Coma' (1968) 205 *Journal of the American Medical Association* 337.

78 The close coincidence of the Committee's work with the first successful heart transplant—one month earlier—may also have provided important context: Chau/Herring, n. 4, 18; Truog, n. 20, 1887.

with the United Kingdom taking a narrower approach in due course,[79] the President's Commission found that 'published criteria for determining cessation of brain functions have been uniformly successful in diagnosing death'.[80] The Sydney Declaration opened by asserting that 'the determination of the time of death is in most countries the legal responsibility of the physician and should remain so', acknowledging the continued relevance in many cases of 'the classical criteria known to all physicians'.[81] Noting the tension between the biological process of gradual cellular death and somatic death, the Declaration adopted a conceptual approach, with clinical interest focused on the 'fate of the person'; what mattered was certainty that this process had, irreversibly, passed beyond resuscitation.[82] Such certainty may involve diagnostic aid, albeit no particular diagnostic criteria were provided,[83] but technological assessment could only facilitate clinical judgement here, never replace it. It was not until 1983, in the aftermath of the President's Commission, that the Declaration was amended to include the importance of determining 'the irreversible cessation of all functions of the entire brain, including the brain stem', but the broader emphasis on clinical responsibility, as the President's Commission also emphasised, and a conception of death focused on the 'fate of the person' remained undisturbed. Both the Harvard Ad Hoc Committee and the drafters of the Declaration identified artificial support mechanisms *and* organ transplantation as drivers for their work.[84]

From the 1960s onwards then, the brain has been central to medical diagnosis of death,[85] with some US states even enacting the Harvard Criteria in the years preceding the UDDA.[86] Some models, such as the United Kingdom's, deploy a unified diagnostic standard, focused on brain function;[87] others, such as the UDDA, use an ostensibly dual standard that explicitly preserves

79 Conference Of Royal Colleges And Faculties Of The United Kingdom, *Memorandum on the Diagnosis of Death* (1979); United Kingdom Health Department, *The Removal of Cadaveric Organs for Transplantation: A Code of Practice* (1979). For discussion of this process, see Skegg, n. 17, 190–95.
80 President's Commission, n. 2, 27.
81 C. Machado, J. Korein et al., 'The Declaration of Sydney on Human Death' (2007) 33 *Journal of Medical Ethics* 699, 701.
82 Ibid., 699–700; Kaan, n. 8, 326–29 on the importance, for legal purposes, of distinguishing between conceptual and diagnostic responses here. Other efforts in this era focused, as in Harvard, on identifying the relevant criteria and tests rather than articulating a conceptual definition: see B. Schöne-Seifert, 'Defining Death in Germany' in Youngner et al., n. 20, 258.
83 Machado, n. 81, 702.
84 Ibid.
85 Laurie, n. 14, 17.09.
86 Kansas was the first to do so; Truog, n. 20, 1888.
87 Academy of Medical Royal Colleges, *A Code Of Practice For The Diagnosis And Confirmation Of Death* (2008), 9. The diagnosis of death 'requires confirmation that there has been irreversible damage to the vital centres in the brain-stem, due to the length of time in which the circulation to the brain has been absent'.

a cardiopulmonary definition distinct from neurological criteria.[88] Within this paradigmatic shift towards 'brain death', debate has centred on the role of brain *stem* death as the required diagnostic foundation.[89] It may be that the latter operates, in effect, as a synonym for the former, with brain stem death 'a convenient marker of the latter': whole brain death,[90] but there is a continued distinction between two broad categories of system; those that rely on whole brain criteria and those for whom brain stem death is sufficient.[91] A degree of pragmatism is inevitably involved in selecting neurological criteria given limitations on what can be measured,[92] and adopting a brain-centred definition does not imply agreement over the relevant function that should be assessed or, indeed, the diagnostic procedures and protocols for doing so.[93] Indeed, work towards internationally harmonising standards for diagnosing death led by the World Health Organisation (WHO)—centred on the brain—has borne no fruit.[94] Equally, that there is disagreement here is not to suggest there are different *types* of death, simply different ways to define the same state. Despite differences, it is noteworthy that the death of the brain, however understood, is widely accepted globally, across a broad range of societies,[95] and evidently now sets the stage for any legal response.

4.3.4 Framing a legal resolution

Moving to how the law can respond, the first challenge is whether it should do so in a general or contextualised manner. There are certainly compelling reasons to avoid competing *legal* resolutions within a single constitutional unit—note the UDDA was intended, in part, to prevent just this—although federal systems may naturally be faced with this situation depending on the relevant principles of *public* law.[96] The risks of ambiguity or stoking the perception that death can, through sleight of law, be sped up in particular contexts

---

88 See also here sec. 2A, Singapore Interpretation Act 1965, as amended (c. 1, 2002 Rev. Ed.).
89 Sec. 1, UDDA, discussed below, has been criticized for its tautological drafting: see Earle, n. 21, 22.34.
90 Laurie, n. 14, ch. 17; Skegg, n. 17, 189.
91 M. Donnelly and B. Lyons, 'Disputing Death: Brain Death in the Courts' (2022) 43 *Legal Studies* 351, 353.
92 Sarbey, n. 11, 750.
93 H.C Chua et al., 'Brain Death: The Asian Perspective' (2015) 35 *Seminars in Neurology* 152, noting the variance between 14 different Asian jurisdictions, despite agreement on either whole or brain-stem death; Sarbey, n. 11, 747ff.; Donnelly/Lyons, n. 92, 353.
94 Laurie, n. 14, 17.21.
95 E.F. Wijdicks, 'Brain death worldwide: accepted fact but no global consensus in diagnostic criteria' (2002) 58 *Neurology* 20.
96 Here different constitutional sub-units may find themselves in tension, as in the cases of Jahi McMath. There, a death certificate issued in California did not prevent continued ventilation in New Jersey. Such plurality, whilst challenging, emphasises the contingent and 'value-laden' process of defining death: Sarbey, n. 11, 747.

are non-trivial,[97] but where a particular context convincingly justifies distinct criteria such risks may be managed. Although a general resolution need not be monolithic: the law may recognise a range of suitable criteria, whether nested or parallel. Consider the UDDA. Focusing on identifying the relevant 'organ systems' rather than a conceptual definition of death, or the required 'operational standards', the President's Commission preserved the traditional approach, but then provided, alternatively, a solution for new complexities, resulting in a bifurcation of standards:[98]

> An individual who has sustained either (1) irreversible cessation of circulatory and respiratory functions, or (2) irreversible cessation of all functions of the entire brain, including the brain stem, is dead. A determination of death must be made in accordance with accepted medical standards.

The separate but mutually supporting responsibilities of law and medicine are clear, the former provides formal, institutional authority, the latter the normative content and assessment. Likewise the UDDA suggests that any definition enshrined in law will need to be abstract enough to be effective across the broad range of circumstances it will have to apply to.[99] Although rooted in 'medical standards', legal force gold-plates that extra-legal framework. The clarificatory power of this choice is obvious; indeed the UDDA has been adopted in some form by nearly all US states.[100] It supplies formal, legal clarity, but the normative responsibility rests with medical practice. But legal force cannot of itself quell medical debate. Certainly, the requirement in (2) is broader than either UK or WHO efforts, which emphasise the brain stem.[101] Likewise, by what 'medical standards' should the relevant assessments be made? By privileging one extra-legal framework over others, law achieves a resolution here, but in doing so leaves key choices beyond obvious legal control or justification.

The UDDA's model is also binary and state-based; one is alive or dead. This reflects law's broader preference for binaries and clarity, eschewing any effort to reflect the scalar nature of the underlying biological process. By contrast, Chau and Herring suggest the legal focus here could be reframed away from these binaries and, embracing death-as-process, instead lie in asking: what is

---

97 A higher-brain criterion could suggest a 'less restrictive standard': ibid., 752. Although whether this would affect donation rates is a different matter: M. Othman et al., 'Public opinion and legislations related to brain death, circulatory death and organ donation' (2020) 413 *Journal of Neurological Sciences* 1.

98 Sarbey, n. 11, 746; A.M. Capron, 'The Bifurcated Legal Standard for Determining Death' in Youngner et al., n. 20, 117.

99 Foster, n. 28, 99–100.

100 Sarbey, n. 11, 746.

101 President's Council On Bioethics, *Controversies in the Determination of Death* (2008), 65–67.

permitted in relation to a body at any given moment?[102] Likewise, the UDDA highlights the challenge of relying on a temporal element here: '*irreversible*' cessation. Whether this is merely a synonym for permanence, or whether certification of death must be postponed until irreversibility is confirmed may remain ambiguous,[103] but a familiar uncertainty can recur in trying to identify the point at which irreversibility has arrived,[104] and, again, the law has a strong incentive towards timely resolution.[105] Yet beyond the confines of intensive care, it has been observed to be 'astonishing how often the moment of "death of the person" is perfectly clear'.[106] Again, if the law intervenes, it is faced with having to resolve a range of different circumstances without disturbing this settled reality, suggesting that flexibility is a necessary quality in any resolution.

Any legal response then appears to engage three overarching distinctions, each overlapping and interlinked. At the foundation there may be tension between legal and lay cultural (including medical) frameworks. Secondly, the biological timeline of the process must contend with a practical need for resolution. Finally, the legal system introduces the distinction between fact and law. The epistemic uncertainty death involves must be resolved with sufficient clarity for legal consequences. If death is a fact this can be demonstrated using extra-legal frameworks. If death is given distinct legal meaning, this must be justified, particularly where distinct from common lay notions.

4.3.5 The baseline in English law

It is perhaps unsurprising that a leading textbook on medical law and ethics commences from the definition of death given in both the Oxford English and Stedman's Medical dictionaries.[107] English law recognises neither a statutory definition of death nor, arguably, a common-law one.[108] Rather, death

---

102 Chau/Herring, n. 4. For a similar conceptual unspooling here see N. Fost, 'The Unimportance of Death' in Youngner et al., n. 20, 161.

103 Gardiner/McGee, n. 3, 147–49.

104 Ibid.

105 G. Williams, *The Sanctity of Life and the Criminal Law*, Knopf 1957, confirming that this was just as much of an issue in the abstract when the focus remained on cardiopulmonary criteria for death. If death was understood to be the cessation of heartbeat 'beyond the known limit of medical recall', this would naturally 'introduce some indeterminacy': 4–5. Skegg was, later, rightly sceptical of Williams' professed dislike for a test that the latter felt would postpone recognition of death 'by reference to a possible resuscitation that does not take place', noting that, in any case, Williams' suggestion would simply shift uncertainty to whether a patient was subsequently resuscitated: Skegg, n. 17, 225–26.

106 Laurie, n. 14, 17.03.

107 Laurie, n. 14, 17.01. See, in a similar vein, reliance on Black's Legal Dictionary: President's Commission, n. 2, 135.

108 See generally here K. Choong, *The Medico-Legal Development of Neurological Death in the UK*, Springer 2022, ch. 3.

is a question of fact reliant exclusively on medical expertise to prove.[109] The law and medicine coincide here,[110] but such coincidence does not assign the law normative responsibility. By the late 1970s UK professional bodies had confirmed the place of diagnosis of death by neurological criteria (DNC), with the necessary protocols revised in due course.[111] The relevant guidance is now captured primarily in the Academy of Royal Colleges' 2008 Code. Whilst the influence of the transplant context cannot be ignored,[112]—albeit the Code clearly stresses that any definition should be unrelated to organ transplantation[113]—advances in life support had already necessitated legal change here in the abolition of the old 'year and a day' rule for homicide.[114] It is presumed that the Scottish position reflects the English law here,[115] providing, in theory, the legal uniformity that legislation might otherwise allow. The focus on courts as the primary legal responders may limit, as common law ultimately does, what can plausibly be achieved here by way of lawmaking. In what follows, both the law's need to respond to medicine's neurological turn, and fact that any response is intimately entwined with determining what treatment, if any, remains appropriate, are clear.

Although it attracted little contemporary attention,[116] in *Re Potter*[117] in 1963—where the accused in a criminal trial had suggested it was the clinicians who had killed the deceased organ donor by removing resuscitation—the court appears to have applied the traditional cardiopulmonary criteria.[118] The likely prospect of artificial life support undermining the traditional criteria, suggested commentary on the case, meant that 'there must be a general threshing out of all the practical, medical, social and legal problems involved'.[119]

---

109 Kaan, n. 8, 310, characterising the common-law approach as treating death as 'a purely factual problem'.
110 Chau/Herring, n. 4, 16.
111 D. Evans, 'The Demise of "Brain Death" in Britain' in M. Potts et al. (eds), *Beyond Brain Death: The Case Against Brain Based Criteria for Human Death*, Springer 2000, 139–40.
112 Ibid.
113 Royal Colleges, n. 87, 9.
114 Law Reform (Year and A Day Rule) Act 1969, on the Law Commission's recommendation. It is notable that none of the cases that follow in discussion below directly engage issues of transplantation; rather, they are squarely grounded in the question of whether continued care should be maintained: see Choong, n. 108, 45.
115 M. Earle and N. Whitty, *Stair Memorial Encyclopaedia*, *Medical Law* (Reissue), LexisNexis 2006, 362.
116 Kaan, n. 8, 313.
117 *The Times*, 26 July 1963.
118 The kidney had been removed under the then Human Tissue Act 1961 following a period of life-sustaining treatment.
119 Elliott, n. 23. An attempt at this duly occurred at a multidisciplinary international symposium in 1966, albeit this was overtaken in effect by the work of the Harvard Ad Hoc Committee: G. Glaves-Innis, 'Organ Donation and Incompetents: Can They Consent – Comparative Analysis of American and Canadian Laws of Consent and Brain Death Determination' (2000) 10 *Touro International Law Review* 155, 182.

Nevertheless, the issue of determining death by reference to neurological criteria only appeared squarely before the High Court in 1992. In *Re A*,[120] a 19-month-old child was admitted to intensive care suffering from serious injuries after a supposed home fall. Although alive when admitted, examination by the same consultant neurologist in line with contemporary guidelines from the Royal Colleges of Surgeons, Physicians and British Paediatric Association diagnosed brain stem death the following day, confirmed the following day using the same protocols.[121] There could be, as Johnson J put it, 'no sensible issue between doctors as to whether or not A was now brain-stem dead'.[122] The legal issue was straightforward: could the court make a declaration that the child was dead for all legal as well as medical purposes, such that ventilation could be legally withdrawn? Relying on the medical evidence, Johnson J found that A had been dead for some days by then. He confirmed the court's power to 'make a declaration that A is now dead for all legal, as well as medical, purposes'.[123] Although not relevant in *Re A*, transplantation was used as a counterfactual to probe the decision A's clinicians had arrived at: were it relevant whether organs could be removed, the consultant would not have hesitated to certify brain stem death.[124] Discussing ventilation, Johnson J noted that the 'function of the court is ... to assist by clarifying the position and not to usurp the discretion of the doctors to do what they think is best'.[125] This clarificatory role, and the evident reliance on medical discretion, was not obviously less relevant in relation to death itself. It is clear that *Re A* provides no legal definition and there was no suggestion that this was the *only* such evidence that would lead to the same result. Likewise, whilst the language in *Re A* suggests death in medical terms was separate from death in legal terms, the better reading is plainly that the legal conclusion flowed directly from the preceding medical one, without suggesting that this was the only *medical* conclusion that would lead to the same result.[126] The court could declare a ventilated patient to, in fact, now *be* dead, but it did not purport to apply any test of its own to do so. *Re A* reveals reliance on the law's institutional weight without engagement in any normative or conceptual assessment. It has been said that the decision can be seen as 'incorporating brain-stem death into the common law', but this

---

120 [1992] 3 Med. LR 303.
121 Ibid., 304.
122 Ibid., 305.
123 Ibid.
124 Ibid., 304.
125 Ibid., 305.
126 Earle, n. 21, 22.39, decrying the fact that *Re A* is sometimes taken as suggesting the comprehensive *legal* definition of death in the United Kingdom is brain-stem death.

is doubtful given no obvious *legal* principle was engaged.[127] It appears more accurate to describe these cases as recognising a given approach to death.[128]

Shortly thereafter, the seminal decision in *Airedale NHS Trust v Bland* arrived,[129] obliquely engaging questions around the legal determination of death. In *Bland*, whilst destruction of his cerebral cortex was clear, the brain stem remained intact. Rather than start from any internal, legal conception of death, as in *Re A*—which went uncited by their Lordships—this work was outsourced as a matter of fact to medical evidence.[130] On that basis, Mr Bland was obviously alive, and the nature of the legal question was significantly different to *Re A*.[131] Their Lordships recognised medicine had wrought a departure from its own traditional certainties. As Lord Browne-Wilkinson put it:

> Until recently there was no doubt what was life and what was death. A man was dead if he stopped breathing and his heart stopped beating. There was no artificial means of sustaining these indications of life for more than a short while … Recent developments in medical science have fundamentally affected these previous certainties.[132]

As in *Re A*, various dicta in *Bland* could be taken to suggest that one might be 'either medically *or* legally' dead.[133] Take Lord Keith's observation that '[i]n the eyes of the medical world *and* of the law a person is not clinically dead so long as the brain stem retains its function'.[134] Or Lord Goff's, that the 'evidence is that Anthony's brain stem is still alive and functioning and it follows that, in the present state of medical science, he is still alive *and should be so regarded* as a matter of law'.[135] Their Lordships understandably acknowledged that death occurs outwith the law,[136] and is something to which the law responds. So, whilst the law could resolve any uncertainty here for itself, there

---

127 Ibid. Such language may have come from a note on the case: I. Kennedy, 'Definition of Death' (1999) 1 *Medical Law Review* 98, 99. As Kaan's own example here reveals, it may be difficult to cast English law's response as involving a legal principle at all: 'the underlying common law *principle* applied … was simply that the determination of death was a determination of fact': Kaan, n. 8, 318.

128 See generally Donnelly/Lyons, n. 91, 355.

129 N. 1.

130 As Donnelly and Lyons nicely put it, the '…legal status of brain stem death was accepted rather than analysed': Donnelly/Lyons, n. 91, 356.

131 'His brain stem is alive and so is he', per Lord Browne-Wilkinson, *Bland*, n. 1, 878; 'I start with the simple fact that, in law, Anthony is still alive', per Lord Goff, ibid., 863.

132 Ibid., 878, per Lord Browne-Wilkinson.

133 Ibid. (emphasis added).

134 Ibid., 856 (emphasis added).

135 Ibid., 863 (emphasis added).

136 As Lord Browne-Wilkinson put it, 'In medicine, the cessation of breathing or of heartbeat is no longer death … The physical state known as death has changed': ibid., 878. With respect, it would be better to suggest that what we recognise as death had changed.

was neither an obvious doctrinal basis for doing so, nor, crucially for these purposes, any real need to develop one if the *medical* reality could be relied on to solve this as a matter of fact. Likewise, *Bland* clearly cannot be taken to suggest approval of higher brain death as a standard for the death of the person.[137]

Recent cases have confirmed that courts remain a forum for resolving uncertainty over death. They inevitably wrestle with whether treatment can be legally withdrawn and commonly arise from difficulties between the parties rather than obvious uncertainty over the law itself; they are the quintessence of what Lord Browne-Wilkinson felt *Bland* heralded.[138] Nevertheless, the baseline established in *Re A/Bland* remains undisturbed.[139] The law looks to the medical guidance as to whether death is established in line with such evidence.[140] The law's task, it seems, was simply to acknowledge and reflect the medical reality, something adduced through evidence not principle. Indeed, despite the rather thin nature of the various dicta, *Bland* has been re-designated as the ultimate authority that brain stem death captures the relevant legal criteria.[141]

4.3.6 Challenging the baseline

Attempts to challenge *Re A/Bland* have proven largely fruitless, but recent years have seen an increase in the issue appearing before the courts.[142] Courts have emphasised the authoritative nature of the medical guidelines:[143] they are not simply personal clinical opinions.[144] Such authority appears beyond contestation when it is ratified in court. In both *Re: A (A Child)* and *Barts Health NHS Trust v Dance* counsel for the respective parents highlighted that the United Kingdom differs from medical practice elsewhere in focusing on

---

137 Earle, n. 21, 22.41.
138 *Re A (A Child)* [2015] EWHC 443, [14], per Hayden J.
139 *Re M (Declaration of Death of a Child)* [2020] Med. LR 165, [13], [91].
140 Whether the 2008 Code (Royal Colleges, n. 87), or additional specialist diagnostic guidance such as the Royal College of Paediatrics and Child Health, *The diagnosis of death by neurological criteria in infants less than two months old* (2015).
141 *Re M*, n. 139, [91]; applied in *North West Anglia NHS Foundation Trust v BN, PS* [2022] EWHC 663 (Fam.), [142]. Donnelly/Lyons, n. 91, 355 suggest *Bland* provided a 'somewhat firmer footing' than *Re A* before it. Given the nature of the actual legal issue at stake in *Bland*, this is best seen as an appeal to the institutional authority of a decision of the House of Lords for later cases: Choong, n. 108, 34, 40.
142 Choong, n. 108, 34, suggesting a recent 'storm' of cases.
143 *Re M*, n. 139, [25]–[37], a permission hearing on *Namiq*, below n. 161ff.; *Barts Health NHS Trust v Dance* [2022] EWCA Civ. 935, [33].
144 *Oxford University NHS Trust v AB (A Minor)* [2019] EWHC 3516, [16], per Francis J. Skegg, n. 17, 185 notes that it would clearly be inappropriate to permit personal medical opinion to govern the legal response.

brain stem death,[145] but such challenges have been flatly rejected.[146] That the courts purport to adopt this position as their own—suggesting that there has been some governing decision to do so, or acknowledging that there is, in theory, a space for the law to acknowledge brain stem death if medical practice abandons it—masks the reality. Key normative decisions are simply beyond legal control. Whether one can say there is a truly *legal* resolution depends—in the absence of any difference between the legal and medical positions—on the weight of this ultimately formal distinction between the two.

Some decisions and commentary have shaded into suggesting brain stem death, arrived at by any route, is now the legal definition of death.[147] Yet the clear direction of influence between law and medicine in *Re A/Bland*, and the explicit reliance on medical guidance, suggest this is overblown.[148] Doubts are only strengthened by examining what is open to a court if the relevant six-stage diagnostic test for brain stem death set out in the 2008 Code cannot be performed. In *Barts Health NHS Trust v Dance*,[149] the very condition of the patient ruled out these tests. Although there was, therefore, no formal medical diagnosis of death, on the basis of the otherwise abundant medical evidence pointing to that conclusion Arbuthnot J found that the child in question was, on the balance of probabilities, brain stem dead, making a declaration as to time and date of death.[150] The parents appealed, in part, on the basis that to take such a decision in the absence of the relevant tests was to have wrongly extended the 'common law definition of death'.[151] As the Court of Appeal noted, the 2008 Code did not provide any alternative basis here.[152] The issue was stark:

> No authority has been produced in which previous judges have declared that death has occurred in an individual whose bodily functioning is

---

145 *Re M*, n. 139, [44]–[45], [64]; *Barts Health NHS Trust v Dance and others* [2022] EWHC 1435, [150].

146 *Re M*, n. 139, [92].

147 Ibid., [91]; see also the short note accompanying the report: C. Hallin [2020] Med. LR 179; *BN*, n. 142, [142], [154], discussing the 'common law definition of death'; likewise, *Dance*, n. 145, [149], per Arbuthnot J: 'Brain stem death became the legal definition of death in the House of Lords case of *Bland*'.

148 *BN*, n. 141, is a good example of this practice here, with almost entire reliance on the 2008 Code over any relevant legal principles.

149 [2022] EWHC 1435 (Fam.).

150 Ibid., [171]–[173], [180].

151 *Dance* (CA), n. 143, [4].

152 Ibid., [33]. Given the Code does acknowledge alternative testing in some circumstances, courts may be forced to decide whether it should, in this sense, be regarded as exclusive or not: see B. Lyons and M. Donnelly, 'A different kind of death? *Barts NHS Trust v Dance and Battersbee*' (2023) 23 *Medical Law International* 159, 167–69. As the authors perceptively note, the crux is that the Code may not be clear enough on what to do when the usual tests *cannot* be relied on.

being mechanically maintained by a ventilator and where death is said to be established on evidence other than testing undertaken in accordance with the Code, or where the judge does not have any medical witness who has diagnosed death. The course that the judge was invited to follow in the present case was, it seems, unprecedented.[153]

Whilst the successful appeal focused on the propriety of Arbuthnot J's best interests assessment—and so a ruling was not made on whether it was *wrong* to make a declaration of death—the Court of Appeal strongly cautioned, necessarily *per curiam*, that judges should not be drawn into making such a diagnosis themselves and that in such circumstances the appropriate course is to instead focus on assessing the presumptively living patient's best interests.[154] Despite the absence of a ruling on the declaration, the remainder of the proceedings therefore took place on the basis that the child was alive.[155] This suggests that far from deploying a legal or 'common law' definition in resolving the uncertainty with which it is faced, the law is truly reliant not only on testing the existence of a medical fact, but a fact arrived at by a *fixed* set of medical procedures.[156] Indeed, at the subsequent best interests hearing Hayden J noted:

Ascertaining death requires the application of clear clinical guidelines. Where they are not met, brain stem death cannot be identified with the certainty that such a conclusion requires. Brain stem death cannot, at least to my mind, be equated with a diagnosis, though I note, that the guidance by the Academy of Medical Royal Colleges is headed '*The Code of Practice for the Diagnosis and Confirmation of Death*'. Death, it seems to me, is a stage beyond diagnosis and thus it follows, that a differential diagnostic approach (i.e., diagnosis by symptoms) is highly unlikely to be appropriate.[157]

The decisive role of medical guidelines this suggests is fully in keeping with previous case law, but further suggests there is no corollary *legal* definition at play. Were this otherwise, there is, respectfully, no coherent reason to suggest that, applying the appropriate standard of proof, a judge could not find facts, as in the ordinary course of any trial, and hold such legal definition satisfied,

---

153 *Dance* (CA), n. 143, [35].
154 Ibid., [37].
155 *Barts Health NHS Trust v Dance & Ors (Re Archie Battersbee)* [2022] EWFC 80, [2], per Hayden J.
156 K.A. Choong and M.Y. Rady, '*Re A (A Child)* and the United Kingdom Code of Practice for the Diagnosis and Confirmation of Death: Should a Secular Construct of Death Override Religious Values in a Pluralistic Society?' (2018) 30 *HEC Forum* 71, suggesting, at 85, that there is 'passive and unquestioning acceptance of the code' by the judiciary.
157 Ibid.

particularly given that this would naturally rely on medical evidence.[158] Yet, it is clearly the case that the mere fact that clinicians pronounce death—as the accidentally entombed of the past can testify—cannot itself suffice to treat someone as dead.[159] It is ultimately the actuality or potential of the *legal* force that will be deployed to reinforce this conclusion if that pronouncement is challenged that purports to settle the issue.

Assuming the relevant tests can be carried out and there are good faith, competent medical witnesses to that effect, there is then, in practice, very little room to challenge the conclusion.[160] The court's narrow, fact-finding process does not engage, as was argued in *Manchester University NHS Foundation Trust v Namiq*, an assessment of whether such conclusion is in the best interests of the person in question,[161] nor the concerns of Article 2 of the European Convention on Human Rights.[162] Indeed, the Court of Appeal has directed that best practice in making a declaration here is for the court to explicitly confirm death, including time and date. If the relevant medical criteria are confirmed, the person is dead and a different—but no less important—set of legal rules are engaged.[163] The petitioner, likely the healthcare institution, bears the burden of proof,[164] and the medical evidence is assessed on the balance of probabilities,[165] with, as Lieven J suggested—adopting the terminology of human rights—'anxious scrutiny'.[166] Given the fraught circumstances, clinical competency may be questioned, but as the relevant diagnostic tests

---

158 A sense of the tension and oddity that the present situation can create can be seen in some of the associated commentary: see Lyons/Donnelly, n. 152, 168: 'On the balance of probabilities, Arbuthnot J may well have been correct in her finding but, although apparently logically founded on the opinions offered by the involved clinicians, it, nonetheless, was a medically unconfirmed diagnosis'. This highlights that such concerns go to the *evidence* on which the judge is basing their conclusion, a matter that—other than by reference to the appropriate procedural rules—is usually unfettered, rather than to the conceptual foundations at play.

159 Skegg, n. 17, 185.

160 See Sir Jonathan Cohen's admirably realistic conclusion in *BN*, n. 141, [21]: 'I really have no alternative but to conclude that death has been diagnosed'.

161 [2020] EWHC 180 (Fam.). Not least because, as confirmed in *Re M*, n. 139, [97], if brainstem death is established, there can be no other realistic answer than that removing ventilation would be lawful. See here also Kennedy, n. 127. Note, however, that the question of death cannot override the necessary attention that any entwined application of a best interests test would require: see *Dance* (CA), n. 143, and discussion below.

162 *Namiq*, n. 161; *Re M*, n. 139, [91]–[96].

163 *Namiq*, n. 161, [32]. As McFarlane P put it in *Re M*, n. 139, [49], 'Once death has been established, then the concept of "best interests" no longer has any legal relevance'.

164 *Namiq*, n. 161, [35].

165 Although it had been suggested, in advance of *Dance*, that, 'if a Court had a doubt as to whether the DNC criteria were met, then it would be most unlikely to grant the declaration sought': *Namiq*, n. 161, [33].

166 Ibid. Further argument in favour of applying the criminal standard of proof, in part on the basis that the civil standard was lower than that applied in the medical decision-making, was again rejected by the High Court in *Dance*, n. 145, [125]–[136]; instead favouring the civil standard and 'anxious scrutiny': [155].

are themselves uncomplicated, such challenges appear unlikely to succeed and would, in any case, speak past the central issue.[167]

4.3.7 Plurality and mitigation in England

As to the potential for plural legal practices in relation to death, English law adopts a narrow focus, eschewing any different approach in different contexts, and appearing to reject other potentially relevant extra-legal frameworks. Formally, section 26(2)(d) of the Human Tissue Act 2004 permits the creation of a framework code of practice for assessing when a donor is dead for the purposes of transplantation. Certainly, then, there is legal scope to resolve uncertainty around death '*for the purposes of this Act*' in a distinct manner, but this has not yet been explored.[168] Guidance published in 2006 suggests, understandably, that brain stem death is the relevant criterion.[169]

There is, however, some evidence that the apparent clarity of legal resolution—and particularly the blunt, binary nature of the conceptual resolution here—is partly mediated in practice by policing the immediate *consequences* of any declaration regarding death. In *Re: A (A Child)*,[170] where a child suffered severe injury after accidentally choking whilst eating, a declaration of death—in reliance on the medical evidence—did not automatically mean that a coroner acquired jurisdiction. Hayden J noted different views in the leading texts over whether jurisdiction could be acquired where a dead body was nevertheless being ventilated.[171] Whilst the judge's sympathy with grieving loved ones is understandable, and the law has good reason to avoid placing coroners and medical practitioners in conflict, the idea that 'dead for the purposes of medicine (and, in effect, legal purposes)' differs from 'dead for the purposes of the coroner's jurisdiction' only serves to highlight the challenge of opting for a state-based, binary resolution at all. Indeed, it is perhaps odd that, having relied on the necessary precision of the medical definition to reach the finding on death, in relation to removal Hayden J instead held that 'insistence on a legally precise definition of death to trigger the involvement of the Coroner, in such challenging circumstances is, in my judgment, so obviously wrong as to be redundant of any contrary argument'.[172] Indeed, Hayden J emphasised that any dispute here was properly to be resolved by the courts, rather than by the coroner themselves, emphasising the institutional role of the court as a forum for airing the potentially distinct normative views of death that might underpin such disputes.[173] Similar efforts towards this can be seen in *BN* where, despite

---

167 *Namiq*, n. 161, [41]; Lyons/Donnelly, n. 152, 165–66.
168 Likewise in Scotland: see Earle, n. 21, 22.35 n. 68.
169 Chau/Herring, n. 4, 17.
170 [2015] EWHC 443.
171 Ibid., [21].
172 Ibid., [24].
173 Choong/Rady, n. 156, 75.

a declaration of death, it was agreed that treatment would be maintained to allow the family a dignified opportunity to say goodbye.[174] Equally, the very entanglement of decisions about death with decisions regarding withdrawal of treatment may itself create space for further dispute. The appeal in *Dance* suggests that making a declaration of death does not necessarily relieve the court of the need to properly undertake a separate best interests test where that is itself contested. Acting on the basis of any declaration can, in effect, be stayed by contesting a *different* but related question. That the declaration was, in effect, overturned is, no doubt, crucial for the individuals involved, but using one to undermine the other risks the clarity of any legal resolution here.[175] If the English courts are, in these cases, mapping a degree of 'reasonable accommodation' it goes too far to suggest that this is in relation to allowing 'alternative views of DNC',[176] but it is certainly the case that both the normative foundation for doing so, and indeed the content and boundaries of such efforts, remain concerningly opaque.[177]

Just as there is little indication of context-specific legal resolutions, there is, likewise, little suggestion that other extra-legal narratives are relevant. In *Re: A (A Child)*,[178] the father had been candid about their hopes of returning to Saudi Arabia on the basis that ventilation would never be withdrawn, in line with their Muslim beliefs,[179] and had challenged 'whether brain stem death is synonymous with clinical/legal death'.[180] The apparent elision of clinical death with legal death fairly reflects the position set out in *Re A/Bland*, but these cases make clear that alternative assessment or frameworks other than medicine are simply not relevant in defining death.[181] In both *AB* and *Namiq*, the parents likewise practised respective faiths but were no more successful

---

174 *BN*, n. 141, [20], per Sir Jonathan Cohen. Likewise *Re M*, n. 139, [106]–[109], per McFarlane P; Donnelly/Lyons, n. 91, 355–59.

175 Donnelly/Lyons, n. 91, 366, arguing this dissonance may suggest the need for greater nuance as to any rights and interests of the dead in DNC cases, drawing on the response to *McKitty* in doing so: see n. 49. As Choong frames it, this might be an 'interest in not having their bodies subjected to indignity', whether through continued ventilation or otherwise: see Choong, n. 108, 44. Concerns over resourcing can also arise here: see Kennedy, n. 127, 100.

176 Donnelly/Lyons, n. 91, 359.

177 See generally Donnelly/Lyons, n. 91, insightfully mapping the potential for 'reasonable accommodation' in the English cases by reference to practice in relevant American jurisdictions.

178 [2015] EWHC 443.

179 Ibid., [17]. Although whether the requirements of Islamic law are broader than brain-stem death is debatable: Earle, n. 21, 22.32 n. 60; Kaan, n. 8, 318–20.

180 *Re: A (A Child)*, n. 178, [10].

181 For a critique of *Re: A (A Child)* on this basis, see Choong/Rady, n. 156. The authors suggest the case appears to be the first such case where the approach to death was challenged on the basis of differing religious beliefs, arguing at root that a 'pluralistic' society such as the United Kingdom ought to better respect cultural and religious beliefs in relation to death. See Choong, n. 108, 42, noting, in discussing *Dance*, that 'the court did not engage in any meaningful sense with the religious arguments'.

on that basis.[182] In reaching beyond itself, the law has clearly chosen to privilege one extra-legal framework over others despite the fact that differences between these frameworks may be critical for the individuals concerned. As has been recently suggested, in doing so, and thereby excluding other frameworks, almost by definition English law recognises there are other approaches to death,[183] but it simply rejects their relevance to its task here.

4.3.8 Justifying law's choices

Whether rooted in individual welfare or collective concerns, an undeniable and regrettable consequence of the English position is the paucity of judicial effort to justify it;[184] as Choong puts it in relation to DNC, an 'accepting and unquestioning attitude can be detected from the beginning'.[185] There is little to suggest such an attitude was any different beforehand. For all its importance, the most consequential policy choice of all—to privilege the medical definition—is rarely openly discussed, appearing, if at all, as a terse syllogism,[186] let alone the precise implications of relying on the currently accepted framework for DNC.[187] The crucial decision to adopt the medical position simply emerged from *Re A/Bland* and casuistic path-dependence has allowed later cases to avoid having to re-assess that choice. But it is important to note that this phenomenon is not English by nature, nor restricted to the common-law tradition. A similar result can be found in Germany: the legal adoption of a standard of brain death well before this was finally captured in the relevant legislation regarding transplantation.[188] This pre-legislative adoption was driven by the same shifts in *medical* practice as elsewhere, with the law tracking these changes accordingly,[189] albeit discussion over what was required to demonstrate brain death continued into the following decades.[190] Indeed, it is

---

182 *AB*, n. 144, [23]. The child's faith was also raised in discussion in *Dance*.

183 Donnelly/Lyons, n. 91, 357–58.

184 Francis J rightly noted that requiring putrefaction would be an affront to those forced to witness it: *AB*, n. 144, [20], [22].

185 Choong, n. 108, 43.

186 In response to one mother contesting withdrawal of ventilation, see Francis J's blunt but unchallengeable reasoning that 'AB is already effectively dead according to the definition from the Code of Practice which I have just read out': *AB*, n. 144, [21].

187 As Donnelly and Lyons put it, the UK courts have generally 'assiduously avoided the normative dimension of DNC': Donnelly/Lyons, n. 91, 364.

188 See §3(2), §5 Transplantation Act 1997. Albeit that preceding period did not lack a measure of public debate in these developments, driven by the *Erlanger* case in particular: see B. Schöne-Seifert, n. 82, 264.

189 A. Laufs, *Arztrecht*, 1st ed., C.H. Beck 1977, 45, noting the protocols provided by the German Society for Surgery. In 1982, the Federal Medical Chamber would issue comprehensive guidance, which remain a touchstone given that §16 of the Transplantation Act enshrines their role here: see C.D. Middel and K. Scholz, 'Transplantationsgesetz-TPG' in A. Spickhoff (ed.), *Medizinrecht*, 4th ed., C.H. Beck 2022, 700, 13 (2847).

190 See generally J. Hoff and J. in der Schmitten (eds), *Wann ist der Mensch Tot?*, Rowohlt 1994.

notable both that, as in the English law, there was no preceding statutory definition despite the generally comprehensive nature of the German *Bürgerliches Gesetzbuch*,[191] nor any obvious bar to the courts simply adopting the medical definition.[192]

Given historical reliance on medical expertise, the simplest, if unarticulated, rationale may be that as dying is unavoidably medicalised in these cases, the medical conceptual analysis best fits that context. But that is a decision that the English law itself has done little to otherwise justify and is one that the necessary legislative process involved in enacting a statutory definition would naturally shine light on.[193] As Skegg suggested, death in law is not simply a 'technical medical issue' given the law must decide to privilege that approach— or any other—in the first place.[194] If it is the case here, as Hayden J has suggested, that 'law and good medical practice will rarely, if ever, diverge', the reason for this requires better explanation, not least as what constitutes 'good' medical practice itself is often subject to legal scrutiny.[195] This may provide a sound reason as to why, at least in a common-law system, one might still advocate to codify existing case law in statutory form: doing so can provide broader democratic input into how law should resolve this uncertainty than courts can ever offer.[196] As is evident in other such medicalised fields, judicial judgement may trump medical judgement.[197] Likewise, a medical context does not automatically mean that medical judgement ought to be privileged.[198] As such,

---

191 In part this might be explained by the view of leading nineteenth-century German jurist F.C. von Savigny: that '[d]eath, as the border of natural legal capacity, is so plainly a natural phenomenon that, like birth, a more precise rendering of its elements is unnecessary. It is only the difficulties of proof that demand positive legal rules': F.C. von Savigny, *System des heutigen Römischen Rechts*, vol. 2, Veit 1840, 17.

192 In later editions, Laufs notes that the medical criteria developed for 'clinical death', that is to say the classic cardiopulmonary definition, provided 'obvious and judicially suitable criteria for death', at least in advance of the neurological turn. But, with it, there is nothing to suggest the basic model of adopting the medical view would be disturbed: see Laufs, n. 189, 144. More cautious views can be found, conscious that one definition may not be able to properly satisfy the myriad different circumstances in which death is legally relevant, see A. Spickhoff, 'Bürgerliches Gesetzbuch' in Spickhoff, n. 189, 70, 1 12 (385). Likewise, A. Laufs and B.-R. Kern (eds), *Handbuch des Arztrechts*, 4th ed., C.H. Beck 2010, 1036.

193 Kaan, n. 8, 310–11.

194 Skegg, n. 17, 187–88, conceding himself that in practice the medical view leads the legal one; Choong, n. 108, ch. 4, exploring the potential legislative advantage here.

195 Such sentiments are, it must be said, hardly new. In response to *Re Potter*, commentators noted that 'death may be important legally but the criteria by which it is judged are for the doctors alone, for any individual case can only be decided on the medical evidence … There can be no distinction between "medical" and "legal" death': 'The Moment of Death' (1963) 31 *Medico-Legal Journal* 195, 195–96.

196 See Kaan's discussion of the issue with Singaporean developments in mind: Kaan, n. 8, 322, 324. See also the role of the Danish Council of Ethics as a provocateur in sparking debate over the introduction of brain death as a relevant criterion: Andreassen Rix, n. 46, 236–37.

197 *Bolitho v City and Hackney Health Authority* [1998] AC 232.

198 *Montgomery v Lanarkshire Health Board* [2015] UKSC 11.

whilst resorting to the courts inevitably harvests certainty from uncertainty, that is won at a price. The inherently vulnerable are placed in direct conflict with medical authority over the factual state of a world both inhabit—and over which views may understandably differ—without obvious explanation as to why one should yield to the other.

The law here is judicially stewarded, but is characterised by both its relative scarcity and, ultimately, its preference to resolve definitional uncertainty through reliance on an extra-legal framework.[199] Although there is no formal legal definition deployed to resolve this uncertainty, this choice allows the underpinning normative medical framework to evolve without risking disruption, even if any evolution would rightly need to be recognised as sufficiently authoritative.[200] A statutory resolution such as the UDDA that, likewise, merely enshrines medical diagnostic practices may achieve little beyond this. Indeed it risks being counterproductive both in re-igniting debate or holding back future developments.[201] Favouring one extra-legal framework over others leaves that framework to justify the relationship between law and public *mores*.[202] Resolving this uncertainty on 'a fact-finding basis' diminishes, if not ultimately rejects, substantive control over and normative responsibility for those facts.[203]

4.4 Conclusions

External events have driven the law here. Advances in medical technology 'created a gap between the body and death'.[204] As Henry K. Beecher, Chairman of the Harvard Committee, suggested, it was, 'desirable … to come to some subtle conclusion as to a new definition of death', at least for medical purposes.[205] Both developments proved crucial in driving legal change. This 'gap' served to highlight and reframe a question of undeniable legal importance: whether

---

199 'Rarely has the judiciary felt the need to pronounce on the issue': Chau/Herring, n. 4, 16. Earle characterises the relevant decision here as a clinical one that the law simply cannot take for itself: Earle, n. 21, 22.35.
200 Skegg earlier suggested that if medical practitioners ever 'come to favour reclassification', statutory intervention rather than parallel judicial evolution might be required. Developments in the case law since suggest the latter may well be possible where medical opinion was sufficiently authoritatively framed: see Skegg, n. 17, 223.
201 *Namiq*, n. 161, [31]; similarly, Laurie, n. 14, 17.34.
202 Skegg, n. 17, 188.
203 *Namiq* n. 161, [28]; *Re M*, n. 139, [51]; Donnelly/Lyons, n. 91, 368–69; Lyons/Donnelly, n. 152, 172; Choong, n. 108, 44 noting that 'the medical profession's definition and criteria for determining death are therefore embraced wholesale and not subjected to critical scrutiny'. The same characterisation of the law's response being 'factual' (distinct in this context from a 'normative' one) can be found elsewhere: see Laufs/Kern, n. 192, 1033, suggesting this is common in European systems more generally.
204 Sarbey, n. 11, 750.
205 G. Belkin, *Death before Dying: History, Medicine, and Brain Death*, OUP 2014, 4.

a person is dead. There was always a need to answer this, whether generally or contextually and whether through reliance on internal or external resolution. Experience in the United States suggests that plural, alternate criteria may suffice here and can be effectively captured in statutory form.[206] Advances in organ transplantation may likewise increase the pressure that uncertainty creates here, acting as a particular context for (re-)definition. Yet, as the United Kingdom demonstrates, it is plausible to proceed without such statutory intervention, albeit with less scrutiny of the underlying policy decisions.

Regardless of how it responds, death remains a fact beyond law. Although the uncertainty stems from an inscrutable, biological process wrapped in a metaphysical choice, in law death is an event that creates a predictable set of legal consequences. Framing death thus, as part of a binary, neatly reflects the binary nature of those legal consequences; one does not become, in law, somehow part widowed as the long day wanes. Depending from such a position, the law can only ever orient itself towards or away from a range of competing extra-legal frameworks responding to the same uncertainty. There is a strong incentive for any legal resolution to acknowledge common social practice and those that adopt a binary model may be particularly attractive. As experience suggests, the law's institutional power rather than its normative convictions may therefore suffice for resolution here. Epistemic uncertainty may reveal turtles all the way down, but it is open to the law to decide where exploration stops.

Focusing on England, it is clear that the normative power is rooted beyond law. If there is a legal *rule* that resolves the uncertainty here it does not engage an internal logic; if anything, the rule is simply to follow medical practice. This adds another footprint to a well-trodden path and is, if anything, a strongly path-dependent response: deploying a medical lens to a question rooted in the body and contextualised by healthcare. This result requires both settled medical practice from which to work, and a practical means of testing it. The former remains the subject of sufficient debate such that global consensus has proven impossible, even if the neurological turn is undeniable. The latter, as captured in the 2008 Code is, likewise, undeniable. As *Dance* suggests, such praxis, once authoritative, may likewise be elevated by law such that other medical views are constrained. The role of other extra-legal frameworks, or individual beliefs, are crowded out entirely. The boundaries of law's response can appear to be medical-evidential ones, rather than legal-conceptual ones given that, where value judgments are required, there is little, if any, internal legal discourse to engage. That the law should strive for clarity is unsurprising—uncertainty here requires resolution—but if the law cannot offer a subtle conclusion of its own, it must likewise acknowledge that such outsourcing ultimately diminishes its role in this most definitive of conclusions.

206 Laurie, n. 14, 17.33.

Part 2

Causation and loss

5 Causal uncertainty in tort law

The special case of mesothelioma

Ken Oliphant

This chapter addresses the issues of causal uncertainty in tort law arising in situations where there are two or more potential causes of the victim's damage, but there is insufficient evidence to determine which was in fact the cause. These have been highlighted in recent times by litigation relating to cancerous mesothelioma attributable to exposure to asbestos. In *Fairchild v Glenhaven Funeral Services*[1] the UK House of Lords moulded a remedy by boldly departing from the established principles of causation; but further high-level judicial decisions and legislative interventions have proved necessary in order to deal with its ramifications. This chapter charts those developments in English law before contextualising the legal issues arising in historical and comparative terms, and highlighting both the still unresolved questions and the anomalies that have ensued from the piecemeal and ad hoc interventions in this area by both judiciary and legislature.

5.1 Historical overview

5.1.1 The magic mineral

It was the 'miracle mineral'.[2] A natural substance composed of soft, flexible fibres that is strong and amazingly resistant to heat, fire, electricity, even decomposition. Amazingly versatile too: it can be woven into a cloth, made into a composite with cement, combined with paper or plastic to make them stronger. We know it as asbestos. Its miraculous properties have been recognised for thousands of years (the Egyptian pharaohs were buried in asbestos cloths to preserve their bodies).[3] But the commercial use of asbestos really began in the late nineteenth century as industrialised mining techniques

---

1 [2003] 1 AC 32.
2 G. Tweedale, *Magic Mineral to Killer Dust: Turner & Newall and the Asbestos Hazard*, revised ed., OUP 2001.
3 D. King, 'History of Asbestos' <https://www.asbestos.com/asbestos/history/> accessed 10.09.2023.

DOI: 10.4324/9781003537526-7

facilitated its extraction and the turbines, motors, vehicles, and construction activities of the modern era provided new opportunities for its use.[4]

The miracle soon turned into a nightmare, however.[5] There are reports of health problems in those working with asbestos from even classical Roman times. But these were overlooked or ignored in the enthusiastic modern embrace of the mineral, soon in widespread use in construction, shipbuilding, motor vehicle manufacture, and many other contexts. Then the reports of illness and deaths began to accumulate. In 1906 a London physician recorded a fatal case of lung disease in an asbestos textile worker who had worked 14 years in the industry. The autopsy confirmed the presence of asbestos fibres in his lungs. In 1924 we have the first medical journal report of asbestosis: a 33-year-old woman who died after working in asbestos textile factories from the age of 13. Her autopsy revealed the lung scarring that we now know to be characteristic of the disease.[6]

Asbestosis is caused by the accumulation of asbestos fibres in the lungs.[7] Over years, the fibres cause inflammation and scarring. It usually takes 15 to 40 years for symptoms to appear: coughing, wheezing, shortness of breath, chest pains. Though a serious condition, only in rare cases is it fatal.

By the 1950s, evidence was emerging of an even more insidious health risk: cancer. Initially the focus was on lung cancer, though the impact of asbestos was difficult to disentangle from that of other carcinogens, notably those in cigarette smoke. Then medical science identified a new type of cancer, mesothelioma, that is almost exclusively linked with exposure to asbestos, though there is scientific uncertainty as to its precise aetiology which makes it impossible to attribute it to specific periods of exposure in individual cases.[8] 'Meso' is a cancer of the lining of the lungs (the pleura) or the lining of other organs. It is extremely aggressive, typically causing death within a year or so of diagnosis, though 10% of patients will survive for five years or more. There is no known cure, so treatment is only to mitigate its effects. Currently, some 2,500 deaths in the UK are attributed to the cancer every year,[9] even though the

---

4 As to the chemical composition, properties, and commercial use of asbestos, see N. Wikeley, *Compensation for Industrial Disease*, Dartmouth 2013, 12–18; UK Asbestos Working Party, 'UK Asbestos – The Definitive Guide', Institute of Actuaries 2004 <https://www.actuaries.org .uk/documents/uk-asbestos-definitive-guide> accessed 10.09.2023, paras 2.1 and 2.3.

5 As to the history of asbestos-related disease, see *Fairchild*, n. 1, [6]–[7] per Lord Bingham; Wikeley, n. 4, 18–25; P.W.J. Bartrip, 'History of asbestos related disease' (2004) 80 *Postgraduate Medical Journal* 72.

6 W.E. Cooke, 'Fibrosis of the lungs due to the inhalation of asbestos dust' (1924) 2 *British Medical Journal* 147, cited by Bartrip, n. 5, 72.

7 As to the various types of asbestos-related disease, see Wikeley, n. 4, 26–30; UK Asbestos Working Party, n. 2, para. 2.2.

8 As to mesothelioma, see *Fairchild*, n. 1, [7] per Lord Bingham; *Sienkiewicz v Greif (UK)* [2011] 2 AC 229, [101]–[102] per Lord Phillips; Wikeley, n. 4, 28–29.

9 HSE/National Statistics, 'Asbestos-related disease statistics, Great Britain 2023', Health and Safety Executive, July 2023 <https://www.hse.gov.uk/statistics/causdis/asbestos-related-dis-

use of asbestos was banned in 1999.[10] Like asbestosis, mesothelioma has an extremely long latency period—20, 30, 40 years or even more—so the deaths today are from exposures decades ago, and their number will reduce with the further passage of time.

5.1.2 Asbestos and the law

The asbestos tragedy prompted a number of legal responses, going beyond the regulatory prohibition of its use.[11] Mesothelioma was prescribed as an industrial disease giving an entitlement to industrial injuries benefit payments. Like other welfare benefits, these are low in value and do not compensate for non-pecuniary losses, so mesothelioma victims and their families began to make tort claims for damages.[12] The potential of tort law could only be unlocked, however, once the law of limitation of actions (time limits) was reformed in 1963 to prevent time running against a claimant for so long as their injury remained latent and unknown.[13] The number of claims that have ensued is very large, numbering in the tens of thousands,[14] though these include multiple claims by the same victim (e.g. against different employers).[15] Most of the claims relate to occupational exposure, though liability has been extended to familial exposure (e.g. where a spouse regularly washed an asbestos worker's work clothes)[16] and even recreational exposure.[17] In total, UK insurers pay out £200 million a year to mesothelioma sufferers.[18]

---

ease.pdf> accessed 10.09.2023, 6. The statistics for 2021, the most recent year for which data is available, fell a little below the ten-year average to 2,268: ibid.

10 Asbestos (Prohibitions) (Amendment) Regulations 1999, SI 1999 No. 2373.

11 As to the history of asbestos-related regulation, see UK Asbestos Working Party, n. 4, para. 2.4; UK Asbestos Working Party, 'UK Asbestos Working Party Upate 2020', Institute of Actuaries 2021, para. 4.5.

12 As to tort litigation for asbestos-related disease, see W.L.F. Felstiner and R. Dingwall, *Asbestos Litigation in the United Kingdom: An Interim Report*, Centre for Socio-Legal Studies, Oxford 1988; Wikeley, n. 4, 37–56.

13 Limitation Act 1963; Wikeley, n. 4, 39–41.

14 The available datasets are limited in their coverage, but it is known that 22,319 mesothelioma claims were reported to the Compensation Recovery Unit (CRU) between 01/01/2007 and 31/12/2015, with a further 10,406 reported to the CRU between 01/04/2016 and 31/10/2019: UK Asbestos Working Party, 'Update 2020', n. 11, 118. A chart showing the number of mesothelioma insurance claims made by year in the period 1968 to 2008 shows the annual number initially close to zero, rising to over 250 by 1975, rising to over 500 in 1980, and first exceeding 1,000 in 1993 and 2,000 in 2002: ibid., 30.

15 For the CRU data cited in the previous footnote, it has been calculated that the two datasets included 15,023 claimants and 6,344 claimants respectively: ibid., 120.

16 *Gibson v Babcock International* [2018] CSOH 78. Cf. *Gunn v Wallsend Slipway and Engineering Co., The Times*, 23 January 1989; *Maguire v Harland & Wolff* [2005] EWCA Civ. 1, [2005] PIQR P21.

17 *Margereson v JW Roberts* [1996] Env. LR 304 (children playing near to factory).

18 Association of British Insurers, 'Mesothelioma and asbestos' <https://www.abi.org.uk/products-and-issues/topics-and-issues/mesothelioma-and-asbestos> accessed 16.10.2023.

Asbestos claims in general, and mesothelioma claims in particular, threw up a wide and varied set of extremely complicated legal issues.[19] The main focus has been on causation, as it can normally be presumed that the person responsible for the exposure owes a duty to potential victims, and even proving breach of that duty has not usually presented problems, at least in employers' liability claims; the risks of heavy occupational exposure to asbestos have been known from the early 1930s.[20] Breach of duty has been a more significant obstacle in claims relating to *non*-occupational exposure as the risks involved were not so immediately apparent and the time of exposure might have preceded the date from which the person responsible for it ought to have known of and guarded against the risk.[21]

The difficulty of attributing causation to a particular period of tortious exposure is largely a product of mesothelioma's uncertain aetiology and its extremely long latency period, combined with the possibility that the victim was engaged in several different activities, for different employers, over the period during which they were at risk. One or more of those employers might now be insolvent or simply have disappeared in the course of the 20, 30, 40 or more years following the relevant periods of employment. Since 1972, employers have been required to take out insurance against their liability to their employees,[22] but the at-risk periods might predate the legislative reform, while many records of past insurance cover proved to be incomplete or missing. Even where the employers' liability insurer was known, they themselves could have become insolvent or otherwise ceased to exist in the intervening years.[23]

5.1.3 Fairchild v Glenhaven Funeral Services *(2002)*

These issues crystallised in *Fairchild v Glenhaven Funeral Services*, which came before the House of Lords in 2002.[24] This was a test case addressing the difficult issues of causation that arise in mesothelioma claims. As explained above,

---

19 See further Felstiner/Dingwall, n. 12; A. Care, 'A century of neglect and 1940s' worker asbestos exposure – chronology and comment' [2005] *Journal of Personal Injury Law* 230; A. McKenna, 'An overview of the legal landscape of negligently inflicted asbestos related conditions' [2011] *Journal of Personal Injury Law* 205. For additional historical background, see Tweedale, n. 2, 233–34 and 261–73. As to the wider legal context in the United Kingdom, see UK Asbestos Working Party, 'Update 2020', n. 11, sec. 5. For a US perspective, see S.J. Carroll et al., *Asbestos Litigation*, Rand Institute for Civil Justice 2005.

20 Wikeley, n. 4, 41–44. See e.g. *Shell Tankers UK v Jeromson* [2001] ICR 1223; but cf. *Williams v University of Birmingham* [2012] PIQR P4.

21 Wikeley, n. 4, 44. See e.g. *Gunn v Wallsend*, n. 16; *Maguire v Harland & Wolff*, n. 16; but cf. *Gibson v Babcock*, n. 16.

22 Employers' Liability (Compulsory Insurance) Act 1969; Employers' Liability (Compulsory Insurance) Act 1969 (Commencement) Order 1971/1116.

23 See generally Felstiner/Dingwall, n. 12, 6 and 10; Wikeley, n. 4, 45–48.

24 *Fairchild*, n. 1.

the typical situation is where an employee has been exposed to asbestos during several different periods of work with different employers; when the mesothelioma is diagnosed 20, 30, or 40 years later, one cannot say which period or periods were causative. Unless a majority of the exposure can be attributed to a single employer, it is not possible to satisfy the normal 'but for' test of causation: would the mesothelioma have arisen but for, i.e. in the absence of, the negligent exposure attributable to the particular employer? If so, the existing orthodoxy would say: no causation.

Fairchild blew this apart by recognising the clear injustice of denying liability where you have a number of negligent defendants, and you know that at least one of them was responsible for the causative exposure, but scientific uncertainty about mesothelioma's aetiology prevents you assigning causal responsibility to any individual defendant on the normal standard of proof, the balance of probabilities. In these circumstances, the House of Lords ruled that any defendant who materially increased the risk to the victim could be deemed to have caused the mesothelioma. This became known as the '*Fairchild* exception'.[25]

5.1.4 The aftermath of Fairchild

The *Fairchild* decision left several important issues of principle unresolved. In particular, was the *Fairchild* exception limited to cases where all the relevant exposure was tortious (thus raising 'the problem of the indeterminate defendant'[26]) or would it extend to situations where some of the exposure was non-tortious? And was liability under *Fairchild* a joint and several liability on every defendant in the full amount of the damage, or only a liability proportional to each employer's share in the total exposure?

The first opportunity to answer these questions arose four years later, in *Barker v Corus (UK)*.[27] The deceased died from mesothelioma after exposure to asbestos in three periods of his working life: one employed by the defendant, another working for another employer, now insolvent, and a third period when he was self-employed. So, this raised the question whether *Fairchild* applies if part of the exposure is non-tortious (here, the period of self-employment). If it did, was the liability on the defendant joint and several in the full amount of the loss, subject to a deduction for the claimant's own contribution? Or was it a proportional liability, commensurate with the fraction of the total exposure for which the defendant was responsible? That would make a big difference to the practical outcome if part of the overall exposure was the fault of another employer who was now insolvent or could not be traced, as was the case in *Barker*.

---

25 *Gregg v Scott* [2005] 2 AC 176, [85] per Lord Hoffmann.
26 *Fairchild*, n. 1, [26] per Lord Bingham.
27 [2006] 2 AC 572.

By majority,[28] the House of Lords ruled that, yes, the *Fairchild* exception did indeed still apply even though part of the exposure was non-tortious. But the liability on each defendant would be proportional to their own contribution to the total exposure. (If a defendant was responsible for x% of the total exposure, they would pay just x% of full damages.) Having bent the rules of causation in favour of the claimant in *Fairchild*, the Law Lords evidently felt they should mitigate the impact on the defendant by departing from the normal rule of joint and several liability. That is the rule that, where multiple defendants are liable for the same damage, the claimant can obtain judgment against any of them for the full amount, and it is left to the defendant who pays to seek financial contribution or an indemnity from the other or others.[29] Proportional damages were envisaged as a way to 'smooth the roughness of the justice' which would otherwise result from the imposition of liability.[30]

As mentioned, the choice between joint and several, and proportional, liability makes a big difference where one of the parties responsible for the damage is insolvent or has disappeared. Under joint and several liability, the claimant gets full compensation from the other defendant(s), who are left out of pocket because they cannot recover a contribution or indemnity from the party who is insolvent or who cannot be found.[31] Under *Barker*'s proportional liability, it is the claimant who is left out of pocket: they get x% of their damages from D1, y% from D2, but go short in respect of the z% for which insolvent D3 would have been liable. Proportional liability transfers the risk of a defendant's insolvency from their co-defendants to the claimant.

This judicial solution did not last for long. The decision in *Barker* was handed down on 3 May 2006. Little more than a month later, following strong protests from unions and Members of Parliament, the then prime minister, Tony Blair, announced the government's intention to reverse *Barker* and impose joint and several liability in *Fairchild* claims.[32] On 17 July, the House of Commons agreed to the amendment of an existing Compensation Bill, introducing a new mesothelioma provision;[33] the Lords accepted the amendment on the following day,[34] and the new clause became sec. 3 of the Compensation Act 2006, which received Royal Assent on 25 July 2006.

---

28 Lord Rodger (dissenting) would have imposed full joint and several liability.
29 Civil Liability (Contribution) Act 1978.
30 *Barker*, n. 27, [43] per Lord Hoffmann. The outcome was also justified by the nature of the defendant's liability as the wrongful creation of the risk; consistency of approach suggested that the damages should be proportional to that risk: [35] per Lord Hoffmann.
31 *Barker*, n. 27, [89] per Lord Rodger, [108] per Lord Walker.
32 'Blair "to change" asbestos ruling', BBC News Online, 13 June 2006 <http://news.bbc.co .uk/1/hi/uk_politics/5074886.stm> accessed 11.09.2023.
33 HC Deb., 17 July 2006, vol. 449, col. 39 ff.
34 HL Deb., 18 July 2006, vol.684, col. 1276.

5.1.5 *Section 3 of the Compensation Act 2006*

Section 3 applies where (sec. 3(1)):

(a) a person ("the responsible person") has negligently or in breach of statutory duty caused or permitted another person ("the victim") to be exposed to asbestos,

(b) the victim has contracted mesothelioma as a result of exposure to asbestos,

(c) because of the nature of mesothelioma and the state of medical science, it is not possible to determine with certainty whether it was the exposure mentioned in paragraph (a) or another exposure which caused the victim to become ill, and

(d) the responsible person is liable in tort, by virtue of the exposure mentioned in paragraph (a), in connection with damage caused to the victim by the disease (whether by reason of having materially increased a risk or for any other reason).

In those circumstances, sec. 3(2) provides:

The responsible person shall be liable—

(a) in respect of the whole of the damage caused to the victim by the disease (irrespective of whether the victim was also exposed to asbestos—

    (i) other than by the responsible person, whether or not in circumstances in which another person has liability in tort, or

    (ii) by the responsible person in circumstances in which he has no liability in tort), and

(b) jointly and severally with any other responsible person.

As noted, sec. 3 thus provides for any 'responsible person' who has, negligently or in breach of statutory duty, contributed to the victim's exposure to asbestos to be liable for *the whole of the damage* caused to the victim by their consequent contracting of mesothelioma (sec. 3(2)(a)). This reverses the *proportional* liability introduced by the House of Lords just weeks before in *Barker v Corus*. Consequently, no matter what proportion of the total exposure was attributable to the responsible person's breach of duty, their liability is for all the damage caused by the mesothelioma. The liability is joint and several with any other responsible person (sec. 3(2)(b)), against whom the right to claim a contribution is expressly preserved (sec. 3(3)(a)).

The main limitation on the scope of the liability is its restriction to cases of scientific uncertainty—specifically, where 'because of the nature of mesothelioma and the state of medical science, it is not possible to determine with certainty ... [which exposure] caused the victim to become ill' (sec. 3(1)(c)). This implicit link with the *Fairchild* liability at common law is confirmed by the further precondition for the application of sec. 3 that the responsible person must already be liable in tort by virtue of the exposure in question, which liability may be one for 'having materially increased a risk' (sec. 3(1)(d)).

Section 3 applies only to mesothelioma claims arising from tortious exposure to asbestos. The victim must have contracted mesothelioma (sec. 3(1)(b)) and the liability is for 'the damage caused to the victim by the disease' (sec. 3(2)(a)). For claims in respect of other asbestos-related disease, or otherwise falling outside the scope of application of sec. 3, the common-law rules continue to apply.[35] The enactment 'left the common law intact, but carved an exception out of it for mesothelioma'.[36]

Though the liability under sec. 3 is joint and several where there is another person responsible for the damage caused to the victim by the disease, there need not be any other responsible person. Indeed, the defendant is liable for the whole damage

> irrespective of whether the victim was also exposed to asbestos—(i) other than by the responsible person, whether or not in circumstances in which another person has liability in tort, or (ii) by the responsible person in circumstances in which he has no liability in tort. (sec. 3(2)(a))

The statutory wording embraces the situation before the House of Lords in *Barker v Corus*, where part of the exposure was indeed 'other than by the responsible person' and non-tortious inasmuch as it related to a period during which the victim was self-employed. However, it is likely that such circumstances would support a successful defence of contributory negligence— explicitly preserved by sec. 3(3)(b).

5.1.6 Sienkiewicz v Greif (UK) *(2011)*

It is important to recall that the scope of the *Fairchild* exception itself is determined by the common-law authorities and not by the statute, whose focus is really the quantum of the liability rather than its existence. One further common-law test of *Fairchild*'s limits remains to be discussed. In *Sienkiewicz v Greif (UK)*,[37] the deceased died of mesothelioma some 20 to 40 years after her employment at the defendants' factory. She worked there mostly in an office but was tortiously exposed to small amounts of asbestos as she moved around the premises. Apart from this 'very light' occupational exposure,[38] there was also low-level exposure to asbestos in the general atmosphere where she lived ('environmental exposure'). The occupational exposure increased the deceased's risk of developing mesothelioma by only 18%. The defendants

---

35 *International Energy Group v Zurich Insurance* [2016] AC 509.
36 Ibid., [179] per Lord Sumption.
37 *Sienkiewicz*, n. 8.
38 Ibid., [60] per Lord Phillips, [116] per Lord Rodger.

argued that this situation did not fall within the *Fairchild* exception because it was not a case where scientific uncertainty prevented the claimant establishing causation; on the contrary, it would have been possible to do so had the tortious occupational exposure more than doubled the risk from the environmental exposure. Further, *Fairchild* should not apply where the only exposure to asbestos other than that for which the defendants were responsible was exposure in the general atmosphere. Rejecting these arguments and affirming the defendants' liability, the Supreme Court ruled that the *Fairchild* exception applies even in a case of single tortious exposure adding to (non-tortious) environmental exposure and that there is no requirement to show that the tortious exposure more than doubled the ambient risk. Under sec. 3 of the Compensation Act 2006, the liability was for the whole of the damage caused to the victim by the disease, it being irrelevant that the defendants were responsible for only a small proportion of the overall exposure—an outcome that Lord Phillips and Lord Brown described as 'draconian'.[39]

5.1.7 The Mesothelioma Act 2014

Sienkiewicz shows that, so long as a mesothelioma claimant is able to sue just one solvent party responsible for their exposure to asbestos, or their insurer, then they recover compensation for the whole of their damage. What of those who are unable to locate *any* solvent party or identify any on-risk insurer? It was to address the compensation demands of this category of victim that Parliament passed the Mesothelioma Act 2014, establishing the Diffuse Mesothelioma Payment Scheme (DMPS).[40] This offers compensation payments equivalent to full tort damages to those exposed to asbestos by their employer in breach of duty (or to eligible dependants) where the first diagnosis of the disease was on or after 25 July 2012 and they are unable to bring an action for damages against any past employer or employers' liability insurer, whether because the latter cannot be found or no longer exist or for any other reason. The scheme is funded by a levy on all active insurers in the employers' liability market, the amount being based on market-share. In eight years of operation since 2014, the DMPS has paid out £254.9 million in compensation to 1,815 successful applicants with the average (mean) payment awarded being around £144,000.[41] Because exposure to asbestos must be through the breach of duty of the victim's employer, it is not possible to claim under the scheme where there was no occupational exposure at all. For victims of para-occupational and environmental exposure, or exposure while self-employed, it

---

39 Ibid., [58] per Lord Phillips, [184] per Lord Brown.
40 See generally N. Wikeley, 'The Diffuse Mesothelioma Payment Scheme 2014' (2014) 21 *Journal of Social Security Law* 65.
41 Department for Work & Pensions, 'Diffuse Mesothelioma Payment Scheme Annual Review 2021–2022', November 2022, 5 <https://www.gov.uk/government/publications/diffuse-mesothelioma-payment-scheme-annual-review-2021-to-2022> accessed 16.10.2023.

is possible to claim a payment under a separate diffuse mesothelioma payment scheme established in 2008,[42] as this entitlement is irrespective of employment status; however, the sums paid are much lower than under the 2014 scheme.[43]

5.2 Scope of the uncertainty problem

The history recounted above problematises the application of established principles of causation in the law of tort to a particular situation of causal uncertainty: there are two or more potential causes of the damage but it is uncertain which of them was (or were) in fact the (or a) cause.

The orthodox approach is to apply the well-known 'but for' test.[44] One asks, for each potential cause in turn, whether the damage would not have occurred but for the cause in question. This is assessed on the ordinary civil standard of proof—the balance of probabilities. In the vast majority of cases, the application of the but for test is unproblematic. However, in a number of scenarios involving multiple potential causes the test produces outcomes that defy common sense:

1. *additional causation*: two (or more) independent events happen simultaneously, each sufficient on its own to bring about the outcome (e.g. bullets from two guns pierce the victim's heart at exactly the same moment);
2. *cumulative causation*: two (or more) independent events contribute to a single causal process, but it is uncertain whether each on its own would have been sufficient to bring about the outcome or known that one or both would *not* have been sufficient without the other (e.g. where there are two intermingled sources of toxic exposure);[45]
3. *pre-empted causation*: two (or more) independent events initiate processes sufficient to bring about the outcome, but the progress of one is pre-empted by the other (e.g. a boy loses his balance while playing on a bridge and instinctively grabs the defendant's dangerously situated high-voltage powerline with fatal consequences; had he not grabbed the powerline, the fall would likely have killed him anyway);[46]
4. *overlapping causation*: two (or more) independent events cause damage to the victim but the effects of that damage overlap (e.g. two successive accidents cause the victim two distinct injuries, each of which on its own

---

42 Child Maintenance and Other Payments Act 2008, Part 4.

43 Wikeley, 'Diffuse Mesothelioma Payment Scheme', n. 40, 65, 68, and 80.

44 *Cork v Kirby Maclean* [1952] 2 All ER 402, 407 per Denning LJ; *Barnett v Chelsea and Kensington Hospital Management* [1969] 1 QB 428.

45 See e.g. *Bonnington Castings v Wardlaw* [1956] AC 613.

46 A slight variation on the facts of *Dillon v Twin State Gas & Electric Co.*, 85 NH 449, 163 A 111 (New Hampshire 1932). The question in such cases is often the extent of the liability of the party responsible for the pre-empting cause. If the pre-empting cause were to have been taken away, the pre-empted cause would have produced the same outcome anyway.

would have rendered them unfit for work;[47] or two successive accidents damage the paintwork on the victim's car, each of which on its own would have necessitated a total respray[48]);

5. *alternative causation*: two (or more) independent events contribute to the risk of the damage but it is not certain which in fact caused the damage that eventuates (e.g. two hunters fire towards the victim at the same time and one of their bullets hits, but it is uncertain whose gun it came from); we are dealing here with a situation of 'either … or …' rather than 'both … and …'.

It is this final category of causal uncertainty that characterises the mesothelioma cases discussed earlier and that provides our focus in this chapter, though the uncertainty regarding mesothelioma's aetiology is scientific, whereas in the hunters' scenario it is merely evidential. It should be noted that the object of study is the causation of the damage that is the gist of the claim, satisfying one of the required elements of liability, as opposed to the quantification of the consequent damages, which is addressed elsewhere in this collection.[49]

5.3 Solutions and policy goals

5.3.1 Historical and comparative perspective

Uncertain alternative causation is a problem confronted by numerous legal systems especially (though not only) in recent years.[50] The parenthetical qualification is required because this uncertainty had already been highlighted in Roman law, as shown by two passages in the Digest cited to the House of

---

47 *Baker v Willoughby* [1970] AC 467; cf. *Jobling v Associated Dairies* [1982] AC 794.

48 *Performance Cars v Abraham* [1962] 1 QB 33.

49 D. Messner-Kreuzbauer, 'Quantifying or avoiding the unknown: damages for future lost earnings in tortious personal injury cases', this volume.

50 For general overviews, see C. von Bar, *The Common European Law of Torts*, vol. 2, OUP 2000, para. 416; B. Winiger et al. (eds), *Digest of European Tort Law, vol. 1: Essential Cases on Natural Causation*, Springer 2007, ch. 6; I. Gilead et al. (eds), *Proportional Liability: Analytical and Comparative Perspectives*, de Gruyter 2013; C. van Dam, *European Tort Law*, 2nd ed., OUP 2013, ss. 1107–8; S. Steel, *Proof of Causation in Tort Law*, CUP 2015; M. Infantino and E. Zervogianni (eds), *Causation in European Tort Law*, CUP 2017. See also, by the present author, K. Oliphant, 'Alternative Causation: A Comparative Analysis of Austrian and English Law' in P. Apathy et al. (eds), *Festschrift für Helmut Koziol*, Jan Sramek 2010; K. Oliphant, 'Proportional Liability' in B. Verschraegen (ed.), *Interdisciplinary Studies of Comparative and Private International Law*, vol. 1, Jan Sramek 2010; K. Oliphant, 'Uncertain Factual Causation in the Third Restatement: Some Comparative Notes' (2011) 37 *William Mitchell Law Review* 159; K. Oliphant, 'Uncertain Causes: The Chinese Tort Liability Act in Comparative Perspective' in L. Chen and R. van Rhee (eds), *Towards a Chinese Civil Code: Historical and Comparative Perspectives*, Brill 2012; K. Oliphant, 'Causal Uncertainty and Proportional Liability in England and Wales' in Gilead et al., above; K. Oliphant, 'Causation in Cases of Evidential Uncertainty: Juridical Techniques and Fundamental Issues' (2016) 91 *Chicago-Kent Law Review* 58.

Lords in *Fairchild* and analysed by Lord Rodger.[51] In the more pertinent of the passages for present purposes, Ulpian considers a situation where a number of people attack a slave, who dies of his wounds. If it is known who struck the fatal blow, that person alone is liable, but if it is not known, then all are liable.[52] Lord Rodger stated:[53]

> I would take from these passages the clear implication that classical Roman jurists of the greatest distinction saw the need for the law to deal specially with the situation where it was impossible to ascertain the identity of the actual killer among a number of wrongdoers. If strict proof of causation were required, the plaintiff would be deprived of his remedy in damages for the death of his slave. In that situation, some jurists at least were prepared, exceptionally, to hold all of the wrongdoers liable and so afford a remedy to the owner whose slave had been killed.

His Lordship admitted that the exact scope of the Roman decisions could no longer be known for sure, but concluded this section of his analysis with this observation:[54]

> The point remains, however, that all these centuries ago considerations of policy plainly led to a departure from what the law would usually require by way of proof of causation.

In modern times, the principal judicial techniques for giving effect to such policy considerations to craft a remedy for the victim are the reversal of the burden of proof, the award of damages for loss of chance, and liability for contribution to risk. They are considered in turn in the following paragraphs.

5.3.1.1 Reversal of the burden of proof

Historically, courts and legislatures in several jurisdictions have resorted to the reversal of the burden of proof in situations of joint action where it cannot be determined which of the joint actors was the actual cause of the damage that ensues. In the well-known hunters' scenario, mentioned briefly above, two hunters negligently discharge their guns and one of them shoots their companion; however, it is not known which hunter fired the bullet that struck them. In such circumstances, the consistent response across different legal systems has been to allow the victim a remedy even though it cannot be shown on the

---

51 *Fairchild*, n. 1, [157]–[160]. See also J.S. Kortmann, 'Ab alio ictu(s): Misconceptions about Julian's View of Causation' (1999) 20 *JLH* 95.
52 Digest 9.2.11.2.
53 *Fairchild*, n. 1, [160].
54 Ibid.

balance of probabilities (or whatever other standard of proof is appropriate) that either of the hunters fired the guilty shot. In California[55] and Canada[56] the technique employed has been to reverse the burden of proof, leaving it to the hunters to exonerate themselves if they are able to.[57] Failing that, they bear joint and several liability. This burden-shifting rule was incorporated in the US *Restatement 2d of Torts* when it was released in 1965[58] and is now to be found in *Restatement 3d*:[59]

> When the plaintiff sues all of multiple actors and proves that each engaged in tortious conduct that exposed the plaintiff to a risk of harm and that the tortious conduct of one or more of them caused the plaintiff's harm but the plaintiff cannot reasonably be expected to prove which actor or actors caused the harm, the burden of proof, including both production and persuasion, on factual causation is shifted to the defendants.

This approach maps neatly onto that already pursued by German law, in whose civil code of 1900 is to be found the following provision:[60]

> If more than one person has caused damage by a jointly committed tort, then each of them is responsible for the damage. The same applies if it cannot be established which of several persons involved caused the damage by their act.

Again, it is left to the participant in the joint conduct to prove they were not the cause of the damage if they can. Similar provisions can be found in the Austrian, Dutch, and Greek civil codes.[61] The Chinese Tort Liability Law of 2010[62] also included an article on alternative defendants that appears to have been modelled on the German approach, and this is now to be found in art. 1170 of the new Chinese Code. Art 1170 reads:[63]

---

55 *Summers v Tice* (1948) 33 Cal. 2d 80, 199 P 2d 1.
56 *Cook v Lewis* [1951] SCR 830.
57 Cf. the approach taken in certain French cases of basing liability on the hunters' collective guardianship of the guns or their participation in a joint venture: see O. Moréteau and C. Pellerin-Rugliano, 'France' in Winiger et al., n. 50, 6a/6.
58 *Restatement (Second) of Torts* (1965) s. 433B(3).
59 *Restatement (Third) of Torts: Liability for Physical and Emotional Harm* (2010) s. 28(b).
60 §830(1) BGB. Translation from <https://www.gesetze-im-internet.de/englisch_bgb/englisch_bgb.html> accessed 10.09.2023.
61 See respectively art. 1302 ABGB (Austria), art. 6.99 BW (Netherlands), and art. 926 CC (Greece). See also art. VI.–4:103 Draft Common Frame of Refence.
62 See generally H. Koziol and Y. Zhu, 'Background and Key Contents of the New Chinese Tort Liability Law' (2010) 1 *JETL* 328. The Tort Liability Law was repealed on the introduction of the Chinese Civil Code on 01.01.2021.
63 Civil Code of the People's Republic of China (adopted at the Third Session of the Thirteenth National People's Congress on 28.05.2020). Translation from <http://en.npc.gov.cn.cdurl

> Where two or more persons commit an act that endangers another person's personal or property safety and the damage is caused only by one or several of them, if the specific tortfeasor(s) can be identified, the tortfeasor(s) shall bear liability, and if the specific tortfeasor(s) cannot be identified, all of the actors shall assume joint and several liability

Moving beyond cases of common conduct, German law also shifts the burden of proof where there is a violation of a protective statute (*Schutzgesetz*) or breach of a judicially recognised safety duty (*Verkehrspflicht*) in circumstances where the damage is such that the duty was intended to protect against.[64] Significantly, this may occur in cases of medical injury where gross negligence is established.[65] There the burden of proof is reversed if the healthcare practitioner contributes more than a minimal risk of harm, even if it is much smaller than the risks associated with the patient's condition or necessarily inherent in the treatment.[66]

In English law, there is no general mechanism for shifting the burden of proof from claimant to defendant in cases of causal uncertainty, though the doctrine *res ipsa loquitur* (the thing speaks for itself) may serve a similar function in situations where it is applicable. In its classic formulation:[67]

> where the thing is shown to be under the management of the defendant or his servants, and the accident is such as in the ordinary course of things does not happen if those who have the management use proper care, it affords reasonable evidence, in the absence of explanation by the defendants, that the accident arose from want of care.

The doctrine has been invoked, for example, to affix liability on an air services company for the unexplained crash of one of its planes,[68] but it has no application where there is a plausible alternative explanation for the accident that occurred,[69] which significantly limits its utility in cases of uncertain alternative causation as by definition at least one alternative cause will have been

---

.cn/pdf/civilcodeofthepeoplesrepublicofchina.pdf> accessed 10.09.2023.

64 For a short overview in English, see van Dam, n. 50, s. 1107–1.

65 See R. Zimmerman and J. Kleinschmidt, 'Germany', in Winiger et al., n. 50, 10/2 (citing Bundesgerichtshof (Federal Court of Justice) 11 June 1968, *Neue Juristische Wochenschrift* 2291, 1968). For further discussion, see G. Schiemann, 'Problems of Causation in the Liability for Medical Malpractice in German Law in L. Tichý (ed.), *Causation in Law*, Faculty of Law, Charles University, Prague 2007, 187–98; M. Stauch, *The Law of Medical Negligence in England and Germany: A Comparative Analysis*, Hart 2008, 87–92.

66 See e.g. Bundesgerichtshof 27 April 2004, *Neue Juristische Wochenschrift* 2011, 2004, noted in Stauch, n. 65, 89–90 (only a 10% chance that proper treatment would have prevented the adverse outcome).

67 *Scott v London and St Katherine Docks Co* (1865) 3 H & C 596, 601 per Erle CJ.

68 *George v Eagle Air Services* [2009] 1 WLR 2133 (Privy Council).

69 See e.g. *Ng Chun Pui v Lee Chuen Tat* [1988] RTR 298 (Privy Council).

identified. That means the maxim will only rarely be relevant in the medical negligence context, other than perhaps in very simple cases.[70] In any event, the effect of the doctrine is not strictly speaking to reverse the burden of proof but merely to describe a situation in which it is proper to draw an inference of negligence.[71]

It should be noted that, in the common law, where the standard of proof is the balance of probabilities, the reversal of the burden of proof only works if the probabilities are equally split between two defendants. If there are more than two, and the probability that each has caused the harm is less than 50%, reversing the burden of proof is insufficient to affix liability to any of them. Each can prove that it was more likely than not that one or other of their co-defendants was responsible. For that reason, reversing the burden of proof would not have been an effective judicial technique on the facts of *Fairchild* itself, given the fragmented nature of the deceased's working life.

5.3.1.2 Damages for loss of chance

Damages for loss of chance are another potential judicial response to the issue of uncertain alternative causation, but English law has so far been unreceptive to their award, at least in cases of physical damage.[72] To date the theory's application has been limited to cases of pure economic loss.[73] Its extension to the area of medical negligence has twice been rejected by the House of Lords, first in *Hotson v East Berkshire Area Health Authority* (1987),[74] then in *Gregg v Scott* (2005).[75]

In *Hotson*, a teenage boy fell from a rope on which he was swinging some distance above ground and was taken to hospital. The medical staff negligently failed to diagnose the severe bone fracture he thereby sustained and so did not discharge their duty of care. The injury led to a serious permanent disability (avascular necrosis). The trial judge found that, if the boy had been diagnosed and treated with reasonable care, there was a 25% chance that the avascular necrosis would not have developed and he awarded damages for the loss of that chance.[76] The Court of Appeal dismissed the health authority's appeal but

---

70 *Ratcliffe v Plymouth & Torbay Health Authority* [1998] PIQR P170.
71 *Ng Chun Pui*, n. 69.
72 See further H. Reece, 'Losses of Chances in Tort Law' (1996) 59 *MLR* 188; M. Stauch, 'Causation, Risk, and Loss of Chance in Medical Negligence' (1997) 17 *OJLS* 205; A. Burrows, 'Uncertainty about Uncertainty: Damages for Loss of a Chance' [2008] *JPIL* 31; K. Oliphant, 'Loss of Chance in English Law' (2008) 16 *European Review of Private Law* 1061; S. Steel, 'Rationalising Loss of Chance in Tort' in S.G.A. Pitel et al. (eds.), *Tort Law: Challenging Orthodoxy*, Hart 2013.
73 See e.g. *Allied Maples Group v Simmons & Simmons* [1995] 1 WLR 1602. As the chance has economic value, it is straightforward to identify its loss as itself constituting damage.
74 [1987] AC 750.
75 *Gregg*, n. 25.
76 *Hotson v Fitzgerald* [1985] 1 WLR 1036.

they then appealed successfully to the House of Lords. The Law Lords ruled that it was a question of past fact whether or not the boy's necrosis could have been avoided by proper medical treatment. The fall had either left him with enough intact blood vessels to avoid the necrosis or it had not. The correct approach to deciding what happened in the past was for the court to decide on the balance of probabilities. The trial judge's finding of a 75% probability that the injury would in any case have followed the same course was thus a decision on the balance of probabilities that the necrosis was inevitable. In effect, the boy was already 'doomed' before he even arrived at the hospital.[77] Their Lordships' reasoning left it open, however, whether the loss of chance analysis might apply where the victim was not doomed in that sense, Lord Bridge noting that there might be cases where 'causation may be so shrouded in mystery that the court can only measure statistical chances'.[78]

In *Gregg v Scott*, the claim was for loss of life expectancy attributable to the defendant doctor's negligent failure to diagnose the claimant's cancer. According to the agreed medical evidence, that led to a delay in treatment that reduced the claimant's chance of cure (defined as survival for ten years from the commencement of treatment) from 42% to 25%. Two Law Lords would have supported liability for loss of chance on the facts,[79] but the majority disagreed, ruling that the reduction of the probability of a favourable outcome for the claimant was not a recoverable head of damage. The facts of the case were unusual in that the claimant was still in fact alive at the time of the House of Lords judgment, some nine years after the commencement of his treatment, so the chance of a bad outcome had not at that time materialised; the chances had not yet resolved. Though it is fair to say that members of the House of Lords majority evinced scepticism about the application of the loss of chance analysis to medical negligence claims even where the bad outcome had occurred,[80] the House of Lords did not unconditionally exclude liability in all such cases in future, so the issue cannot be considered finally determined.

In contrast with the somewhat unwelcoming stance of English law, damages for loss of chance are to be found in one form or another in most other European legal systems.[81] However, the application of the analysis to claims relating to physical injury is mainly limited to jurisdictions in the Romantic legal tradition, such as France, Belgium, Spain, and Italy.[82] Damages for loss

---

77   *Hotson*, n. 74, 792 per Lord Ackner.
78   Ibid., 782. See also ibid., 786 per Lord Mackay.
79   Lord Nicholls and Lord Hope.
80   See e.g. *Gregg*, n. 25, [88]–[90] per Lord Hoffmann, [170] per Lord Phillips, [224]–[225] per Baroness Hale.
81   See T. Kadner Graziano. 'Loss of Chance in European Private Law: "All or Nothing" or Partial Liability in Cases of Uncertain Causation' (2008) 16 *European Review of Private Law* 1023.
82   See Winiger et al., n. 50, ch. 10; I.C. Durant, 'Belgium' in H. Koziol and B.C. Steininger (eds), *European Tort Law 2008*, Springer 2009, para. 31ff.; J. Ribot and A. Ruda, 'Spain',

of chance in respect of medical negligence have also gained traction elsewhere, now being recognised in a majority of US states[83] as well as in Japan.[84]

Unlike the reversal of the burden of proof, which results in the unsuccessful defendant's liability for the entire damage suffered by the victim, damages for loss of chance result in proportional recovery. In principle, they are calculated on the basis of the victim's pre- and post-accident chances, rather than as an estimate of the proportion of the overall risk for which the defendant was responsible. As such, minor changes in the probability of the defendant's negligence being the cause of the damage may result in significant changes in the quantum of damages.[85]

5.3.1.3 *Liability for contribution to risk*

So far eschewing the alternative techniques considered above, English law's approach—encapsulated in the *Fairchild* decision—has been to solve the problem of uncertain alternative causes by basing liability on the defendant's contribution to the risk whose materialisation has caused the victim's damage. To that extent it adopts the analysis advanced by the California Supreme Court in *Rutherford v Owens-Illinois Inc*, which concerned the liability of asbestos manufacturers.[86] European civil law jurisdictions have also sought to resolve such problems with reference to the defendant's contribution to risk or some cognate idea, albeit not as yet in great number; the main examples so far are Austria and the Netherlands.[87] As under the post-*Fairchild* common law, in contrast with sec. 3 of the Compensation Act 2006, the liability in such cases is proportional to the defendant's contribution to the risk, which is also the approach taken in the Principles of European Tort Law.[88]

In the United States, there is considerable diversity as between state approaches to apportionment.[89] An extensive scholarly literature argues in

---

ibid., para. 27ff. The award of damages for loss of chance is expressly contemplated in the Draft Common Frame of Reference: see PEL Liab. Dam. art. 2:101 cmt. 15 (suggesting that the chance could be recognised as an interest worthy of legal protection).

83 See the overview provided in *Matsuyama v Birnbaum* (2008) 890 NE 2d 819, 828–29 (Mass.).

84 R.B Leflar, 'The Law of Medical Misadventure in Japan' (2012) 87 *Chicago-Kent Law Review* 79, 95.

85 L. Bieri and P. Marty, 'The Discontinuous Nature of the Loss of Chance System' (2011) 2 *JETL* 23.

86 (1997) 67 Cal. Rptr. 2d 16.

87 For Austria, see OGH 4 Ob. 554/95, *Juristische Blätter* 1996, 181; Oliphant, 'Austrian and English Law', n. 50, 802–3. For the Netherlands, see *Karamus/Nefalit*, Hoge Raad 31.03.2006, RvdW 2006, 328; M.G. Faure and T. Hartlief, 'The Netherlands' in H. Koziol and B.C. Steininger (eds), *European Tort Law 2006*, Springer 2008, para. 22ff.

88 Principles of European Tort Law, arts 3:103 and 3:106. See further European Group on Tort Law, *Principles of European Tort Law: Text and Commentary*, Springer 2005, 61–64, 71–74.

89 See M. Green, 'A Future for Asbestos Apportionment' (2005) 12 *Connecticut Insurance Law Journal* 315.

favour of proportional liability[90] but in practice it is largely limited to 'market share' product liability cases.[91] The English courts have yet to rule on the market share theory; in *Fairchild*, Lord Hoffmann stated that the issue should be left for consideration when an appropriate case arose.[92]

5.3.2 *The approach taken in* Fairchild

The comparative analysis offered above is particularly pertinent in that, in *Fairchild*, the House of Lords actively sought out comparative, especially European, resources to assist in their resolution of the case.[93] Their Lordships' survey of the material demonstrated that, although the problem underlying such cases was universal, the solutions to it were not; most jurisdictions, however, would grant a remedy whether by treating an increase in risk as equivalent to a material contribution, by reversing the burden of proof, by enlarging the ordinary approach to acting in concert, or otherwise.[94] This analysis 'fortified'[95] the Law Lords in concluding that the problem they were facing was a genuine one and in need of solution in the interests of justice.

In fact, the Law Lords repeatedly underlined the unfairness, in circumstances where the damage was undoubtedly tortious, of depriving a claimant of a remedy simply because it was impossible to identify which particular wrongdoer had caused it. Such an outcome would be 'deeply offensive to instinctive notions of what justice requires and fairness demands'.[96] The balance of justice and injustice favoured the tortiously injured claimant over the tortiously acting defendant. Their Lordships acknowledged the injustice in imposing liability on an employer who could not be shown to have caused the victim's mesothelioma, but found that this was 'heavily outweighed by the injustice of denying redress to a victim' where the harm could only have resulted from a breach of duty by at least one of the victim's employers, all of

---

90   See especially J.H. King Jr., 'Causation, Valuation, and Chance in Personal Injury Torts Involving Pre-existing Conditions and Future Consequences' (1981) 90 *Yale Law Journal* 1353; D. Rosenberg, 'The Causal Connection in Mass Exposure Cases: A "Public Law" Vision of the Tort System' (1984) 97 *Harvard Law Review* 849; D.A. Farber, 'Toxic Causation' (1987) 71 *Minnesota Law Review* 1219; J. Makdisi, 'Proportional Liability: A Comprehensive Rule to Apportion Tort Damages Based on Probability' (1989) 67 *North Carolina Law Review* 1063; C.H. Schroeder, 'Corrective Justice and Liability for Increasing Risks' (1990) 37 *UCLA Law Review* 439. For criticism, see M.D. Green, 'The Future of Proportional Liability: The Lessons of Toxic Substances Causation' in M. Stuart Madden (ed.), *Exploring Tort Law*, CUP 2006.

91   See especially *Sindell v Abbott Laboratories* (1980) 26 Cal. 3d 588.

92   *Fairchild*, n. 1, [74].

93   See further K. Oliphant, '*Fairchild v Glenhaven Funeral Services Ltd* (2002)' in C. Mitchell and P. Mitchell (eds), *Landmark Cases in the Law of Tort*, Hart 2010.

94   *Fairchild*, n. 1, [32] per Lord Bingham, [156] per Lord Rodger.

95   Ibid., [34] per Lord Bingham.

96   Ibid., [36] per Lord Nicholls.

whom had breached their duty to the victim.[97] This 'balance of justice' consideration[98] was supported by the perceived need to reinforce the employer's duty of care by providing an effective liability in cases of breach: if the law were to apply the but for test to each employer's breach of duty, that would empty the duty of its practical content and so be contrary to policy (the 'empty duty' argument).[99]

5.3.3 Fairchild's field of application

The Law Lords sitting in *Fairchild* underlined repeatedly that they wished to resolve the case before them on the narrowest possible basis, without seeking to define the precise scope of the principle they applied.

One important question is the scope for invoking the decision in respect of conditions other than mesothelioma. The legitimacy of doing so was implicit in *Fairchild* itself as the House of Lords expressly invoked by way of support for their analysis their earlier decision in *McGhee v National Coal Board*.[100] That was a case of industrial dermatitis contracted through the occupational exposure of the victim to brick dust in the course of his employment in a brick kiln. It was accepted that some exposure to brick dust was unavoidable for kiln-workers. However, some of the exposure resulted from the employer's failure to provide workplace showering facilities in breach of duty. So there was 'guilty' as well as 'innocent' exposure. But it was uncertain whether the kiln-worker contracted the dermatitis from his cumulative exposure to the dust or merely from a single abrasion. In the latter eventuality, it could not be established on the balance of probabilities that the employer's breach of duty had contributed to the injury at all. Nevertheless, the House of Lords upheld the claim on the basis that the breach of duty had at least contributed *to the risk* of the injury.

As *McGhee* is to be regarded as a case of *Fairchild* liability *avant la lettre*,[101] it is clear that the scope of the *Fairchild* exception stretches beyond cases of mesothelioma. That has been confirmed by the more recent decision of the Court of Appeal in *Heneghan v Manchester Dry Docks*, applying the *Fairchild* principle in a case of lung cancer.[102] The potential causes of the cancer were exposure to asbestos and smoking. The outcome was not uncontroversial.[103] For now it is sufficient to note that *Heneghan* goes further than *McGhee* inasmuch as the 'alternative' cause of the damage was not additional 'innocent'

---

97 Ibid., [33] per Lord Bingham. See also [39]–[42] per Lord Nicholls, [63] per Lord Hoffmann, [155] per Lord Rodger.
98 Cf. *Sienkiewicz*, n. 27, [197] per Lord Kerr.
99 *Fairchild*, n. 1, [62] per Lord Hoffmann, [155] per Lord Rodger.
100 [1973] 1 WLR 1.
101 *Barker*, n. 27, [13] per Lord Hoffmann.
102 [2016] 1 WLR 2036.
103 Cf. the criticism of S. Green (2017) 133 *LQR* 25.

exposure to the same harmful agent but an entirely different source of risk (the victim's smoking). Whether that extension of *Fairchild* liability can withstand possible future challenge is beyond the scope of the present chapter.

We know though that the impact of *Fairchild* is not just on mesothelioma claims, nor even just on claims for asbestos-related disease. Yet the courts have repeatedly underlined that the *Fairchild* liability is exceptional.[104] Where are its boundaries to be drawn and how does the exception fit with other established principles and other decisions of unchallenged authority? A remaining conundrum is how *Fairchild* is to be reconciled with the 1988 decision of the House of Lords in *Wilsher v Essex Area Health Authority*.[105] The infant claimant was born prematurely in the defendant's hospital and some time later he became nearly totally blind. It was argued on his behalf that the blindness resulted from the hospital's negligence in administering excessive levels of oxygen to him after his birth. However, the blindness might also have been attributed to alternative causes, given the other conditions that premature babies commonly suffer. It was found on the facts that there had been exposure to unduly high levels of oxygen pressure on six distinct occasions; the defendants bore responsibility for only one of the six. The House of Lords consequently ruled that, on the balance of probabilities, the defendant's negligence had not made a material contribution to the infant's blindness. It was not enough merely to show that the defendant had materially contributed to the risk of blindness. *Wilsher* preceded *Fairchild*, but the Law Lords in the later case clearly thought that it would not have fallen within the scope of the new principle that they there laid down.[106] On what basis was it distinguishable?

The same question might be posed in respect of English law's so far consistent rejection of claims for loss of chance in the medical context.[107] As the chance of avoiding damage can be considered to be simply the reflection of the risk of suffering it,[108] why does the *Fairchild* liability for contributing to the risk not apply?

In their attempt to limit the field of *Fairchild*'s application, and reconcile it with established principle, the English courts have relied on two considerations. First, it is proposed that the claimant's inability to prove causation on the balance of probabilities must be on account of scientific, more specifically aetiological, uncertainty, not merely a lack of evidence about knowable facts.[109] This would certainly preclude *Fairchild*'s application in *some* medical

---

104 See e.g. *Barker*, n. 27, [1] per Lord Hoffmann, [57] per Lord Scott.

105 [1988] AC 1074.

106 See in particular *Fairchild*, n. 1, [22] per Lord Bingham, [70] per Lord Hoffmann, [170] per Lord Rodger.

107 *Hotson*, n. 74; *Gregg*, n. 25.

108 G.O. Robinson, 'Probabilistic Causation and Compensation for Tortious Risk' (1985) 14 *Journal of Legal Studies* 779, 793.

109 See e.g. *Fairchild*, n. 1, [2] per Lord Bingham ('because of the current limits of human science'), [61] per Lord Hoffmann ('medical science cannot prove whose asbestos ... caused

cases as the uncertainties in such cases are not always aetiological. But that will not be true in all medical cases—and it does not account for the refusal to apply *Fairchild* in *Gregg v Scott*, as the aetiology of cancer is a matter of considerable scientific uncertainty. Further, a requirement of aetiological uncertainty would wholly preclude the rule's application in the hunters' scenario considered above, which seems remarkable given the centrality of that example to the Law Lords' reasoning in *Fairchild*.[110]

Second, it is sought to limit the scope of the *Fairchild* exception to cases where each potential alternative cause involves the exposure of the victim to a risk of the same or at least a similar nature.[111] Again, this consideration may be enough to distinguish *many* typical medical negligence cases, as the background risk associated with the patient's condition may well involve a different causative agency than that associated with the defendant's breach of duty. However, it does not seem apt to reconcile *Fairchild* with the loss of chance cases, *Hotson* and *Gregg*, as the doctor's failure to diagnose and treat serves to exacerbate the existing risk the patient was facing, not to add in a new risk involving a different sort of causal agency.

5.3.4 *Mitigating the cost on employers and insurers*

Putting aside the unresolved issues about *Fairchild*'s scope of application, we now turn to a perhaps under-appreciated feature of the joint and several liability regime established by sec. 3 of the Compensation Act 2006. Recall that the *Fairchild* liability was determined in *Barker* to be proportionate to the defendant's contribution to the overall risk, not for the whole of the damage resulting from the risk's materialisation. But, as explained above, Parliament quickly intervened to reverse this for mesothelioma claimants. We are left in a situation where the responsible person bears full liability under the statute where the claim is one for mesothelioma and otherwise incurs only proportional liability at common law.

As the statutory scheme was designed (in a hurry) with the full involvement of the insurance industry, it is no surprise that it contained a mitigation

---

the disease'), [170] per Lord Rodger ('the current state of the relevant science leaves it uncertain exactly how the injury was caused and, so, who caused it').
110 See especially ibid., [27] per Lord Bingham, [38]–[39] per Lord Nicholls, [164] per Lord Rodger.
111 See e.g. ibid., [170] per Lord Rodger ('the same agency ... [or] an agency that operated in substantially the same way'); *Barker*, n. 27, [24] per Lord Hoffmann ('it is an essential condition for the operation of the exception that the impossibility of proving that the defendant caused the damage arises out of the existence of another potential causative agent which operated in the same way'), [114] per Lord Walker ('The principle must in my view be restricted to ... conditions having the same distinctive aetiology and prognosis'). For criticism, see K. Wellington, 'Beyond Single Causative Agents: The *Fairchild* Exception Post-*Sienkiewicz*' (2013) 20 *Torts LJ* 1; G. Turton, *Evidential Uncertainty in Causation in Negligence*, Hart 2016, 212–15

to make its impact more palatable. Buried in sub-section (7) of the new section was the power for the Treasury to make provision by regulation for the compensation of a responsible person unable to obtain a contribution from another person liable to a contribution under the joint and several liability the section imposes. Regulations duly followed in December of the same year, providing for compensation to be paid through the Financial Services Compensation Scheme.[112] This is the insurance-industry-funded scheme that, amongst other things, acts as guarantor for insurance pay-outs where the liable insurer has become insolvent. This protection is now extended to employers and others liable under the *Fairchild* exception, where their co-defendant is insolvent and they are otherwise unable to recover the financial contribution to which they would be entitled.

It is worth underlining that this compensation made available in *Fairchild* situations is not for mesothelioma victims unable to establish causation because of the scientific uncertainty, but for the defendants whose liability has been stretched in order to protect those victims.

The protection benefits the responsible person 'irrespective of whether the victim was also exposed to asbestos ... other than by the responsible person' (Compensation Act 2006, sec. 3(2)(a)). Of course, if there were no exposure other than that attributable to the responsible person's breach of duty, then that breach of duty would be *the sole* cause of the victim's mesothelioma. The qualifying language ('irrespective of ...') was intended to refer to two further scenarios. One is where there was additional 'innocent' exposure that the responsible person caused or permitted to be caused—but not in breach of duty. A possible situation would be where the initial exposure cannot be shown to have been in breach of the responsible person's common law or statutory duties, but increased knowledge of or heightened sensitivity to the risks associated with asbestos means that the exposure is to be regarded as tortious from a particular date onwards. The second scenario is where there is additional exposure 'other than by the responsible person'. The further explanatory wording ('whether or not in circumstances in which another person has liability in tort') suggests that we are dealing with four more specific situations:

1. where there is other exposure for which another person has liability in tort ('guilty exposure');
2. where there is other exposure which is caused or permitted by another person who is not the victim, but for which they do not have liability in tort ('innocent exposure');

---

112 Compensation Act 2006 (Contribution for Mesothelioma Claims) Regulations 2006/3259, reg. 2(3), inserting into Financial Services and Markets Act 2000 (Transitional Provisions, Repeals and Savings) (Financial Services Compensation Scheme) Order 2001 (SI 2001/2967) a new reg. 9A.

3. where there is other exposure which is caused or permitted by the victim ('self-exposure');
4. where there is other exposure that cannot be shown to have been caused or permitted by another person at all ('environmental exposure').

In all four of these situations, the statutory liability *in respect of the whole of the damage* is to apply. Note that it is only in the case of guilty exposure that the liability is joint and several as only here is there another responsible person. Where the totality of the other exposure is innocent exposure, self-exposure,[113] or environmental exposure, or a mix of the three, there is no other responsible person to bear that liability, whether jointly or severally, and consequently no right to reimbursement from the Financial Services Compensation Scheme. This seems to have been the situation in *Sienkiewicz* (considered in Section 5.1.6 above), prompting the Justices' comments that the outcome was 'draconian'.

5.4 Conclusions

The historical and comparative survey undertaken above shows clearly that the issues of causal uncertainty faced by the UK courts in *Fairchild* and subsequent cases are timeless and universal. They are not unique to mesothelioma or to asbestos-related disease more generally. But it was the terrible impact of mesothelioma on tens of thousands of workers and their families that provided the context in which the Law Lords in *Fairchild* were led to forge an innovative solution to the causal challenges that so many of the victims were facing, and mesothelioma was also the explicit focus of the ensuing legislative intervention—designed in particular to protect victims' compensation entitlements against the risk that one or more of the responsible parties might be untraceable or insolvent. Section 3 of the Compensation Act 2006 saw to it that each responsible party would have joint and several liability for the whole of the damage suffered, meaning that, so long as one responsible party could be traced and was either solvent or insured, the victim would recover damages to the full extent of their legal entitlement. And if there was no such party, the victim's claim would be satisfied by the Diffuse Mesothelioma Payment Scheme established under the Mesothelioma Act 2014.

We are left with a patchwork of legal rules addressing the tragic situation of the victims of mesothelioma, with radical judicial development of the common law intertwined with successive gap-filling efforts on the part of the legislature. There is now a mood in the judiciary that *Fairchild* itself was a wrong step and that it would have been better to acknowledge the injustice caused by the application of established common-law principles and to call on Parliament to intervene on a more considered and comprehensive basis.

---

113 Though here there may be a reduction in the damages by reason of contributory negligence.

Writing extra-judicially some years after his judgments in *Fairchild* and *Barker*, Lord Hoffmann affirmed that the House of Lords in *Fairchild* should 'have adhered to established principle, wrung their hands about the unfairness of the outcome in the particular case, and recommended to the Government that it pass appropriate legislation'.[114] Instead, it created 'confusion in the common law by trying to legislate for special cases'.[115] In like vein, Lord Neuberger and Lord Reed reflected in *International Energy Group v Zurich Insurance* that

> [f]or the courts to develop the law on a case-by-case basis, pragmatically but without any clear basis in principle, as each decision leads to a new set of problems requiring resolution at the highest level, as has happened in relation to mesothelioma claims, is not satisfactory either in terms of legal certainty or in terms of public time and money.[116]

I would draw the opposite conclusion from the history recounted above. It has been the Parliamentary intervention that has caused the real problems by reversing the proportional liability established at common law in *Barker* and establishing joint and several liability in the whole damage for—and only for—mesothelioma claims satisfying the requirements of sec. 3 of the Compensation Act 2006.[117] There is no convincing reason for making mesothelioma a special case in that respect. Further, the mismatch between the statutory scheme and the common-law principles has resulted in unintended and draconian outcomes, exemplified by *Sienkiewicz v Greif*,[118] where very light occupational exposure resulted in liability for the whole of the damage resulting from the victim's mesothelioma even though much the larger part of her exposure was environmental and not attributable to another tortfeasor. The intended financial mitigation through the Financial Services Compensation Scheme was seemingly unavailable because that is premised on the putative right to claim a contribution from another responsible person (s. 3(7)) whereas the statutory liability for the whole of the damage results 'whether or not … another person has liability in tort' (s. 3(2)(a)(i)). If there is no other liability in tort, there is manifestly no other responsible person from whom a contribution might be sought, and so no right to the statutory compensation.

'Leaving it to the legislator' is not a responsible judicial reaction to a clear injustice resulting from the application of established common-law principle.

---

114 Lord Hoffmann, '*Fairchild* and After', in A. Burrows, D. Johnston, and R. Zimmermann (eds), *Judge and Jurist: Essays in Memory of Lord Rodger of Earlsferry*, OUP 2013, 68.

115 Ibid.

116 [2016] AC 509, [210].

117 In addition to the cases discussed in the text, consider also the following decisions on the insurance and reinsurance issues arising in this context: *Durham v BAI (Runoff)* [2012] 1 WLR 867; *International Energy Group v Zurich Insurance* [2016] AC 509; *Equitas Insurance v Municipal Mutual Insurance* [2020] QB 418.

118 *Sienkiewicz*, n. 37.

Even when the courts have called for legislative intervention in the past, Parliament has not always heeded the request.[119] In the present context, the legislature's crafting of an ad hoc and piecemeal solution for (some) mesothelioma claims only gives rise to no confidence at all that its future interventions, if they do in fact ensue, will address the issues in comprehensive and coherent fashion. It is crucial that the courts remain willing to take on the responsibility themselves of developing the law in principled fashion, even if this entails bold deviations from previous practice. As Lord Burrows has written, albeit before assuming his current judicial role:[120]

> it is an abdication of judicial responsibility for judges, at least in the law of obligations, to decline to develop the common law on the grounds that legislation is more appropriate. Even if a statutory solution would be better, no-one can predict whether legislation will, or will not, be passed. It is therefore preferable for judges to proceed as they think fit, whether the decision be in favour or against a development, knowing that the Legislature is free to impose a statutory solution if the common law position is thought unsatisfactory or incomplete.

---

119 See K. Oliphant, 'Against Certainty in Tort Law' in Pitel et al., n. 72, 9–11.
120 A. Burrows, 'The relationship between common law and statute in the law of obligations' (2012) 128 *LQR* 232, 258. See also 248.

6 Known unknowns

Loss of a chance and intractable connections

Samantha Schnobel and Judith Skillen

Coherence and simplicity have much to recommend themselves to the common law. There exists a certain comfort in areas which are free from exception or appeals to practical justice, and are instead buttressed by enduring statements of principle; 'damage is the gist of negligence'[1] is an example. The doctrine on loss of a chance, however, yields none of these creature comforts.

Itself an exception to the traditional requirements of 'but for' factual causation—a 'notoriously inadequate'[2] test in Stapleton's eyes—claimants here can at best assert that they have lost a chance at achieving a better outcome or of avoiding a future loss because of the defendant's breach. Evidencing on the balance of probabilities that, 'but for' the defendant's breach, they would not have suffered their harm is simply not on the cards. In asserting the loss of a chance argument, claimants challenge orthodox constructs of damage and press the courts to make sense of temporal uncertainties surrounding past fact or epistemic uncertainties surrounding the aetiology of disease or injury. A notoriously vexing question for UK tort law, then, is the extent to which (if at all) a claimant who cannot establish *sine qua non* causation because of these uncertainties is permitted to circumvent the traditional rule for factual causation and recover compensation through framing their claim as one for loss of a chance.

The response has been complex and fragmented, and, in some instances, the uncertain state of the law is such that attempts to bring claims for lost chances are now all but barred. Efforts thus far in the UK courts to make loss of a chance a defensible doctrine—whether this be through a reliance on statistics, through a strict adherence to orthodox forms of actionable damage, or an uncomfortable pairing of the two—has resulted in the opposite. We now

---

1 'It is now hornbook law that damage is the gist of the action in negligence', per Baroness Hale, *Gregg v Scott* [2005] UKHL 2 (hereafter *Gregg*), [193]. See also Lord Scarman in *Sidaway v Board of Governors of the Bethlem Royal Hospital and the Maudsley Hospital* [1985] AC 871, 883 and J. Stapleton, 'The Gist of Negligence' (1988) 104 *LQR* 389.

2 J. Stapleton, 'Reflections on Common Sense Causation in Australia' in S. Degeling et al., *Torts in Commercial Law*, Thomson Reuters, Pyrmont 2011, 338.

DOI: 10.4324/9781003537526-8

find that the doctrine lacks both centralising principles and a coherent thread, both to maintain the boundaries of the doctrine itself and also to properly regulate conduct for those who may be responsible for lost chances. By contrast, continental jurisprudence from Belgium and France offers an alternative approach, by grounding an action in the loss of the chance itself and adapting the remaining liability requirements to match.

We put forward that, whilst present-day loss of a chance cases concerning economic and physical interests share a common ancestry, the crux of the uncertainty problem lies in medical negligence claims involving physical and, as will be seen, relational interests. Our focus will therefore be placed on pulling these uncertainties to the fore and advancing the position that the current state of the law in this area fails adequately to serve those harmed. Reform here matters because chances matter, and whilst one of the greatest strengths of the common law system is its ability to evolve, a considered re-focus is needed.

At the risk of becoming outflanked by the many directions of analytical travel, we begin by first by exploring the contractual origins of loss of a chance claims and then move to consider the (ill) effects of expanding the doctrine into the realm of medical negligence claims. Actions in this category combine, in different makes and measures, medical uncertainties running the entire course from the aetiology of a disease to its consequences; hypothetical patient conduct and choice; a practitioner's intervention or non-intervention; and, lastly, a sometimes unruly application of social policy considerations by the courts. Whilst expansion into the realm of medical negligence was no doubt expected, it brought with it a fundamental shift in causal uncertainty; one which unsettled orthodox notions and frustrated developing ones. From this intractable entanglement we turn to consider a simpler possibility adopted by France and Belgium.

6.1 Historical overview

6.1.1 *Contractual origins*

The origins of loss of a chance actions in English law can be found in the law of contract. *Chaplin v Hicks*[3] is widely regarded as the first case in which damages for loss of a chance were recognised.[4] In *Chaplin*, the claimant Eva Chaplin had entered a competition, organised by the defendant and run in a local newspaper. The competition called for women who wished to be actresses to submit their photographs to the newspaper, with the prize being theatrical employment by the defendant. The rules of the competition stated that the public would vote for finalists from photographs of the candidates published

---

3 [1911] 2 KB 786 (hereafter *Chaplin*).
4 The case is 'generally regarded as having introduced the loss of a chance doctrine into the law of England' and Wales: J. Edelman et al. (eds), *McGregor on Damages*, 21st ed., Sweet & Maxwell 2020, 10-041 (hereafter *McGregor*).

in the newspaper, and the winners would be selected by the defendant and his committee following an interview. The claimant received enough public votes to qualify as a finalist. However, at the time when a letter inviting her to interview was sent to her home address in London, Eva Chaplin was acting in Dundee. By the time the invitation was forwarded to her in Scotland, it was too late for her to be interviewed. After unsuccessful attempts by the claimant to make a further appointment with the committee, she sued for damages. The jury awarded her £100 in damages.[5] In its decision, the court reasoned that 'a jury may well take the view that such a right … would have been of such a value that every one would recognize that a good price could be obtained for it'.[6] The decision in *Chaplin* has been likened to opening Pandora's box in introducing loss of a chance into the law.[7] However, as colourfully illustrated in *McGregor on Damages*: '[f]or some decades after *Chaplin v Hicks* loss of a chance remained quiescent; no evil spirit flew out of Pandora's box'.[8]

It was almost half a century before the next significant loss of a chance case came before the courts in *Kitchen v Royal Air Force*.[9] Here, despite the events which led to the claimant's husband's death being 'fraught with mystery',[10] the court nonetheless awarded damages of £2,000 when the defendant solicitors representing the claimant negligently failed to initiate proceedings within the limitation period. Once it was found that the claimant had established negligence on the part of the defendants, the question turned to whether 'the [claimant] lost some right of value, some chose in action of reality and substance'.[11] On this point, Lord Evershed MR found it 'impossible to say that there was here no valuable right, which was lost by the negligence'[12] and proceeded to award the claimant the equivalent of two-thirds of the maximum she might have recovered under the Fatal Accidents Acts.

In both *Chaplin* and *Kitchen*, the court viewed the contractual right itself, whether that be the right to participate in the contest or the right to exercise a valid chose in action, as something of substance or something for which a good price could be obtained. It could, in essence, form the gist of an action regardless of whether the claimant's litigation in *Kitchen* or the claimant's interview in *Chaplin* would have resulted in successful outcomes.

---

5 See W. Miao and J.L. Gastwirth, 'Estimating the Economic Value of the Loss of a Chance: A Re-Examination of *Chaplin v Hicks*' (2018) 17 *Law, Probability and Risk* 279 for an interesting argument that the sum awarded to the claimant was too low. In this article, the authors develop a more complex probability model taking into account the high number of votes received by Ms Chaplin compared to other finalists.

6 *Chaplin*, n. 3, 793.

7 *McGregor*, n. 4, 10-042.

8 Ibid., 10-043.

9 [1958] 1 WLR 563 (hereafter *Kitchen*).

10 Ibid., 576.

11 Ibid., 575.

12 Ibid.

6.1.2 *Pure economic loss and lost chances*

In the mid-1990s, *Spring v Guardian Assurance*[13] and *Allied Maples Group v Simmons & Simmons*[14] affirmed that damages for loss of a chance may be awarded in negligence where the claim is for pure economic loss. In *Spring*, the claimant's ex-employer negligently wrote a bad reference, with the result that the claimant did not get the post which he sought. *Spring* is routinely taught in law schools mainly through the lens of pure economic loss, with much less emphasis being placed on the fact that it is also about loss of a chance. Indeed, this is not really discussed much in the case either, except by Lord Lowry, who said:

> Once the duty of care is held to exist and the defendants' negligence is proved, the [claimant] only has to show that by reason of that negligence he has lost a reasonable chance of employment (which would have to be evaluated) and has thereby sustained loss: *McGregor on Damages*, 14th ed. (1980), pp. 198-202, paras. 276-278 and *Chaplin v. Hicks* [1911] 2 K.B. 786.[15]

In the later case of *Allied Maples*, it was clarified by the Court of Appeal that, where the chance is dependent on the actions of a third party, there must have been a real and substantial chance of success as between the claimant and the third party, and not merely a speculative one. In this case, it was argued that the defendant solicitors had been negligent in failing to advise the claimant about potential liabilities stemming from a business purchase. The claimants were later exposed to these liabilities. The court held that, to establish liability, it was not necessary that the claimants show that with the proper advice they would have successfully negotiated with the seller to obtain protection from the liabilities; rather, that a substantial chance of success existed. Thus, the claimant had to show a) on the balance of probabilities that they would have taken steps to renegotiate the terms of purchase and b) as a 'matter of causation that a *real or substantial chance* as opposed to a speculative one'[16] existed that the third party would have accepted the more protective terms— the chance element.

Conversely, where a claim rests upon the hypothetical or future conduct of the claimant, it must be shown on the balance of probabilities that the chance would have occurred. Where the hypothetical outcome rests on the conduct of a third party, a claimant must show a real or substantial chance of obtaining the desired outcome. The obvious justification for this distinction is that it is

---

13 [1994] 2 AC 296 (hereafter *Spring*).
14 [1995] 1 WLR 1602 (hereafter *Allied Maples*).
15 *Spring*, n. 13, 327. This was also approved by Stuart-Smith LJ in *Allied Maples*, n. 14, 1613.
16 *Allied Maples*, n. 14, 1614 (emphasis added). See also *Davies v Taylor* [1974] AC 207 (hereafter *Davies*).

not overly onerous to expect a claimant to prove what they would have done on the balance of probabilities, whereas it is too burdensome to expect claimants to prove with certainty how a third party with their attendant free will would have acted.[17] This distinction was affirmed recently by the UK Supreme Court in *Perry v Raley's Solicitors*.[18] After endorsing the distinction in *Allied Maples*, Lord Briggs went on to describe the distinction as 'sensible, fair and practicable'.[19]

The cases discussed so far in Section 6.1.2 have been for losses of a chance in the economic sphere. As we shall see later, in Section 6.2.1, the law is far more complex and restrictive in allowing loss of a chance of avoiding personal injury. How might we explain this difference in treatment? Tony Weir offered a defensible rationale for the courts being more receptive to loss of a chance claims where the chance is financial gain:

> If I deprive you of a chance of a monetary gain, I deprive you of a gain, though a lesser one than the gain you were deprived of the chance of making. The chance and the thing—the stake and the prize—are … entirely comparable, in the way that the chance of not being crippled and being actually crippled are not.[20]

As such, according to Weir, because chances are economic in nature they can be *compared* to economic loss. Whereas a *chance* of personal injury is not the same as *actual* personal injury and so they cannot be so easily compared. Another possible explanation—one put forward by Lord Hoffmann in *Gregg v Scott*—is that the economic loss cases have tended to rest on the hypothetical conduct of persons, and because people have free will, these outcomes are not causally predetermined, unlike the progression of physical injury in the body.[21] Instead, the law generally requires a claimant to wait and see whether an actionable personal injury arises, and then where actionable personal injury or death *has occurred* (i.e. it is now a past fact by the time of trial) the claimant must prove, on the balance of probabilities, that the defendant's negligence caused the injury. Then, consequent uncertainties as to the claimant's future (e.g. loss of earnings or the chances of an injury improving or getting worse) are assessed according to chance at the quantification stage. But loss of a chance is—generally—not a head of loss in itself.

---

17 This rationale for the distinction is endorsed also by A. Burrows, 'Uncertainty about uncertainty: damages for loss of a chance' (2008) 1 *JPIL* 31, 36–37; *McGregor*, n. 4, 10-065.
18 [2019] UKSC 5.
19 Ibid., [21].
20 T. Weir, *A Casebook on Tort*, 10th ed., Sweet & Maxwell 2004, 214.
21 *Gregg*, n. 1, [79]–[83] (Lord Hoffmann). This case will be discussed in detail below in Section 6.2.1.

6.2 Scope of the uncertainty problem

Damages for loss of a chance may be awarded where there is 'uncertainty as to hypothetical events or the future' but claimants invoking the doctrine have had less success where the uncertainty relates to past facts.[22] Uncertainties as to past facts must generally be resolved not by way of chances but by the balance of probabilities test. As memorably put by Lord Hoffmann, here '[t]he law operates a binary system in which the only values are 0 and 1',[23] 'all or nothing', whereby if a claimant succeeds in showing that it is more likely than not (>50% likelihood) that the defendant's breach of duty caused the damage complained of, the claimant will have established their case. The claimant will then recover damages in full. By contrast, where courts are in the realm of hypothetical or future events, then the 'all or nothing' approach is jettisoned in favour of assessing damages proportionately.

Lord Burrows, then Andrew Burrows QC, summarised the general approach to proof in *Palliser v Fate (In Liquidation)*:

> The correct picture of the law on proof in relation to damages is therefore that where the uncertainty is as to past fact, the 'all or nothing balance of probabilities' test applies. Where the uncertainty is as to the future, proportionate damages are appropriate. Where the uncertainty is as to hypothetical events, the correct test to be applied depends on the nature of the uncertainty: if it is uncertainty as to what the claimant would have done, the all or nothing balance of probabilities test applies; if it is as to what a third party would have done, damages are assessed proportionately according to the chances.[24]

Where there are intractable uncertainties around past facts—for instance, whether an asbestos fibre was a cause of mesothelioma—a claimant may not be able establish causation on the civil standard of proof. One potential route around uncertainties as to past facts is to reframe the claim as one for loss of a chance in order to avoid their claim failing for want of causation. Thus, a further important distinction should be made as between where loss of a chance is the *gist* of damage being pleaded, or the actionable head of damage on which a claim rests, compared to courts evaluating chances as consequential

---

22 Burrows, n. 17, 33. See also *McGregor*, n. 4, 10-044.

23 *In Re B (Children) (Care Proceedings: Standard of Proof)* [2008] UKHL 35, [2]. Writing extrajudicially, Lord Hoffmann further explained, '[i]f the evidence that something happened satisfies the burden of proof … then it is assigned a value of 1 and treated as definitely having happened. If the evidence does not discharge the burden of proof, the evidence is assigned a value of 0 and treated as definitely not having happened. There is no forensic space for the conclusion that something which has to be proved *may* have happened': L. Hoffmann, 'Causation' in R. Goldberg (ed), *Perspectives on Causation*, Hart 2011, 7–8.

24 *Palliser v Fate (In Liquidation)* [2019] EWHC 43 (QB), [27].

losses upon other actionable damage at the quantification of damages stage of litigation.[25] This distinction is evident in Lord Diplock's speech in *Mallet v McMonagle*:

> The role of the court in making an assessment of damages which depends upon its view as to what will be and what would have been is to be contrasted with its ordinary function in civil actions of determining what was. In determining what did happen in the past a court decides on the balance of probabilities. Anything that is more probable than not it treats as certain. *But in assessing damages which depend upon its view as to what will happen in the future or would have happened in the future if something had not happened in the past, the court must make an estimate as to what are the chances that a particular thing will or would have happened and reflect those chances, whether they are more or less than even, in the amount of damages which it awards.*[26]

As Harvey McGregor QC explained, when quantifying damages, 'chances are all-important, and an assessment of damages is entitled, indeed is required, to take into account all manner of risks and probabilities'.[27] Quantifying damages requires the courts to consider future or hypothetical events, and as such proportionate damages reflecting the claimant's chances are appropriate and are routinely awarded. As outlined in Section 6.1.2, in cases involving future or hypothetical events, courts do not expect a claimant to prove their case on the balance of probabilities. Lord Reid in *Davies v Taylor* puts the point well:

> When the question is whether a certain thing is or is not true—whether a certain event did or did not happen—then the court must decide one way or the other. There is no question of chance or probability. Either it did or it did not happen ... *You can prove that a past event happened, but you cannot prove that a future event will happen and I do not think that the law is so foolish as to suppose that you can. All that you can do is to evaluate the chance.*[28]

In Section 6.2.1, we examine the law's response where loss of a chance is not being sought at the quantification of damages stage, but rather at the liability stage of an action: where the lost chance (or increased risk) is said to be actionable damage. We place particular focus on medical negligence claims as these

---

25 The importance of this distinction has been noted by various scholars, such as J. Morgan, 'A Chance Missed to Recognize Loss-of-a-Chance in Negligence' [2005] *LMCLQ* 281; H. McGregor, 'Loss of Chance: Where Has It Come From and Where Is It Going?' (2008) 24 *Professional Negligence* 2.

26 *Mallett v McMonagle* [1970] AC 166, 176 (emphasis added).

27 McGregor, n. 25, 5.

28 *Davies*, n. 16, 213 (emphasis added).

cases illustrate vividly the relationship between damage and causation when loss of a chance responds to intractable uncertainties as to past facts.

6.2.1 *Questions of scope in medical negligence actions*

Loss of a chance in the clinical negligence sphere came before the House of Lords in *Hotson v East Berkshire Health Authority*.[29] In *Hotson*, the claimant was a 13-year-old boy who fell out of a tree and suffered a hip fracture. He then encountered a negligent delay in treatment by the defendant hospital. Ultimately, the claimant suffered avascular necrosis of his hip. The trial judge, Simon Brown J, found that, even if the injury had been properly diagnosed and treated, there was a 75% chance that the disability would have developed. Or, to put it another way, no matter what the defendant did, once the claimant fell from the tree and damaged his hip, it was more likely than not that the damage would have occurred anyway. Despite this finding of fact, the trial judge and Court of Appeal awarded the claimant damages to reflect the 25% chance of 'recovery' of which the claimant was deprived by the defendant's negligence. However, the House of Lords reversed this award on the basis that it was the fall rather than the defendant's negligence which caused the avascular necrosis. Nevertheless, their Lordships also took the occasion to consider loss of a chance more broadly. According to Lord Bridge, there are 'formidable difficulties' in the way of accepting the 'superficially attractive analogy' between cases awarding damages for a loss of a financial chance and awarding damages 'for the lost chance of avoiding personal injury or, in medical negligence cases, for the lost chance of a better medical result which might have been achieved by prompt diagnosis and correct treatment', but his Lordship held that *Hotson* was not the suitable occasion for reaching a 'settled conclusion'.[30]

In the subsequent case of *Gregg v Scott*, however, a settled conclusion rejecting a role for loss of a chance in relation to personal injuries was ultimately reached; The case itself was noted by Lord Hope as 'an anxious and difficult' one, taking eight months to hand down. In 1994, the claimant developed a lump under his left arm. He went to his doctor, the defendant, who negligently misdiagnosed the claimant and told him the lump was nothing to worry about. Had the defendant acted with due care and referred the claimant to hospital at that stage, where the lump would have been found to be cancerous, the claimant would have started treatment in April 1994 and had a 42% chance of his cancer being 'cured' (defined as being ten years in remission).

---

29 [1987] AC 750.
30 Ibid., 782–83. Lord Mackay also refused to lay down a hard-and-fast rule against loss of a chance relating to physical injuries, stating that 'it would be unwise in the present case to lay it down as a rule that a [claimant] could never succeed by proving loss of a chance in a medical negligence case': ibid., 786.

What happened, however, is the cancer went untreated and it spread. The claimant suffered delay in treatment until January 1996, which reduced his chances of being 'cured' to 25%. Importantly, then, even if the defendant had acted with reasonable care, the claimant would not be able to prove on the balance of probabilities that his cancer would be cured. Thus, the causal link between the defendant's breach and the personal injury occasioned could not be established. As with *Hotson*, in *Gregg* we see the damage being reframed in light of difficulties around proving causation: the claimant sued the defendant on the basis that his negligence reduced his chances of being cured by 17 percentage points, from 42% to 25%. By the stage of the decision in the House of Lords, the claimant was six years into remission so it was unknown whether he would be 'cured' of cancer or not. The outcome was not already known, unlike *Hotson*, so *Gregg* was not necessarily bound by this previous decision; nonetheless, the loss of a chance argument was also rejected by a majority of 3:2.

Arguably, there are various reasons why the result in *Gregg v Scott* is justifiable. Recognising loss of a chance of injury would, for example, unsettle orthodox notions of 'damage' in negligence. A lot turns on what we are prepared to recognise as actionable damage, and the law has decided that *an increased risk of physical injury* or *losing the chance of avoiding physical injury* is not so considered.[31] Loss of a chance in the context of personal injuries demonstrates the conservative approach taken by the court as to what constitutes 'damage' in the tort of negligence.[32] Damage is said to be the gist of negligence,[33] and in this context has been defined by Lord Hoffmann in *Rothwell v Chemical & Insulating Co.* as being 'worse off, physically or economically, so that compensation is an appropriate remedy'.[34]

In *Gregg*, however, Lord Nicholls dissented from the majority and was prepared to broaden the ambit of actionable damage in negligence to include loss of a chance of avoiding an injury. One of the reasons provided by his Lordship was that losing a chance of avoiding injury is 'something of importance and value' and 'a real loss' for a claimant.[35] It is difficult to locate with more precision what Lord Nicholls means by 'real loss' or the patient being 'worse off' here, and the reasoning is somewhat circular on this point, but there are similarities to some of the earlier contract cases discussed above. We wonder if the reference to 'importance and value' denotes that what is actually behind Lord Nicholls' sense of loss looks something more like a personal sense of disappointment and disempowerment suffered by, or distress caused to, the

---

31 *Gregg*, n. 1, [20] (Lord Nicholls).
32 For instance, recent attempts to introduce loss of autonomy as a head of damage have been rebuffed: *Shaw v Kovac* [2017] EWCA Civ. 1028.
33 *Gregg*, n. 1, [193].
34 *Rothwell v Chemical & Insulating Co.* [2008] 1 AC 281, [7]. In addition, at [8] Lord Hoffmann emphasised that being worse off must surpass a *de minimis* threshold.
35 *Gregg*, n. 1, [3].

claimant by his reduced chances of survival. If so, this would be in tension with well-established authorities which have affirmed that mere distress or unpleasant emotions are insufficient to ground an action in negligence.[36]

Accepting loss of a chance as the actionable damage element in claims involving physical harms also brings particular causation problems. As we noted at the beginning of Section 6.2, in an action, if a claimant suffers actionable damage, they must prove that damage was caused by the defendant's negligence on the balance of probabilities. If a claimant cannot pass this hurdle, they will not recover damages—not unless the law relaxes the rules of causation. As we have indicated in our discussion of *Hotson* and *Gregg*, another route to recovery for a claimant is not to seek to amend the rules of causation, but to push at the edges of what the law recognises as damage. If a claimant cannot prove on the balance of probabilities that their personal injury was caused by the defendant, then they might be able to show that the defendant increased their risk of injury, or put another way, was a cause of their *loss of a chance* of avoiding personal injury. As we have indicated in this section, accepting loss of a chance as damage would be unorthodox for the law of negligence.[37] Further, our discussion of causation and the *Fairchild* exception below in Section 6.2.2 indicates that, when faced with intractable uncertainties as to past facts, the law has shown more willingness to amend the rules of causation than to permit loss of a chance or increased risk as damage.

6.2.2 *Further complications: the* Fairchild *exception and causal expansion*

The mirror image of loss of a chance of a positive outcome is the increase of risk of a negative outcome occurring. As risk and chance are necessarily intertwined, discussion of loss of a chance in English law would be incomplete without consideration of *Fairchild v Glenhaven Funeral Services*, in which the House of Lords created an exception to the normal application of 'but for' causation and instead held causation to be satisfied where a defendant materially increased the *risk* of harm to the claimant.[38] In *Fairchild*, the claimants were negligently exposed to asbestos dust during periods of employment by different defendants. The claimants then went on to develop mesothelioma, a form of cancer. Uncertainty in scientific knowledge about the aetiology of mesothelioma made it impossible for the claimants to prove that any single breach of duty by a defendant was more likely than not to have caused their mesothelioma. Rather than permit the injustice of denying claims brought by those unfortunate enough to have been negligently exposed to asbestos by a

---

36 For example, *Hicks v Chief Constable of South Yorkshire* [1992] 2 All ER 65.
37 See also *Gregg*, n. 1, [196]–[199] (Baroness Hale).
38 *Fairchild v Glenhaven Funeral Services* [2002] UKHL 22 (hereafter *Fairchild*). See further K. Oliphant, 'Causal uncertainty in tort law: the special case of mesothelioma', this volume.

number of employers, the House of Lords instead created an exception to the normal 'but for' rule of establishing causation.

This decision on 'but for' causation in *Fairchild* no doubt encouraged the radical argument seen in *Gregg*: that merely losing a chance of avoiding injury, or increasing the risk of injury developing in the future, is actionable.[39] If we look at contemporary reactions to *Fairchild* we can see that legal scholars questioned the wide-ranging implications that *Fairchild* may hold for the law generally. For instance, Tony Weir questioned whether *Hotson* would be reversed in light of the decision, given that 'in certain cases it may not even be necessary to show that the defendant's fault probably contributed to the actual occurrence of harm if it is clear that it has contributed to the risk of harm'.[40] Soon after *Fairchild*, Kumaralingam Amirthalingam argued that the House of Lords had attributed 'causal responsibility for damage that was not in fact proved to have been caused by the defendant'—and did so to advance a case for recognition of loss of a chance as a head of damage in English law.[41] Sarah Green, again writing soon after *Fairchild*, viewed the decision as recognising the gist of the wrongdoing was increasing *risk* of injury and that this was welcome, at least where the risk materialised into actual injury.[42]

Undoubtedly, since *Fairchild*, the courts have been tasked with keeping the exception within bounds. For instance, since *Fairchild* we have seen that the exception may apply where the claimant was exposed to one of the similar agents innocently or through their own negligence.[43] We have also seen the exception apply outside of mesothelioma to other industrial diseases.[44] Importantly, however, the House of Lords in *Gregg* did not adopt risk-based reasoning in the context of clinical negligence. In *IEG v Zurich*, Lord Hodge viewed *Gregg* as a bulwark to the expansionist tendencies of the *Fairchild* exception when stating that the 'House of Lords in *Gregg v Scott* [2005] 2 AC 176 has been careful not to allow the relaxation of the established rules of causation more widely by applying a weak rule of causation outside the *Fairchild* enclave'.[45]

Of course, an initial obvious difference between *Gregg v Scott* and *Fairchild* is that no actionable injury materialised in *Gregg* by the time of trial, whereas in *Fairchild* the mesothelioma had arisen. Thus, the claimant's attempts in *Gregg* to rely on *Fairchild* can easily be rebuffed as conflating a rule about causation (*Fairchild*) and a rule about what the law accepts as actionable damage.

---

39 A point acknowledged by Lord Hoffmann in *Barker v Corus (UK)* [2006] 2 AC 572 (hereafter *Barker*), [5].

40 Weir, n. 19, 12.

41 K. Amirthalingam, 'Loss of Chance: Lost Cause or Remote Possibility' (2003) 62 *CLJ* 253, 254–55.

42 S. Green, 'Winner Takes It All' (2004) 120 *LQR* 566, 569–71.

43 See *Barker*, n. 39.

44 *Heneghan v Manchester Dry Docks* [2016] EWCA Civ. 86 (lung cancer).

45 *IEG v Zurich Insurance UK* [2015] UKSC 33 (hereafter *IEG*), [109].

However, the explanation of *Fairchild* as being purely an evidential rule where proof of causation of the actionable damage suffered on the balance of probabilities is impossible and where the damage was caused by a single agent was made more uncertain by the later decision of the House of Lords in *Barker v Corus*.[46]

Fairchild itself did not determine the extent of the defendants' liability, that is whether defendants are liable in full joint and severally (as is normal when a claimant proves that a defendant's negligence caused personal injury), or in proportion (which is the type of liability we tend to associate with probability or chance rather than proof). That question arose in *Barker*, which further muddied the waters by arguably introducing a limited role for loss of a chance into the realm of personal injury. Similar to *Fairchild*, in *Barker* two of the three claimants had been negligently exposed to asbestos by a series of employers and suffered mesothelioma, and another claimant had been exposed during periods of employment and self-employment. The House of Lords, instead of opting for the orthodox principle of holding defendants joint and severally liable for damage they caused, imposed liability *in proportion to the risk created* by the defendants. Looking at the *Fairchild* exception post-*Barker*, it is therefore arguable that a defendant's liability corresponds not to the physical injury which the claimant suffers, but rather the *risk of injury* created by the defendant (though the damage still does have to occasion).[47]

Some of the speeches in *Barker* seemed to acknowledge risk of injury as the damage. Take, for example, Lord Hoffmann in *Barker*, who seemed to suggest that the *Fairchild* exception permitting liability for risk of harm was essentially indistinguishable from the loss of a chance claim being attempted in *Gregg*. His Lordship claimed that *Gregg* was decided

not on the ground that there was some conceptual objection to treating the diminution in the chances of a favourable outcome or (putting the same thing in a different way) the increase in the risk of an unfavourable outcome as actionable damage.

Rather, reasoned Lord Hoffmann, 'the adoption of such a rule in *Gregg v Scott* would have effectively extended the *Fairchild* exception to all cases of medical negligence, if not beyond ... I regarded *Fairchild* as an example of the very rule which the minority wished to apply [in *Gregg*]'.[48] Similarly, Lord Rodger's powerful dissent in *Barker* was premised on his understanding of the majority's approach as reframing harm as *risk* rather than injury.[49] Lord Phillips

---

46 *Barker*, n. 39.
47 A point made in *McGregor*, n. 4, 10-057. See also Green, n. 42.
48 *Barker*, n. 39, [39].
49 Ibid., [80]–[85].

(albeit in the minority) in the *'Trigger' Litigation*[50] also read *Barker* as such. However, the role (if any) for loss of a chance in the realm of personal injuries after *Barker* has been curtailed by more recent Supreme Court decisions in the *'Trigger' Litigation* and *IEG v Zurich*,[51] which held that the *damage* in *Fairchild* cases is the industrial disease suffered, not the risk of incurring injury.

As argued by Sandy Steel and Nick McBride, the damage in the *Fairchild* line of cases is the *disease* suffered by the claimant, not the risk of the disease emerging.[52] The *Fairchild* exception is, therefore, just that: a broader notion of causation responding to evidential gaps. Steel writes that

> *Barker*, as currently interpreted, does not conceive of the loss which the claimant suffered as an increase in risk of mesothelioma. It is better thought of as creating proportionate liability in proportion to the chance that the defendant has caused the mesothelioma. Damages are for the chance of causation, not causation of a lost chance.[53]

In light of these more recent authorities, we should therefore be cautious in viewing *Fairchild* as a true inroad to the position of English law: that there can be no claim for loss of a chance in relation to personal injuries. Drawing threads together, when faced with intractable uncertainties as to past facts, the law has permitted an exception to the 'but for' causation requirement in negligence—at least where claimants have found it impossible to satisfy the normal causal rule due to a lack of scientific knowledge, and also where the potential causes of the injury operate in a substantially similar way.[54] The courts have been more conservative in their approach to actionable damage, where loss of a chance (or increase of risk) has not been recognised. It may be that causation, with its close ties to ideas of responsibility for wrongdoing, seems like the more natural doctrine to refine (rather than actionable damage) in order to accommodate concerns about unfairness arising out of intractable uncertainties faced by claimants. Another plausible reason why causation rather than damage is being refined in such cases is that liability for physical damage (such as property damage or personal injury) in negligence is more easily established than liability for intangible harms (such as a pure economic loss or psychiatric harm). Liability for *risk* of harm, then, falls outside the physical damage core of

---

50 *Durham v BAI (Run Off)* [2012] UKSC 14, [123]–[130]
51 *IEG*, n. 45.
52 N. McBride and S. Steel, 'The Trigger Litigation' (2012) 28 *Professional Negligence* 285; S. Steel, 'Rationalising Loss of a Chance in Tort' in S. Pitel et al. (eds), *Tort Law: Challenging Orthodoxy*, Hart 2012, 241–43; S. Steel and D.J. Ibbetson, 'More Grief on Uncertain Causation in Tort' (2011) 70 *CLJ* 451, 459–60.
53 Steel, n. 52, 242.
54 *Fairchild*, n. 38. This also explains the unsuccessful outcome in *Wilsher v Essex Area Health Authority* [1988] AC 1074.

negligence, and, to that extent, it is unsurprising that risk as damage has been treated with scepticism by the courts.

6.2.3 *Potential for an overall adverse effect on personal injury claimants in general*

Allowing loss of a chance of avoiding injury to constitute actionable damage might have a further adverse impact on claimants who *can* prove their case on the balance of probabilities. Say in a case like *Gregg* that the courts *were* prepared to award damages in proportion to the 17-percentage point (42%–25%) loss of chance. Now take a case where a claimant proves on the balance of probability that the defendant's tort did cause their personal injury, and we can assess that probability at 75%. Would it not be open for counsel to begin to press against the orthodox line and seek to reduce the claimant's damages by 25% to reflect the 75% probability? This was an argument which found favour with Baroness Hale in *Gregg v Scott*. Making reference to Tony Weir's plea to avoid the tendency to state matters of proof in terms of percentages, Baroness Hale reminded us that, once persuaded that an injury was 'more likely than not' caused by the defendant's negligence, a judge awards a claimant the full value of the damage caused.[55] That the law requires proof of harm on the balance of probabilities, not just probability, cuts both ways:

> If it is more likely than not that the defendant's carelessness caused me to lose a leg, I do not want my damages reduced to the extent that it is less than 100% certain that it did so. On the other hand, if it is more likely than not that the defendant's carelessness did not cause me to lose the leg, then the defendant does not want to have to pay damages for the 20% or 30% chance that it did. A 'more likely than not' approach to causation suits both sides.[56]

Having said this, Lord Nicholls in his dissent clearly thought that it was fairly arbitrary that a claimant whose prospects of surviving cancer could be assessed at 60% and who, because of the negligent delayed treatment, now has a 40% chance of survival would be able to sue, whereas a patient who starts off with a 40% chance of survival and then has this chance reduced to nil by the negligence is unable to sue.[57]

55 *Gregg*, n. 1, [194].
56 Ibid., [195].
57 Ibid., [46].

6.3 Solutions and policy goals

Of course, England is not the only jurisdiction to deny loss of a chance claims for personal injury. The High Court of Australia in *Tabet v Gett*[58] and the Supreme Court of Canada in *Laferrière v Lawson*[59] similarly denied claims involving loss of a chance on the basis that it infringed the orthodox understanding of factual causation. Whilst the previous section made clear the full range of intractable issues arising from the current approach to loss of a chance, this final section will explore possible solutions to reconceptualise its application.

To begin, we turn to two continental jurisdictions by way of example: those of France and Belgium. The favourable treatment of loss of a chance claims in these countries is important for two reasons. First, this provides an opportunity to glean insight into the overarching mechanics of how claims brought for loss of a chance have been decided where the damage involved is a lost chance. Second, courts in these jurisdictions have gone some way to articulating why lost chances matter to claimants, which reminds us to be similarly alive to the claimant's articulation of their harm. Perhaps unsurprisingly, the reasons advanced by claimants in these cases are not dissimilar to what claimants (and dissenting judges) in England have articulated, albeit to date unsuccessfully. In taking this forward, we look at developing the idea that the loss of a chance is something of value—retaining the reasoning of earlier English cases and present-day continental cases—and that a more robust understanding of the connection between damage and duty may provide a solution through which to better understand why losses of a chance remain an important area within the tort of negligence.

6.3.1 A comparative perspective: the claimant-friendly approach of France and Belgium

At present, both France and Belgium allow loss of a chance claims. In these countries, the loss of a chance itself is considered the actionable harm, with the result that 'the law does not try to solve such problems in terms of causation between the tortious activity and the harm finally suffered'.[60] In both jurisdictions, claims for loss of a chance can be brought in a wide range of areas, including negligent professional advice, medical negligence, and omissions liability, to name a few. More controversially, it does also seem fairly

---

58 (2010) HCA 12.
59 [1991] 1 SCR 541. It should be noted that this action was, however, 'saved' by Canada's claimant-friendly approach to psychiatric injury; namely, the psychological harm suffered by the claimant need not be medically recognised to ground a claim. In a way, then, the claimant still received some measure of recognition for the harm she suffered, even though it was not framed specifically as a loss of a chance: see below n. 89.
60 N. Jansen, 'The Idea of a Lost Chance' (1999) 19 *OJLS* 271, 274.

well decided that both jurisdictions permit loss of a chance claims in situations where the claimant alleges they have lost the chance of obtaining a benefit and where they have lost the chance to avoid a particular harm.[61] Whilst there has been opposition to the acceptance of the latter construct in the Belgium courts[62] and by French scholars[63] on the ground that it seeks to circumvent causation requirements, decisions in both jurisdictions seem to have resolved the conflict in favour of a more expansionist approach.

This appetite for expansion and openness in these two systems is intrinsically linked to the focus which is placed on victims who have suffered a harm at the hands of another.[64] Art. 1240 (previously art. 1382) of the French Civil Code, for example, states that every human act which causes damage to another obliges the person by whose fault the harm has occurred to make reparation for it[65]—this, of course, representing the flipside of the coin to art. 4 of the Declaration of the Rights of Man 1789, which reads, 'liberty consists in being able to do anything which does not harm another person'.[66] The incredibly broad scope of art. 1240 and two hundred years of rapid social change meant that it was ultimately the courts that intervened and interpreted the law liberally[67] and with *équité* in an effort to keep pace with a changing society. The result is that there are very few limitations on the types of damage which can be used to form the basis of a claim—as Borghetti states, 'in principle, all types of loss or damage can be compensated'.[68] Further, the concept of 'fault' which is central to the negligence inquiry is similarly broad, focusing primarily on a type of abnormal behaviour or failing to do something one ought to, as adjudged by a standard of reasonableness;[69] yet another way in which French

---

61 See generally W.T. Nuninga et al., 'Chances as Legally Protected Assets' (2020) 28 *European Review of Private Law* 375. Broadly defined, the loss of a chance in French law refers to an actual and certain disappearance of a favourable eventuality. See: 'Cass. Civ. 1 4 June 2007,' no. 05-20.313 and art. 1238 para 1 of the 2020 Bigot-Reichhardt Reform Bill.

62 B. Dubuisson et al., 'Belgium' in B. Winiger et al. (eds), *Digest of European Tort Law, Vol. 2: Essential Cases on Damage*, de Gruyter 2011, 26/7 nos. 6–12.

63 P. Jourdain, 'La perte d'une chance, une curiosité française' in P. Wessner et al. (eds), *Pour un droit equitable, engage et chaleureux: mélanges en l'honneaur de Pierre Wessner*, Helbing Lichtenhahn 2011; more generally, G. Viney et al., *Les Conditions de la Responsabilité*, LGDJ 2013.

64 See generally J.-S. Borghetti, 'The Culture of Tort Law in France' (2012) 3 *JETL* 158.

65 Art. 1241 (previously art. 1382) CC makes it clear that liability attaches where damage is caused by the negligence of another.

66 For this point, see J. Bell et al., *Principles of French Law*, 2nd ed., OUP 2008, 367.

67 P. Giliker, 'Codification, Consolidation, Restatement? How Best to Systemise the Modern Law of Tort' (2021) 70 *ICLQ* 271, 283.

68 Borghetti, n. 64, 158.

69 Previously, the bon pere de famille, translated as 'the good father of the family', taken from Roman origin of the *paterfamilias*. This would roughly translate to the standard of the 'reasonable man' in the common law, though the concept is considerably more dynamic than the 'venerable ... reasonable man, who was born during the reign of Victoria but remains in vigorous health ...'. See *Healthcare at Home v The Common Services Agency* [2014] UKSC 49, [1] per Lord Reed.

courts afford themselves a level of flexibility and adaptability to meet changing social conditions.[70] For now, at least, Belgian law has tracked closely to its French counterpart, applying the Civil Code with a similar level of interpretivism guided by changing social norms. It is with these principles and cultural mindsets, then, that we move to consider some examples.

6.3.1.1 Examples from the case law

6.3.1.1.1 BELGIUM

The claimants in the selected action inherited a horse, 'Prizrak' ('Ghost'), from their late father. When the defendant veterinarian was called to inspect the horse, he negligently failed to consider a gastric probe, which, based on the presentation of the horse and in accordance with the expert evidence given, ought to have been undertaken. Had a gastric probe been performed, it would have been possible to start appropriate treatment and Prizrak's death, by way of gastric rupture, could have been avoided. Had the appropriate treatment been applied, Prizrak stood a high chance of recovery based on evidence provided by experts, which the appellate court took to represent a 'real chance'. In the eyes of the court, there was no doubt as to the causal link between the fault and the damage, namely the loss of the chance of survival. The veterinarian appealed against this finding, arguing that the link between his faulty conduct and the damage was not certain.

The Court of Cassation rejected this and found that the loss of a real chance of cure or survival is compensable if there is a *conditio sine qua non* link between the fault and the loss of chance. It went further and stated, 'the court may award compensation for the loss of a chance to obtain an advantage or the avoidance of a disadvantage if the loss of this chance is attributable to a fault'.[71] Thus, it can be taken that the Court of Cassation accepts the loss of such a chance as actionable damage and that, provided causation between the wrongful act or omission and the damage is established, compensation can be awarded.

6.3.1.1.2 FRANCE

The first of the two cases considered here concerns the duty of a doctor to warn of inherent risks to particular forms of medical surgery, the purpose of which is to allow informed consent. The second is used to demonstrate that,

---

70 Bell et al., n. 66, 367.
71 Cour de Cassation de Belgique, 5 Jun. 2008, C.07.0199.N., ECLI:BE:CASS:2008: ARR.20080605.5. The original reads: 'Le juge peut accorder une réparation pour la perte d'une chance d'obtenir un avantage ou d'éviter un préjudice si la perte de cette chance est imputable à une faute'.

whilst courts in France (and Belgium) are liberal in their acceptance of the loss of a chance as actionable damage, there are limitations.

In the first case, decided in 1990,[72] the patient underwent surgery to correct a case of acute sinusitis. During the surgery, a rupture of the right orbital wall occurred and the patient was left with severe vision problems. The rupture itself was not due to a surgical error on the part of the doctor; however, the claimant argued that the doctor had not informed him of this risk, which itself was not characterised as exceptional. The court permitted the action on the basis that the information would have allowed the claimant the chance to avoid that harm. A later argument put forward by the claimant was rejected: that, had he known of the risk, he would have refused the operation, thus forming a link between the personal injury sustained and the doctor's breach. The chance itself was taken as the actionable harm and it was on that basis that damages were later awarded.

The second case involved the death of the claimant's son in a road traffic accident.[73] The defendants represented the wrongdoer's insurance company. The claimant sought damages in line with her lost chance of obtaining financial support from her son in her later life. This claim was rejected by the court on the basis that the only records of the son's employment were a four-month fixed-term contract in the hotel industry and approximately seven months of service in the military. Further, at the time of the fatal accident, the claimant's son was listed as unemployed. The claim for loss of a chance was denied, as the court determined that, at the relevant time, there was no real chance (or real prospect) of the victim's being able to support his mother.

6.3.1.2 What do those cases tell us about loss of a chance as damage for the purposes of English law?

Together, these cases tell us a number of things which can be brought forward into the next discussion. First, the requirement that the damage be real and serious embraces both a tangible value-capable quality, which extends to economic loss, but which also embraces a harm assessment which is more personal to the claimant, such as one's interest in self-determination and dignity.[74] As to whether the 'chance' in question is considered real and legitimate, courts may as a matter of procedure rely on evidence provided by appointed, impartial experts, as seen in the Belgian case.[75] However, there admittedly remains a lack of clarity in the cases considered as to why and under what

---

72 Cass. civ. 1, 7 Feb. 1990, no. 88-14.797, Bull. civ. I no. 39, 30. This can also be seen in a more recent decision: Cass. civ. 1, 6 Dec. 2007, no. 06-19.301, Bull. civ. I no. 380.

73 Cass. civ. 2, 5 Jan. 1994, no. 92-14.463.

74 See also Cass. civ. 1, 9 Oct. 2001, no. 00-14.564, Bull. civ. I no. 249, 157, which reads, 'dans l'exigence du respect du principe constitutionnel de sauvegarde de la dignité de la personne humaine'.

75 See, for example, art. 962, Belgian Judicial Code.

circumstances harms that impact dignity and self-determination matter where losses of chances are concerned.

What does come across in the cases considered, particularly in the medical context, is the willingness of courts to use loss of a chance as an instrument to ensure some level of compensation for victims where establishing a claim along traditional lines, involving physical injury, fault, and causation, would be incredibly difficult, if not insurmountable. Art. L.1111-2 of the French Public Health Code enshrines the rights of patients to have risks disclosed as a matter of personal autonomy and self-determination. Moreover, the professional Code of Deontology makes clear in great detail the duties doctors owe to fully and meaningfully discuss those risks, so as to allow the patient the chance of avoiding a further loss.[76] Where the allegation is that a doctor has failed to adhere to these principles, the burden is placed on the doctor to produce evidence through notes, meeting records, letters, etc. to rebut this.[77] Factual causation, which otherwise requires a standard of 'near-absolute certainty'[78] is relaxed and mirrors the damage, which, as long as the lost chance was a real and serious one, is unlikely to pose significant barriers for victims.

Lastly, it is worth noting that, despite it being the case that courts in France and Belgium are quite liberal in the acceptance of lost chances as compensable damage, this is not absolute, and courts are willing to interrogate the construction of the lost chance to ensure its 'realness'. Where submissions fail to meet this threshold, claims can and will be rejected.

6.3.2 Reining in another unruly horse

On loss of a chance, it has been said that 'the Belgians and the French criticize the doctrine for providing a bypass of the causation requirement, whilst the English reject its application apparently in fear of it becoming such a bypass'.[79] However, at least as regards Belgium and France, this criticism does not come from judges; it comes predominantly from academia. The natural question then arises: 'why?' Why might it be the case that courts have accepted the doctrine of loss of a chance in its current form, whilst academics remain steadfast in their scepticism? Perhaps it is indeed the case that causation is being bypassed or circumvented, but this may well be a policy choice of a different colour. If 'but for' causation has shown itself to be an imprecise tool for dealing with what are accepted as legitimate legal harms presented by claimants, then it is

---

76 S. Taylor, *Medical Accident Liability and Redress in English and French Law*, CUP 2015, 118–20.

77 Ibid., 125; see Bell et al., n. 66, 373.

78 Nuninga et al., n. 61, 379.

79 Ibid., 395.

worth considering whether some traction can be gained by re-shifting focus to other elements within the inquiry so that they can deliver.[80]

6.3.2.1 A 'chance' as something of 'value'

If we are to accept in English law that the loss of a chance can itself constitute actionable damage (and, later, the basis of the factual causation inquiry), as has been accepted in some continental jurisdictions, we need some level of clarity as to the types of harm it encompasses. Damage remains a centralising force within the negligence inquiry, linking the duty of care element, breach, and factual and legal causation. As such, a robust level of specificity is required so that realistic controls can be maintained and to ensure that negligence law does not unduly restrict people's freedom of action.[81] Having said this, the element of actionable damage, it is recognised, has historically been ignored or repackaged as a question of causation or even duty.[82] That we lack systematic internal legal argument in the realm of loss of a chance,[83] in particular at the damage stage, means that in re-thinking our approach, a willingness to openly consider what damage here comprises is needed. For present purposes, it is not contested that the starting point for this assessment begins with *Rothwell* and with the idea that the claimant must be worse off; a change alone is insufficient. It is also accepted that one can be made worse off where the harm consists of a loss of the chance to obtain an advantage or avoid a disadvantage. Further interrogation is needed, however, when we consider what it means to have been made worse off by a lost chance.

That the claimant's narrative around the harm that they have suffered should be prioritised as a means of understanding the nature of the damage has been argued by a number of commentators.[84] Even saying that damage is the gist of an action is to invite an assessment of its substance or its essence. In working to understand a lost chance as damage, understanding and being open to this narrative is a key element.[85] 'Chance' has been described by commentators and

---

80 'But for' causation has, of course, been expanded numerous times in the United Kingdom on the basis of policy, and achieving practical justice at the detriment of coherence. See, for example, *Chester v Afshar* [2005] 1 AC 134; *Fairchild*, n. 38. Of course, *Fairchild* was itself described as a 'sort of juridical version of chaos theory' by Lords Neuberger and Reed in *IEG*, n. 45, [191].

81 For this final point, see D. Nolan, 'New Forms of Damage in Negligence' (2007) 70 *MLR* 59, 79.

82 Ibid., 59.

83 On this point see Jansen, n. 60, 275.

84 For this second point on prioritisation, see, for example, N. Priaulx, 'Humanising Negligence: Damaged Bodies, Biographical Lives and the Limits of Law' (2012) 33 *Adelaide Law Review* 177; Nolan, n. 81.

85 Also key to this would be to understand *when* the alleged damage occurred within this narrative. This will be important in understanding the claimant's loss and also assessing the defendant's possible duties around this.

judges in a multitude of ways; it stands to reason that claimants themselves would offer similarly personal and sometimes experiential accounts of what it means to lose a chance. What does seem to come across with great prevalence is that the chance was something held by or belonging to the claimant, either as a right[86] or, as put forward by Nuninga et al., 'an asset';[87] something the deprivation of which could translate to being made worse off. It will be recalled that Lord Nicholls in *Gregg* argued that the claimant's lost chance represented 'something of importance' and was a 'real loss' to him.[88]

Chance was also explicitly *not* blind luck in the eyes of Moisan J in the Quebec Court of Appeal decision in *Laferrière*, and was capable of *being shaped* to some extent by will and self-determination.[89] Yet it must also be recognised that, in speaking about a chance as being something 'real' or 'an asset' or something capable of being shaped, we must also question judges' attempts to bring chance into the realm of orthodox understandings of tangible damage. Where appeals to qualities of 'realness' and tangibility attempt to do this, we should also question whether this is ultimately desirable. That judges have been willing to engage in discourse around the edges of orthodox damage is positive and it is also not to say that chances cannot be articulated in such language. Having said this, perhaps there is also something to be said for acknowledging the limitations of current constructs and expanding the

---

86 This can also be seen in the early contract cases discussed above: *Chaplin*, n. 3, and *Kitchen*, n. 9, for example. Rights-based discussions also extend to cases of disclosure of risk and informed consent. For example, the Quebec Court of Appeal in *Laferrière* found the right to be one to take decisions that affect one's life and health, and equated it to sec. 7 of the Canadian Charter of Rights and Freedoms: *Laferrière v Lawson* [1989] RJQ 27 (QCCA) per Gonthier J. See too, in France, Cass. civ. 1, 6 Dec. 2007, no. 06-19.301, Bull. civ. I, no. 380. Similarities may also be drawn with autonomy-based arguments in the UK courts.

87 Nuninga et al., n. 61, 396. This point is also discussed in Steel, n. 52, 265.

88 *Gregg*, n. 1, [3].

89 *Laferrière*, n. 86. It should also be noted that whilst loss of a chance was denied in the Supreme Court (*Laferrière v Lawson* (SCC), n. 59), Gonthier J, with whom the majority agreed, concluded, 'I am convinced that Mrs. Dupuis experienced a *type of psychological suffering* which was directly related to the appellant's failure to inform his patient of her condition. From 1975 until her death, she experienced the horrible rhythms of her disease and the regular and seemingly ineffectual treatments and medications in the knowledge that things might have been different had she known earlier and been treated earlier. Her chances may not have been sufficient for the law, but they were *very real to her, no doubt* ... While she was a person who was concerned with her health and prepared to seek the best medical evidence and abide by it, she was denied the opportunity and choice of doing so by reason of the appellant's failure to inform her' (emphasis added). Canada has of course taken the position that for psychological injury to meet the threshold necessary for actionable damage, the claimant must establish serious and prolonged psychological injury, which has had a significant impact on the claimant's life, but which need not be diagnosed: see *Mustapha v Culligan of Canada* [2008] SCR 114 and *Saadati v Moorhead* 2017 SCC 28. Much of the language used by Gonthier J in *Laferrière* is not dissimilar from the language used in the present discussion on the meaning and value of a chance, and focuses on taking seriously the narrative regarding the harm suffered by the instant claimant.

language around loss of a chance, prioritising the claimant's voice about where their harm actually lies.

Importantly, just as the chance can itself be seen as something real and of substance to that claimant, so too is it the case that it also be of *value* to that claimant, so that, when it is lost, the claimant is worse for it. We agree with Steel that value in these circumstances is not well conceived through the lens of the claimant's subjective preferences or desires,[90] but rather that 'we … care about our chances because we care about the *things to which chances relate*'.[91] It may well be, for example, that the value to which the chance relates is monetary in nature (e.g. the market value of the horse in the Belgian example above); however, this will not always be the case. It may be that the value to which a chance relates is to be found in something more abstract, such as the exercise of qualities central to how an individual exists and participates in society; for example, making an autonomous decision or exercising self-determination. These are arguably valid and can be observed in the continental cases discussed above, yet analysis around why autonomous decision-making is important when considering lost chances is lacking. Perhaps part of the answer lies in looking beyond the 'things' to which chances relate (e.g. material injuries), to the *relationships* to which chances relate.

6.3.2.2 'The duty of care is a sine qua non of negligence'[92]

An element shared by very nearly all of the cases considered in this piece is that the relationships involved are 'special'; that is, relationships between doctors and patients, employers and employees, veterinarians and owners, clients and solicitors, etc. Within the common law, these special relationships have traditionally come with more burdensome, positive obligations, which are largely justified on the basis that one party (the defendant) possesses a greater level of knowledge, holds a greater amount of bargaining power, or is in some way able to determine or control, whether through action or inaction, an individual's life path in a particular circumstance. Where it is taken that a duty owed attaches to a specific person in a particularised way, interactions and expectations within these relationships will be different, not only amongst those similarly considered 'special' (though there are also similarities), but in particular, say with a stranger. When we think, then, about what lost chances mean in the context of these special relationships, perhaps part of the answer lies in the point that harm suffered to *that* relationship can itself represent damage in those circumstances.

---

90 S. Steel, n. 52, 261–62. Note as well the etymology of the word 'real' being 'realis' or 'res'— the idea of belonging to a thing.
91 Ibid., 263 (emphasis added).
92 J. Conaghan and W. Mansell, *The Wrongs of Tort*, 2nd ed., Pluto 1999, 13.

In the realm of employers and employees, for example, employment laws now represent an 'evolution of pragmatic attempts to balance the logic of the market system with the liberal aspiration to ensure that individuals are treated with respect and justly, and that they have the opportunity to construct meaningful lives'.[93] When a negligently compiled letter of reference is completed by a former employer, it may not only be the future prospects of employment that are damaged. It may also represent a violation of these relational expectations that an employee be treated respectfully and that from this they can build and construct a sense of purpose in their working life. Looking at the roles that professionals undertake, the work they perform has been said to carry an intrinsic value because of the weighty impact their efforts have on both an individual and a societal level, and their commitment to certain moral principles.[94] In a similar vein to the employment relationship, when lost chances occur in the professional negligence context, it may also be the case that what is harmed contains a relational element central to that chance. Take, for example, disclosure of risk in the medical context. This area has changed significantly in recent decades to recognise the importance of mutual, productive communication, which places the patient at the centre of the conversation.[95] As a result, professionals and employers hold positions of responsibility and carry obligations that go beyond non-injuriousness. And where patients, clients, and employees are concerned, matters of human dignity and trust lie at the centre.

The fact that much of the debate on the (im)permissibility of recovering for lost chances in the United Kingdom has focused on 'but for' causation and the difficulties of attaching this to orthodox heads of damage (e.g. physical injury and economic losses), and not on the damage and duty link, where the lost chance itself represents the actionable damage, means that the 'why permit lost chances in the first place?' question has not been sufficiently addressed. Analysing these latter issues is, however, fundamental to any attempt to make sense of, or resolve, the legal uncertainties surrounding the doctrine. Within the duty analysis, questions as to whether the defendant owed an obligation to protect against a particular type of lost chance would likely fall to an assessment

---

93 H. Collins, *Employment Law*, OUP 2010, 5.
94 See Lord Justice Jackson, 'The Professions: Power, Privilege and Legal Liability' (Peter Taylor Memorial Lecture to The Professional Negligence Bar Association, London, 21 April 2015), 2.6 and 3.2–3.6. For example, a perhaps rather hyperbolic extract from A.M. Carr-Saunders and P.A. Wilson, *The Professions*, Clarendon Press 1933, 497, reads, 'They engender modes of life, habits of thought and standards of judgment which render them centres of resistance to crude forces which threaten steady and peaceful evolution... The family, the church and the universities, certain associations of intellectuals, and above all the great professions, stand like rocks against which the waves raised by these forces beat in vain'.
95 This has also been extensively analysed in the French context. Discussions here led to the creation of art. L.1111-2, Public Health Code in an effort to rebalance and give greater meaning to the doctor-patient relationship. See generally Taylor, n. 76, ch. 6.

of the scope of the defendant's duty in assessing each party's expectations within that relationship. Whether a duty is found is ultimately a question for the courts, and yet much could still be learned about relational expectations in these scenarios whichever way the court ultimately determines.

6.4 Conclusions

When it comes to lost chances, causation in fact has played a notoriously influential role; indeed, for Conaghan and Mansell, causation in large part 'determines who wins and loses in "the forensic lottery"'.[96] Courts and commentators have also acknowledged, however, that strict adherence to factual causation might sometimes lead to unjust outcomes, the most obvious area being where evidential uncertainty makes it impossible for a claimant to prove their claim on orthodox principles.

Whilst courts seem fairly content to bend the strict application of 'but for' causation where the loss of a chance concerns the loss of a particular financial gain—this turning on now fairly well-established rules on future hypotheticals concerning either the claimant's or defendant's conduct—the picture is significantly obscured in the medical context. Here, the law in the United Kingdom has worked its way into an intractable quagmire, uncertain as to whether it is causation or damage that is guiding the inquiry, and on what basis orthodox principles are to be extended or vigorously defended. As we have seen in *Fairchild*, rather than allowing an undesirable outcome for the claimants, the courts have found causation to be satisfied where the defendant's breach materially contributed to the *risk* of the injury occurring. In such cases, however, one could argue that the increased risk of injury (or loss of a chance of avoiding it) is the gist of the complaint in the absence of the claimant being able to establish causation through orthodox 'but for' principles. Although this interpretation of the law has since been rejected by the Supreme Court in *IEG*, it is notable that the courts were more comfortable introducing at least some limited role for increased risk through amending the rules of causation rather than expanding notions of harm.

And yet, a glimpse to the continental jurisdictions of Belgium and France, where doubts about causal uncertainty are decided instrumentally with a claimant-centric focus in mind, along with a clear acceptance of loss of a chance as damage, provides a starting point capable of inspiring future thought in the United Kingdom. As our own case law indicates, lost chances are important and they represent a harm to the claimant involved. In some instances, this may be because the claimant regards the chance as something of tangible economic value, whilst in others the value may exist in something to which the chance itself attaches: a protected interest in something or potentially a relational expectation. To get to grips with this, focus ought to be placed on

---

96 Conaghan/Mansell, n. 92, 62, citing T.G. Ison, *The Forensic Lottery*, Staples Press 1967.

the contours of the damage requirement and its connection with the duty of care, before proceeding through breach and causation. Reconstituting the negligence inquiry to accept this broader starting position would no doubt represent a development in the law and a movement away from historic conservativism in permitting new forms of actionable damage. However, to adopt the words of Lord Nicholls, 'so be it'.[97]

97 *Gregg*, n. 1, [45].

7 Quantifying or avoiding the unknown?

Damages for future lost earnings in tortious personal injury cases

David Messner-Kreuzbauer *

It is a well-known ideal of the law of tort that courts should seek, when award-ing compensatory damages, to place the injured party in the position they were in before the commission of the tort: compensation *in full* is the goal.[1] This is particularly so with respect to pecuniary loss, where it seems that a per-son's losses could, at least ideally, be calculated down to pounds and pence, or euros and cents.[2] Such rigour is also the theoretical ideal for compensation of lost earnings following severe personal injuries, which will be the focus of this paper. As Lord Goddard explained in *British Transport Commission v Gourley*:

> [T]he basic principle so far as loss of earnings ... are concerned is that the injured person should be placed in the same financial position, so far as can be done by an award of money, as he would have been had the accident not happened.[3]

How can tort law put this commitment into practice where, although a wrong is clearly established,[4] the extent of pecuniary loss is *unknown* in the way inevi-

---

* Emily Gordon contributed a substantial amount of preparatory research and initial drafting for what became this chapter, elements of which are reflected in the final text. I am grateful to her for generously allowing me to make use of her work when circumstances obliged her to retire from the project and I continued as sole author of this piece.

1 See e.g. *Livingstone v Rawyards Coal* (1880) 5 App. Cas. 25, 39 (Lord Blackburn).
2 For non-pecuniary losses flowing from personal injury, such as pain and suffering, it is (more) apparent that setting this aim would be misleading. See *The Mediana* [1900] AC 113, 116 (Lord Halsbury): 'Nobody can suggest that you can by any arithmetical calculation establish what is the exact amount of money which would represent such a thing as the pain and suffer-ing which a person has undergone'.
3 [1956] AC 185, 206.
4 This chapter does not discuss the situation where a detriment required to establish a wrong ('actionable damage'), rather than losses as the subject of compensatory damages, is uncertain. On the problem, and drawing a distinction, see D. Nolan, 'Rights, Damage, and Loss' (2017)

DOI: 10.4324/9781003537526-9

tably true of future lost earnings? While losses that have already manifested at the date of trial may be easy enough to identify and measure—things such as lost wages from a particular employment—a much more challenging task is assessing what might have happened in the claimant's career if not for the tort, and how their circumstances will change in the future. This problem is especially clear where the claimant is a child. If the courts do not want to 'sacrifice physically injured claimants on the altar of the certainty principle',[5] they need a strategy for dealing with this uncertainty.

This chapter will compare the English rules of the twentieth and twenty-first centuries with those of two Germanic jurisdictions: Germany and Austria. Comparing the rather different rules on assessment and award of uncertain losses in these jurisdictions proves enlightening, and the conclusion to the paper will try to make sense of these clear differences and what may be learned from them.

7.1 Historical overview

Uncertainty may now appear as a central problem in assessing lost earnings, but this is a relatively recent phenomenon in England. This is so because, for a considerable time, English law's emphasis on a precise 'full compensation' of financial loss, shown by *British Transport Commission v Gourley*, was less pronounced than it is today.[6]

Although this development towards a precise measurement of assets is a general phenomenon in European tort law, it is particularly distinct in England, because assessment of damages lay in the hands of the jury until 1933.[7] An ideal of strictly measured damages would have been difficult to implement until then. After all, lay bodies can hardly be expected to deliver empirically grounded and mathematically precise predictions of financial loss. It also seems, as far as is apparent, that indeed judges did not expect this: they would only intervene with a verdict if there were apparent irregularities, or if the sum awarded was perceived to be extravagant or outrageous.[8] The general view was that damages could not be calculated with precision; the instruction

---

37 *OJLS* 255; A.J. Bell, *Damages for Non-pecuniary Loss in the Tort of Negligence*, Ph.D. thesis: University of Birmingham 2018, 92–137.

5 J. Edelman, *McGregor on Damages*, 21st ed., Sweet & Maxwell 2022, no. 40-037.

6 See generally D. Ibbetson, 'Tortious Damages at Common Law' in R. Gamauf (ed.), *Ausgleich oder Buße als Grundproblem des Schadenersatzrechts von der lex Aquilia bis zur Gegenwart*, Manz 2017, 97; B. Markesinis et al., *Compensation for Personal Injury in English, German and Italian Law*, CUP 2005, 8–10; and more generally A.J. Bell and J. McCunn, 'Known unknowns: uncharted waters', this volume, 1.2.3.1.

7 By sec. 6, Administration of Justice (Miscellaneous Provisions) Act 1933, there was a right to trial in limited circumstances (for negligence cases, at the court's discretion). See also *Ward v James* [1965] 1 QB 273, 290 (Denning MR). By 1965, civil trials with a jury were rare.

8 Ibbetson, n. 6, 102–4; M. Lobban, 'Personal Injuries' in W.R. Cornish et al. (eds), *OHLE*, vol. XII, 958–1000, 990.

often given to juries was that they should give what they considered to be a 'fair' sum, given all of the circumstances.[9] Juries were, it seems, occasionally even discouraged from basing awards too closely on information such as average annual income; such a practice was perceived to be unfair, and juries were also to bear in mind the blameworthiness of the defendant in arriving at a sum.[10] In *Rapson v Cubitt*, an 1841 action brought by a butler injured in a gas explosion, Lord Abinger summed up for the jury as follows:

> For the damages—I never knew the aggravation of them attempted in so unreasonable a manner as in this case. Where the accident is a calamity, and the defendant is not particularly to blame, a more favourable view should be taken of his fault. If it be asked that the jury are to give damages equal to an annuity, it may be demanded what right has the plaintiff to calculate that he would have continued in office to the end of his life. I think it would be absurd to make the value of the annuity the measure of the damages.[11]

Even after the use of juries in negligence cases fell away after 1933, courts would award damages without identifying the reasons for arriving at a particular sum. But matters have since changed significantly. In a development initiated by *Jefford v Gee*,[12] courts were required to provide detailed itemisation of awards.

Moreover, the traditional award in English law is a once-and-for-all sum, but, since 1988, legislative intervention has increasingly provided for alternatives, such as provisional awards and periodical payments.[13] These instruments, discussed below, allow for a more precise compensation of lost earnings.

What can be learned from these developments? It may be tempting to assume that law in the past did not possess knowledge and resources sufficient to address uncertainty in any more nuanced way than leaving it to the discretion of laypersons. David Ibbetson concludes that '[i]t was not until the disappearance of the jury in the middle of the twentieth century that England can be said to have begun to have a true law of damages for personal injury'.[14] This implies that a 'true law of damages' required a rational approach towards assessment better represented by a judge with legal experience and procedural instruments at their command.

But it is important to point out that, at least according to a common interpretation, this rational approach did not *only* require more experience and

---

9 Lobban, n. 8, 990.
10 Ibbetson, n. 6, 102–3, 107; Lobban, n. 8, 990–91.
11 *Rapson v Cubitt* (1841) C & M 64, 68.
12 [1970] 2 QB 130. See further Edelman, n. 5, nos. 40–060-061.
13 See R. Lewis, 'The Politics and Economics of Tort Law: Judicially Imposed Periodical Payments of Damages' (2006) 69 *MLR* 418, 420.
14 Ibbetson, n. 6, 107.

instruments for dealing with the facts. It also required a previously non-existent level of clarity over the *goal* of tort law compensation being, at a fundamental level, to put the claimant in the financial state they would be in absent the wrong. Lord Abinger's speech in *Rapson* seems to show different concerns when he refers to the defendant's fault,[15] because this factor obviously has no relation to the change in assets. This can be interpreted in a variety of ways. It might mean that punitive and other elements, known from now-exceptional awards of exemplary damages, were not clearly distinguished from other awards. Or it might mean that awards were based on altogether different views on what losses should be or how they should be compensated. As these interpretations show, strategies to deal with uncertainty and normative views on compensable loss are not easily separated. This problem remains relevant even today.[16] As this paper will show, for loss of earnings it is still often possible to dispute whether apparently less precise rules simply represent a diminished effort to deal with uncertainties, or else an altogether different understanding of what the relevant loss is and how it should be compensated.

7.2 Scope of the uncertainty problem

A first step in understanding potential solutions to the problem of uncertain lost earnings is to distinguish more clearly between several types of uncertainty relevant to damages.[17]

First, loss of earnings may be uncertain because courts never have complete access to *facts about the future* ('what will be'); for instance, what deteriorations the claimant's health may suffer in years to come, further diminishing their actual earnings. I label this *predictive uncertainty*. For present purposes, this may be understood broadly, so it does not matter whether the future development is presently unknowable or whether the courts only lack access to knowledge that would already predict it.[18] For instance, sometimes current

---

15 Even Lord Blackburn in *Livingstone v Rawyards Coal Co* (1880) 5 App. Cas. 25, defining the now-orthodox approach, still referred to a possibility of assessing damages in light of the tortfeasor's fault in cases other than the innocent trespass which was the subject of that decision.

16 Some theorists of tort law assume that compensation should be 'fair and reasonable' rather than 'full': J.C.P. Goldberg and B.C. Zipursky, *Recognizing Wrongs*, Harvard University Press 2020, 163–68 (for reasons inherent to tort concepts); P. Cane and J. Goudkamp, *Atiyah's Accidents, Compensation and the Law*, 9th ed., CUP 2018, 131–32 (for policy reasons). Under this assumption, it is obviously less of a concern to make an estimation of uncertain losses down to the last penny or cent.

17 A general typology of uncertainty is provided in Bell/McCunn, n. 6, 1.2.1.

18 Predictive uncertainty is thus a convenient broad category coextending with the concept of 'risk' in a commonly used, fact-related but otherwise broad sense. See e.g. S.R. Perry, 'Risk, Harm and Responsibility' in D. Owen (ed.), *Philosophical Foundations of Tort Law*, OUP 1995, 321 (distinguishing objective and epistemic risk). The present paper also does not distingish between 'risk' and (true) 'uncertainty' in the sense of (un-)ascertainable probabilities introduced by F. Knight, *Risk, Uncertainty, and Profit*, Riverside Press 1921, 231–32.

methods are insufficient to detect how severely a person is infected by a disease in its early stages, although strictly speaking the deterioration is causally determined and therefore in a sense 'knowable'. The point of singling this kind of uncertainty out is that it may *be reduced or eliminated through the lapse of time*. Thus, a focus on lump-sum awards makes predictive uncertainty challenging, while instruments to postpone the (final) award of damages are a potential avenue to resolve or avoid predictive uncertainty.

Second, a very relevant type of uncertainty in loss of earnings cases is how a victim's life *would have* developed but for the harmful event. Consider, for instance, the question whether an injured child would have had a successful, high-earning career or would have become unemployed with barely an income if they had not been harmed. This is a case of *counterfactual (modal) uncertainty*, where a court will have to investigate what the editors of the present book call 'inherently speculative, hypothetical alternative histories'[19] rather than the present or future facts about the actual world. Such an inquiry comes with different difficulties and methodological baggage from an inquiry into present or future facts.[20] Lapse of time does not necessarily help in resolving counterfactual uncertainties. (It can at best provide a better general understanding of natural rules, psychological patterns, or the individuals involved in a case.[21])

Third, aside a court's knowledge of actual or counterfactual developments, there may still be *normative (legal) uncertainty* over whether a detriment should be recognised as a loss in tort.[22] Debates over non-pecuniary loss demonstrate this well, but questions of this kind occasionally also arise for pecuniary losses, because the general rule that loss is a (factual) difference in assets does not always give satisfactory answers. For instance, does voluntary nursing provided to a victim by a family member represent a loss, although they did not lose any paid income?[23] This type of uncertainty is resolved through legal discourse rather than evidence. It should be distinguished from the others but will not be the focus of this chapter.

Finally, since this paper is primarily interested in predictive and counterfactual uncertainties, its subject seems to differ from the *ex post uncertainties* that

---

19 Bell/McCunn, n. 6, 2.1.3.

20 On knowledge about modal facts in general, see e.g. A. Mallozzi et al., 'The Epistemology of Modality' in E.N. Zalta (ed.), *The Stanford Encyclopedia of Philosophy* (Summer 2023 edition), https://plato.stanford.edu/entries/modality-epistemology/ (last accessed 10.2024).

21 It is only slightly too strong if authors write that assessments under this kind of uncertainty 'obviously cannot be verified or falsified by subsequent events' (Cane/Goudkamp, n. 16, 118).

22 For theories of normatively relevant loss, see e.g. V. Tadros, 'What Might Have Been' in J. Oberdiek (ed.), *Philosophical Foundations of the Law of Torts*, OUP 2014, 171; H. Stoll, *Haftungsfolgen im Bürgerlichen Recht*, C.F. Müller 1993, 236–80.

23 It does in England under *Lowe v Guise* [2002] QB 1369; see text to n. 84.

are the focus of other chapters.[24] But on closer inspection it turns out to be a borderline case. Relevance will attach throughout this paper to the fact that, if loss is understood not as a change in assets ('loss of earnings'), but a reduction in *earning capacity* ('loss of earning capacity'), the problem of predictive and counterfactual uncertainties appears greatly reduced. While loss of earnings will only manifest in the future, this view treats a loss from the same tort as something certain lying in the past. It also tends to produce normative uncertainty over how a loss in earning capacity should be measured. This shows how a shift in normative perception is sometimes linked to a shift in the relevant type of uncertainty.

7.3 Solutions and policy goals

7.3.1 English law

7.3.1.1 Overview

As a roadmap for what follows, it is useful to first sketch the rules dealing with predictive and counterfactual uncertainty in personal injury awards in English law. There are two kinds to consider: those relating to how damages are *awarded* and those relating to how losses are *assessed*.

First, the award itself:

1. *Lump sum over periodical payment.* The standard approach of English courts is to award a one-time sum. Periodical payment orders are an exception.
2. *Rigid awards over flexibility.* Generally, damages for future losses are awarded on a once-and-for-all basis. Only if uncertainty proves very high can the once-and-for-all approach be abandoned in favour of provisional awards or a reservation for the revision of periodical payments.

Second, assessment of damages:

1. *General shift to probabilistic approach.* Ordinarily, damages are awarded for a particular loss. However, as far as compensation for future lost earnings is concerned, it is accepted that such loss would be impossible to prove with sufficient certainty. The courts therefore generally rely on a probabilistic assessment, resulting in compensation based on the mean expected loss.
2. *Shifts away from mathematical precision.* As far as possible, the probabilities relevant to the claimant's loss will be assessed by way of induction from statistics, as would be appropriate for actuarial assessment. However, if the evidential basis is too weak, courts increasingly rely on less formal,

24 Bell/McCunn, n. 6, 2.1.3.

general experience and, ultimately, adopt an 'impressionistic' approach to determining an appropriate amount.

3. *Exceptional shift to denial.* In (only) some limited situations, evidence is so weak that any award seems too arbitrary. For some scenarios where this is frequently the case, a legal rule exists to bar claims for damages for those losses entirely. An example of this is where children are denied damages for 'lost years'.

This taxonomy does not mean to deny that there is an important interplay between assessment and award. For instance, the award of a once-and-for-all sum prevalent in English law means that the courts face a high degree of predictive uncertainty, which is not the case where awards are flexible. This is also why this chapter foregrounds those rules.

7.3.1.2 Rules regarding the award

7.3.1.2.1 BASIC RULE: RIGID LUMP SUM

It is still the basic rule of English law to award damages for future lost earnings by way of a once-and-for-all assessment and in the form of a lump sum.[25] Since heads of damages for personal injury are united in one cause of action,[26] the claimant has to file the claim in order to avoid limitation, and it is problematic to wait until the extent of their disability becomes clear. The challenges this approach produces in assessing uncertain losses will be discussed below with assessment.

The justification provided for this position is that finality in litigation is desirable: the rule avoids the possibility of disputes carrying on indefinitely and thereby putting pressure on both courts and litigants.[27]

7.3.1.2.2 SHIFT TO FLEXIBILITY AND PERIODICAL PAYMENTS

As noted already, there are now exceptions to the once-and-for-all rule.

Very occasionally, it may be possible to postpone the assessment itself. The appellate courts have a discretionary power to extend the time in which permission to appeal may be sought, and this mechanism may be used to vary a damages award if the claimant's position changes soon after the original trial.[28] Even more extensively, in *Cook v Cook*,[29] Eady J ordered that assess-

---

25 See *Lim Poh Choo v Camden & Islington Area Health Authority* [1980] AC 174, 182–83 (Lord Scarman).
26 See Edelman, n. 5, no. 11–024.
27 See e.g. Cane/Goudkamp, n. 16, 118.
28 See e.g. ibid., 123, citing CPR 52.12; *Murphy v Stone-wallwork (Charlton)* [1969] 1 WLR 1023; *Mitchell v Mulholland* [1971] AC 666 (care costs).
29 [2011] EWHC 1683 (QB). See also *A v National Blood Authority* [2002] Lloyd's Rep. Med. 487.

ment of damages for a ten-year-old's brain injury be halted until solid evidence was available on the basis of Civil Procedure Rule 3.1.(2), though he admitted that this was 'a very exceptional course to take'. The ruling thus remains controversial.[30]

By sec. 32A, Senior Courts Act 1981, where the claimant has suffered injuries giving rise to a chance that, at some time in the future and as a result of the tort, the claimant will develop a serious disease or suffer a serious deterioration of their condition, the court can make a *provisional award*. Here the court makes an award on the basis that the deterioration will not occur, but the door is left open for the claimant to apply, once only,[31] for further damages if it does. This mechanism creates the possibility of an *increase* in the award, not a decrease. This claimant-friendly rule is grounded in the idea that, if it were possible to reduce the damages, this might hinder the claimant's recovery.[32] It would also be difficult, in practical terms, to secure repayment of a lump sum that has been invested.[33]

Since an application for further damages is not open to all claimants, but instead conditional on the court having declared the award 'provisional', this mechanism provides an avenue to redress future deterioration only where *its risk is known at the time the award is made*. General uncertainty does not suffice, it has to be specific. This option will also not apply to instances of gradual deterioration, because it has been interpreted as capturing significant changes only: in *Willson v Ministry of Defence*,[34] it was held that an award of provisional damages was available in cases where there was a risk of a 'clear and severable' medical event in the future, not in cases involving continuing deterioration of a condition, like the arthritis developing in that case. Uncertainties as to how a condition would generally develop were said to be sufficiently accounted for in the making of the lump-sum award.

More recently, the Courts Act 2003 and Damages (Variation of Periodical Payments) Order 2005 have made it possible for courts to award *periodical payments* for future pecuniary losses. The courts may make such an award even without the consent of the parties, although their wishes are one factor to be considered.[35] Indeed, courts are now required to consider whether to make such an order with respect to future economic loss flowing from personal injury.

A periodical payment order does not require the court to calculate a lump sum. Instead, the court arrives at an amount to be paid each year and the

---

30 See Edelman, n. 5, no. 52–058, with criticism.
31 See CPR 41.3.
32 Cane/Goudkamp, n. 16, 124.
33 Ibid.
34 [1991] 1 All ER 638.
35 See secs. 100–101, Courts Act 2003 and attendant 41B PD; see also Edelman, n. 5, nos. 52–036-038; Lewis, n. 13.

defendant is left to work out how to meet this obligation.[36] Before making a periodical payment order (PPO), the court must be satisfied that the defendant is likely to meet the payments required—that the stream is secure.

Perhaps the most significant development[37] is that these periodical payments might also be varied if the claimant's circumstances change.[38] However, PPOs are not quite the flexible instruments they might, at first, appear to be: the general rule is that they are *not flexible* unless the court orders otherwise. In some respects, PPOs may therefore remain as insensitive to unknown future developments as lump-sum awards.

In one respect, however, PPOs are always more flexible than a lump sum. Under the Damages Act 1996, they are generally indexed. The default reference is the retail price index,[39] but for loss of earnings, the courts usually make use of their powers to order otherwise and refer to the Annual Survey of Hours and Earning (ASHE), which better reflects the development of earnings in the claimant's field.[40] The indexation represents a clear improvement in accuracy over the discount approach for lump sums.

Moreover, the court may order an increase or decrease for specified events, like changes in the claimant's care costs, educational circumstances, or expected dates of promotion.[41] The court may also order further variations under the Damages (Variations of Payment) Order 2005 if the claimant might, in future, either develop 'some serious disease or suffer some serious deterioration' or 'enjoy some significant improvement in his physical or mental condition'.[42] Unlike with provisional awards, the flexibility rules for PPOs also apply to *reduce* the amount payable where there is an *improvement* in conditions.

However, an order for variable periodical payments still cannot be tailored to account for each and every uncertainty. As with provisional awards, whether variation is necessary is determined at the time of trial and there needs to be some specified risk. Precise dates for changes must be specified in the original order.[43] Thus, even PPOs cannot simply leave the door open for all unforeseen changes. Moreover, changes can only be made to the amount payable to reflect the claimant's condition; the rules do not extend to cover changes in, for example, a general increase in costs of medical care on the market.[44]

---

36 Lewis, n. 13, 428; Cane/Goudkamp, n. 16, 129–30.

37 See Lewis, n. 13, 419 and sources there cited.

38 Sec. 2B, Damages Act 1996; Damages (Variation of Periodical Payments) Order 2005, SI 2005/841.

39 Secs, 2(8), 2(9).

40 *Actuarial Tables with Explanatory Notes for Use in Personal Injury and Fatal Accident Cases*, 8th ed., Government Actuary's Department 2020, [167]–[172]; Edelman, n. 5, nos. 40–021-026.

41 41B PD 2.2.

42 See art. 2, Damages (Variation of Periodical Payments) Order 2005.

43 Lewis, n. 13, 428.

44 See Edelman, n. 5, no. 40–033.

The resulting position is that, while compensation by variable periodical payment is possible, the circumstances in which a variation to the payment might take place are limited. This and certain procedural weaknesses have resulted in a relatively limited use of PPOs, and lost earnings awards are over-whelmingly made as lump sums.[45]

7.3.1.3 Assessment of losses

7.3.1.3.1 GENERAL SHIFT TO PROBABILISTIC APPROACH

Ordinarily, evidence is expected to prove a specific loss. Of course, the compensation of a specific loss still depends on probability in the sense that, for it to be proven, it must be more likely than not, but the consequence is that the court treats the full loss as the relevant fact and awards its full sum.

By contrast, this approach would often be fruitless with losses dependent on the future and on counterfactuals, for their precise extent is unknowable and even to prove a preponderance of probabilities for a specific sum impossible. Therefore, the standard requires modification. In *Mallet v McMonagle*,[46] Lord Diplock observed:

> The role of the court in making an assessment of damages which depends upon its view as to *what will be* and *what would have been* is to be contrasted with its ordinary function in civil actions for determining *what was*. In determining what did happen in the past the court decides on the balance of probabilities ... But in assessing damages which depend upon its view as to what will happen in the future or what would have happened in the future if something had not happened in the past, the court must make an estimate as to what are the chances that the particular thing will or would have happened and reflect those chances, whether they are more or less than even, in the amount of damages which it awards.[47]

Lord Diplock refers to a replacement of an all-or-nothing decision based on ordinary evidentiary standards with a probabilistic assessment resulting in proportional awards where the extent of loss depends on predictive knowledge or knowledge on counterfactuals. For instance, in *Langford v Hebran*,[48] the claimant recovered for the 20% possibility that he would have become a kickboxing champion. Functionally, if not conceptually, this means that tort law

---

45 Cane/Goudkamp, n. 16, 130.
46 [1970] AC 166.
47 Ibid., 176 (emphasis added). See also *Davies v Taylor* [1974] AC 207, 213 (Lord Reid) and, further, Edelman, n. 5, nos. 10–044-046.
48 [2001] EWCA Civ. 361.

compensates the loss of a chance once the claimant successfully proves the basic elements of a tort.[49]

The tendency of English law to award damages by way of a lump sum rather than postponing the award makes this probabilistic approach a complex enterprise. At the end of a trial, a court is required both to make a final prediction as to how the claimant's future health will develop, how much money they will be able to earn, and how much the claimant would have earned if not for the injury suffered. In *Gourley*, Lord Reid described the severity of the problem:[50]

> If [a claimant] had not been injured he would have had the prospect of earning a continuing income, it may be, for many years, *but there can be no certainty as to what would have happened. In many cases the amount of that income may be doubtful even if he had remained in good health, and there is always the possibility that he might have died or suffered from some incapacity at any time.* The loss which he has suffered between the date of the accident and the date of the trial may be certain, but his prospective loss is not. Yet damages must be assessed as a lump sum once and for all, not only in respect of loss accrued ... but also in respect of prospective loss. *Such damages can only be an estimate, often a very rough estimate, of the present value of his prospective loss.*

Damages for future economic losses are typically determined using the 'multiplier' method. This approach is used for calculating all future economic losses, including earnings and expenses. This involves multiplying the claimant's net annual loss by the number of years this loss will be suffered.[51] Calculation must therefore commence by determining the relevant *multiplicand*—the net annual loss.

The court decides what the claimant's annual income might have been, but for the injury, taking into account matters such as the claimant's prospects of promotion. The court has to determine the chance, as a percentage, that the claimant would have been promoted, calculate a new multiplicand for this period, and then discount it to reflect the fact that it was not a certainty.[52] The court then deducts from this 'no-tort annual income' sums representing what would have been the claimant's necessary expenditure, including income tax and pension scheme contributions.[53] The courts do not, however, speculate

---

49 On the loss of a chance doctrine and its relation to *Mallet v McMonagle*, see S. Steel, 'Rationalising Loss of a Chance in Tort' in S.G.A. Pitel et al. (eds), *Tort Law: Challenging Orthodoxy*, Hart 2013, especially 243–46.

50 [1955] AC 185, 212 (emphasis added). See also *Lim Poh Choo v Camden & Islington Area Health Authority* [1980] AC 174, 182–83 (Lord Scarman).

51 For a useful overview of this process, see A. Burrows, 'Damages' in M.A. Jones (ed.), *Clerk & Lindsell on Torts*, 23rd ed., Sweet & Maxwell 2023, nos. 27–29-30.

52 See Markesinis et al., n. 6, 125.

53 *British Transport Commission v Gourley* [1956] AC 185; Burrows, n. 51, no. 27-28.

as to future taxation rates, but use the rate that is applicable at the time of calculation. If the claimant can still work in some capacity, any income they are likely to receive in the future must also be deducted.[54] If there is a risk of further complication in the future—for example, epilepsy in brain injury cases—the court will calculate a sum to compensate the claimant if the risk does materialise, but awards a percentage of this sum to reflect the risk.[55]

Even in modern times, female claimants are more likely to take breaks in their career to raise children. This is something on which the court might hear evidence. Another, more significant, challenge arises where the claimant is a child with no career yet at all. The court will hear evidence as to the child's educational record and any career aspirations.[56] If the claimant is a very young child, the court may find such a process altogether too speculative and, instead, use national average earnings and the employment undertaken by the claimant's family to determine the relevant multiplicand.[57] For example, in *Croke v Wiseman*,[58] Griffiths LJ noted that:

> The [trial] judge assessed the future loss of earnings at £5000 per annum. He arrived at this figure by taking the national average wage for a young man. In my view, he was justified in doing so. This child came from an excellent home, the father is an enterprising man starting his own business and the mother is a qualified teacher; they have shown the quality of their characters by the care they have given their child.[59]

Once determined, the court multiplies the loss per annum (multiplicand) with a figure which represents the number of years for which the loss will be suffered (*multiplier*). The court will need to determine: 1) the claimant's post-tort life expectancy, and 2) how long the claimant would have lived but for the tort.[60] The courts use a set of actuarial tables, known as the Ogden Tables, which furnish an applicable multiplier based on the claimant's circumstances.[61] The court is also able to consider evidence about matters such as, for example, the particular retirement policies of a specific employer.[62]

The multiplier is likely to be less than the number of years for which the loss is said to be suffered. This is for several reasons. The court will reduce the figure to account for 'general vicissitudes'—things that may have happened

---

54 See e.g. *Billingham v Hughes* [1949] 1 KB 634.
55 Cane/Goudkamp, n. 16, 119.
56 Markesinis et al., n. 6, 125.
57 Ibid., 126; see also *Croke v Wiseman* [1982] 1 WLR 71.
58 Ibid.
59 Ibid., 83.
60 *Pickett v British Rail Engineering* [1980] AC 136.
61 *Actuarial Tables with Explanatory Notes for Use in Personal Injury and Fatal Accident Cases*, 8th ed., Government Actuary's Department 2020.
62 Markesinis et al., n. 6, 124.

to the claimant anyway, like sickness or redundancy. Unless the claimant is working in a particularly hazardous occupation, such reductions are likely to be small.[63] Low multipliers are used for young children to account for the fact that there is too much uncertainty—they might never have become wage earners at all.[64]

Another reason for reducing the multiplier is that income flows from investment of the lump sum, and the sum is intended to be exhausted at the end of the claimant's life.[65] The leading case is *Wells v Wells*,[66] where the House of Lords held that the discount rate should reflect the rate of return on index-linked government stocks (ILGS)—at the time, this was 3%. The main reason for this preference[67] is that injured claimants are not in the same position as ordinary investors; they must rely on the income for their everyday needs and cannot 'wait out' periods of market decline.[68] However, calculation of the discount rate through the ILGS rate has been replaced by the Lord Chancellor exercising powers to fix the rate under the Damages Act 1996.[69] From 2001, the prescribed discount was reduced from 4–5%[70] to 2.5%; in 2017 it was reduced to negative 0.75%; and in 2019 it became negative 0.25%.[71] The latter increase marked a move away from the assumption that claimants will invest in very low-risk instruments, as successful claimants frequently receive financial advice and invest in 'diversified portfolios' resulting in higher returns.[72] The courts are obliged to use the rate thus set, though may, in exceptional circumstances, depart from it.[73]

7.3.1.3.2 SHIFTS AWAY FROM MATHEMATICAL PRECISION

A general question is the extent to which the multiplier method means relying on an actuarial approach. Any prediction of the claimant's circumstances requires some degree of individual assessment, and the courts acknowledge

---

63 See e.g. *Herring v Ministry of Defence* [2003] EWCA Civ. 528.
64 *Croke v Wiseman* [1982] 1 WLR 71, 83 (Griffiths LJ).
65 Markesinis et al., n. 6, 120.
66 [1999] 1 AC 345.
67 For a useful discussion of further arguments regarding the suitable rate, see Burrows, n. 51, no. 27-32.
68 See e.g. *Wells v Wells* [1999] 1 AC 345, 367 (Lord Lloyd).
69 See sec. 1, Damages Act 1996.
70 This had been the prior figure, though in *Wells v Wells* [1999] 1 AC 345 the House of Lords used 3%.
71 See Damages (Personal Injury) Order 2017, SI 2017/206; Damages (Personal Injury) Order 2019, SI 2019/1126.
72 Ministry of Justice, *The Personal Injury Discount Rate: How It Should Be Set in Future*, Cmnd 9500, HMSO 2017.
73 *Warriner v Warriner* [2002] 1 WLR 1703.

this.[74] However, ordinary uncertainties in assessing loss of earnings are no reason for English courts to abandon general reliance on the multiplier approach, and therefore the aim of mathematical precision for significant parts of the award. Per Lord Scarman:

> Though arithmetical precision is not always possible, though in estimating future pecuniary loss a judge must make certain assumptions (based on the evidence) and certain adjustment, he is seeking to estimate a financial compensation for a financial loss.[75]

In assessing the probabilities where no actuarial information is available, the courts must depend on expert opinion. For instance, the court relied in *Langford v Hebran*[76] on the testimony of a forensic accountant who modelled four possible career paths in amateur boxing, and in *Clarke v Maltby*[77] on a legal recruitment consultant assessing the claimant's career prospects as a solicitor.

The judge's experience also plays a role. In *Langford* the Court of Appeal found an arithmetical error in the trial judge's calculation, but declined to interfere, because of the trial judge's 'indefinable yet vital "feel" for the case'. Under some scenarios, however, the weakness of available evidence is so manifest that the courts, instead of trying to engage in multiplier-multiplicand calculation, openly prefer what the relevant author in *Clerk & Lindsell* calls an 'educated impressionistic guess',[78] and do not use any formalised multiplication.

The prime example is a young child claimant who has therefore never earned anything. In such cases, courts have preferred to avoid any attempt at the conventional approach.[79] Yet, the 'impressionistic' approach to damages has also been used in cases not involving child claimants. In *Blamire v South Cumbria Health Authority*,[80] there was nothing particularly unusual about the claimant's situation. However, the trial judge considered that there was too much uncertainty as to 1) what the claimant would have earned during her life, and 2) her future pattern of earnings, for the multiplier-multiplicand approach to be used. The claimant had been 22 and working as a nurse when

---

74 See e.g. R. Lewis et al., 'Court Awards of Damages for Loss of Future Earnings: An Empirical Study and an Alternative Method of Calculation' (2002) 29 *Journal of Law and Society* 406, 410, citing Lord Oliver in *Hodgson v Trapp* [1989] 1 AC 833: 'average life expectancy can be actuarially ascertained, but to assess the probability of future political, economic and fiscal policies requires not the services of an actuary or an accountant but those of a prophet'.
75 *Pickett v British Rail Engineering* [1980] AC 136, 168.
76 [2001] EWCA Civ. 361.
77 [2010] EWHC 1201 (QB).
78 Burrows, n. 51, no. 27-37.
79 See e.g. *Joyce v Yeomans* [1981] 1 WLR 549.
80 [1993] PIQR Q1.

she was involved in a lifting accident at work. She thereby permanently injured her back. Over the next five years she worked on and off due to flare-ups in her condition, moved to part-time employment, and changed jobs several times. She also took time out to have children. On appeal, the defendant argued that the judge should have started with the multiplicand-multiplier approach to assessment. The Court of Appeal held that the judge had been entitled to take the view that the conventional mode of assessment was inappropriate and adopt a different approach. Balcombe LJ agreed that there were 'far too many imponderables here for the judge to have been bound to take the conventional approach'. Since *Blamire*, awards of this kind have been made in a variety of situations.[81]

For certain heads of loss requiring a separate award, like a claimant's disadvantage in the employment market, where assessment is altogether too speculative, courts similarly occasionally award a sum thought to best represent the loss suffered. This is true for what are known as '*Smith v Manchester*' awards, made where a claimant is able to remain in their current employment but would be disadvantaged in the employment market if they were to lose it.[82] Without using the multiplicand-multiplier approach, the court assesses how long the claimant will likely be out of work before finding new employment and awards net earnings for that period.[83] Similarly, where a victim's relatives provide voluntary care to them as a consequence of the tort, the courts do not attempt to calculate the statistical chances that the relative would have had another income in the period help is likely to be given. Instead, they award the market value of the relevant services.[84]

Both 'impressionistic' awards and references to market value can seem like a flashback to the approach of 'fair compensation' awarded by a jury, noted above. Just as for the historical discretion in jury awards, there are at least two possible justifications for 'impressionistic' awards. They may simply be an answer to particularly problematic uncertainties where no other means are available, but might also be understood as a different approach to what the relevant loss is. Some speak of '*loss of earning capacity*' rather than loss of earnings,[85] the former being the capacity to work as such, the latter being the loss of what the claimant would have earned.

---

81 See e.g. *Ward v Allies and Morrison Architects* [2012] EWCA Civ. 1287; *Irani v Duchon* [2019] EWCA Civ. 1846.

82 See *Smith v Manchester Corporation* (1974) 17 KIR 1.

83 Markesinis et al., n. 6, 126.

84 *Lowe v Guise* [2002] QB 1369.

85 See e.g. D. Réaume, 'Rethinking Personal Injury Damages: Compensation for Lost Capacities' (1988) 67 *Canadian Bar Review* 82 (arguing for a difference); Burrows, n. 51, no. 27-37 (arguing nothing depends on the concept). Compare also other jurisdictions, below 7.3.2.3.2.

7.3.1.3.3 EXCEPTIONAL SHIFT TO DENIAL

Generally, it is the task of the trial judge to assess whether, under the probabilistic approach of *Mallet*, there is sufficient evidence to arrive at a reasonable sum at all. However, there are also certain situations in which the courts have opted for a *general rule* that no compensation should be awarded where calculation is deemed too speculative. A clear example is the 'lost years' for child claimants.

Lost year awards are made if an injury has reduced the claimant's life expectancy. *Pickett v British Rail Engineering*[86] clarified that a claimant may receive compensation for the income that they would have earned during the years now lost because of the tort. Living expenses are deducted from this sum.[87] Though justified, in theory, by the idea that the claimant must be compensated in full, in reality this type of award is given for the benefit of the claimant's dependants.[88]

Such a claim for 'lost years' cannot be made where the claimant is a seriously injured child. In *Croke v Wiseman*,[89] the Court of Appeal explained this position's basis in policy; as compensation for 'lost years' was intended to benefit the claimant's dependants, the exercise was too speculative for a child who would never have dependants:

> In attempting to assess the value of a claim for the lost years, the court is faced with a peculiar difficulty. Not only does it have to assess what sum the plaintiff might have been earning, but it also has to make an assessment of the sum that would not have been spent upon the plaintiff's own living expenses and would have, therefore, been available to spend upon his dependants. In the case of a living plaintiff of mature years ... there are compelling social reasons for awarding a sum of money that he knows will be available for the support of his dependants after his death ... In the case of a child, however, there are no dependants ... and, if the injuries are catastrophic, equally there will never be any dependants ... *In such circumstances, it seems to me entirely right that the court should refuse to speculate as to whether in the future there might have been dependants for the purpose of providing a fund of money for persons who will in fact never exist.*[90]

---

86 [1980] AC 136.

87 *Harris v Empress Motors* [1984] 1 WLR 212.

88 See e.g. Cane/Goudkamp, n. 16, 136. This also means that a claim by an estate under the Law Reform (Miscellaneous Provisions) Act 1934 will not include damages for 'lost years'—dependants have a claim for support under the Fatal Accidents Act 1976.

89 [1982] 1 WLR 71.

90 Ibid., 82 (Griffiths LJ) (emphasis added).

Where such rules exist, the court does not engage with the predictive and counter-factual uncertainties of the case directly; instead, these become the *rationale of a rule* that prevents a damages award altogether. Such rules raise the question why precluding an individual assessment of evidence by the trial judge is preferable to relying on the courts' discretion over the sufficiency of a claimant's evidence as to loss. Why should a claimant be denied compensation where, in a perhaps exceptional case, they do reach a sufficient standard? It is thus unsurprising that courts forced to apply *Croke* have repeatedly criticised it.[91] In *Iqbal v Whipps Cross University Hospital NHS Trust*,[92] the court followed *Croke* but suggested that it was inconsistent with *Pickett* and the aim of providing full compensation to the claimant. For Gage LJ, it was difficult to accept that it is possible to assess prospective loss of earnings for a young child, but impossible, as too speculative, to assess damages for the 'lost years'.[93] Similarly, in *Totham v King's College Hospital*, Laing J explained that she found the rule to be inconsistent with the principle of full compensation.[94]

Nonetheless, it is clear that there are currently rules that exclude damages for certain heads of losses categorically, fully or in part because of predictive and counterfactual uncertainty.

7.3.2 German and Austrian law

7.3.2.1 Background

This section will generally focus on the German legal system and add remarks on interesting features of the Austrian legal approach.

This will first require some background information for these jurisdictions. Germany and Austria have civilian legal systems and most rules of private law are set down in their civil codes, the BGB and ABGB respectively. However, comparatists' routine warnings against overestimating this difference from common law systems[95] are well justified in the present context, because the German rules governing personal injury are to a considerable extent judge-made; partly because relevant legislative provisions leave much room for

---

91 E.g. *Iqbal v Whipps Cross University Hospital NHS Trust* [2007] EWCA Civ. 1190 at [46]; *Totham v King's College Hospital NHS Foundation Trust* [2015] EWHC 97 (QB) at [46].
92 [2007] EWCA Civ. 1190.
93 Ibid., [46].
94 *Totham v King's College Hospital NHS Foundation Trust* [2015] EWHC 97 (QB) at [47].
95 See generally S. Vogenauer, 'Sources of Law and Legal Method in Comparative Law' in M. Reimann and R. Zimmermann (eds), *Oxford Handbook of Comparative Law*, 2nd ed., OUP 2019, 896–99.

interpretation,[96] partly because courts regard themselves as primarily bound to the values of the system as a whole rather than the letter of the law.[97]

As in England, a fundamental principle guiding application of the law is the principle of full compensation. Friedrich Mommsen is famous for spearheading the idea that this means *undoing a change in assets* when he defined an interest—by which he meant compensable loss—as:

> the difference between the value of the estate of a person, as it is at a certain point in time, and the value which this estate would have without the intervention of a particular damaging event at the time in question.[98]

But there has always been a minority critical of this basic rule,[99] and we will see that Austrian law places less emphasis on Mommsen's principle.

Two major differences between German and English tort litigation should be mentioned. One is the stronger presence of the social security system.[100] With regard to lost earnings, victims with diminished earning capacity are generally eligible for annuities based on their earnings or a minimal rate, the only conditions for a claim being sufficient time within, and contributions to, the system,[101] in which most people are insured. Where it applies, it not only mitigates victims' needs, but—to this extent like in England[102]—it is also the social security institution that primarily interacts with the tortfeasor or their liability insurer, because it takes over the victim's tort actions to the extent social security has provided compensation.[103] This lessens the pressure on the courts to address uncertainties, though they must still do so where social security institutions do not provide compensation or litigate a recourse claim.

A second, much-debated difference between English and Germanic law relevant to personal injury is the different standard of proof in civil litigation. While a *preponderance of probabilities* is generally sufficient for proof in English civil procedure, Germanic law requires the court to be *convinced* of the facts that are the basis of its decisions (§286, German Civil Procedure Ordinance, *Zivilprozessordnung*, German ZPO; §272, Austrian ZPO). This

---

96 See e.g. B. Markesinis et al., *Markesinis's German Law of Torts*, 5th ed., Hart 2019, 193, 196–97.
97 Defining the limits of statutory interpretation is a central problem of continental legal methodology (*Methodenlehre*). See e.g. F. Bydlinski, *Juristische Methodenlehre und Rechtsbegriff*, 2nd ed., Springer 1991, 553–71.
98 F. Mommsen, *Zur Lehre von dem Interesse*, Schwetschke 1855, 3 (my translation).
99 For a critical discussion, see e.g. N. Jansen, *Die Struktur des Haftungsrechts*, Mohr Siebeck 2003, 509–12; Stoll, n. 22, 147–81.
100 J. Fedtke, 'The Culture of German Tort Law' (2012) 3 *JETL* 201.
101 VII §43, Social Security Code (*Sozialgesetzbuch*) (generally, the applicant must have been with the scheme for five years, with contributions in three of those).
102 On the interactions in England, see e.g. R. Lewis, 'England and Wales' in U. Magnus (ed.), *The Impact of Social Security Law on Tort Law*, Springer 2003, 56–73.
103 See X §116, Social Security Code; Markesinis et al., n. 96, 193.

standard is notoriously difficult to translate into chances, but it is likely at least a rather high probability.[104] The standard represents a comparatively uncertainty-averse approach of Germanic law more generally.

7.3.2.2 *Rules regarding the award*

7.3.2.2.1 BASIC RULE: FLEXIBLE PERIODICAL PAYMENT

There is a significant difference between the German and English basic approaches to awards for lost earnings: the basic German rule is to award a flexible periodical payment rather than a once-and-for-all sum. The central source for this approach lies in the BGB:

§843 Annuity in money or lump sum settlement

(1) If, in consequence of an injury to body or health, the earning capacity of the injured person is eliminated or diminished or an increase of his necessities arises, compensation must be made to the injured party by the payment of a money annuity …

(3) Instead of an annuity the victim may demand a lump sum settlement, if a serious reason exists for it.[105]

The rule provides the opposite of the English approach: the annuity is standard; lump sums an exception. Moreover, the exception is not the court's alone to make; rather the *victim must request* a lump-sum payment based on a *serious reason*.

In practice, most personal injury cases are nonetheless apparently resolved by lump-sum compensation.[106] Yet this statement is only true because it counts awards by alternative dispute resolution, in particular by institutional players (social insurance institutions and liability insurers). In court decisions, lump-sum awards under §843 (3), BGB remain an exception. Initiatives to change

---

104 See e.g. H-W. Laumen in G. Baumgärtel et al. (eds), *Handbuch der Beweislast*, vol. I, 5th ed., Heymanns 2023, no. 5/8-12. This paper generally assumes a genuine difference, though this is very controversial: see Bell/McCunn, n. 6, 1.2.3.1.

105 Translation in Markesinis et al., n. 96, 214. In Austria, §14, Railway and Motor Vehicle Liability Act 1959 (*Eisenbahn- und Kraftfahrzeughaftpflichtgesetz*, hereafter EKHG) introduces a very similar rule, which the courts (exemplifying the approach introduced above) apply by analogy to all personal injuries.

106 Some authors cite a figure of 90%; see e.g. H. Lang, 'Chancen und Risiken beim Abfindungsvergleich/der Kapitalisierung von Ansprüchen' in Deutscher Verkehrsgerichtstag (ed.), *57. Deutscher Verkehrsgerichtstag 2019*, https://www.deutscher-verkehrsgerichtstag.de/images/pdf/57_Dokumentation_VGT_2019.pdf, 139.

this, in particular through expanding the claimant's right to claim a lump sum, have not yet found enough support.[107]

Apart from this starting point, German annuity awards also differ from periodical payment as exceptionally awarded under English law in an important respect. They may *always be varied* in both directions where circumstances change significantly; the affected party will bring an action for amendment (*Abänderungsklage*; §323, ZPO).[108] In a remarkable contrast to the English approach, developments that allow for such an action only include those *not considered* at the time of the first judgment.[109] An amendment may thus not only reflect an exceptionally bad recovery or deteriorating condition,[110] but also unexpected developments in living costs or higher salaries.[111]

A German preference for variability is also evident in the fact that, even where the claimant cannot prove any loss at a given time, they may always wait for new developments. It follows from the general civil procedure rules that, even where a claim in damages is dismissed because no damage could (yet) be proven, the claimant may reopen a trial if they base the claim on new facts, or evidence that did not previously exist, such as a deterioration in their health. In the meantime, if the claimant has a legitimate interest in ascertaining responsibility for future harm, they may also file a declaratory action (*Feststellungsklage*; §257, ZPO) to prepare the basis for a later follow-up claim in damages. Claimants may also use this device where sufficient evidence for damages would already be available, but the parties prefer a basis for settlement.[112]

7.3.2.2.2 SHIFT TO A LUMP SUM AND RIGIDITY

Where courts award lump sums, they take an approach similar to English courts, and base it on the available evidence regarding further developments and a discount rate based on a prognosis of future interest rates, vicissitudes of life, tax differences, etc.[113] Moreover, a lump-sum payment is *never variable*. Thus, a lump sum and rigidity only arise in combination, and there is no basis

---

107 See generally F. Pardey, 'Personenschäden' in K. Haag (ed.), *Geigel: Der Haftpflichtprozess*, 24th ed., Beck 2024, 233; for a recent plea to change the law see C. Huber, 'Kapital oder Rente—Erfordernis eines gesetzlichen Abfindungsanspruchs' in Deutscher Verkehrsgerichtstag (ed.), *57. Deutscher Verkehrsgerichtstag 2019*, https://www.deutscher-verkehrsgerichtstag.de/images/pdf/57_Dokumentation_VGT_2019.pdf, 116–20.

108 The same rule applies in Austria based on general procedural principles. See E. Sole and W. Veith, 'Aspekte der Schadensrente' in C. Huber et al., *Festschrift für Karl-Heinz Danzl*, Manz 2017, 203, 215.

109 *MünchKomm⁹/Wagner, §843 no. 52.

110 BGH, 09.07.1968, *Versicherungsrecht* (hereafter *VersR*) 1968, 1066.

111 BGH, 20.12.1960, *NJW* 1961, 871; BGH, 08.01.1981, *NJW* 1981, 818.

112 *MünchKomm⁹/Wagner, §843 no. 40.

113 The current recomendation is 3 to 4%, depending on how far into the future harm is expected to reach (Pardey, n. 107, nos. 239–41).

for provisional awards as known to English law. The courts and commentators compare the lump-sum award to a settlement and assume that one of its functions is finality in litigation.[114] In an odd contrast to this strict approach, a lump sum settled upon by the parties *voluntarily* is subject to limited *ex post* judicial review in light of new developments.[115] Although an application of the famous general rule under which contract terms violating good faith are void (§138, BGB), the assessment of good faith takes unequal positions of the parties involved into account, and thus the courts arguably decided this way not least because insurance companies seemed to have a relatively superior capacity of risk-assessment.

Courts have accepted the following justifications for switching to a lump-sum award: establishing a business or trade,[116] the victim's fragile health (which may be impacted by the uncertainty of an annuity),[117] changed needs requiring adaptation of the victim's property (insofar as the annuity does not cover this),[118] and reasons related to the defendant, including the defendant irritating the victim through petty behaviour in managing the annuity.[119] The questionable future solvency or probable evasion of the defendant are other reasons, although the main safeguard here is a security, which the court may require of the defendant (§843 (2), BGB).

Clearly these reasons all concern the disadvantages produced by stretching payment over several years. By contrast, the courts do not accept an interest in finality of litigation as a sufficient justification for the shift to a lump sum by itself. Therefore, absent concurring further grounds for a shift, the claimant can only achieve this aim by a settlement with the defendant.

Austrian 'abstract annuities' for lost earning capacity, discussed below,[120] are an exception where the award becomes rigid but does not take the form of a lump sum. However, a modest amount of flexibility is provided by the fact that, like any periodical payment, the annuity is indexed. Apart from this, it differs from English market value awards (such as *Smith v Manchester* damages) only in the form of payment.

---

114 See e.g. OLG Celle, 30.11.2011, *Neue Zeitschrift für Verkehrsrecht* (hereafter *NZV*) 2012, 547; *MünchKomm⁹*/Wagner, §843 no. 35.
115 The leading case is BGH, 28.02.1961, VI ZR 95/60; *VersR* 1961, 382 (child developing epilepsy).
116 RG, 26.01.1933, *Juristische Wochenschrift* 1933, 840.
117 RG, 23.05.1910, RGZ 73, 418.
118 BGH, 19.05.1981, *VersR* 1982, 238.
119 OLG Cologne, 11.08.2011, *VersR* 2012, 907 (with comment by Jaeger).
120 7.3.2.3.2.

7.3.2.3   *Assessment of losses*

7.3.2.3.1 FREQUENT SHIFT TO PROBABILISTIC APPROACH

Where the courts apply ordinary rules to loss of earnings, the claim's success depends on full proof of not only the existence, but also the precise extent, of the difference in assets, under a standard of proof stricter than under English law.

Somewhat surprisingly, the courts assume that this is possible. An important reason for this is that, as previously discussed, Germanic law awards lost earnings as *flexible periodical payments*, which significantly lowers the predictive uncertainties the court has to address. The rule allows courts to focus on the near future, and they will therefore frequently regard evidence on precise earnings as sufficiently certain where the claimant had a stable income or clear career path. For instance, in a recent case the Austrian Supreme Court regarded it as fully (!) proven that the long-time mayor of a small town would have won re-election absent his injury.[121]

Nonetheless, like English law, Germanic law treats the uncertainties involved in an award of damages as a special case and allows for an easing of the general rules of proof. Under §287 (1), German ZPO and §273 (1), Austrian ZPO, the judge decides on the extent of damages by 'free conviction' after considering all circumstances. They need not take evidence where the judge exercises their discretion (Germany) or where obtaining it would be impossible or disproportionate (Austria).

§287, German ZPO and §273, Austrian ZPO are usually understood as provisions allowing an 'estimation' (*Schätzung*) of damages. Their precise understanding is subject to many overlapping theoretical disputes, for instance on whether (as the German Federal Supreme Court assumes) they introduce a lower standard of proof.[122] These discussions cannot be unravelled in detail here. For present purposes, it is more important to emphasise a functional effect, which is either presupposed or introduced by the provisions: the court may award damages *based on probability* although it cannot (or cannot effectively) obtain evidence on the precise extent of losses. Even though Austrian lawyers speak of 'discretion', it is clear that this award still depends on an assessment of likelihood based on the facts.[123] Thus, for instance, application

---

121 OGH, 28.01.2021, 8 Ob. 98/20z.
122 BGH, 25.04.1972, *NJW* 1972, 1515; more recently e.g. BGH, 29.01.2019, *BGHZ* 221, 43; see further C. Koller, 'Beweisfragen bei kapitalmarktrechtlichen Prozessen in Österreich' (2020) 133 *Zeitschrift für Zivilprozess* (hereafter ZZP) 435–40.
123 See e.g. W. Rechberger in W. Rechberger and H. Fasching (eds), *Zivilprozessgesetze*, 3rd ed., Manz 2017, §273 ZPO no. 11; P. Gottwald, *Schadenszurechnung und Schadensschätzung*, Beck 1979, 214–26.

of this provision can result in a deduction for such things as the chance of unemployment.[124]

To this extent, German civil procedure rules allow for probabilistic assessment not very different from *Mallet v McMonagle*. But note that these rules apply *even to past and present uncertainty* and are therefore not limited to predictive or counterfactual uncertainty. It is, however, necessary that at least the basis of liability (the wrong) has been proven.[125] To what extent this in itself already requires proof of some extent of loss or legal harm is controversial.[126]

Whether the general rules or §286/§273 apply, it is not strictly determined how the relevant probability is found, and thus also whether damages are assessed by actuarial numbers or by way of less formalised considerations. We turn now to the extent of reliance on actuarial data.

7.3.2.3.2 SHIFTS AWAY FROM MATHEMATICAL PRECISION

German courts aim for precision in putting the 'difference principle' into practice. Consequently, courts try to assess what children might have earned based on their previous education, efforts, social situation, and aims. As the BGH emphasised in the case of a 23-year-old who worked on and off, even §287 ZPO does not provide a basis to make an abstract guess on the extent of lost earnings.[127]

To what extent they rely on actuarial data, and how much is inevitably determined by experience, is not rigidly prescribed, however.[128] There are no official tables like the Ogden tables for assessing lost earnings. Only where nothing relevant is known, as when the claimant is a young child, has it been suggested that courts must accept very general statistics on average earnings as their only evidence.[129] Generally, the courts use a combination of actuarial guidance, expert opinions, and individual experience, using their powers under §287, German ZPO to determine what evidence will be most appropriate and effective. A good example is provided by the 2010 case of a German language teacher who, 39 years old when injured, had made preparations to obtain a doctoral degree, while at the same time the employment market for teachers in Hesse had become more uncertain.[130] The BGH ordered the appellate court to reassess the prospects of a person of the claimant's age on the job market, for which, the BGH said, expert opinion would be necessary. But the

---

124 K. Schmidt, 'Beweisführung und Beweiswürdigung' in K. Haag (ed.) *Geigel: Der Haftpflichtprozess*, 24th ed., Beck 2024, 62.
125 BGH, 13.12.1951, BGHZ 4, 192; OGH, 12.07.1950, 1 Ob. 391/50.
126 See H. Koziol, *Österreichisches Haftpflichtrecht*, vol. I, 4th ed., Jan Sramek 2020, D.9 nos. 13–15; Koller, n. 122, 435–37.
127 BGH, 17.01.1995, *NJW* 1995, 1023.
128 See, critically, Gottwald, n. 123, 214–26.
129 H. Lange and G. Schiemann, *Schadensersatz*, 3rd ed., Mohr Siebeck 2003, 315–16.
130 BGH, 09.11.2010, *NJW* 2011, 1145.

case was too unique for meaningful statistics and one can imagine that even the expert would only assess the claimant's loss on the basis of general professional experience.

The Austrian approach presents a contrast to German law, insofar as it allows for reliance on the judge's individual experience alone. First, the courts openly assume that §273 (1), Austrian ZPO does allow for discretion on the basis of the judge's life experience.[131] Second, courts exceptionally award something close to 'impressionistic' damages: an 'abstract annuity' (*abstrakte Rente*). (That this is an *annuity* rather than a lump sum was discussed above.[132])

The courts award such annuities where proof exists of a permanent reduction in the claimant's earning capacity, and future harm of a particular kind is likely, but *no particular harm* that they have suffered or will suffer as a result can be proven.[133] The results are sometimes similar to those of English *Smith v Manchester* awards:[134] claimants who become disabled but do not (immediately) lose their employment receive an award for their disadvantage in the labour market.[135] Sometimes, the awards go beyond this: those working on and off may also receive compensation for the reduction of their capabilities,[136] so results are sometimes similar to *Blamire*. However, the Supreme Court now regards this kind of award as exceptional and is strict regarding the extent of uncertainties acceptable for making such an award. In 2016, it declined to award an abstract annuity to a 16-year-old schoolboy who had taken initial steps to become a technician:[137] the judges held that it was too uncertain whether he would actually have proceeded on this career path. There need to be particular indications that the claimant would have worked in the future; otherwise, they do not receive compensation.

Austrian academics understand the annuity as compensation for the isolated market value of *earning capacity*. The dominant view has the aim of such awards as compensating detriments to *a person's entitlement* to earning capacity as such, rather than their loss of earnings.[138] This thought is itself based on the Austrian version of the continuity thesis (*Rechtsfortwirkungsgedanke*).[139]

---

131 See e.g. OGH, 28.01.1999, 2 Ob. 13/99x.
132 For a history and defence of this approach in Austrian doctrine, with references, see OGH, 12.09.2003, 2 Ob. 143/03y.
133 OGH, 05.06.2002, 2 Ob. 133/02a.
134 See text to nn. 82–83.
135 E.g. OGH, 12.09.2003, 2 Ob. 143/03y.
136 OGH, 29.04.2009 , 2 Ob. 234/08p.
137 OGH, 19.01.2016, 2 Ob. 230/15k.
138 E. Karner, 'Fragen der objektiv-abstrakten Schadensberechnung', in S. Perner et al. (eds), *Festschrift für Attila Fenyves*, Verlag Österreich 2013, 202; H. Koziol, *Österreichisches Haftpflichtrecht*, vol. II, 3rd ed., Jan Sramek 2018, A.5 nos. 75–81.
139 H. Koziol, ibid., A.5 no. 79. The underlying theory was developed by W. Wilburg, 'Zur Lehre von der Vorteilsausgleichung' (1932) 82 *Jherings Jahrbücher für die Dogmatik des bürgerlichen Rechts* 51, 125–48.

The general idea is that entitlements assign a kind of value to persons that may not be reduced to their purely financial value.

An alternative view is familiar from the section on English law. Academics have suggested that case law does not move from assessing a change in assets. Rather, it understands 'abstract annuities' as an educated guess on lost earnings.[140] This would approximate English 'impressionistic' awards and, potentially, mean that these cases are also indistinguishable from the reliance on 'life experience' under §273, Austrian ZPO. That the Supreme Court insists on a 'known unknown'—namely a risk of actual, but unmeasurable lost earnings—as a condition for awarding an abstract annuity arguably fits better with this rationale than the abstract value claim.[141] Moreover, the courts only award abstract annuities where no particular harm can be proven, so the victim is not free to choose, whereas supporters of abstract annuities would allow such a choice.[142]

Germanic scholars sometimes debate whether German law really knows no 'abstract' damages. Test cases in this debate include housekeepers with no paid income and home care provided to the victim by a family member instead of a professional. The ordinary focus on the development of a victim's assets would not allow the court to go beyond compensation for loss of an income they can prove that they would likely have received. However, in a pattern not limited to Germany, this solution has struck most as unjust and dismissive of such work.[143] Thus, German law exceptionally allows for compensation based on the service's estimated market value, no matter whether individual evidence or statistics support an assumption that the relative would otherwise have earned anything. In such cases, they speak of 'normative loss' (*normativer Schaden*) rather than 'natural loss' (*natürlicher Schaden*). Critics have repeatedly suggested that this is in fact compensation for lost earning capacity in disguise.[144]

7.3.2.3.3 EXCEPTIONAL SHIFT TO DENIAL

The discussion so far has shown that German courts not only use a higher ordinary standard of proof than their English counterparts, but also resort to a broad-brush approach more restrictively (Austria) or not at all (Germany). Thus, it seems they emphasise certainty rather more. Considering this, it is perhaps unsurprising that they are also more often prepared to categorically deny compensation than their English counterparts.

---

140 R. Welser, 'Fragen der zivilrechtlichen Haftung aus Verkehrsunfällen' (1978) *Zeitschrift für Verkehrsrecht* *30, *35–37.

141 Koziol, n. 138, nos. 79–83.

142 See OGH, 12.11.2009, 2 Ob. 176/09k.

143 See Markesinis et al., n. 96, 196. For England, see also text to n. 84.

144 Cf. e.g. Lange/Schiemann, n. 129, 378–81; Karner, n. 138, 202–3, with references. Cases of this kind are also used by Réaume, n. 85, 88–90.

In cases where a person loses earnings due to their premature death, German and Austrian courts do not award damages to the primary victim themselves. A claim for the earnings in 'lost years' does not exist *at all*.[145] Heirs are only entitled to damages insofar as they have lost maintenance (§844, BGB). This produces the awkward situation that a person who survives but has to retire early may claim lost earnings, while killing a person on the spot may not result in any similar damages. A commonly given, but not very convincing reason for this rule is that new claims cannot accrue to a dead person.[146] A better explanation may be that German law generally considers it too speculative to ask whether the victim would really have kept their estate together and passed it to persons who would have benefitted, i.e. the victim's heirs. For Hans Stoll, this is 'no more than a vague perspective' that 'evades assessment as such'.[147] Someone who merely retires earlier can at least still make the personal decisions over their fortune that they would probably have made in any case; a court making an award for lost years has to reconstruct such decisions through assumptions. Still, it is hard to see how drawing the line at death is always coherent, since a comatose person produces similar difficulties.

One might think that at least Austrian law would allow functional compensation of lost years via compensation of the earning capacity that is destroyed in a person's death. However, the power to pursue such claims is considered to be rooted in a personal entitlement and therefore limited to the holder of the entitlement.[148]

7.4 Conclusions

What conclusions can be drawn from this comparative survey? Insofar as it is representative, there is a general tendency for German and (to a lesser extent) Austrian law to be more hesitant in awarding damages in cases of uncertainty than English law. One reason for this is certainly the different basic rules on how to make the award: variable periodical payments remove pressure to arrive at an immediate assessment of damages. But this can hardly be the only reason, because postponing awards does not solve every problem. It may of course be that the greater or lesser willingness to take imprecision into account produced by these options also 'spills over' to cases where leaving the award flexible does *not* help, such as counterfactual uncertainty. But there are also other possible factors, such as reducing pressure through social security awards and background legal culture.

---

145 See H. Koziol, 'Die Tötung im Schadenersatzrecht' in H. Koziol and J. Spier (eds), *Liber Amicorum Pierre Widmer*, Springer 2003 (reviewing German, Austrian, and Swiss law); *Staudinger BGB*⁸/Röthel, §844 no. 211.

146 See H. Stoll, 'Der Tod als Schadensfall' in E. von Caemmerer et al. (eds), *Festschrift für J. Zepos*, Katsikalis 1973, 687–88, 691.

147 Ibid., 691.

148 Koziol, 'Die Tötung im Schadenersatzrecht', n. 145, 208–13 considers, but rejects an award.

This general tendency aside, it will be useful to again discuss rules on awards first and assessment of losses second.

7.4.1 Rules regarding the award

In the jurisdictions studied, there has already been much discussion on the choice between lump sums and periodical payments, or rigidity and flexibility.[149] The survey above supports the usual conclusion that all of the conceivable combinations should be used. Thus, the problem is to determine which rule should apply by default and what circumstances should justify a departure.

Lump sums are often said to have 'twin weaknesses':[150] they may be too lavishly spent and they do not account for future developments. But the above survey shows that one of these weaknesses—the spending problem—is produced by the *form of payment*, while the other is produced by the *rigidity* of the award. As the Austrian example shows, regular payments can be rigid, and English provisional awards show that lump sum payments can be designed to be sensitive to changing circumstance.

The investment aspect has been discussed frequently and no extensive reproduction is needed here. It suffices to say that the Germanic approach grants the victim security and so eliminates the chance that 'a victim might squander a lump sum and be left in dire financial straits',[151] whereas the English approach generally prefers to give the victim autonomy[152] and flexibility over how to invest their capital in light of their new situation. In any case, and in spite of different basic rules, Germanic and English law differ only in degree, because both offer—sometimes limited—possibilities to claim the other kind of award.

As to the choice between flexibility and rigidness, a rigid-award recipient bears the risk of future negative developments, the defendant the risk of positive developments. From an economic point of view, it often seems best to make a rigid award. But even this is only true if the court arrives at a meaningful figure taking all uncertainties into account; otherwise, the structural effects of entirely random over- and under-compensation will also cause economic harm.

---

149 See Lewis, 'The Politics and Economics of Tort Law', n. 13, 420–41; Lord Chancellor's Department, *Damages for Future Loss: Giving the Courts the Power to Order Periodical Payments for Future Loss and Care Costs in Personal Injury Cases*, Consultation Paper (March 2002); B.A. Koch and H. Koziol, 'Comparative Analysis' in B.A. Koch and H. Koziol (eds), *Compensation for Personal Injury in Comparative Perspective*, Springer 2003, nos. 75–77 and the references in n. 107.

150 Edelman, n. 5, no. 40-004.

151 S. Sugarman, 'Damages' in C. Sappideen and P. Vines, *Fleming's Law of Torts*, 10th ed., Thomson Reuters 2011, no. 10-20. Similarly, 470 *Beilagen zu den Stenographischen Protokollen des Nationalrats*, VIII. GP (1958) 13, on §14 EKHG.

152 See also the internal critique of German law by Huber, 'Kapital oder Rente', n. 107, 121–22.

More importantly, from the perspective of the individual claimant, in some cases there is a legitimate interest in leaving open the possibility of returning to court. This is true especially where a person's basic maintenance is at stake. English law might not take this into consideration often enough, and the comparison with German law at least gives reason to rethink the approach. One point not further stressed here is the narrow limits of preliminary awards, which do not compare favourably even internally, considering that variable English PPOs offer more flexibility. However, the variable payment order is itself not as flexible as the German counterpart, since the latter is sensitive to unforeseen developments. In cases where known unknowns loom large and the claimant is justified in not taking risks—e.g. because their maintenance is at stake—it does not seem entirely fair if the defendant must accept a potentially more efficient, but also more risky award that does not permit, even as a variable order, a reassessment in the event of unexpected developments. Thus, the power of the court to define the scope of acceptable changes could be expanded.

It may also be helpful to reconsider whether the award can be postponed where the court would otherwise have to decline to award any damages, rather than order a provisional sum, or where the problem is that it is not yet clear whether the loss will be significant. German declaratory judgments and rules on the binding effects of judgments make this possible.

There is room to learn from the perspective of Germanic law. For instance, English law provides some reason for adding to the scenarios where rigid awards may be made, either sought by the claimant or awarded of the court's own motion. The interest in finality is not respected by the current rule, and suggestions for improvement deserve support.

7.4.2 Assessment of losses

In all the systems discussed, an important exception to the general requirement of a proven specific loss is available to claimants: the probabilistic approach in *Mallet v McMonagle* and the German and Austrian ZPO, which contrasts with the individual assessment generally used for pecuniary loss.

This does not determine how probability is assessed. This may include use of formalised actuarial evidence, expert knowledge and the judge's experience, and an intervention by way of a general rule that bars damages. These methods represent more general ways of assessing probabilities under uncertainty: statistics, experienced probability, and acknowledging that probability is unknowable.[153] English, German, and Austrian law all show a combination of them.

---

153 See generally J. Steele, *Risks and Legal Theory*, Hart 2004, 18–24, 31–33; and, on the alternatives to frequency interpretations, A Hájek, 'Interpretations of Probability' in E.N. Zalta (ed.), *The Stanford Encyclopedia of Philosophy* (Winter 2023 edition), https://plato.stanford.edu/entries/probability-interpret/ (last accessed 10.2024).

In the assessment of chances, there is a general tendency to use actuarial evidence to the extent it seems reliable. But it is not possible or desirable to deal with all cases through the frequencies reported by such evidence, for many cases are too unique to do so. It does, however, remain possible to assess probabilities even absent clear patterns or regularities.[154] It is difficult to arrive at a general rule as to when these probabilities should be assessed by expert opinion and when this should be left to the judge. The latter approach seems to find more favour under English and Austrian law, which do not in every case insist on a calculation, but allow for an award based on the judge's experience. It is also possible to interpret market value awards—*Smith v Manchester*, voluntary nursing under *Lowe v Guise*, Austrian abstract annuities, and German normative damages—as a similar method, as a simplification of otherwise near-impossible assessments. German courts, by contrast, at least in theory emphasise an approach to assessing the difference in assets based on statistics and expert opinion.

In some cases, probabilities are unknowable,[155] and damages must thus be denied. Such a denial is left in any particular scenario to the trial judge, but it may also be prescribed by a general legal rule. But, as noted above, it is then a legitimate question why a categorical exclusion is necessary. The rationale appears to be that trial judges are not in the best position to assess this, or that a general line is more efficient (evidence on which is often missing).

With the lost-years example in this paper, English courts rarely seem to take this approach, while Austrian and German law do so more frequently. It may be mentioned that the legislator appears to be especially tempted to introduce such rules where they intervene in tort law by way of statutes, as has been the case in Australia.[156] The aim of statutory bars and caps on damages may be to de-fang cases where the assessment of loss seems highly speculative; these are then close to the denial rules discussed in this paper. Of course, they can also serve to suggest that the claimant does not deserve compensation to the full extent or that the responsibility of the defendant is deemed too weak for it. In any event, reasons for such rules should be clear and they should aim to provide consistent lines, which has not usually been the case.[157]

It is worth noting that it is easier to justify such shifts in assessment by reference to *counterfactual uncertainty*, such as the uncertain alternative history

---

154 See Steele, n. 153, 31–33 (referring to I. Hacking).

155 Ibid., 31–33 (referring to B. Wynne's 'indeterminacy': causal chains, networks, and processes defy prediction).

156 See J. Goudkamp, 'Reforming English Tort Law: Lessons from Australia' in E. Quill and R.J. Friel (eds), *Damages and Compensation Culture: Comparative Perspectives*, Hart 2016, 75–94.

157 For a positive assessment of caps, based on the controversial claim that tort law aims to secure minimal living standards, see ibid., 78–81. Continental lawyers and theorists arguing from private law concepts usually regard such caps as too arbitrary; see e.g. Koziol, *Österreichisches Haftpflichtrecht*, vol. I, n. 126, C.3 nos. 29–30; Goldberg/Zipursky, n. 16, 174–78.

of child claimants. By contrast, solving problems of predictive uncertainty by a broad reference to a judge's experience, or even by denial, produces a question: why would it not be more proportionate to wait the uncertainty out by leaving the door open for later litigation or making the award flexible? This is true, for instance, for *Smith v Manchester* awards and their Germanic counterparts, insofar as they are an answer to predictive uncertainty, e.g. about possible future unemployment. Following that interpretation, the approach means awarding damages for a chance that cannot be assessed. It is possible to justify such assessment on other grounds—on deontological reasons or grounds of efficiency—but it requires careful arguments. A general legal rule denying damages for losses just by virtue of their predictive uncertainty would seem even more excessive.

7.4.3 Final remarks

This survey's focus has been on uncertainty. The aim was to describe what measures address what kinds of uncertainties. It was not the focus of this paper to analyse in detail whether their various costs—in terms of under- and over-compensation, litigation fees, etc.—are worth paying. That question turns on many factors.

One issue is what weight the entitlement of the claimant has.[158] Even today, the concessions a jurisdiction is ready to make in cases of uncertainty rise with the stakes. The importance of physical integrity and earning capacity seems to be a weighty reason for the variety of instruments discussed in this paper, which are not usually so developed for other kinds of economic loss.

A second concern is whether the costs may be shifted to the defendant, and whether defendants deserve to carry this burden. A rationale for the general probabilistic approach to lost earnings, which necessarily results in over- or under-compensation, is that the cost of false assessment may fall on the shoulders of a defendant who committed a tort. A similar justification is relevant for the rule that a defendant has no influence on the decision between lump sum and annuity. Thus, it seems the historical idea to award more and to be more flexible in cases of grave violations is not entirely dated.

Finally, choices between various answers to uncertainties have social costs. Allowing guesses on the basis of judges' experience, rather than statistical evidence or expert opinion, is an obvious instance where a rule of assessment increases the incidence of misjudgments, but saves in terms of fees and allows more potentially justified cases to be successful.

This is not to say that the relevant factors are always sufficiently considered. But a principled approach in English, German, and Austrian law seems possible, and this paper suggests refining the available means of assessment and award further is the way forward.

---

158 This is observed for Austrian awards by Koziol, *Österreichisches Haftpflichtrecht*, vol. I, n. 126, D.2 nos. 19–21.

Part 3

Meanings and intentions

8   Contractual interpretation and *ad hominem* rules of construction

Joanna McCunn

This chapter explores the problem of intractable uncertainty about the meaning of a contract. Legal systems have attempted to solve this problem for millennia, though few have sought to pin down its precise nature or boundaries. One popular solution is the use of *ad hominem* rules of construction, which require us to choose the meaning that is more or less favourable to one of the parties; for example, construing the contract against a drafter or in favour of a debtor. Vogenauer describes such rules as 'apparently universal'. Several originated in Roman law, spread throughout Europe, and continue to play an important role in national and international legal systems today.[1] As Troje notes, these rules have been used for 'diverse, even conflicting' reasons over time.[2] For most of their history, they were consistently framed as rules of last resort, which addressed only intractable uncertainty about contractual meaning. More recently, however, *ad hominem* rules of construction have been repurposed as consumer protection rules, and policy concerns have come to overshadow the core uncertainty problem.

8.1 Historical overview

The imprecise nature of human language means that uncertainty about meaning is a perennial problem when people make contracts.[3] It is possible that some styles of legal drafting may successfully reduce uncertainty,[4] but it is unlikely

---

1 *HKK*/Vogenauer, §§305-310, no. 13. Such rules have spread to legal systems outside Europe and to international law, while a similar rule even exists in the laws of chess: S. Vogenauer, 'Interpretation of Contracts and Control of Unfair Terms in Asia: A Comparison' in M. Chen-Wishart and S. Vogenauer (eds), *Studies in the Contract Laws of Asia III: Contents of Contracts and Unfair Terms*, OUP 2020, 498–99; T. Just, *US Chess Federation's Official Rules of Chess*, 7th ed., 2020, 19F.

2 H.E. Troje, 'Ambiguitas Contra Stipulatorem' (1961) 27 *Studia et documenta historiae et iuris* 93, 96.

3 G. McMeel, *The Construction of Contracts*, 3rd ed., OUP 2017, 5; F. Terré et al., *Droit Civil: Les Obligations*, 12th ed., Dalloz 2018, 681; K. Zweigert and H. Kötz, *An Introduction to Comparative Law*, T. Weir tr., 3rd ed., Clarendon Press 2011, 400.

4 J. Morgan, *Contract Law Minimalism*, CUP 2013, 233.

DOI: 10.4324/9781003537526-11

that any approach could ever completely excise it.[5] Even if the language of the contract is clear, it may be difficult to apply it to facts that the parties did not anticipate.[6] Given the prevalence of problems about the meaning and effect of contractual language, it is important that any legal system provide interpretive rules to solve them.[7] In some cases, however, the meaning of a contract will be unclear even after applying these ordinary rules of interpretation. It is in such cases that the law may recognise an intractable uncertainty about the contract's meaning, and institute a special rule to resolve the impasse.

In continental Europe, lawyers have recognised and sought to resolve such intractable uncertainties for millennia. Ancient Roman lawyers instituted special *ad hominem* rules of construction for 'obscure or ambiguous' contracts, which applied only after all other interpretive principles had failed. These rules were later generalised by the glossators into the maxim that ambiguous words should be construed *contra proferentem*, against the party who had proffered them. Having been adopted by canon lawyers, this maxim spread across Europe, and versions of it were included in many continental codes. The rule had made it to England by the fourteenth century, but it was not until the early modern period that common lawyers recognised the existence of intractable uncertainty about the meaning of a contract.[8]

The idea of intractable uncertainty about meaning therefore has a long pedigree in the European legal tradition. However, lawyers have never precisely clarified the nature of such uncertainty, or grappled with delineating its boundaries. This has left *ad hominem* rules of construction as hostages to fortune, their scope liable to expand and contract as understandings of the uncertainty problem evolve. Across legal systems, this flexibility was exploited during the nineteenth and twentieth centuries. Legislators and judges seized on *ad hominem* rules as one solution to the increasing use of exploitative standard-form contracts. Concern with intractable uncertainty fell by the wayside, as the rules were repurposed to address any kind of uncertainty in unequal contracts.[9]

By the late twentieth century, most European legal systems had enacted substantive controls on unfair contract terms. As a result, *ad hominem* rules of construction were restored to their place as rules of last resort to resolve uncertainty, though they were still often only applied to unequal contracts. In this realm, they continue to thrive, thanks partly to a 1993 EEC Directive mandating the construction of ambiguous consumer contracts in favour of consumers.[10] Their application to freely negotiated contracts tends to be viewed with

---

5 Contrast smart contracts, which are written in unambiguous computer code: S. Green, 'Smart Contracts, Interpretation and Rectification' [2018] *LMCLQ* 234, 240.

6 McMeel, n. 3, 5–8; Terré et al., n. 3, 682; Zweigert/Kötz, n. 3, 400.

7 McMeel, n. 3, 4; A. Etienney-de Sainte Marie, 'Les principes, les directives et les clauses relatives à l'interprétation' [2016] *Revue des contrats* 384, 384.

8 See below 8.2.1.

9 See below 8.2.2.

10 Art. 5, Council Directive 1993/13/EEC on unfair terms in consumer contracts.

more suspicion, perhaps because modern lawyers associate them more with public policy than with the problem of intractable uncertainty.

8.2 Scope of the uncertainty problem

8.2.1 *Kinds of uncertainty*

Contractual interpretation inevitably involves grappling with some kind of uncertainty about meaning. However, legal systems have often identified a special degree of uncertainty that goes beyond ordinary interpretive uncertainty.[11] The nature and boundaries of this special uncertainty are difficult to pin down. They are rarely discussed directly; instead, the uncertainty is largely defined by the rules that are used to resolve it. If ordinary principles of construction fail to resolve an uncertainty, a special tiebreaker rule can be used to dissolve the impasse. The existence of such tiebreaker rules presupposes a new level of uncertainty, which is intractable insofar as it cannot be resolved by other means.

Such intractable uncertainty about meaning has been recognised by legal systems since ancient times. Roman law, for example, provided specific *ad hominem* rules for the interpretation of contracts that were 'obscure or ambiguous'.[12] These rules were subsidiary to other principles of construction, and were only to be used as a very last resort.[13] Lawyers of the *ius commune* followed suit. The glossator Bassianus formulated a highly influential hierarchy of interpretive criteria; the *contra proferentem* rule, generalised from these Roman *ad hominem* rules, came in last place, and was only to be applied when all other interpretive criteria had failed.[14] Writers of the early modern *usus modernus* continued to make lists of maxims, with the *contra proferentem* rule again generally falling at the end.[15] Faber, for example, observed that the rule should only be used if the judge was left with nothing better to say, a stance Troje describes as 'not very encouraging'.[16] In the eighteenth century, Pothier still followed the outline of Bassanius' scheme.[17] All of these writers identified a hierarchy of interpretive rules and thus assumed the existence of a hierarchy of interpretive uncertainties.

---

11 In England, this may be referred to as 'ambiguity': see K. Lewison, *The Interpretation of Contracts*, 7th ed., Sweet & Maxwell 2020, 8.01–8.04.
12 Digest 2.14.39.
13 Vogenauer, §§305–310, n. 1, no. 16; Troje, n. 2, 97.
14 Troje, n. 2, 99; E.J.H. Schrage, 'Contra Proferentem' [2005] *Vermogensrechtelijke Analyses* 34, 41.
15 Vogenauer, §§305–310, n. 1, no. 20.
16 Troje, n. 2, 104 (with relevant citations).
17 R.J. Pothier, *Traité des Obligations*, vol. 1, Debure l'aîné 1761, 106–14; see Schrage, n. 14, 43.

Eighteenth- and nineteenth-century codifications duly continued to emphasise this hierarchy, and *contra proferentem* as a rule of last resort.[18] In Austria, for example, the Codex Theresianus (1766) provided that the rule would only apply when the meaning of a term could not otherwise be established 'by any means'.[19] The Prussian ALR (1794) offered a list of interpretive rules; the contract was only to be interpreted against the *proferens* if it 'cannot be interpreted' using any other rule.[20] The Saxon BGB (1863) provided that the rule should only be used if 'a conclusion cannot be reached' by other means.[21]

More recently, this hierarchical system has fallen out of favour. Neither the French *Code civil* nor the German BGB lays down a hierarchy of interpretive maxims to be applied in a strict order. Rather, these subsidiary principles are simply seen as offering commonsense advice to judges as they interpret contracts.[22] The *contra proferentem* rule is the exception here: it is the only maxim that still comes attached to a level of uncertainty, a relic of the old hierarchical system. The rule in the Austrian ABGB, for example, has been described as 'incomparably lowly' compared to other principles of interpretation,[23] and the French rule has a 'subsidiary character'.[24]

In contrast to this, the common law did not initially recognise different levels of uncertainty about the meaning of a contract. Instead of compiling hierarchical lists of interpretive principles, medieval and early modern common lawyers dealt with all interpretive questions in a single stage. If the contract remained ambiguous, it was meaningless, and so void. The *contra proferentem* rule had been adopted by common lawyers, but was initially given equal weight with other interpretive principles.[25] Bacon may have been the first English writer to position it as a tiebreaker rule: in his collection of maxims, which was heavily influenced by civilian scholarship,[26] he wrote that the rule was 'the last to be resorted to, and is never to be relied upon but where all other rules of exposition of words fail'.[27] He thus identified a level of intractable uncertainty about meaning in the same way as civilian writers.

Bacon's approach was influential: his explanation was adopted almost word for word by Blackstone in the eighteenth century,[28] and subsequently by many

---

18 Schrage, n. 14, 44; Vogenauer, §§305–310, n. 1, no. 25.

19 III.2.179, Codex Theresianus[1766].

20 I.5.§266, ALR[1794].

21 §813, Saxon BGB[1863].

22 Terré et al., n. 3, 688; S. Vogenauer, 'Interpretation of Contracts: Concluding Comparative Observations' in A. Burrows and E. Peel (eds), *Contract Terms*, OUP 2007, 131.

23 Troje, n. 2, 110.

24 N. Martial-Braz, 'L'objectivation des méthodes d'interprétation: la référence à la "personne raisonnable" et l'interprétation in favorem' [2015] *Revue des contrats* 193, 197–98.

25 See e.g. *Throckmerton v Tracy* (1555) Plow. 145, 160.

26 F. Bacon, *The Elements of the Common Lawes of England*, More 1630, 17; P. Stein, *Regulae Iuris: From Juristic Rules to Legal Maxims*, Edinburgh University Press 1966, 170.

27 Bacon, n. 26, 16.

28 W. Blackstone, *Commentaries on the Laws of England*, vol. 2, Clarendon Press 1766, 380.

later writers and judges.[29] Powell, for example, wrote that the rule would only apply 'if there be in the terms of a contract any obscurity or dubiousness, which cannot be cleared up by the intention of the contracting parties or any other circumstance, and all other rules of exposition of words fail'.[30] English lawyers thus accepted the notion of an intractable uncertainty that required special rules to resolve, even though they did not adopt the more general hierarchy of interpretive rules.

The existence of such an intractable uncertainty has only rarely been doubted. One possible nineteenth-century English sceptic was Jessel MR, who argued that if 'the ordinary and proper rules of construction' failed to find its meaning, the contract would simply be void.[31] Declaring a contract void for uncertainty is an option in many legal systems.[32] On one view, it is not a response to intractable uncertainty about meaning, but an acceptance that the contract is meaningless.[33] By doubting the existence of 'last resort' rules of construction, Jessel MR may therefore have been doubting the existence of intractable interpretive uncertainty.[34]

European legal systems, however, have generally recognised the existence of intractable uncertainty about contractual meaning. What they lacked was any discussion of how such an intractable uncertainty could be recognised, aside from the fact that it could not be resolved by ordinary principles of interpretation. Perhaps as a result, it was difficult for lawyers to keep their 'rules of last resort' in check. The sixteenth-century French jurist Cujas complained that the *contra proferentem* rule was too hastily used in practice to save the bother of further interpretation.[35]

During the nineteenth and twentieth centuries, this ambiguity was further exploited. Lawyers began to elide intractable uncertainty about the meaning of a contract with other kinds of uncertainty, in order to expand the ambit of the tiebreaker rules. In particular, they blurred the boundaries between rules that dealt with intractable uncertainty and separate rules that mandated the narrow

---

29 See e.g. J. Chitty, *A Practical Treatise on the Law of Contracts Not Under Seal*, Sweet 1826, 21; S.M. Leake, *Principles of the Law of Contracts*, A.E. Randall (ed), 4th ed., Stevens 1902, 149; *Lindus v Melrose* (1858) 3 H & N 177, 182; *Birrell v Dryer* (1884) 9 App. Cas. 345, 350.

30 J.J. Powell, *Essay upon the Law of Contracts and Agreements*, vol. 1, Johnson and Whieldon 1790, 395.

31 *Taylor v Corporation of St Helens* (1877) 6 Ch. D 264, 270–71.

32 See e.g. Lewison, n. 11, 8.131–8.135; *KBB⁵*/Bollenberger, §915, 1031; A.L. Corbin, *Corbin on Contracts*, vol. 3, 2nd ed., West 1960, §559.

33 See *Fawcett Properties v Buckingham County Council* [1961] AC 636, 670–71.

34 On another view, holding a contract void is a response to intractable uncertainty about meaning; it is simply not an attempt to salvage any meaning from the contract. For reasons of space, however, it will not be considered as a response to uncertainty in this chapter.

35 Cited in Troje, n. 2, 101–2.

construction of exclusion clauses.[36] In Germany, for example, the courts began to apply the *contra proferentem* rule to exclusion clauses that were not really ambiguous at all.[37] Commenting on this proclivity, Raiser argued that the courts were trying to save themselves the difficulty of assessing whether a term was really ambiguous.[38] In England, the courts continued to insist that the *contra proferentem* rule would only apply when a contract was ambiguous. However, where in the early twentieth century they had firmly distinguished true ambiguity from mere difficulty of construction,[39] they were soon holding that a contract would be ambiguous unless it was 'perfectly clear'.[40]

The courts were motivated to smudge the nature of uncertainty by their concern to protect consumers from exploitative terms in unequal contracts.[41] In the latter half of the century, this concern was addressed by other means, as legislatures enacted substantive controls on unfair contract terms.[42] As a result, the courts were able to refocus on the issue of intractable uncertainty about meaning. In Germany, for example, it is now generally accepted that the *contra proferentem* rule may not be used in just any case of interpretive difficulty, but only if a doubt remains after all other interpretive principles have been applied.[43] The English courts have also held that the *contra proferentem* rule is 'very much a last refuge, almost an admission of defeat, when it comes to construing a document'.[44] It must not be the starting-point of analysis, but may only be invoked when a term is 'genuinely ambiguous'.[45] The focus has now shifted back to instances of truly intractable uncertainty.

The 1993 EEC Directive on Unfair Contract Terms, meanwhile, mandates that interpretation be made in favour of a consumer 'where there is doubt about the meaning of a term'.[46] The English courts have described this as a 'rule or principle of last resort' and as a 'tie-breaker', which 'is limited to cases

---

36 Vogenauer, §§305–310, n. 1, no. 33; *John Carter v Hanson Haulage* [1965] 2 QB 495, 504; *Adams v Richardson & Starling* [1969] 1 WLR 1645, 1653. Rules about exclusion clauses were previously distinct from the *contra proferentem* rule: Vogenauer, §§305–310, n. 1, nos. 10–12. They may have originated in maritime law: *Czech v The General Steam Navigation Company* (1867) LR 3 CP 14, 19.

37 Vogenauer, §§305–310, n. 1, no. 31.

38 L. Raiser, *Das Recht Der Allgemeinen Geschäftsbedingungen*, Hanseatische Verlagsanstalt 1935, 265.

39 *London and Lancashire Fire Insurance v Bolands* [1924] AC 836, 848.

40 *Jaques v Lloyd D George & Partners* [1968] 1 WLR 625, 632; see also *Alder v Moore* [1961] 2 QB 57, 68.

41 See below 8.3.2.

42 See below 8.3.2.

43 Vogenauer, §§305–310, n. 1, no. 36.

44 *BNY Mellon Corporate Trustee Services v LBG Capital No 1* [2016] UKSC 29, [53].

45 *Transocean Drilling UK v Providence Resources* [2016] EWCA Civ. 372, [20]; see also *R & S Pilling t/a Phoenix Engineering v UK Insurance* [2019] UKSC 16, [51].

46 Art. 5, Council Directive 1993/13/EEC on unfair terms in consumer contracts. This has been implemented by, e.g., sec. 69(1), Consumer Rights Act 2016; the new art. 1190 CC; and what is now §305c (2) BGB.

of genuine interpretative doubt or ambiguity'.[47] International instruments provide similar rules where a term is 'unclear'[48] or subject to 'doubt'.[49]

Legal systems, then, have consistently recognised the existence of intractable uncertainty about contractual meaning, which can only be resolved by using an *ad hominem* rule of construction to break the tie. The question of how to identify and circumscribe this uncertainty is, however, rarely addressed. Is it a qualitatively different kind of uncertainty to ordinary uncertainty about meaning, or is it simply uncertainty with a vituperative epithet? As Abrahams observes, the condition of ambiguity alone is fundamentally 'opaque', providing 'no guidance' to an interpreter other than an 'I know it when I see it' test.[50] Intractable uncertainty about meaning has thus proved to be a highly malleable concept, and has frequently been exploited by legal systems seeking to mould it to their present needs.

8.2.2 *Kinds of contract*

Legal systems have not always been equally concerned with uncertainty in all kinds of contract; they have often chosen to focus only on problems with some particular contracts. In Roman law, for example, *ad hominem* tiebreaker rules were instituted for only some kinds of ambiguous contract: stipulations, sales, and leases.[51] In the second half of the twelfth century, the glossators expanded these rules into a general principle of interpretation: all doubtful contracts and expressions were to be interpreted against their speaker.[52] Commentators like Bartolus discussed the rule in relation to all kinds of contract.[53] For later jurists, up to the nineteenth-century Pandectists, it was similarly clear that the rule could be generalised from the Digest fragments to any kind of contract.[54]

The natural law codifications also tended to draw on this intellectual tradition and to address uncertainty in all forms of contract together.[55] For example, the Prussian ALR referred simply to 'a contract' that could not be explained by any other rule.[56] In the Austrian ABGB, provision was made for doubts about the meaning of unilateral contracts and for unclear expressions in synallagmatic

---

47 *AJ Building and Plastering v Turner* [2013] EWHC 484 (QB), [53].
48 Art. 4.6, UNIDROIT Principles of International Commercial Contracts (2016).
49 C. von Bar and E. Clive (eds), *Principles, Definitions and Model Rules of European Private Law: Draft Common Frame of Reference*, OUP 2010 (hereafter DCFR), II. – 8:103(1); arts. 64(1) & 65, Proposal for a Regulation of the European Parliament and of the Council on a Common European Sales Law, COM (2011) 635 (hereafter CESL).
50 K.S. Abraham, 'A Theory of Insurance Policy Interpretation' (1996) 95 *Michigan Law Review* 531, 538–40.
51 Vogenauer, §§305–310, n. 1, no. 14.
52 Ibid., no. 17. This principle was found to be too broad: Troje, n. 2, 96.
53 Troje, n. 2, 100; Vogenauer, §§305–310, n. 1, no. 17.
54 Vogenauer, §§305-310, n. 1, nos. 20–21.
55 Ibid., no. 25.
56 I.5.§266, ALR[1794].

contracts.[57] The French *Code civil* was something of an outlier, as it included two rules relating to uncertain contracts. Art. 1162 required any doubtful contract to be construed against the stipulator; it was drawn almost word for word from Pothier's gloss on the Roman sources.[58] Art. 1602, meanwhile, was more specific, providing that obscure or ambiguous pacts were to be interpreted against the seller. Again, the Roman influence is clear.[59] The German jurist von Savigny, meanwhile, emphasised that the *contra proferentem* rule was 'only applicable to the interpretation of contracts' and not to unilateral instruments, as only in contracts had the *proferens* taken responsibility for representing the other party.[60]

In England, meanwhile, early modern lawyers were prepared to apply the *contra proferentem* rule to deeds, pleadings,[61] and grants of the King,[62] but not to wills[63] or statutes.[64] There were two kinds of deed that were used to make formal contracts in this period: deeds poll, single deeds that bound only their maker,[65] and indentures, which bound all of the parties.[66] Some lawyers argued that the *contra proferentem* rule applied only to deeds poll, since it could not be said that an indenture had a single *proferens*.[67] It does not seem that this argument was ever successful: the courts were generally happy to apply the rule to all kinds of contract made by deed.[68] Nonetheless, it was repeated by Blackstone,[69] and it is still often asserted by English lawyers that the rule is concerned only, or most centrally, with the problem of uncertainty in unilateral contracts.[70] This offers an interesting contrast with Savigny's views.

As we have seen, however, concerns about the uncertainty problem shifted decisively in the nineteenth century. As early as 1789, common lawyers were arguing that it was 'peculiarly necessary' to construe fire insurance policies *contra proferentem* because they were 'entered into without examination, and

---

57 §915, ABGB[1812].
58 Vogenauer, §§305-310, n. 1, no. 23.
59 C. Krampe, *Die Unklarheitenregel*, Duncker und Humblot 1983, 18.
60 F.C. von Savigny, *Das Obligationenrecht Als Theil Des Heutigen Römischen Rechts*, vol. 2, Veit 1853, 195.
61 E.g. YB (1430) Mich. 9 Hen. VI pl. 31 fol. 49b–50b, 50b. See also Bacon, n. 26, 19. The rule applied to writs in Scotland, but only if they were drawn up by 'skilful persons': J. Viscount of Stair, *The Institutions of the Law of Scotland*, 2nd ed., Anderson 1693, 691.
62 E.g. YB (1493) Trin. 8 Hen. VII pl. 1 fol. 1a–5a; *The Case of Mines* (1568) Plow. 310, 330–32; Lewison, n. 11, 7.98–7.100.
63 Bacon, n. 26, 24; 'Contra Proferentem' (1897) 6 *Michigan Law Journal* 213, 214.
64 Bacon, n. 26, 24. See *Reniger v Fogossa* (1550) Plow. 1, 11 for an unsuccessful attempt.
65 J.M. Kaye, *Medieval English Conveyances*, CUP 2009, 8.
66 Ibid.; see T. Littleton, *Littleton Tenures in Englishe*, Tottell 1556, 80v.
67 YB (1480) Mich. 20 Edw. IV pl. 2 fol. 8b–9a, 8b; *Browning v Beston* (1555) Plow. 131, 135; *Saunders & Starkey v Stanfourde* (undated) Hunt. MS El. 482 fol. 70, 72v.
68 See generally J. McCunn, 'The Contra Proferentem Rule: Contract Law's Great Survivor' (2019) 39 *OJLS* 483, 486–89.
69 Blackstone, n. 28, 380.
70 Leake, n. 29, 150; Lewison, n. 11, 7.66.

without any previous negotiation'.[71] Throughout the nineteenth and twentieth centuries, the common law courts held that the rule applied 'strongly' to standard-form contracts like insurance policies.[72] By 1967, one commentator could observe that exclusion clauses in standard-form contracts provided 'the most frequent illustrations of the *contra proferentem* rule'.[73]

The same was true on the continent. In Germany, the courts initially applied the uncodified *contra proferentem* rule to all kinds of ambiguous contract.[74] However, in 1931, the *Reichsgericht* held that it applied only to standard forms.[75] In systems like Austria and France, general *ad hominem* rules of construction had been codified, but were now applied increasingly often to standard-form contracts such as insurance contracts.[76] In Austria, §915 required ambiguous synallagmatic contracts to be interpreted against the drafter, which naturally tended to work in favour of consumers.[77] In France, art. 1162 had mandated interpretation in favour of an obligor and against a stipulator. This was more difficult, insofar as the obligor was generally the provider of the standard form; the problem was solved by reinterpreting 'stipulator' to mean the drafter of the contract.[78]

Many more recent statutory rules explicitly apply only to standard-form or consumer contracts. In 1942, Italy became the first jurisdiction in Europe to codify special rules for standard-form contracts, providing, inter alia, that ambiguous clauses prepared by one party must be interpreted in favour of the other.[79] Germany followed suit with its AGB-Gesetz in 1977, which laid down a similar rule for business terms that were preformulated for multiple contracts.[80] The 1993 EEC Directive, meanwhile, applied a default rule to contract terms concluded between a seller or supplier and a consumer where these were not individually negotiated.[81] In England today, there are two *ad hominem* rules of last resort. The rule derived from this Directive applies only to contracts between a trader and a consumer,[82] while the common law rule applies in principle to all contracts. In practice, the courts have emphasised

---

71 *Routledge v Burrell* (1789) 1 H Bl. 254, 256.
72 *Etherington v Lancashire and Yorkshire Accident Insurance Company* [1909] 1 KB 591, 596.
73 G. Dworkin (ed), *Odgers' Construction of Deeds and Statutes*, 5th ed., Sweet & Maxwell 1967, 98.
74 Vogenauer, §§305–310, n. 1, no. 28.
75 Ibid., no. 31.
76 Krampe, n. 59, 23, 61; Troje, n. 2, 110.
77 Bollenberger, n. 32, 1031.
78 Terré et al., n. 3, 690.
79 §1370, *Codice civile*; see generally P. Nebbia, *Unfair Contract Terms in European Law: A Study in Comparative and EC Law*, Hart 2007, 31–34.
80 §§1(1), 5, *Gesetz zur Regelung des Rechts der Allgemeinen Geschäftsbedingungen* (hereafter *AGB-Gesetz*).
81 Arts. 3(2), 5, Council Directive 1993/13/EEC on unfair terms in consumer contracts. The German provisions have been updated accordingly: see §310(3) Nr. 2 BGB.
82 Secs. 61(1), 69(1), Consumer Rights Act.

that it has 'a very limited role' in the interpretation of 'commercial contracts, negotiated between parties of equal bargaining power'.[83] In international model rules, *ad hominem* rules of construction are generally provided only for contract terms that have not been individually negotiated.[84]

8.2.3 The locus of uncertainty

Intractable uncertainty about meaning can arise in different kinds of contract and term; it can also arise in different ways. The glossators, for example, sought to distinguish ambiguity, which related to unclear speech, from obscurity, which was concerned with words that had multiple meanings.[85] This scheme shifted over time: Cujas and Faber argued that obscurity was the general concept and ambiguity a special case in which one of two meanings must be chosen.[86] One common lawyer, meanwhile, has distinguished vague words, which have an unclear application to marginal cases, from ambiguous words, which have multiple different applications.[87] The *contra proferentem* rule has been applied to both kinds of uncertainty in England.[88] It has also been applied to cases involving ambiguous syntax[89] and conflicting or inconsistent contract terms.[90]

The nature of uncertainty about meaning may also be understood differently according to broader views about the nature of interpretation. Some legal systems ask what the parties to the contract intended; some, what the contract itself means.[91] Thus, some will view uncertainty about meaning as uncertainty about the historical fact of the parties' intentions, a fact that can never be directly known.[92] For others, the uncertainty is about what a reasonable person would understand the contract to mean, and arises from difficulties

---

83 *Persimmon Homes v Ove Arup & Partners* [2017] EWCA Civ. 373, [52].
84 See e.g. art. 4.6, UNIDROIT Principles of International Commercial Contracts (2016); arts. 64(1) and 65, CESL; II. – 8:103(1), DCFR.
85 Troje, n. 2, 97–98.
86 Ibid., 103.
87 E.A. Farnsworth, '"Meaning" in the Law of Contract' (1967) 76 *Yale Law Journal* 939, 953.
88 For the former, see *Young v Sun Alliance* [1977] 1 WLR 104 (meaning of 'flood'); for the latter, see *Birrell v Dryer*, n. 29, (meaning of 'St Lawrence').
89 E.g. *Re Drake Insurance* [2001] Lloyd's Rep. IR 643.
90 E.g. *The Governors of the Peabody Trust v Reeve* [2008] EWHC 1432 (Ch.); though cf. *Parker-Grennan v Camelot UK Lotteries* [2024] EWCA Civ 185, [58].
91 H. Kötz, *European Contract Law*, G. Martens and T. Weir trs., 2nd ed., OUP 2017, 92; Vogenauer, 'Interpretation of Contracts: Concluding Comparative Observations', n. 22, 125.
92 C. St German, *Doctor and Student*, T.F.T. Plucknett and J.L. Barton eds, Selden Society 1974, 230; YB (1477) Pas. 17 Edw. IV pl. 2, fol. 1a–2b, 2b; *Brogden v Metropolitan Railway* (1877) 2 App. Cas. 666, 692; A. Giuliani, 'Civilian Treatises on Presumptions, 1580–1620' in R.H. Helmholz and W.D.H. Sellar (eds), *The Law of Presumptions: Essays in Comparative Legal History*, Duncker und Humblot 2009, 59.

in the complex process of identifying meaning.[93] We will see below how these different conceptions of uncertainty can affect justifications for *ad hominem* rules of construction.[94]

8.2.4 Overview

Uncertainty, then, can arise and be conceptualised in different ways. Beyond this, though, we can see clear shifts in focus over time. Until the nineteenth century, lawyers were concerned with the issue of intractable uncertainty in all kinds of contract. This was initially part and parcel of a general hierarchical approach to interpretation. However, even as this hierarchical system faded away, the concern with intractable uncertainty remained. In the nineteenth century, attention shifted to the problem of uncertainty more broadly, but only in unequal standard-form or consumer contracts. In recent decades, unequal contracts have remained the primary object of concern, but intractable uncertainty has once again been disentangled from general uncertainty about meaning.

In the next section, we will see that these developments were driven by policy goals. However, they were facilitated by the difficulty of identifying intractable uncertainty about meaning. The distinction between intractable uncertainty and mere interpretive difficulty is hard to pin down and rests on 'an almost completely intuitive' judgment.[95] Legal systems have never really addressed this problem, enabling the scope of 'rules of last resort' to wax and wane as policy concerns demand.

8.3 Solutions and policy goals

8.3.1 Ad hominem *rules*

Thanks to the influence of Roman law, *ad hominem* rules of construction have generally been the chosen responses to intractable interpretive uncertainty in the European legal tradition. Such rules require us to choose the meaning of the contract that is more or less favourable for one of the parties, an approach that is often simply taken for granted. Savigny, for example, wrote that 'the resolution of the doubt must invariably turn out to the advantage of the one party and so to the disadvantage of the other'; the only question was which party to favour.[96] European legal systems have thus followed the form of the Roman rules fairly consistently, but the precise aspects emphasised have shifted over time.

---

93 A. Kramer, 'Common Sense Principles of Contract Interpretation (and How We've Been Using Them All Along)' (2003) 23 *OJLS* 173, 175.
94 See below 8.3.2.
95 Abraham, n. 50, 540.
96 Savigny, n. 60, 192.

In Roman law, a stipulation was to be construed against the stipulator,[97] a sale against the vendor,[98] and a lease against the lessor.[99] In the *ius commune*, these rules were generalised into the maxim that all contracts were to be construed against the *proferens*, a notion that continued to dominate legal scholarship until the nineteenth century.[100] The most popular alternative to the *contra proferentem* rule has been *contra creditorem* or *favor debitoris*, which derived from Bartolus's gloss on the Roman texts and mandates construction against a creditor, vendor, or other obligee.[101] These two rules often coexist. In Austria, for example, doubts about unilateral contracts are to be resolved in favour of the obligor, and synallagmatic contracts against the party who made use of the ambiguous term.[102] In France, following the 2016 reforms, an ambiguous contract that was negotiated by the parties is interpreted against the creditor and in favour of the debtor, while a standard-form contract is interpreted against the party who put it forward.[103]

In a number of early Germanic codes, these basic rules were glossed. The Codex Theresianus, for example, specified construction against the party in whose power it was to express themselves more clearly and intelligibly.[104] In Prussia, a contract was to be interpreted against the party who had used the ambiguous expression, especially if they sought 'unusual advantages' from it.[105] The Saxon BGB, meanwhile, provided that an ambiguous provision would be interpreted against the party who would have derived a greater benefit from it,[106] and the proposed Bavarian BGB that ambiguous contracts be interpreted to the disadvantage of the party 'in whose interest it was to secure a clearer expression'.[107]

As attention shifted to the problems of standard-form contracts, new variations of the rule emerged. For example, general interpretive maxims were excluded from the German BGB at its promulgation.[108] Only in 1977 was an *ad hominem* rule of construction codified, establishing that 'doubts in the interpretation of standard business terms are resolved against the user'.[109] Since 1993, meanwhile, the construction of doubtful consumer contracts in

---

97 Digest 34.5.26; Digest 45.1.38.18; Digest 45.1.99.pr.
98 Digest 2.14.39; Digest 18.1.21; Digest 50.17.172.pr.
99 Digest 2.14.39.
100 Vogenauer, §§305–310, n. 1, no. 21.
101 Troje, n. 2, 101.
102 §915.
103 Art. 1190 CC.
104 III.2.179, Codex Theresianus[1766].
105 I.5.§§266–67, ALR[1794].
106 §813, Saxon BGB[1863].
107 I.4.Art. 77, *Entwurf eines bürgerlichen Gesetzbuches für das Königreich Bayern*[1861].
108 Vogenauer, §§305–310, n. 1, no. 30.
109 §5, *AGB-Gesetz*. In 2002, this rule was integrated into the BGB: §305c (2) BGB. See *HKK/Hofer*, §§305–310 (I), no. 34.

favour of the consumer has been mandatory across the EU.[110] In France, a rule to this effect was enacted in 1995, supplementing the existing, more general, Code provisions.[111]

In England, lawyers from the fourteenth to eighteenth centuries held that a deed should be interpreted against its maker[112] and a grant against the grantor.[113] There was, however, continued controversy over the position of a deed that contained multiple grants or was made by more than one party.[114] In the nineteenth century, treatise-writers referred to the contractor[115] or 'the party who used' the words,[116] although difficulty remained: the courts insisted that some terms were 'in substance … attributable to both parties alike' and thus not susceptible to the *contra proferentem* rule.[117] The situation became clearer as focus shifted to standard-form contracts, which had an obvious *proferens*. Today, two tiebreaker rules exist side by side in England. The statutory consumer protection rule mandates construction in favour of a consumer,[118] while the common law *contra proferentem* rule is still plagued by the problems of identifying a *proferens*, a process that modern judges have described as 'abstruse'[119] and 'bewildering'.[120]

Many different kinds of *ad hominem* rule, then, have been used to resolve uncertainties about the meaning of contracts. These have tended to be variations on either the Roman rules or the glossators' general rule, requiring construction against a drafter, seller, grantor, creditor, or obligee. Sometimes the rules have been glossed: for example, by shifting the focus to the party who would have benefitted from the provision or from clearer drafting. More recent rules seek construction against a user of standard-form contracts or in favour of a consumer. In some instances, the rule does not apply at all if the parties were equally sophisticated.[121]

---

110 Art. 5, Council Directive 1993/13/EEC on unfair terms in consumer contracts.

111 Art. L133-2, *Code de la consommation*.

112 *Plessington v Mowbray & Ellerton* (1382) Mich. 6 Ric. 2 pl. 17 (1996 AF 147–51) 148; YB (1440) Mich. 19 Hen. VI pl. 7 fol. 3b–4b, 4a; *Reniger v Fogossa*, n. 64, 10; *Drinkwater v Corporation of the London Assurance* (1767) 2 Wils. KB 363, 364.

113 YB (1429) Trin. 7 Hen. VI pl. 21 fol. 43b–44a, 43b; *Throckmerton*, n. 25, 152; *Miller and Johns v Manwaring* (1633) Cro. Car. 397, 152; M. Bacon, *A New Abridgment of the Law*, Lintot 1736, 665.

114 See McCunn, n. 68, 486–92.

115 J. Chitty, *A Practical Treatise on the Law of Contracts Not Under Seal*, 2nd ed., Sweet 1834, 80.

116 W.R. Anson, *Principles of the English Law of Contract*, Clarendon Press 1879, 242; F. Pollock, *Principles of Contract*, 5th ed., Stevens 1889, 245.

117 *Birrell*, n. 29, 354.

118 Sec. 69(1), Consumer Rights Act 2015.

119 *K/S Victoria Street v House of Fraser (Stores Management)* [2011] EWCA Civ. 904, [68].

120 *Oxonica Energy v Neuftec* [2008] EWHC 2127 (Pat.) [89]. See *North v Marina* [2003] NSWSC 64, [57]-[72]; Lewison, n. 11, 7.73–7.85.

121 In early twentieth-century Germany, the *contra proferentem* rule did not apply if both parties were equally familiar with the contract terms (e.g. where the defendant consumer was also a

It will also be noticed that some forms of these rules require an ambiguity to be construed against one party, while others mandate that it be taken in favour of the other. Thus, for example, the German BGB requires construction against the user of standard business terms, while the equivalent Italian provision enjoins construction in favour of the party who did not prepare the terms.[122] Sometimes, the point is expressed both ways: early modern English lawyers explained that a lease was 'to be taken strictly for the lessor and most favourably for the advantage of the lessee',[123] and the French *Code civil* requires negotiated contracts to be interpreted 'against the creditor and in favour of the debtor'. It is not clear whether these different framings reflect any broader preference for penalising one party or protecting the other party, and it is often assumed that they are two sides of the same coin.[124] However, it is certainly conceivable that, where there are more than two possible meanings of a term, the meaning most favourable to one party will not be the least favourable to the other; the different rules could then lead to different outcomes.

8.3.2 Justifications

Ad hominem rules of construction have changed over time, as have the nature and scope of the uncertainty that they address. Both of these shifts are intimately connected to justifications for the rules themselves, and to the policy aims that have been projected onto them. When justifications for the rules are relatively weak, they are expressed in general terms and apply only to truly intractable uncertainties. However, when the rules are seen to address pressing policy concerns, their scope can be stretched by legislators and courts so that they bite on a broader range of uncertainties. The rules might also be reformulated to attack these concerns more directly, or to focus on some specific kinds of problematic contract.

Since lawyers have tended to take the existence of their *ad hominem* rules for granted, and have paid little attention to the nature of the problem that they solve, few writers have made arguments for the necessity of default rules per se. Instead, they have generally focused on justifying specific versions of the rules. One exception was the nineteenth-century English jurist Pollock; he wrote that 'any rule not inconsistent with justice is better than uncertainty, and it matters little whether the reasons ... for a rule be convincing or not'.[125]

---

director of the claimant bank): O. Prausnitz, *The Standardization of Commercial Contracts in English and Continental Law*, Sweet & Maxwell 1937, 129. See also the suggestion made by Roberts CJ in *Lamps Plus v Varela* 139 S. Ct. 1407 (2019), 1417. In contrast, the ECJ has held that the key issue is the capacity in which the party is acting, not their personal characteristics: see Case C-110/14 *Costea v SC Volksbank România* [2015] OJ C354/6.

122 §1370, *Codice Civile*.
123 *Moyes v Grigge* (1600) BL Add. MS 25203 fol. 200v.
124 Lewison, n. 11, 7.106.
125 Pollock, n. 116, 245.

Prior to the nineteenth century, the main explanation offered for *ad hominem* rules was that the party who drafted the contract should take responsibility if it was ambiguous. Thus, the Roman law rules were justified on the basis that the terms had been formulated by one of the parties, who could have avoided the ambiguity.[126] Papinian, for example, wrote that an ambiguous contract should be construed against the seller or lessor 'because it was in their power to have stated the terms of the contract more clearly'.[127] This was clearly the case for the formal stipulation,[128] while it has been suggested that the rules applying to sales and leases developed, and were only applied, before these became consensual contracts.[129] One theory about the ultimate origin of the rules posits that they grew out of the word formalism of sacral law. Ambiguous vows were to be avoided at all costs, since the gods would construe them as strongly as possible against their makers.[130]

In the canon law *Liber sextus* (1298), the rule was likewise that 'interpretation is to be made against the one who had the power to speak more clearly'.[131] Later jurists offered similar arguments. One popular explanation in fifteenth-century England was that the drafter had been foolish to leave an ambiguity in his contract, and the law was not in the business of rewarding folly.[132] In France, Faber explained that the party who took the initiative in setting the contract's terms was responsible for expressing them clearly.[133] The Scottish jurist Erskine wrote that 'doubtful clauses in obligations are to be interpreted against the granter', because 'he did not express his mind more clearly when it was in his power'.[134] In the eighteenth century, one English judge held that 'in a doubtful case ... the turn of the scale ought to be given against the speaker, because he hath not fully and clearly explained himself'.[135] Savigny, meanwhile, argued that the party who took responsibility for the contract's terms 'bears the blame, if his opponent was mistaken about the meaning'.[136]

Others put a slightly different spin on *ad hominem* rules of construction. Bartolus connected them with allocations of the burden of proof, writing that interpretation is made against a party who cannot prove his intention.[137] Demolombe later argued along similar lines: an obligee must be able to prove

126 Krampe, n. 56, 12–14.
127 Digest 2.14.39; see also Digest 18.1.21.
128 See R. Zimmermann, *The Law of Obligations: Roman Foundations of the Civilian Tradition*, OUP 1996, 68.
129 Vogenauer, §§305–310, n. 1, no. 15.
130 Zimmermann, n. 128, 640 n. 121.
131 *Liber sextus* 5.13.57.
132 YB (1462) Pas. 2 Edw. IV pl. 6 fol. 2a–4a, 2a; YB (1494) Hil. 9 Hen. VII pl. 11 fol. 17a–18a, 17b; *Colthirst v Bejushin* (1550) Plow. 21, 29.
133 Troje, n. 2, 103; see also A. Loysel, discussed in Krampe, n. 59, 63.
134 J. Erskine, *An Institute of the Law of Scotland*, vol. 2, Bell 1773, 482.
135 *Drinkwater*, n. 112, 364.
136 Savigny, n. 60, 193.
137 Vogenauer, §§305–310, n. 1, no. 17.

the existence of the obligation, just as any party who asserted a fact bore the burden of proving it.[138]

Another view was first suggested by Cujas: that the *contra proferentem* rule should only be applied where the *proferens* was actually capable of avoiding the ambiguity. If he could have expressed himself more clearly and failed to do so, he must have been either negligent or deceitful.[139] The *Reichsgericht* described the use of ambiguous clauses as 'not in accordance with the customs of honest business'.[140] Other jurists focused less on the party's fault than on his attempt to benefit himself. Thus, Bartolus argued that if the *proferens* could not be identified, ambiguous expressions should be interpreted against the party who would have benefitted from them.[141] Some scholars have read a similar position into the Roman sources.[142] This view was also current in nineteenth-century Germany,[143] and we have seen that a number of Germanic codes focused on identifying the party who would have benefitted from the ambiguous term.[144]

This shaded into another concern, for protecting the presumptively weaker party to the contract.[145] It is likely that a Roman buyer or lessee was in a weaker position than a vendor or lessor; the same may have been true of the *promissor* in a stipulation.[146] The early modern French lawyer Loysel explained the *contra venditorem* rule on the basis that 'there are more foolish buyers than foolish sellers'.[147] Indeed, Kötz criticised the original *Code civil* provisions for reflecting 'the widespread, but inaccurate, belief that... debtors and buyers are always weak and poor and in need of protection'.[148]

Until the nineteenth century, all of these justifications were relatively weak. As a result, the rules that they supported were confined to cases of truly intractable uncertainty. However, concerns about the exploitation of weaker contracting parties grew as economically powerful actors began to abuse standard-form contracts. During the nineteenth century, consumer transactions increased dramatically.[149] Large enterprises, such as railway and insurance companies, began to deal with the public *en masse* using standard-form

---

138 C. Demolombe, *Traité des Contrats*, vol. 2, Durand 1869, 23–24.
139 Troje, n. 2, 102; see also J. Domat, discussed in Vogenauer, §§305–310, n. 1, no. 19.
140 *Reichsgericht*, 03.06.1921, RGZ 102, 227, 228.
141 Vogenauer, §§305–310, n. 1, no. 17.
142 Ibid., 1488–89.
143 Krampe, n. 59, 15.
144 See above 8.3.1.
145 In Vietnamese law, a rule of construction explicitly protects the 'weaker party' to a transaction: Vogenauer, 'Interpretation of Contracts and Control of Unfair Terms in Asia: A Comparison', n. 1, 499.
146 Vogenauer, §§305–310, n. 1, no. 15.
147 Cited in Krampe, n. 59, 63.
148 Kötz, n. 91, 99.
149 *OHLE*, vol. XII, 325–28.

contracts,[150] a category that was itself first defined in the 1930s.[151] Often, consumers were unaware of the terms they had ostensibly agreed to, or had no realistic choice but to sign up to disadvantageous contracts.[152]

Lawyers saw an urgent policy imperative to protect the weaker parties to these transactions. *Ad hominem* rules of construction were accordingly repurposed to balance unequal contracts, ensuring that their terms were interpreted as favourably as possible for the parties who had been forced to accept them.[153] The reach of the rules was increased by applying them to a broader range of ambiguities, not just to terms that were intractably uncertain. Meanwhile, the question of uncertainty in all kinds of contract fell by the wayside as lawyers focused primarily on unequal contracts.

Explanations of the rules were now explicitly policy-based. Raiser observed that the German courts were using the *contra proferentem* rule as a means 'to come to the aid of the economically weaker contracting party as far as possible'[154] and 'to adjust many onerous provisions in favour of the consumer'.[155] Scholars observed that substantive controls were effectively being imposed on standard-form contracts, although this was not explicitly acknowledged by the courts themselves.[156] In England too, courts were generally wary of expressing a policy basis for their decisions.[157] However, some were more open: Lord Denning MR described judges using 'all their skill and art' to 'cut down the ordinary meaning of the words and reduce them to reasonable proportions', simply because they disliked 'unreasonable' clauses.[158]

Judges became less interventionist after these policy concerns were addressed by consumer protection legislation. Following the enactment of the Unfair Contract Terms Act 1977, for example, Lord Denning observed that the courts would no longer have to 'go through all kinds of gymnastic contortions' when construing contracts in order to protect the 'little man' from the 'big concern'.[159] Moore-Bick J explained that, while 'past judges have tended to invoke the *contra proferentem* rule as a useful means of controlling unreasonable exclusion clauses', it may now only be used to 'resolve cases of

---

150 Krampe, n. 59, 22; Vogenauer, §§305–310, n. 1, no. 5.

151 Krampe, n 59, 23; S. Hedley, 'From Individualism to Communitarianism? The Case of Standard Forms' in T.G. Watkin (ed), *Legal Record and Historical Reality*, Hambledon Press 1989, 237.

152 Prausnitz, n. 121, 16; F. Kessler, 'Contracts of Adhesion—Some Thoughts about Freedom of Contract' (1943) 43 *Columbia Law Review* 629, 632.

153 H. Kötz and A. Flessner, *European Contract Law*, vol. 1, T. Weir tr., Clarendon Press 1997, 115.

154 Raiser, n. 38, 251.

155 Ibid., 101.

156 Vogenauer, §§305–310, n. 1, no. 32.

157 S.M. Waddams, 'Unconscionability in Contracts' (1976) 39 *MLR* 369, 382.

158 *Gillespie Brothers & Co v Roy Bowles Transport* [1973] QB 400, 415. See also *Kelly v Cornhill Insurance Co* [1964] 1 WLR 158, 168.

159 *George Mitchell (Chesterhall) v Finney Lock Seeds* [1983] QB 284, 297–99.

genuine ambiguity'.[160] Similarly, the German legislator emphasised that the *contra proferentem* rule was now only to be used as a last resort.[161]

Yet while *ad hominem* rules of construction are once again used to address intractable uncertainties, they are still primarily justified in policy terms. For example, the main objective of the 1993 EEC Directive is 'the effective protection of consumers as the typically weaker party'.[162] The rationale for construction in favour of consumers is that they are a vulnerable group in need of protection. In England, both courts and commentators have described the *contra proferentem* rule as one of 'public policy';[163] Sedley LJ argued that its 'origin and first purpose' was 'to limit the power of a dominant contractor'.[164] In France, interpretation against a *proferens* or creditor is seen as a tool of 'social justice', which can rebalance a contract in favour of the weaker party.[165]

A rather different policy rationale is that the *contra proferentem* rule incentivises better contractual drafting. Bacon described the rule as 'a schoolmaster of wisdom and diligence in making men watchful in their own business',[166] while William Blackstone wrote that it would 'make men sufficiently careful, not to prejudice their own interest by the too extensive meaning of their words'.[167] In 1921, the *Reichsgericht* argued that the application of the rule would discourage businesses from their 'propensity to create unclear relationships through the choice of unclear words'.[168] A similar justification was given for the inclusion of the rule in the *AGB-Gesetz*.[169] One objective of the EEC Directive was to deter traders from using problematic contract terms,[170] and the rule therein has been described as a 'sanction for the lack of clarity' in drafting.[171] In recent years, a number of law and economics scholars have praised the *contra proferentem* rule for incentivising clarity and promoting an efficient allocation of drafting risks.[172]

---

160   *Taberna Europe CDO II v Selskabet AF1* [2016] EWCA Civ. 1262, [23].

161   Krampe, n. 59, 27.

162   European Commission, 'Guidance on the interpretation and application of Council Directive 93/13/EEC on unfair terms in consumer contracts' (2019/C 323/04), 1.1.

163   *Egan v Static Control Components (Europe)* [2004] EWCA Civ. 392, [37]; McMeel, n. 3, 312.

164   *Association of British Travel Agents v British Airways* [2000] 2 All ER (Comm.) 204, 220.

165   Etienney-de Sainte Marie, n. 7, 387, 390; Martial-Braz, n. 24, 194, 196–97.

166   Bacon, n. 26, 11.

167   Blackstone, n. 28, 380.

168   *Reichsgericht*, 03.06.1921, RGZ 102, 227, 228.

169   Krampe, n. 59, 27.

170   European Commission, 'Guidance on the interpretation and application of Council Directive 93/13/EEC on unfair terms in consumer contracts' (2019/C 323/04), 1.1.

171   M. Tenreiro and E. Ferioli, 'Examen Comparatif Des Législations Nationales Transposant La Directive 93/13/', p. 9 <https://ec.europa.eu/consumers/archive/cons_int/safe_shop/unf_cont_terms/event29_01.pdf> accessed 08.12.2021.

172   Kötz/Flessner, n. 152, 115; E.A. Posner, 'There Are No Penalty Default Rules in Contract Law' (2006) 33 *Florida State University Law Review* 563, 580; R.A. Posner, *Economic Analysis of Law*, 7th ed., Aspen Publishers 2007, 109; P. Cserne, 'Policy Considerations in

Given this policy-based reasoning, it might be asked whether the rule is really one of interpretation at all.[173] Demolombe, for example, strongly refuted this. Interpretation, he wrote, seeks to 'discover the hidden meaning of the contract and to recognise the true intention of the parties', but the *contra proferentem* rule does no such thing. It is 'interpretation avowing itself powerless before the impenetrable obscurity of the contract', cutting the knot instead of untying it,[174] and only marginally better than drawing straws.[175] Similarly, one modern South African scholar has written that the rule 'does not help solve the difficulty of knowing what the parties intended; it cuts the Gordian knot and arbitrarily determines against the stipulator'.[176]

It has generally been recognised that *ad hominem* rules of construction are poor guides to the true intentions of the parties.[177] In systems that take a subjective approach to interpretation, presumptions have traditionally been understood as a means to access the parties' historical intentions.[178] However, it is difficult to maintain that *ad hominem* rules can pick out the actual common intention of the parties when they function to prefer one party over the other.[179] Such systems may therefore give *ad hominem* rules of construction a special status, recognising that they serve a different purpose.[180] For example, the Italian *contra proferentem* rule is regarded as an 'objective' rule of interpretation, one that does not seek to identify the subjective intentions of the parties.[181] In France, principles of contractual interpretation are generally regarded simply as rules of thumb to guide the judge of fact to the parties' intentions,[182] but the consumer protection rule has always had an exceptional status as a binding rule of law based on 'equity'.[183] Other *ad hominem* rules may share this status.[184]

Contract Interpretation: The Contra Proferentem Rule from a Comparative Law and Economics Perspective' [2007] *Hungarian Association for Law and Economics Working Papers* 14; P. Torbert, 'A Study of the Risks of Contract Ambiguity' [2014] *Coase-Sandor Institute for Law & Economics Working Paper* No. 686, 80.

173 Vogenauer, §§305–310, n. 1, no. 36.
174 Demolombe, n. 138, 20–21.
175 Ibid., 23.
176 J.W. Wessels, cited in C. Lewis, 'Interpretation of Contracts' in R. Zimmermann and D. Visser (eds), *Southern Cross: Civil Law and Common Law in South Africa*, Clarendon Press 1996, 214.
177 Etienney-de Sainte Marie, n. 7, 386; Martial-Braz, n. 24, 194. For exceptions, see e.g. YB (1406) Trin. 7 Hen. IV pl. 9 fol. 16b–17a, 16b; *Miller and Johns*, n. 113, 399.
178 Zimmermann, n. 128, 638; Giuliani, n. 90, 59.
179 E. Hake, *Epieikeia: A Dialogue on Equity in Three Parts*, D.E.C. Yale (ed), Yale University Press 1953, 54; Terré et al., n. 3, 690.
180 Such rules may even be entirely rejected: see e.g. Troje, n. 2, 114.
181 Nebbia, n. 79, 55.
182 Terré et al., n. 3, 688.
183 Ibid., 691.
184 Etienney-de Sainte Marie, n. 7, 388–89; Martial-Braz, n. 24, 198.

In other systems, an objective approach to interpretation holds sway; the search is for the reasonable meaning of the contract, rather than the parties' actual intentions. Here, it may be easier to fold *ad hominem* rules into the ordinary interpretive process. For example, a reasonable reader might expect a party to speak clearly if she really does wish to benefit herself.[185] Thus, the US writer Corbin distinguished between rules of interpretation, which identify the meaning of language, and rules of construction, which determine its legal consequences.[186] He argued that the *contra proferentem* rule 'is hardly to be regarded as truly a rule of interpretation; its application does not help to determine the meaning' of the contract. Instead, it directs the court to choose between meanings 'on the basis of their legal operation'.[187]

Finally, it is worth noting that compromise solutions have not been attempted in this area. It is generally thought that words must be given a single, legally correct meaning, even if reasonable people could ordinarily understand them in different ways.[188] No attempt has been made to split the difference between the meanings contended for by rival parties. This may relate to the fact that no clear water is recognised between construing against the *proferens* and construing in favour of the proferee: the picture is of two rival interpretations with no middle ground. One exception is the argument that the standard *contra proferentem* rule only enjoins the court to choose a construction that is favourable to the proferee, while the EEC rule is different because it mandates the 'most favourable' construction for the consumer. On this view, the ordinary version of the rule may indeed represent some kind of compromise.[189]

8.3.3 Overview

It is striking how consistent, yet how flexible, *ad hominem* rules of construction are. They have been ubiquitous in the European legal tradition as solutions to intractable uncertainty about meaning. However, they have almost never been justified solely as such. Rather, they have been suffused with other policy ideas: penalising foolishness, negligence or deceit; protecting the weak or exploited; or incentivising efficient drafting. These justifications can be strong enough to

---

185 McCunn, n. 68, 503–4. See e.g. *Tam Wing Chuen v Bank of Credit and Commerce Hong Kong* [1996] BCC 388, 394. The drafters of the BGB considered a similar 'probability'-based rationale for the rule, but found it unconvincing: Krampe, n. 59, 21. Such explanations have also been rationalised as part of a subjective approach: Martial-Braz, n. 24, 195.

186 Corbin, n. 32, §534.

187 Ibid., §559.

188 *McConnel v Murphy* (1873) LR 5 PC 203, 219; *Slim v Daily Telegraph* [1968] 2 QB 157, 171–72. But compare *Financial Conduct Authority v Arch Insurance* [2021] UKSC 1, [325].

189 Tenreiro/Ferioli, n. 171, 9. See also Law Commission & Scottish Law Commission, *Unfair Terms in Contracts*, Law Com. CP No. 166, Scot. Law Com. DP No. 119, HMSO 2002, 3.74.

influence the forms of the rules themselves: instead of simply mandating interpretation against a *proferens*, legal systems might specify construction against the party who sought to gain from the uncertainty, or in favour of the party in a weaker bargaining position. As we have seen, pressing policy considerations also enable systems to take their eye off the ball of intractable uncertainty.

Can the justifications offered for these rules tell us any more about the nature of our core uncertainty problem? It may be possible to draw out two lessons. Firstly, there is a strong tendency to see *ad hominem* rules as policy-based, rather than as part of the ordinary process of interpretation. This may suggest that the uncertainty they address is not simply ordinary uncertainty turned up to 11; instead, it is a truly intractable uncertainty that can only be resolved by an exceptional tiebreaker rule. Secondly, there is very little focus on the problem of intractable uncertainty itself. This tends to be mentioned as a limiting factor that keeps the application of *ad hominem* rules in check, rather than as an explanation for the existence of the rules in the first place. Again, the impression is that lawyers have taken both the rules and the relevant uncertainty for granted, without thinking too deeply about the nature of the latter.

8.4 Conclusions

The *ad hominem* rules of construction instituted by the Romans have been enormously influential across Europe and beyond. Thanks to the glossators' framing of these rules, European lawyers understood interpretation to involve levels of uncertainty, which were to be resolved using a hierarchy of principles. At the nadir stood an intractable uncertainty that could only be dissolved with an *ad hominem* tiebreaker rule. The rest of this system gradually fell away, but the rules that addressed intractable uncertainty remained. If a decision is not wholly avoided by declaring the contract void, the deployment of an *ad hominem* rule of construction is still the standard response to an intractable interpretive uncertainty. Yet because they have largely taken its existence for granted, lawyers have made few attempts to interrogate the nature and boundaries of this uncertainty, or to explore other possible solutions.

The lack of clarity here means that *ad hominem* rules of construction are highly malleable, and the core uncertainty problem is easily supplanted. This was the case in the nineteenth and twentieth centuries, as lawyers became more concerned with protecting weaker parties than with intractable uncertainty. As they gained new weapons to use against exploitative contracts, they allowed *ad hominem* rules to shrink back to their original domain of true uncertainty. Still, however, there is little interest in pinning down exactly how far this extends. Lawyers willingly accept *ad hominem* rules of construction if they seem to have an obvious practical use. However, they have little interest in the problem of intractable uncertainty about meaning, nor in *ad hominem* rules as solutions to this problem. Perhaps any clarification of these matters would only reduce the flexibility, and practical utility, of *ad hominem* rules.

9   Unmixing intangible assets

*Benjamin Douglas and Lorenzo Maniscalco**

It is common in commercial life that assets become separably but unidentifiably mixed and need 'unmixing'. Withdrawals from the mixture will occur, and parties with interests in it assert individual ownership over the withdrawals. The problem is most acute for intangible assets, like choses in action, which are but reified rights to take legal action and have no 'natural' or physical comparator on which to base rules for unmixing. The shares of contributions to the mixture can be known with certainty, but once mixed, there is uncertainty about the ownership of any withdrawals from the mixture.

No value–neutral standard can allocate property rights on unmixing. The law must create and apply its own rules. Current English case law addresses this problem piecemeal using three standards: intentions, culpability, and commercial fairness. Intention is the most emphasised factor, but is particularly difficult to pin down. It is not always possible to know another's intention with certainty; the relevant intention may not even have been formed; or parties may have formed different intentions at different times. To resolve this factual uncertainty problem, the leading case[1] imposes an irrebuttable presumption of 'honest' intention. However, the intentions of the parties often appear to be at odds with the law's presumption. In practice, the law's presumed intention reflects what the court thinks is the most just outcome, thus overlapping with the other two standards.

Since the allocation problem is broader than the problem of uncertainty about intention, factual and legal uncertainties cut across each other here. In this chapter we examine whether the various standards used to solve the problem of unmixing intangible assets can be made coherent across the different types of mixtures the law encounters, namely consensual mixing (traditionally viewed in England as an issue of certainty of subject) alongside innocent and wrongful mixing (traditionally viewed as tracing issues).

* To unmix the mixed authorship of this chapter: Dr Maniscalco was primarily the author of 9.1–9.2 and 9.3.4–9.4; Mr Douglas of 9.3–9.3.3.
1 *Re Hallett's Estate* (1880) 13 Ch. D 696, 731.

DOI: 10.4324/9781003537526-12

We argue that, in the common law, coherence can be brought to understanding the legal uncertainty problem by centring the rules for unmixing intangible assets around the creation and enforcement of trusts and fiduciary relationships. These are governed by party intentions, raising the factual uncertainty problem. Intention has two distinct roles to play. When mixtures are consensually made under a fiduciary relationship, the parties' intention sets the terms of the relationship and gives the trustee certain powers with definite limits. Providing the fiduciary acts within the lawful limits of their powers, their intentions govern any unmixing. If the fiduciary acts outside their powers, the trustee's intention is subordinated to that of the beneficiary, whose *ex post* intention allocates ownership.[2] Any third party who wrongfully acquires the assets and mixes them receives them subject to this power of the beneficiary, and so the wrongful third party's intentions also become irrelevant. When assets are accidentally, innocently mixed, there is no reason to subordinate one party to the other, so the intentions of the mixing party allocate ownership. If there are no actual intentions, an intention is presumed.

This chapter focuses on English law. We then examine US law's different approach before turning to the very different way these issues are conceptualised and resolved in civil-law jurisdictions.

9.1 Historical overview

Intangible assets cannot strictly speaking be 'mixed' in the same way as tangible fungibles.[3] The interplay between the law governing these two types of mixtures is not, however, straightforward. In England, the rules governing intangibles developed earlier than (and influenced) those governing tangibles. This seems surprising, especially since many jurisdictions would not regard intangibles as capable of 'mixing'.[4] The reason is that the English law of tangible fungible mixtures did not involve, for most of its history, issues of co-ownership, and thus any difficulties with attributing withdrawals. Fox has shown that this resulted from the absence of any remedies in the form of account or otherwise that co-owners of goods could have brought against one another.[5] An account only became available in 1705, but the rules remained underdeveloped and uncertain.

Mixtures of intangibles involve the substitution of a chose in action[6] for another held in common by the contributing parties. The history of the rules

---

2 *Re Sutherland; French Caledonia Travel Service* (2003) 59 NSWLR 361, [84].

3 A. Waghorn, 'Sorting out Mixtures of Property at Common Law' (2021) 84 *MLR* 61.

4 See below 9.3.4.2.

5 D. Fox, 'The Reception of Roman Law into the Anglo-American Common Law of Mixed Goods', University of Cambridge Faculty of Law Research Paper No. 23/2016, <https://ssrn.com/abstract=2795098> accessed 15.08.2023.

6 *Colonial Bank v Whinney* (1885) 30 Ch. D 261, 285–87; *Torkington v Magee* [1902] 2 KB 427, 430.

governing the identification and unmixing of such developed as the law of tracing. Though its origins are complex, rules of tracing arguably developed by extension from the rules allowing trust beneficiaries to claim substitutes of trust assets in cases of wrongdoing by trustees.[7] Since a beneficiary has historically been recognised as having a proprietary right in the trust assets from time to time—and thus a right to the substitutes of assets leaving the trust fund—this proprietary reasoning could be extended to identifying as the beneficiary's property any substitutes of trust property, regardless of whether they were held by a trustee or third parties.[8]

Since any mixtures of money, shares, or other intangibles involve 'mixed substitutions', it is only the possibility for each contributor of asserting a claim to such substitutes that has made it possible historically to think meaningfully about proprietary rights in these mixtures. It is precisely the existence of tracing, and the survival of proprietary rights in mixed substitutes, that allows the conceptual parallel to be drawn between such cases and 'physical' mixtures. Jurisdictions that have not developed a law of tracing find it impossible to approach these issues from a proprietary outlook or regard them as having anything in common with 'mixtures'.[9]

9.2 Scope of the uncertainty problem

We are concerned with circumstances in which intangibles, like bank accounts, shares, and other choses in action, held by different parties, contribute or are 'mixed' together in the creation of a substitute asset of which the contributors are seen as co-owners. Contributions to this mixture are known with certainty, but the ownership of withdrawals from the mixture is unknown or unknowable by any natural means. Practical reasons force the law to develop a rule to 'unmix' the mixture, allocating the withdrawal's ownership.

Whether the idea of a 'mixture' is even appropriate to intangible assets is questioned. When tangible assets are mixed, there is physical continuity from separate assets to mixture. The difficulty of unmixing is, theoretically, evidential only. But intangible assets are purely legal creations. There is no physical basis to see any 'mixing' when, say, two people transfer part of a bank account balance into a new 'mixed' account. Formerly there were two choses in action. Subsequently there is a third chose in action. The term 'mixed substitution' has been suggested as a more accurate description of this scenario, since the apparent pooling of assets results in the creation of a new right, substituting

---

7 P. Millett, 'Proprietary Restitution' in S. Degeling and J. Edelman (eds), *Equity and Commercial Law*, Lawbook Co. 2005, 315; L. Smith, 'Philosophical Foundations of Proprietary Remedies' in R. Chambers et al. (eds), *Philosophical Foundations of the Law of Unjust Enrichment*, OUP 2009, 299–301.

8 R.C. Nolan, 'Property in a Fund' (2004) 120 *LQR* 108.

9 See below 9.3.4.2.

itself to the previous one.[10] What is it that is mixed? The current authoritative explanation is that 'value' is what persists between substitutions.[11] This has been challenged in recent scholarship,[12] which emphasises the susceptibility of the property to the mixing party's power to exchange the asset.[13] As discussed below, powers are critical to our understanding of the role of intention in this area, though its role has been hidden in the case law's development.

The common law approaches the uncertainty involved in mixtures of intangibles in compartments reflecting historical categories in which the rules developed (the law of tracing and of creation of trusts). Viewed from the perspective of the uncertainty problem, we can distinguish:

- consensual mixtures;
- wrongful mixtures; and
- innocent accidental mixtures.

Within these categories, the law uses various standards to determine how any mixtures are to be unmixed. They include:

- intentions;
- culpability (or wrongfulness); and
- standards of commercial practice (and other policy considerations).

These standards are not mutually exclusive. Culpability and general policy concerns overlap. Intention, however, is more difficult to pin down. It overlaps significantly with the other standards. Looking at the case law, we want to see whether there is any consistency and relationship between these three standards, or whether courts apply them ad hoc in response to the justice of any situation. If the latter, it will be difficult to discern any overarching principles in this area. If the former, it will be desirable to clarify how the standards apply with some consistency.

9.2.1 Consensual, wrongful, and innocent accidental mixtures

The first category of cases where this uncertainty arises are cases of consensual mixtures—cases where two parties decide to pool their money or other

---

10 Waghorn, n. 3, 82.
11 *Foskett v McKeown* [2001] 1 AC 102, 127–28, adopting L. Smith, *The Law of Tracing*, OUP 1997, 67.
12 T. Cutts, 'Tracing, Value and Transactions' (2016) 79 *MLR* 381; J. Edelman, 'Understanding Tracing Rules' (2016) 16 *Queensland University of Technology Law Review* 1; A. Nair, *Claims to Traceable Proceeds*, OUP 2018, ch. 2; M. Raczynska, *The Law of Tracing in Commercial Transactions*, OUP 2018, ch. 3, [Con.04]–[Con.08]; C. Mitchell, 'Book Review' (2018) 12 *J Eq.* 123.
13 Nair, n. 12, [2.143]–[2.145]; Raczynska, n. 12, [3.12], [Con.08].

intangibles in a single account owned jointly at law, or in only a single party's name.

Perhaps the most common situation is the case of a joint bank account—and the rules governing the withdrawal of money are among those most studied.[14] Another example is a party who agrees to a trustee mixing trust assets with the trustee's own personal assets. The normal rule is that a trustee should keep a beneficiary's assets separate. That is precisely to prevent uncertainty as to whether trust assets or personal assets are being dealt with.[15] However, a mixture may be unavoidable where trusts are declared over part of a trustee's own interest in some shares.[16] This would also involve cases where a party holds money or other assets for investment for his own and another's benefit.[17] More generally, the same issues of uncertainty arise in all cases where a party holds an account in which part of the assets belong to the account-holder in equity and part to a third party—whether both fall under the same trust or are held in different capacities.

Property may also be mixed without the consent of both parties. These mixtures will generally take two forms: innocent and wrongful.

A wrongful mixture is where a party's money or other intangibles are mixed with a wrongdoer's current account. This may happen where a trustee mixes a beneficiary's money with their own;[18] where a party transfers another's assets in their own name pursuant to their own fraud;[19] or where a party knowingly receives trust money or assets from another in circumstances where it would be unconscionable not to return them.[20] Generally this extends to all cases where a party is or should be aware that they have no title to part of the assets they hold in their account and fails to return them to the relevant beneficiary. Sometimes wrongfulness derives from interfering with an existing fiduciary relationship, and the rules for mixing can be seen as enforcing the beneficiary's rights under that relationship. Sometimes there is no pre-existing relationship but there is clearly one wrongful party. Here, equity imposes the equivalent result of a fiduciary relationship upon the wrongful party and applies the same rules for the purposes of unmixing the mixture.

A final category concerns cases where a party receives, without consideration, assets from a third party pursuant to a fraud or other vitiating factor of

---

14 M. Bridge et al., *The Law of Personal Property*, 3rd ed., Sweet & Maxwell 2021, [2-048]–[2-050].

15 *Pennell v Deffell* (1853) 4 De GM & G 372, 386, 392.

16 *Hunter v Moss* [1994] 1 WLR 452; *White v Shortall* (2006) 68 NSWLR 650.

17 *Re Beatty* [1990] 1 WLR 1503; *Citibank v MBIA Assurance* [2007] EWCA Civ. 11; C. Mitchell, 'Good Faith, Self-Denial and Mandatory Trustee Duties' (2018) 32 *TLI* 92, nn. 61–64; J.E. Penner, 'Distinguishing Fiduciary, Trust, and Accounting Relationships' (2014) 8 *J Eq.* 201, 206–8.

18 *Re Hallett*, n. 1.

19 *Foskett v McKeown*, n. 11.

20 *Re Diplock* [1948] Ch. 465, 539; *Commerzbank v IMB Morgan* [2005] 1 Lloyd's Rep. 298.

which they are unaware. If the receiving party has no defence against rescission of such a transaction or the assertion of a third-party interest (e.g. they are a volunteer who received a gift voidable for mistake), then this is an involuntary mixture of intangibles, albeit both contributor and recipient are innocent.

Different policy considerations apply to the rules that one might exercise when dealing with an uncertainty created by a wrongdoer, against cases where both parties have taken the risk of creating such an uncertainty or, indeed, where the mixture occurred through an innocent mistake.

9.2.2 *The withdrawing party's intentions*

The withdrawing party's intentions provide a further layer of difficulty, present in both voluntary and involuntary mixtures. This question cuts across the one examined above.

A first case category involves a party being unaware that there is a mixture at all, and therefore unable to form an intention as to whose money to withdraw from it. Note that in such cases a party may nevertheless be able to form an intention to withdraw any particular share of the fund on a different basis,[21] but not on the basis that they belong to any particular party. Such cases will often overlap with accidental mixtures, but also cover a thief breaking into a trust account of shares held by a number of beneficiaries and withdrawing money. Finally, there may be circumstances where assets are lost or transferred purely accidentally, without the intervention of any party, as with transfers caused by computer error, or otherwise interfered with by a remote third party without trustee or beneficiary fault.

A second category involves cases where a party is aware that there is a mixture. Here they can form an intention to appropriate money belonging to one or other party. The effect of the withdrawing party's intentions may depend on the prior question of how the mixture was created, and whether the intention to withdraw is lawful. That is, should the basis on which a mixture was made affect the way in which the withdrawer's intentions can resolve the uncertainty? If a fund was initially created consensually on the basis that neither party should draw on their own share, but a contributor has later withdrawn from the fund intending to deal only with their own share and make a profitable investment, what relevance should the consensual set-up of the mixture have to resolving the uncertainty of allocating ownership to the withdrawals, and what relevance should attach to the intention of the withdrawing party? This further complicates the uncertainty in the law's treatment of intention when dealing with unmixing.

As we shall see in the next section, these issues of uncertainty are currently addressed by English courts through a combination of rules giving relevance to the parties' intentions, and others operating by presumption when no

---

21 E.g. as in *Re Diplock*, ibid.

evidence of the intention can be identified, or where a party is prevented from relying on a wrongful intention. The courts have not yet approached intention in a unified and consistent manner across these situations.

9.3 Solutions and policy goals

Turning to the present state of English law, we will examine non-consensual mixtures before consensual mixtures, mirroring the law's historical development. We shall see later that the law on consensual mixtures provides the overall terms of the relationship between the parties and determines whether a fiduciary relationship exists. Only after considering that can the overall function of intention be seen together with its interaction with culpability.

9.3.1 Innocent and wrongful mixtures

9.3.1.1 Clayton's case (FIFO)

The earliest rule applied to mixtures of intangibles is the so-called rule in *Clayton's* case:[22] withdrawals from a mixed fund should be resolved on a 'first-in, first-out basis' (FIFO). The rule in *Clayton's* case, despite early success, became increasingly side-lined, almost (not quite) to vanishing point. Adapting Lord Birkenhead, 'it may, without excessive irony, be said that it has been distinguished with more zest than it has been followed'.[23]

Clayton's case itself did not concern the unmixing of asset mixtures. It involved a set of parties with changing membership (a banking partnership) which became liable for debts multiple times while the membership changed. The partnership owed several separate debts to creditors and made payments without specifying which debts they were discharging. This mattered: only one of the initial members of the set was solvent. *Clayton's* case involved identification of a debtor,[24] not unmixing assets. The payment was never mixed. The issue was identification of payment to obligor.[25]

Clayton's case decided that a payment to a creditor would by presumption discharge the oldest debt first, unless it was shown that the debtor had intended to discharge another debt or that the creditor had allocated it to one debt specifically. The reasoning was 'probably' inspired by a Roman-law rule[26] that, absent evidence of the parties' intentions, the debtor was presumed to intend to make payment in the way most beneficial to him, and, if all debts

---

22 *Devaynes v Noble* (1816) 1 Mer. 529.
23 *Portman v Viscount Portman* [1922] 2 AC 473, 488.
24 *Re Sutherland*, n. 2, [23].
25 See A. Televantos, *Capitalism Before Corporations*, OUP 2020, 157–60.
26 Digest 46.3.5. See *Clayton's* case, n. 22, 605 (older cases made no reference to civil law: e.g. *Dawe v Holdsworth* (1791) Peake 89).

were equal, to attribute the credit to the oldest debt.[27] Doubtless this rule commended itself to judges as possessing twin advantages: antiquity and continued commercial sense. Older debts would have accrued more interest; actual intentions more likely been forgotten; and witnesses become less reliable. The Chancery, which was perpetually sorting out accounts, doubtless found a rule that kept accounts tidier and easier to read instinctively appealing. It accords with a natural human instinct to keep things in an apparent state of intellectual tidiness. This was reinforced by a contemporary tendency to view bank accounts as a series of independent debts, rather than a single debt as today.[28]

Often where a judge gives many alternative reasons it becomes difficult to know where the limits of the case should lie. This applies to *Clayton's* case. FIFO was probably later applied to mixed funds of intangibles because Grant MR gave very general reasons in his judgment:

> [A]ll the sums paid in form one blended fund the parts of which have no longer any distinct existence ... In such a case, there is no room for any other appropriation than that which arises from the order in which the receipts and payments take place ... Presumably, it is the sum first paid in, that is first drawn out. It is the first item on the debit side of the account, that is discharged, or reduced, by the first item on the credit side. The appropriation is made by the very act of setting the two items against each other. Upon that principle, all accounts current are settled.[29]

Thus, *Clayton's* case was taken as establishing a general rule applicable to withdrawals generally from a mixed bank account, rather than the narrower issue actually dealt with.[30]

9.3.1.2 FIFO's rise and fall in wrongful mixtures

The first applications of *Clayton's* case to mixed funds involved fiduciaries mixing beneficiary moneys with their own. In *Pennell v Deffell*,[31] it was applied to the case of a trustee and in *Brown v Adams*,[32] a solicitor.

Pennell reveals a tension between the principles felt to be involved between fiduciaries and beneficiaries and the then-perceived operation of *Clayton's* case. For the Court, principle favoured subordinating the fiduciary to the beneficiary. Knight Bruce LJ gave an example of a trustee who mixed a beneficiary's

---

27 *Clayton's* case, n. 22, 605–6.
28 *Re Sutherland*, n. 2, [31]–[32], [149]–[152]; D. Fox, *Property Rights in Money*, OUP 2008, [1.46]–[1.51].
29 *Clayton's* case, n. 22, 608 (see also 610).
30 *Pennell*, n. 15, 391; *Re Hallett*, n. 1, 731; *Equity Trust (Jersey) v Halabi* [2022] UKPC 36, [202].
31 n. 15.
32 (1869) LR 4 Ch. App. 76.

physical money with his own in a chest and then withdrew money for his own purposes:

> what he so took would be solely or primarily ascribed to those contents of the repository which were in every sense his own. He would, *in the absence of evidence that he intended a wrong*, be *deemed* to have intended and done what was right; and if the act could not in that way be wholly justified, it would be *deemed* to have been just to the utmost amount possible.[33]

This treats unmixing as a question of intention. It assumes that actual intentions govern the allocation, even if wrongful. There is a loose presumption of honest intention, but it is qualified, only operating in the *absence* of evidenced, actual intention, giving intention primacy over culpability.

Despite this promising start, *Pennell* held that *Clayton's* case 'inexorably'[34] applied to a bank account, based on the then-prevailing legal understanding of a bank account as a series of individual loans and repayments.[35] FIFO was therefore briefly established as the rule applicable to withdrawals from mixed funds.

Re Hallett's Estate[36] ended that. A fiduciary had mixed client money with his own. After several withdrawals, the question was what proportion of the money remaining in the account was still held on trust for the clients, so that they could claim in priority to unsecured creditors.

Re Hallett had the weighty task of overruling a decision of a court of coordinate jurisdiction. It did this by holding that *Pennell* was right in principle on trusts law but wrong in its application of *Clayton's* case to trusts.[37] Placing intention front and centre was crucial. *Clayton's* case was held to be an intention-based rule, applicable only 'unless there is evidence either of agreement to the contrary or of circumstances from which a contrary intention must be presumed'.[38] Then, a wrongdoer was held to have a *presumed* intention of 'honest' or 'rightful' conduct. *Pennell* thus erred because *Clayton's* case was displaced by the presumption of honest intention. In the process, intention changed from an actual intention in *Pennell* to an irrebuttable[39] presumed intention in *Re Hallett*. Intention, nominally the legal standard, was in substance supplanted by culpability.

33 n. 15, 382–83 (emphasis added).
34 Fox, n. 28, [1.50].
35 Ibid.; *Re Sutherland*, n. 2, [149]–[151].
36 n. 1.
37 Ibid., 729, 737–45.
38 Ibid., 728 (also 738–39).
39 Ibid., 727, 737–43.

The principle in *Re Hallett* developed further in *Re Oatway*.[40] A trustee, rather than dissipating the trust fund, first made profitable investments from it before depleting the fund. If *Re Hallett*'s formal intention-based reasoning were applied with severity, regardless of its policy, then at the time the first withdrawal was made, the trustee must be presumed to have acted honestly and withdrawn their own money; they had *at that time* no right to withdraw the beneficiary's. Subsequently, when the trustee 'honestly' exhausted all their money, they can only be taken to have used the beneficiary's money, which on this logic would be attributed to the dissipated withdrawals. So applying the presumption of honest intention would leave the trustee the profits from his investments merely because they were made with an earlier withdrawal. It plainly contradicts the true policy of the presumption: that the fiduciary is to be subordinated to the beneficiary.

Joyce J rejected the argument that the presumption of honesty meant that the trustee had first withdrawn their own money to make the investment and then, once only beneficiary money remained, must be taken as dissipating the beneficiary's money:

> [H]e never was entitled to withdraw the [money for the investment] from the account, or, ... he could not be entitled to take that sum from the account and hold it or the investment made therewith, freed from the charge in favour of the trust, unless or until the trust money paid into the account had been first restored, and the trust fund reinstated.[41]

This reasoning focused attention on, not rights or presumptions at a particular time, but the overall problem of an unauthorised mixing. Joyce J was guided by lack of title or right rather than a formal presumption of honesty, putting the law in terms that simply stated the allocation between the parties:

> [W]hen the private money of the trustee and that ... held in a fiduciary capacity have been mixed in the same banking account, from which various payments have ... been made, then, in order to determine to whom any remaining balance or any investment that may have been paid for ... ought to be deemed to belong, the trustee must be debited with all the sums that have been withdrawn and applied to his own use so as to be no longer recoverable, and the trust money in like manner be debited with any sums taken out and duly invested in the names of the proper trustees. The order of priority in which the various withdrawals ... may have been respectively made is wholly immaterial.[42]

---

40 [1903] 2 Ch. 356.
41 Ibid., 361.
42 Ibid., 360–61.

The last sentence must be part of the *ratio*. In Australia's *Re Sutherland*, Campbell J, having characteristically exhaustively reviewed the authorities, said of *Re Oatway*: 'this is the language of ex post facto accounting, not of presumption of intention'.[43] The beneficiary elects at the time of trial with the benefit of hindsight. *Re Hallett* says that unmixing from a wrongfully mixed fund is determined by a presumption of the fiduciary's honest intention, but the effect of that presumption according to *Re Oatway* is that it is actually the *ex post* intention of the *beneficiary* that governs the proprietary allocations of unmixing.

   Re Oatway was only a first-instance decision. It boldly loosed itself from the formal reasoning in *Re Hallett*, though it is entirely consistent with the principle underlying the presumption of honest intention: that, by wrongful conduct, the trustee is precluded from asserting rights in priority to the beneficiary. The principle was so stated shortly thereafter by Lord Parker in *Sinclair v Brougham*.[44] His discussion of tracing was treated as authoritative in *Re Diplock*.[45] In the United States, in *Primeau v Granfield*,[46] Learned Hand J explained the presumption of honest intention entirely in policy terms as 'merely a way of giving an explanation by a fiction of the right of the beneficiary to elect to regard his right as a lien'. He saw no inconsistency between *Re Oatway* and *Re Hallett*. Similarly, in *Foskett v McKeown*,[47] Lord Millett spoke to general principle:

> As against the wrongdoer and his successors, the beneficiary is entitled to locate his contribution in any part of the mixture and to subordinate their claims to share in the mixture until his own contribution has been satisfied.

This general principle is sometimes termed the principle of subordination.[48] As recently as 2003, in *Shalson v Russo*,[49] *Re Oatway* was said to support a beneficiary's rights to 'cherry-pick' withdrawals. But in 2005, in *Turner v Jacob*,[50] Patten J interpreted *Re Oatway* narrowly so that it did not apply if the balance of the mixed account remained above the beneficiary's notional amount, in which case the beneficiary was said to be limited by *Re Hallett* to

---

43 *Re Sutherland*, n. 2, [79].
44 [1914] AC 398, 442 (still authoritative: *Westdeutsche Landesbank Girozentrale v Islington LBC* [1996] AC 669, 713–14 overruled *Sinclair* but expressly preserved the authority of *Re Diplock*, where Lord Parker's reasoning was relied upon). Lord Parker's language echoes Joyce J in *Re Oatway*, n. 40.
45 n. 20.
46 184 F. 480, 484–85 (SDNY 1911).
47 n. 11, 132.
48 L. Tucker et al. (eds), *Lewin on Trusts*, 20th ed., Sweet & Maxwell 2020, [44-033].
49 [2005] Ch. 281, [144].
50 [2006] EWHC 1317 (Ch.).

the account balance and could not claim any withdrawals. This interpretation goes against the broad principle of subordination identified above. It is opposed by Lord Parker, Learned Hand J, Lord Millett, Campbell J, Rimer J, and most commentators.[51]

This state of confusion is probably due to the uncertain role that intention plays in wrongful mixtures. It seemingly illustrates what Learned Hand J described as 'the usual injustice which fictions do bring, when pressed logically to their conclusion'.[52] *Re Hallett* can be seen as using 'intention' as a way to disapply *Clayton's* case and overrule *Pennell* without disrespecting precedent. The presumed intention is said to be based on what the trustee 'honestly' or 'rightfully' could do. What is acting honestly? It must be acting in accordance with the terms of the fiduciary relationship. Thus, setting the terms of the fiduciary relationship is logically prior to the presumption of honesty. What sets the terms of the fiduciary relationship? It depends how the relationship arises. In the majority of cases, the intentions of the parties in forming their fiduciary relationship will set the terms. In a minority of cases, equity will impose the equivalent result of a fiduciary relationship on the parties *de novo* through a constructive trust. In those cases, the reason will be the various policies that lead equity to impose constructive trusts.[53]

9.3.1.3 FIFO and innocent mixtures

After *Re Hallett*, the rule in *Clayton's* case could only operate, if at all, over innocent mixtures,[54] i.e. when an innocent party receives without notice or consideration property belonging to another.[55] The co-owners of the mixed fund are innocent as against one another,[56] and there are dicta that *Clayton's* case is applicable between multiple beneficiaries.[57]

The most important authority on innocent mixtures is *Re Diplock*.[58] Money was mistakenly paid by an executor under a void bequest to 139 charities. When the mistake came to light, the money had been mixed with the charities' assets and partially or wholly spent. The court treated the charities as innocent volunteers who had mixed beneficiary money with their own.

---

51 C. Mitchell et al., *Goff & Jones: The Law of Unjust Enrichment*, 10th ed., Sweet & Maxwell 2022, [7-53]; P. Matthews et al., *Underhill and Hayton: Law of Trusts and Trustees*, 20th ed., LexisNexis 2022, [90.28]; Bridge et al., n. 14, [31–044]. But cf. *Lewin*, n. 48, [44-083].

52 n. 46. Learned Hand J seemingly treats the presumption of honest intention as a 'hard fiction': L. Shmilovits, *Legal Fictions in Private Law*, CUP 2022, [2.6.4].

53 *Westdeutsche*, n. 44, 705; *Beatty v Guggenheim Exploration Co.*, 225 NY 380, 386; 122 NE 378, 380 (1919).

54 *Re Hallett*, n. 1, 743.

55 Purchasers of the legal estate for value without notice take free of competing equities: *Pilcher v Rawlins* (1872) LR 7 Ch. App. 259, 269.

56 *Foskett*, n. 11, 132.

57 *Hancock v Smith* (1889) 41 Ch. D 456, 461–62.

58 n. 20.

Clayton's case was applied to Dr Barnardo's Homes[59] which placed the money into their current account and continued to operate. The Court of Appeal chose to apply *Clayton's* case over a rateable approach:

> It might be suggested that the corollary of treating two claimants on a mixed fund as interested rateably should be that withdrawals out of the fund ought to be attributed rateably ... But in the case of an active banking account this would lead to the greatest difficulty and complication in practice and might in many cases raise questions incapable of solution. What then is to be done? In our opinion, the same rule as that applied in *Clayton's* case should be applied.[60]

This is the sole modern authority that applies *Clayton's* case to a mixed bank account between innocent parties. *Clayton's* case was chosen over a rateable approach as the solution that best avoided practical 'difficulty and complication'. While those difficulties were not enumerated, one can speculate: Barnardo's was and is a going concern. This makes it unlike most modern authorities, which involve insolvent investment schemes where there is a definite end-point to the account.[61] A rateable approach applied to a going concern with a busy current account would involve the beneficiary asserting a proportional share of every withdrawal, theoretically indefinitely. Each deposit of the volunteer's own money would diminish the beneficiary's share in subsequent withdrawals, but the beneficiary's portion of the mixed account, while ever diminishing, would, theoretically, never be eliminated (although doubtless a practical end-point could be drawn). The sheer number of transactions potentially impugned by a rateable approach would be inconvenient. The advantage of FIFO for a busy going concern's running account is that it allocates the beneficiary's money to a discrete period and pushes it cleanly *out* of the mixed bank account. The number of withdrawals affected is minimal. That is advantageous for commercial certainty. If the entity operates normally, the beneficiary is subjected to the risks inherent in the volunteer's trade.

Re Diplock also dealt with how the withdrawing party's actual intention might govern withdrawals. The National Institute for the Deaf (NID) had innocently received and mixed £1,500 in its current account. It then earmarked that sum as being withdrawn and transferred to its capital account. FIFO would have allocated the Diplock money to withdrawals that dissipated the money, inconsistently with the NID's own intention. The Court said:

> A volunteer who mixes what turns out to be trust money with his own can surely himself 'unmix' it subsequently ... And as the operation of

---

59 And to St George's Hospital without further discussion: ibid., 550.
60 ibid., 553–54.
61 *El Ajou v Dollar Land Holdings (No 2)* [1995] 2 All ER 213, 219.

equity is directed to preventing the volunteer doing what is unconscionable, surely it would be unconscionable for the volunteer who, for his own purposes, has earmarked the trust money to assert that what he has earmarked is not trust money.[62]

This enables the mixing party to control the ownership of the withdrawals. But that ability must be subject to a limitation that the unmixing must not be in bad faith, otherwise a volunteer could earmark and withdraw to defeat any potential adverse claims. It was acceptable in *Re Diplock* because the charities acted in ignorance of the executor's mistake.

Clayton's case was not applied to the Royal Sailors' Orphan Girls' School and Home,[63] who, in Dickensian fashion,[64] applied their charitable funds, not to food, clothes, or toys for the children, but to purchasing War Stock. There was evidence that the School used its War Stock as something like a fund, adding to its holdings and selling it as needed to fund expenditure. The Court refused to apply *Clayton's* case outside the context of banking accounts, instead applying a rateable approach. This shows that the fairest neutral allocation preferred by courts unfettered by authority is a rateable approach.

In modern times, *Clayton's* case has been distinguished further to the point of practical elimination. The most important authority is *Barlow Clowes International v Vaughan*,[65] which involved innocent victims of a failed investment scheme. The innocent parties' assets were mixed by a party who was not a contributor. The Court of Appeal held that allocating withdrawals on a FIFO basis would contradict the parties' 'presumed intentions', because it would lead to an arbitrary distribution of losses and profits. In principle it would be fairer to adopt a *pari passu* or 'rolling charge' distribution method. A rolling charge means that each time a withdrawal is made from the mixed account, the withdrawal should be deemed to affect a rateable share of the contributors' money at that time.[66] This method was evidentially impracticable in *Barlow Clowes*, because too many payments in and out had been made over the applicable period for an accurate calculation to be possible; the court decided, as a compromise, simply to allocate the total amount between the contributors determined at the time of judgment.[67] The *pari passu* approach has since been treated as the better presumption in cases where a party (innocent or not) deals with a fund co-owned by others.[68]

---

62 ibid., 552.
63 ibid., 555.
64 C. Dickens, *Oliver Twist*, Bentley 1838.
65 [1992] 4 All ER 22.
66 Ibid., 39.
67 Per Woolf LJ, ibid.: 'pari passu ex post facto'.
68 *Russell-Cooke Trust v Prentis* [2003] 2 All ER 478; *Commerzbank*, n. 20; *NCA v Robb* [2015] Ch. 520, [64]; *Charity Commission v Framjee* [2015] 1 WLR 16.

We again see a reference to 'presumed intention' at the core of the Court's reasoning. What are these intentions? Lord Diplock explained this concept of intention in *Gissing v Gissing*:[69]

> [E]ffect is given to the inferences as to the intentions of parties to a trans-action which a reasonable man would draw from their words or conduct and not to any subjective intention or absence of intention which was not made manifest at the time of the transaction itself. It is for the court to determine what those inferences are.

In *Barlow Clowes*, Leggatt LJ put it pithily: 'The court goes by what must be presumed to have been the intention'.[70] In the absence of express writ-ten terms in any mixing arrangement, the court is to infer 'intentions' from the arrangement's terms and the parties' conduct, standing in the shoes of a reasonable person. If we remove the anthropomorphism, 'intention' means the most commercially reasonable solution that fits the facts. Hence in *Barlow Clowes* the Court held that, because the transaction involved a common fund, allocations to individual investors were not intended and therefore *Clayton's* case was inapplicable.[71] This followed Learned Hand J's reasoning in *Re Walter J Schmidt & Co., Ex parte Feuerbach*,[72] refusing to apply *Clayton's* case to allocate a loss between two trust beneficiaries:

> The rule in *Clayton's Case* is to allocate the payments upon an account. Some rule had to be adopted, and though any presumption of intent was a fiction, priority in time was the most natural basis of allocation. It has no relevancy whatever to a case like this. Here two people are jointly interested in a fund held for them by a common trustee. There is no reason in law or justice why his depredations upon the fund should not be borne equally between them. To throw all the loss upon one, through the mere chance of his being earlier in time, is irrational and arbitrary, and is equally a fiction as the rule in *Clayton's Case*. When the law adopts a fiction, it is, or at least it should be, for some purpose of justice. To adopt it here is to apportion a common misfortune through a test which has no relation whatever to the justice of the case.

Barlow Clowes picked up this idea of a 'common misfortune'.[73] Woolf LJ went further than his brethren, stating that in all circumstances involving a common

69 [1971] AC 886, 906.
70 *Barlow Clowes*, n. 65, 46.
71 Ibid., 41, 45–46.
72 298 F. 314, 316 (SDNY 1923).
73 See *Re Stanford International Bank* [2019] UKPC 45, [75]–[76].

misfortune, the parties would not have intended FIFO but equal distribution.[74] This is the most results-oriented reasoning utilising a presumed intention.

There are nevertheless limits to the common misfortune reasoning. First, it seems still to depend on a 'common misfortune' and suggests that equality is not unfair because of the large number of investors who expect equal treatment as a group.[75] When there are fewer parties with substantially unequal situations, and the issue is allocating amongst a range of withdrawals, not 'salvaging' the situation, FIFO might not be inapplicable,[76] as with Barnardo's in *Re Diplock*.

The role of intention is in reality smaller in this area than might be supposed. Subjective intentions of a single withdrawing party are irrelevant if they countermand the overall investment scheme's design. But if there are express arrangement terms, the court will be bound to give them effect as a matter of objective construction. Presumed intentions are a means for the court to find a commercially reasonable outcome.

9.3.2 *Consensual mixtures and intentions*

For consensual mixtures, the parties' intentions govern the withdrawals' identification. Intention is not just a legal mechanism for achieving a just outcome, and cannot be attacked as a 'fiction'. It sets the terms of the consensual relationship, and within those limits the intentions of the withdrawing party allocate ownership of withdrawals.

Where parties have by common intention mixed intangibles in a fund, withdrawals from the fund will, absent contrary evidence, be interpreted consistently with that initial common intention. Alternatively, in substance synonymously, the withdrawing party will be deemed to have dealt with the fund 'honestly'; i.e. in accordance with the terms set with the relationship governing the mixture.

The most common instance in the case of intangibles is a joint bank account.[77] *Re Bishop* summarised the applicable principles:

[I]n the absence of some circumstances or some evidence of intention that the joint account was to have a limited operation or was set up and kept up for some special purpose, each [party] has power to draw on the joint account not only for the benefit of the [parties] but for his or her own benefit.[78]

---

74 *Barlow Clowes*, n. 65, 41.
75 *Equity Trust*, n. 30, [204].
76 *Re Allanfield Property Insurance Services* [2015] EWHC 3721 (Ch.), [130]–[131].
77 *Re Young* (1885) 28 Ch. D 705, 707; Bridge et al., n. 14, [2-044].
78 [1965] Ch. 450, 458–59 (Stamp J).

Intention has a twofold role: it sets the overall terms of the account, and can limit it to 'some specific or limited purpose'. Within those limits, the intentions of each withdrawing party determine the shares affected.[79] If an intention to withdraw from the fund is unlawful, it will sever the joint tenancy in equity, and the withdrawing party will be deemed to have dealt with the fund 'honestly', drawing on their own share.[80]

A novel situation arose in the late twentieth-century case *Hunter v Moss*,[81] where a person with a fund of fungible intangible assets purported to declare a trust over part of it in favour of another. The narrow issue was whether there was sufficient certainty of subject over part of the shares. The reasoning was severely criticised,[82] but the outcome has generally been accepted.[83] One defence of *Hunter* was that, where a trustee holds assets consensually mixed with beneficiary assets, if the trustee chooses to withdraw, the tracing rules applicable to wrongful mixtures should apply, because the trustee 'becomes under a duty to segregate the trust assets from his own'.[84] It is not clear why such a duty to separate should arise if the beneficiary has agreed to the mixture (or it was part of the terms of a gift).

This reasoning shows that equity lawyers are more familiar with the rules for wrongful than consensual mixtures, putting the cart before the horse. Before one can identify what is right or wrong (for the honesty presumption), the relationship's terms must be known. It is circular to deduce those terms from principles for wrongdoing. Therefore, the principles for consensual mixtures must be logically prior to those for wrongful mixtures.

An acceptable judicial solution to *Hunter* was supplied in New South Wales' *White v Shortall*,[85] and adopted in England.[86] Campbell J analysed a purported declaration of trust over 222,000 of 1.5 million shares as in substance a trust over the whole fund of shares for both parties.

> The declaration of trust left [the trustee] free to deal with the parcel of 1.5 million shares as he pleased, provided that it was not reduced below [222,000], ... at least 222,000 were left unencumbered, and ... the plaintiff was entitled to call for the transfer of 222,000 shares at any time...

---

79 E.g. ibid.; *Jones v Maynard* [1951] Ch. 572; *Heseltine v Heseltine* [1971] 1 WLR 342.
80 E.g. *Williams v Hensman* (1861) 1 J & H 546, 558; *Re Hewett* [1894] 1 Ch. 363; *Re Sharer* (1912) 57 SJ 60.
81 n. 16.
82 D. Hayton, 'Uncertainty of Subject Matter of Trusts' (1994) 110 *LQR* 335.
83 P. Parkinson, 'Re-Conceptualising the Express Trust' [2002] *CLJ* 657, 657–76; R. Goode, 'Are Intangible Assets Fungible?' [2003] *LMCLQ* 379.
84 J. Martin, 'Certainty of subject matter: a defence of *Hunter v. Moss*' [1996] *Conv.* 223–27.
85 n. 16.
86 *Pearson v Lehman Brothers Finance* (*Lehman Rascals*) [2010] EWHC 2914 (Ch.), [232].

Whether any such sale was a breach of trust on his part, is an entirely different question. Under the trust the defendant declared, he has no power to sell those shares that he held on trust for the plaintiff. Thus if he were to sell any shares, with the intention of thereby diminishing the number of shares he held in trust, ... his action would be a breach of trust. If he were to sell some of his shareholding, and ... did not identify whether the shares that he sold were beneficially his own, the same presumption as is used in tracing would be applied, so that he would be presumed to be acting in accordance with his obligations as trustee, and thus to be selling his own shares.[87]

This analysis shows that a trustee can form an actual intention about what to do with the mixed property, providing it is within the limits of their *power* under the trust. The terms of the trust enable a court to determine whether the trustee is in breach of trust; thus the rules on unmixing closely resemble the presumption of honesty. However, there is a major difference. Unlike under the honesty presumption, a trustee can form an intention to affect the beneficiary's interests if it would not breach the trust.

9.3.3 Overarching principles

As shown, there are two different scenarios where the law has developed solutions for unmixing funds in equity, with minimal crossover between them. The judicially developed solutions for wrongful and innocent accidental mixtures include an opaque use of intention (at times, seeming to involve actual intentions and at others, determined by policy) and culpability or wrongfulness (involving subordination based on an irrebuttable presumption of honesty). Consensual mixtures involve giving effect to parties' actual intentions in the creation of their initial relationship, which in turn sets the mixing party's powers, within which their intentions as to individual decisions operate. The factor seemingly present in all types of mixtures is some form of intention. This section will explain how intention, together with culpability, provides an overarching explanation for the rules for mixing and unmixing assets.

The doctrine of subordination might be explicable as an equitable version of the common-law rule that evidential uncertainties should be construed against the party who wrongfully created them.[88] However, this would depend on whether a fund was wrongfully mixed *ab initio*, so that the wrongdoer is clearly responsible for creating the uncertainty about future withdrawals, or else mixed accidentally or consensually, and later wrongfully interfered with by the withdrawing party. Another explanation would then be needed for

---

87 *White*, n. 16, [210], [257].
88 The evidential rule is found in *Armory v Delamirie* (1722) 1 Str. 505 and was applied to mixtures of tangibles in *Indian Oil Corp. v Greenstone Shipping* [1988] QB 345, 370.

wrongful interferences with consensually created mixtures. But the explanations for *Hunter* suggest that one single or two similar principles are involved here. Moreover, the common-law evidential rule was not part of the reasoning in *Re Hallett* or *Re Oatway* where the explanation involved a presumption of honesty or right to withdraw (though used early as a basis for tracing by Lord Eldon[89] and recently by Lord Millett *obiter*[90]).

There are two clues to the overarching doctrine in *Re Hallett*: first, the repeated reference to a fiduciary relationship; second, the language of the presumption.

The references to a fiduciary relationship have proved controversial, because later authority, notably *Re Diplock*,[91] treated the existence of a fiduciary relationship as a pre-requisite to trace in equity.[92] Televantos has explained[93] that the meaning of 'fiduciary' has narrowed over time; at the time of *Re Hallett* the meaning was much broader than the modern understanding.[94] Nineteenth-century fiduciaries are described as '[p]artaking of the character of a trustee'.[95] In *Re Hallett*, Jessel MR defined a fiduciary relationship as:[96]

> one in respect of which, if a wrong arise, the same remedy exists against the wrongdoer on behalf of the principal as would exist against a trustee on behalf of the *cestui que trust*.

Though references to fiduciaries abound in the framing of the tracing rules, these suggest that the central case is that of a trustee.

The second clue is the presumption of honesty. The terms in *Re Hallett* are 'honesty',[97] 'rightfully',[98] and 'lawfully'.[99] What is right or wrong can only be determined by some *rule* that is or is not breached. That must be, on *Re Hallett*'s definition of a fiduciary, some rule governing the fiduciary relationship, i.e. the trust's terms. With a passive trust, where the duty is simply to hold the property separately for the beneficiary, most dealings by the trustee with the assets, unless instructed by the beneficiary, will be a breach of trust and therefore wrongful conduct. But in more complex trusts the trustees will have extensive powers. Authorised exercises of trustees' powers over the trust

---

89 *Lupton v White* (1808) 15 Ves. 432. See Nair, n. 12, [2.38]–[2.66].
90 *Foskett*, n. 11, 132.
91 n. 20, 523.
92 This impliedly excluded absolute titles from the protection of equity's ability to trace, weakening their overall protection, despite an absolute title being English law's highest-known title.
93 A. Televantos, 'Losing the Fiduciary Requirement for Equitable Tracing Claims' (2017) 133 *LQR* 492.
94 *Bristol & West Building Society v Mothew* [1998] Ch. 1.
95 *Foley v Hill* (1848) 2 HL Cas. 28, 35.
96 *Re Hallett*, n. 1, 712–13.
97 Ibid., 735–43.
98 Ibid., 727–28.
99 Ibid., 699.

assets overreach the beneficiary's interest in those assets.[100] So there can be no tracing if the trustee's mixing is pursuant to an express power, even if it were otherwise a breach of trust, because the presence of the power means the trustee's actions are not wrongful, and therefore the beneficiary's proprietary rights are validly altered by the trustee's actions.[101]

The reasoning in *White v Shortall* illustrates how the powers of the trustee determine the unmixing. The trustee and beneficiary have interests in the whole fund. Questions of withdrawals are not governed by pre-existing proprietary rights in the individual assets but by the obligations of the trustee. The trustee has a power to deal with the whole fund except for the number allotted to the beneficiary, which must be kept aside unencumbered. If the trustee acts *intra vires*, their intention in each decision governs the unmixing. Two intentions are involved: the decision will accord with the intentions that set the terms of the relationship and the intention as to the individual transaction. If the trustee acts *ultra vires*, the decision is void in equity,[102] the beneficiary's interest is not overreached and persists. The fiduciary principle[103] (established as part of the relationship from the intentions of the parties) subordinates the trustee to the beneficiary. The beneficiary has the ability to elect *ex post* how to allocate the ownership to the withdrawal.[104]

The net result of this is that it is equally correct to speak of the intention of the parties and the fiduciary relationship governing the unmixing of the account, insofar as the parties' intention determines the terms of the fiduciary relationship and the trustee's actions are characterised by reference to the trustee's powers and duties defined by that relationship. The trustee's intentions with respect to each individual transaction are only effective if they are within the scope of the trustee's powers and duties.[105]

When, rarely, there is a mixture and the mixing party is not a fiduciary to the other parties (as in *Re Diplock*) the parties are innocent and neither is subordinated to the other. The question of unmixing is left to the parties' intentions, which, owing to the likely absence of any actual objective intentions, must be found by the court as 'presumed' intentions. As discussed, these can be viewed as the imposition of commercially fair outcomes.

---

100 *Independent Trustee Services v GP Noble Trustees* [2013] Ch. 91, [104]; *State Bank of India v Sood* [1997] Ch. 276.

101 Cf. the *ratio* of *Space Investments v Canadian Imperial Bank of Commerce Trust Co. (Bahamas)* [1986] 1 WLR 1072.

102 *Pitt v Holt* [2013] 2 AC 108.

103 *Mothew*, n. 94.

104 See text accompanying n. 43.

105 Nolan has a similar, more developed argument: R.C. Nolan, 'The administration and maladministration of funds in equity: making a coherent set of choices' in P.G. Turner (ed.) *Equity and Administration*, CUP 2016, 73. Cf. D. Whayman, 'Obligation and Property in Tracing Claims' [2018] *Conv.* 157.

The explanation given so far has centred around an express trust or trust arising from a consensual fiduciary relationship where the parties' intentions set the powers of the mixing party and thus the standard of wrongful dealings. However, this picture is complicated insofar as equity also creates constructive trust relationships and other proprietary interests in response to wrongdoing absent a pre-existing fiduciary relationship,[106] e.g. a constructive trust over stolen property,[107] or upon rescission.[108] This suggests that intention alone cannot be a single overarching principle for all mixtures, because 'fiduciary' relationships (within the meaning in *Re Hallett*) can arise in opposition to wrongful conduct. Nevertheless, the constructive trust is conceptually reliant on the existence of express trusts for its content. The best that can be said then is that neither intention nor culpability is separately a complete explanation for the rules for unmixing mixed funds. Neither can subsume the other, but neither is intelligible alone. Of the two, intention gives the most overall structure to the rules for unmixing mixtures of intangibles.

9.3.4 A comparative perspective

It is interesting, in light of the many difficulties surrounding the development of English law in matters of mixed intangibles, to consider briefly the range of answers provided to these problems in other jurisdictions.[109]

9.3.4.1 US law

Perhaps the approach most useful to compare is that of the United States, both in terms of case law (closely resembling English law) and commentary in the *Restatement (Third) of Restitution and Unjust Enrichment* (R3RUE).[110] US law governing tracing through mixed funds of intangibles is complex, mostly due to variation across states.[111] In terms of its case-law development, the principles, like England's, are in a state of confusion. There is similar ambiguity about the applicability of a doctrine of subordination to wrongful mixtures.[112] US case law also influenced English law, introducing the *pari passu*

---

106 Nair, n. 12, [6.18]–[6.20].
107 *Westdeutsche*, n. 44, 716; *Fistar v Riverwood Legion & Community Club* (2016) 91 NSWLR 732, [37]; Fox, n. 28, [4.93].
108 *Shalson*, n. 49, [122]–[126].
109 Commonwealth responses are closely comparable to England's; we therefore omit detailed discussion.
110 American Law Institute 2010.
111 G.E. Palmer, *The Law of Restitution*, vol. 1, Wolters Kluwer 1978, [2.16]–[2.18].
112 See text to nn. 49–52. Palmer, n. 111, [2.16], 203–5; *Mitchell v Dunn*, 211 Cal. 129; 294 P 386 (1930); *Primeau*, n. 46; *Re AO Brown & Co.*, 189 F. 432, 434 (SDNY 1911) (broader reading of subordination doctrine). Cf. *Republic Supply Co. v Richfield Oil Co.*, 79 F 2d 375 (9th Cir. 1935) (lien over purchased property only); and *Re Redpath*, 224 Neb. 845; 402 NW 2d 648 (1987) (minority view, denying even lien).

approach to allocating withdrawals where a party draws from a fund made up of innocent third-party moneys.[113] Seemingly, in US law the intentions of the withdrawing party play no role for *Diplock* recipients, and an innocent party drawing on a fund partially composed of their own and others' assets will be found to deplete their own share first.[114]

A set of solutions to the same problems faced by English law, but taking an entirely different approach, has recently been adopted in R3RUE. The R3RUE rules involve a radical divergence from English principles, resolving the scenarios above (wrongful, innocent, and other *Diplock* mixtures) independently from the intentions of any parties involved, except insofar as they may elect between different remedies. Wrongful mixtures are governed by a full subordination rule, allowing victims to find the most advantageous marshalling of payments from the fund.[115] The identification of withdrawals from a fund in the hands of an unknowing, innocent recipient are instead made dependent on restitution and unjust enrichment, so that the contributing claimant may trace into profitable investments only insofar as that is compatible with the recipient's duty to make restitution of consequential gains from their unjust enrichment. Where assets belonging to innocent claimants are mixed, but not with the withdrawing party's money, any attributions must be made on a rateable basis.[116]

There is a theoretical problem in the unmixing rules which English authorities have not addressed. Presumptions and intentions may theoretically come into irreconcilable conflict. Suppose T is trustee for B. T has a personal bank account. T adds £1,000 (B's trust money) to this account. T then innocently receives money belonging beneficially to X and adds it to the same account. There is now a mixture of money belonging to T, B, and X. How should the presumptions operate? T is clearly subordinated to B. T and X are equally innocent, so there should be no subordination. But B and X are also equally innocent. X cannot be equal to both T and B. If X is held equal with T, then X is subordinated to B. But if X is held equal to B, T is subordinated to X.[117] English law would probably reach a conclusion that involves applying ordinary rules of priority as articulated in *Re Diplock*.[118] B has priority over T. B and X have equal equities; in terms of unconscionability, X must admit B's claim, but need not prefer it. Therefore, B and X must have equal priorities. While T and X prima facie have equal equities, X cannot be deprived of equality with B.

---

113 Palmer, n. 112 [2.18], 216. *Re Walter J Schmidt*, n. 72; *Matter of Reece*, 122 Misc. 2d 517; 470 NYS 2d 974 (1983); *Ruddle v Moore*, 411 F 2d 718 (DC Cir. 1969); *Murry v Hale*, 203 F Supp. 583 (ED Ark. 1962).

114 *Loring v Baker*, 329 Mass. 63; 106 NE 2d 434 (1952); A.W. Scott, 'Comment: Following the Res and Sharing the Product' (1953) 66 *Harvard Law Review* 872, 875.

115 R3RUE, n. 110, §59(1)–(2).

116 Ibid., §59(3).

117 Cf. the works of M.C. Escher.

118 n. 20, 539.

Therefore, T also becomes subordinated to X, because of T's wrong to B. Put differently, it is not unconscionable for X to receive priority over T because X is wholly innocent in the mixture, whereas T, as a wrongdoer, loses priority to B *and those with equal priority to B.*

R3RUE addresses issues of priority between rules, finding that, where a remedy based on the doctrine of subordination would interfere with the protection of innocent third-party interests, a victim of wrongdoing has a claim in priority to other innocent contributors.[119] The editors reject any reference to the parties' intentions as necessarily fictional:[120]

> The rules for tracing through a commingled fund are often called 'tracing fictions,' and they are sometimes criticized as arbitrary. The rules will indeed appear fictional if they are explained ... as presumptions about the intent of the person making withdrawals ... Outside the narrow scope of §59(2)(b),[121] however, the tracing rules have nothing to do with anyone's intent. They are formal in operation, in that they employ presumptions to answer an otherwise unanswerable question: namely, the extent of the claimant's ownership of the commingled fund or its product. But the answers supplied are not arbitrary: they make a rough, practical compromise between the competing interests of the restitution claimant and of the other persons with an interest in the fund ... The balance initially struck by the tracing rules is graduated, moreover, to reflect the equitable position of the persons at whose expense restitution is awarded.

Therefore the R3RUE commentary on mixed substitutions significantly differs from the case law, both US and English. The R3RUE statement is an interesting example of how rules in this area can be reframed explicitly on the basis of policy, rather than the parties' intentions. (The downside is the loss of flexibility which acting through presumed intentions gives judges.) These principles also offer a straightforward solution to the problems concerning overlaps between the various principles, as they explicitly identify an order of priority for the applicable rules. They should be taken as a useful instrument of comparison by judges and commentators exploring mixtures cases.

However, two criticisms may be tentatively levied against a completely intentions-independent model. Firstly, viewing a party's intentions to unmix their own money when withdrawing from a mixed fund as 'fictional' seems

---

119 R3RUE, n. 110, §59(4).
120 Ibid., §59 cmt b, echoing *Re Kountze Bros.*, 79 F 2d 98, 101–2 (2nd Cir. 1935).
121 §59(2)(b): 'Subsequent contributions by the [wrongdoer] do not restore property previously misappropriated from the claimant, unless the [wrongdoer] affirmatively intends such application'. (Equivalent in England: *James Roscoe (Bolton) v Winder* [1915] 1 Ch. 62.)

inappropriate—an example is *Re Diplock*;[122] a party dealing with a mixed fund may meaningfully form an intention to unmix money coming from a certain source. Another, perhaps more common, example is a party managing a consensually created mixed fund, and forming an intention to act alone so as to sever any joint tenancy.[123] In cases involving wrongdoing, intentions may appear fictional because a party is not permitted to rely on a wrongful intention, but this is otherwise when the withdrawing party acts lawfully or innocently. The reason is that, when there is a consensual mixture, the trusts' terms give the trustee power to deal with the mixed assets within the power's limits. When there is no pre-existing relationship between innocent parties to limit their intentions, why should the parties' intentions, if objectively manifested, not be relevant, as is usual in other property transactions?

The second criticism is that basing the proprietary claim of a party claiming from a mixed fund on rules of restitution puts the remedial cart before the tracing horse. The issue in these cases is precisely whether one can identify money used from a fund as that which belonged to the contributing party— only if the money can be so identified will a claim in restitution follow. Indeed, if a recipient holds two separate bank accounts, one (A) empty and the other (B) containing the recipient's own £1,000, if the innocent contributor puts their money into A, it will be entirely determined by the recipient's intention whether the money from A or B is used to pay for a certain asset. If the innocent recipient's intentions can be relevant in this case, it is unclear why a similar intention, proved by different means, should not determine the identification of withdrawals where the two funds are mixed.

Nevertheless, R3RUE shows that the uncertainty of withdrawals from mixtures of intangible assets can be entirely addressed by rules explicitly rooted in policy and does not require an overarching legal framework of intention: thus avoiding the factual uncertainty entirely. But it does so at the expense of seeing a unity between cases of consensual and wrongful mixtures, which as discussed place the trust's terms at the centre of both rightful and wrongful unmixing.

9.3.4.2 *Civil law jurisdictions*

The approach in civil law is not as straightforward to compare. In civil-law systems, if a party holds a fund of money or other intangibles for another, the conceptual framework is that of a custodian or—for jurisdictions recognising this status—a fiduciary acting under a mandate for another. In these cases, it is far from straightforward that the principal has any proprietary right assertable

---

122 See above 9.3.1.3.
123 See n. 80.

against the fund,[124] but useful analyses may be drawn from the law governing the separation of patrimonies held by an individual.[125] A person's patrimony is the collection of their assets.[126] A party may hold assets in separate patrimonies, so that one of the two is held for a principal and ringfenced from potential creditors' claims.[127] Some jurisdictions achieve a similar effect, not by using separate patrimonies, but by distinguishing the 'material' and 'economic ownership' (*wirtschaftliches Eigentum*) of assets held by a mandatary.[128] In these cases, the outcome is the same, and the principal, holding the 'economic ownership', is able to claim a 'right of separation' of the assets held by the 'material owner' to claim them in priority to the latter's creditors.[129] Both scenarios give priority to the principal for whom the assets are held when claiming back the assets they transferred to the patrimony's holder. However, a further step is required to trace the money held by a mandatary for another into assets purchased with the money so held.

This takes us to the second point. Civilian legal systems do not recognise a right to trace as a corollary of property rights in funds in the same way as apparently recognised in common-law systems—therefore, the rules will instead depend on the civilian doctrine of real subrogation.[130] Briefly, real subrogation is the set of rules at civil law that allows property held for another to be substituted for assets obtained in exchange. As we shall see, however, real subrogation usually depends on the agreement between principal and mandatary—so that one is faced with great difficulties if a mandatary uses money or other assets held for a principal in an unauthorised transaction. Generally, however, rules governing tracing have been developed in much finer detail in common-law systems than in civilian systems.[131]

Finally, we are not presently concerned with analogies between civilian patrimonies/real subrogation and common-law trusts/tracing, but with the corollaries of that system for cases involving mixed substitutions of intangibles. Here, various further difficulties arise. While the analogy with *confusio* is at

---

124 E.g. A. Pretto, 'Comparative Personal Property: The Case of Shares' (2001) 1 *Global Jurist Advances* 1, 60–65.

125 For differences between 'patrimony' and 'trust' see L. Smith, 'Trust and Patrimony' in R. Valsan (ed.) *Trusts and Patrimonies*, Edinburgh University Press 2015, 42–61.

126 Though the term may also be used to include a party's liabilities as well as assets.

127 Smith, n. 125, 42–61.

128 E.g. Austrian law: see W. Kastner and P. Doralt, *Gesellschafts- und Unternehmensrecht*, Manz 1982, 608ff; M. Graziedei et al. (eds), *Commercial Trusts in European Private Law*, CUP 2005, 286–87.

129 For the right of separation see e.g. Austria's §44, *Konkursordnung* (Insolvency Act) (see now §44, *Insolvenzordnung*); Graziedei et al., n. 128, 285–87.

130 M. Raczynska, 'Parallels between the civilian separate patrimony, real subrogation and the idea of property in a trust fund' in L. Smith (ed.), *The Worlds of the Trust*, CUP 2013, 454–80.

131 E.g. E. von Caemmerer and P. Schlechtriem (eds), *International Encyclopedia of Comparative Law Volume 10*, Brill 2007, [8-83]–[8-87].

least arguable at common law,[132] civil-law jurisdictions do not view cases of mixed substitutions of intangible assets as mixtures of any kind.[133] The question depends instead on whether a separate patrimony, or a party's 'economic ownership' of assets, can be identified where a mandatary mixes the money or other intangibles received by a principal with their own. This means we must consider (i) whether a principal can separate and claim in priority against a mandatary's creditors assets transferred to the mandatary when such a mixture occurs, (ii) whether assets belonging to the principal have been dissipated by the mandatary's withdrawals, and (iii) whether real subrogation allows such a principal to claim substitute assets held by the mandatary, and in what shares against other innocent contributors or the mandatary themselves.

9.3.4.2.1 PRIORITY CLAIMS INTO MIXED FUNDS

Most European jurisdictions, including Austria, Belgium, Denmark, Finland, Germany, the Netherlands, and Portugal do not recognise the possibility of economic ownership or a separate patrimony surviving a mixture with a party's assets.[134]

Among few exceptions, French law seemingly only allows it in the narrow case of a *consignation* or *sequester*, i.e. a payment with a depositee of a sum disputed between two parties pending judgment in relation to it.[135] In Italian law, mixed moneys and other unidentifiable intangibles can be claimed as 'moveable assets that are in the possession of the insolvent' only if the depositee has not been granted the right to dispose of them, and if they remain unmixed with the depositee's own.[136] Commentary on this issue remains divided,[137] but judgments of the highest court have consistently held that an asset needs to be 'ascertained in its specific and precise individuality' to be claimed, and that a *confusion* of the money with that of the mandatary or depositee would defeat such a claim.[138] The one notable exception in this sphere is Spanish

---

132 *Foskett*, n. 11.

133 Rules governing mixtures of tangibles, even fungibles, are kept conceptually distinct as concerning straightforwardly proprietary issues: see C. von Bar et al. (eds), *Principles, Definitions and Model Rules of European Private Law: Draft Common Frame of Reference (DFCR)*, Bk. 8, pt. 5:202, 4291–99, <http://www.transformacje.pl/wp-content/uploads/2012/12/european-private-law_en.pdf> accessed 15.08.2023.

134 Graziedei et al., n. 128, 287–93, 298–302.

135 Cass. com., 13 Nov. 2001, no. 97–16.652, Bull. civ. IV no. 177 and Cass. com., 24 Apr. 2007, no. 06–16.215, Bull. civ. IV no. 114; A. Touzain, *La Consignation*, Panthéon-Assas 2022, [617].

136 RD 16 March 1924, no. 267, art. 103.

137 App. Milano, 15 February 1985, Fallimento, 1985, 793.

138 G. Bozza, 'Le domande di rivendica e restituzione' in A. Jorio and B. Sassani (eds), *Trattato delle procedure concorsuali*, a cura Giuffré 2014, 973; Graziedei et al., n. 128, 314–15. See, for the general principle regarding appropriation, Cass., 14 June 2018, no. 15703, *Società*, 2018, 1058.

law's approach: where money is given to a fiduciary mandatary, the mandatary receives only 'formal ownership' and, despite a mixture with the fiduciary's own fund, the assets are seemingly deemed separate for insolvency purposes.[139] There is still a divide among Spanish commentators about the extent to which such a division is recognised,[140] but the doctrine of separation of property has been applied by the Spanish Supreme Court on numerous occasions.[141]

9.3.4.2.2 DISSIPATIONS BY THE FUND-HOLDER

As all the jurisdictions examined above, except Spain, do not contemplate the possibility of a proprietary claim to intangibles surviving in cases of mixture with a mandatary or other fiduciary, the funds will be at the risk of the principal if the fiduciary violates the mandate and unlawfully mixes them with their own.[142]

Spain is therefore the only jurisdiction identified where rules determining attributions of outward payments would be relevant, especially since the goods are protected from insolvency under the Commercial Code, which allows recovery of the property on the basis that the transferor retains title.[143] This proprietary base for the claim might cause concern where it is argued that the mandatary disposed of the principal's assets; however, the solution is more likely the simpler one, that as long as sufficient money remains in the account to satisfy the principal, the claim will have priority over the remaining creditors.[144]

9.3.4.2.3 TRACING

For most civil-law jurisdictions, notably excepting Spain, the only case of 'mixture' that needs addressing is that of moneys or other intangibles belonging to

---

139 S. Cámara Lapuente, 'Operaciones fiduciarais o *trusts* en Derecho Español' (1999) *Revista Crítica de Derecho Immobiliario* 1807, n. 181, cited in Graziedei et al., n. 128, 330, n. 169. The correct characterisation of this institute remains disputed, see e.g. A. Martín León, 'Negocios fiduciarios y usucapión' (2013) 66 *Anuario de Derecho Civil* 3, 1163–276, 1179–80.

140 E.g. B. Rodríguez Rosado, *Fiducia y pacto de retro en garantía*, Marcial Pons 1998, 120; R. de Ángel Yágüez, 'Problemas que suscita la venta en garantía en relación con los procedimientos de ejecución del deudor' (1973) *Revista Crítica de Derecho Inmobiliario*, Jan–Feb, 53; J. Garrigues Díaz Cañabate, *Negocios fiduciarios en el Derecho mercantil*, Civitas 1978, 67.

141 E.g. SSTS, 25 February 2013, 8 October 2012, 4 October 2011, 5 December 2005.

142 Most of these jurisdictions respond to the injustice that may result through specific legislation relating to the guarantees and insurance that parties acting as agents or in other fiduciary capacities must put in place. See Graziedei et al., n. 128, 287 (Austria), 290 (Belgium), 293 (Denmark).

143 Art. 908. RD, 22 August 1885, Código Comercio; Graziedei et al., n. 128, 330.

144 This seems to be the approach taken for granted under the *fiducia cum amico*: Cámara Lapuente, n. 139.

several principals, deposited in a fund kept separate from that of the mandatary, amounting to a separate patrimony. The rules governing these cases are, however, much more restrictive than the common-law rules—principals have a prima facie[145] pro rata claim to the funds in priority to the mandatary's unsecured creditors. If the money has been used to purchase assets, approaches to tracing vary. Some systems only allow contributors to claim the traceable proceeds of the assets if the mandatary intended to use the money for the principal's purposes.[146] Here, the basis of the principal's property right in the traceable assets is the mandatary's authority to act for the principals, not the proprietary basis in the moneys themselves, and if the mandatary intended to use the assets for his own purposes, or was acting outwith his authority, this will leave the principals with a mere unsecured personal claim for compensation.[147] In other systems, the mere existence of the mandate suffices to allow tracing, but the source of the property right, even in these systems, is the ratification of the agent's conduct—not the proprietary base in the moneys used.[148] Thus, in all these systems, tracing leads to the mandators' contractual right to have title to the fund-purchased assets transferred into their name, but until this happens the right is merely personal, binding no third parties.[149] In any case, as soon as the moneys, whether belonging to a single or numerous different principals, are mixed with the fiduciary's own, this results in a type-(ii) situation and any priority is lost, with the fiduciary deemed the sole owner of the full sum. The innocent contributors are thereafter treated as unsecured creditors.

In Spain, the situation is slightly closer to that in England, insofar as arts. 1717 and 1720 of the Commercial Code allow for tracing into assets purchased by a mandatary when they are purchased with another's (in this case, material or economic) property,[150] and the 'formal' title acquired by the mandatary has been described by the Supreme Court as provisional only.[151] This raises potential tracing issues that would need addressing by Spanish lawyers and courts; however, the question of what approach would be adopted in cases of money mixed with those of the trustee remains unaddressed in both case law and commentary, leaving a gap in Spanish doctrine.

Reviewing these civil-law jurisdictions shows that the uncertainty arising in English law is largely a function of how the initial issue of whether and how property rights are capable of being mixed is viewed. No helpful

---

145 Subject to e.g. applicable statutory exceptions, like preference rules.
146 Seemingly so in Belgium, Finland, France, Greece, the Netherlands, Scotland, and Sweden: Graziedei et al., n. 128, 369–403.
147 Some jurisdictions emphasise intentions, others the objective scope of the agent's authority: ibid., 404.
148 See e.g. Austria, Germany, Italy, Luxembourg, and Portugal in ibid., 369–403.
149 Ibid., 370 (Austria), 380 (France).
150 Arts. 1717, 1720, RD, 22 August 1885, *Código Comercio*; Graziedei et al., n. 128, 399.
151 STS, 22 May 1964, STS 15 May 1983; Graziedei et al., n. 128, 399.

doctrinal structures exist here to aid in interrogating English policy or inten-tion-interpreting discussions. Quite differently based risk decisions are made in the civil law because of the different proprietary starting point, demon-strating that the factual uncertainty problem need not exist. But, where it does, there is no more developed solution than that discussed above for the common law.

9.4 Conclusions

This chapter shows that there are multiple levels of uncertainty in common-law treatments of withdrawals from mixtures of intangible assets. First, the law must determine how to allocate withdrawals in the absence of a physical coun-terpart on which a natural or value-neutral rule could be drawn. The review of civil-law jurisdictions shows that the very ability to see intangible property as capable of mixing and unmixing is what allows the uncertainty to arise at all. It need not exist unless property law rules allow it. In that sense, the uncertainty is a legal or normative uncertainty, and the rules for unmixing are really issues of legal policy and the application of legal standards.

A second uncertainty problem is created by the standards applied by English law to resolve the factual uncertainty of mixing. The common law evolved sev-eral solutions, many relying on the concept of intention. This creates a new factual uncertainty, as the relevant intention needs ascertaining. Intention is treated inconsistently by courts and has been criticised as a legal fiction.

We have shown that intention is a consistent standard so long as it is under-stood in multiple senses, with consensual mixtures placed at the centre of the puzzle. In the central case of an express trust, intention sets the terms of the trustee's powers and duties in dealing with the assets. When the trustee acts in conformity with these, their intention determines the ownership of with-drawals from the fund. If the trustee exceeds their powers, their intention is subordinated to the beneficiary, who can elect how to treat their property after the fact, in substance giving effect to the beneficiary's *ex post* intention. When there is no fiduciary relationship between the parties, and they are innocent as against each other, the mixing party's intentions nominally govern the own-ership, but in practice this requires the courts to find a presumed intention. Finally, equity will sometimes impose the equivalent of fiduciary relationships non-consensually on parties in response to wrongful conduct. This is an excep-tion to the central explanatory place of intention. But once the non-consen-sual relationship is imposed, it operates remedially in the same manner as a consensual fiduciary relationship.

US law shows that the concept of intention can be discarded in favour of explicit policy-based rules in the context of wrongful and innocent mix-tures. This explanation sidesteps the factual uncertainty problem, but does not work for consensual mixtures. Intention therefore cannot be wholly jettisoned from the resolution of the uncertainty created by mixtures of intangible assets. Although the use of intention at times does seem to be a mask for policy-based rules, this is no different to the general way in which intention is used in the common law in other situations.

Part 4

Broader perspectives on law and uncertainty

10 A spectrum of uncertainty

Matthew Dyson

The chapter explores legal uncertainty, taking criminal law as an example.[1] The earlier chapters in this book show how law is applied when facts are imperfectly known; here we fold in the reality that laws themselves are often uncertain. This chapter argues that both factual and legal descriptions exist on a spectrum, from certain to uncertain. Indeed, they are on the *same spectrum*. More than that, legal actors even respond to them in the same way. Where the outcome of the legal actor's operation is binary, liability or no liability, many of the same techniques are used to respond to factual and legal uncertainty. Since a decision-maker has to decide whether the legal conditions for liability are met by the facts, the decision sometimes turns on which is more malleable, law or fact. Legal uncertainty has been formulated, guided, and obscured in ways that tell us something valuable about legal reasoning more generally. In particular, the shared use of some of the same techniques to address factual and legal uncertainty suggests two things. First, it highlights how the uncertainty is thought to be capable of being remediated by the same means, regardless of whether it is fact or law. Second, it suggests that legal uncertainty can be as intractable as proving facts such as events or mental states. The criminal law has used many legal techniques, some foundational, such as the fiction that criminal law itself originated in a breach of the King's Peace.[2] This chapter particularly looks at examples from English law concerning presumptions and deeming provisions.

10.1 A spectrum of fact and law

Uncertainty is inherent in human decision-making. Decisions in the face of uncertainty have particularly significant consequences where the state also

---

1 Decisions of legal actors lead to binary outcomes beyond the criminal law but criminal law provides enough examples to substantiate the claim. In addition, in the common law tradition, facts need to be proven to a higher standard in criminal law than in civil law, suggesting that the factual units on the spectrum, if satisfied by criminal law, would be satisfied by civil law.
2 See e.g. P. Alldridge, 'Some Uses of Legal Fictions in Criminal Law' in M. Del Mar and W. Twining (eds), *Legal Fictions in Theory and Practice*, Springer 2015.

DOI: 10.4324/9781003537526-14

asserts the authority to punish. Part of the rationale of criminal law hinges on claims about that uncertainty, claims that there are ways to manage it. In English law, the claims most commonly articulated focus on the process of adjudication being fair. For at least a hundred years, this has included the premises that both sides have 'equal arms'; lay justice is administered fairly; the prosecution must prove beyond reasonable doubt that the offence was committed; and there is some system of review or appeal. These are most often discussed with reference to *factual uncertainty*. It is not clear there that those claims are always about finding truth, and thus, rendering uncertain facts certain. They might instead demonstrate only a legitimacy of enquiry and decision-making, not objective certainty. Indeed, while there are mechanisms to prevent cases which are under-evidenced proceeding through the courts, there is a wide range of cases that are left, and, it is thought, should be left, to the predominantly lay fact-finders. Within that range, legal actors tend to operate on the basis that the facts are sufficiently known at the point of application of the law. However, how resolved they are depends on the purpose they are to be put to. Hence, *legal uncertainty* is just as key to resolving the application of the law. In legal contexts, the uncertainty is also assumed to be resolved at the point of application, and again often is not. Criminal law hides some uncertainty, since some of the determinations about how law is applied do not have to be explained by reasons: juries need not give reasons, and the reasoning of magistrates need not be extensive. In addition, the criminal law itself can rely on open-textured concepts, including with respect to foundational ones such as fault doctrines and causation. Similarly, while the standard and burden of proof of facts are well known, there is no such trite standard for showing what the law is, and what it means to a particular set of facts. Beyond this, *law* has the significant difference of potentially applying beyond any particular dispute. The process of removing or reducing legal uncertainty is far more contentious than factual uncertainty.

Many of the techniques traditionally associated with deciding legal outcomes for factual uncertainty are also able, and have been used, to provide outcomes for legal uncertainty. These techniques differ in whether they are substantive techniques, describing legal rules claiming to concern doctrine, or procedural techniques, shaping how doctrinal rules are applied in practice. They also range in how openly legal actors acknowledge the uncertainty. But, remarkably, the most significant substantive examples, especially presumptions and deeming provisions, have all been applied to resolve both factual and legal uncertainty. If a particular fact that would challenge legal actors' understanding or acceptance of a legal rule cannot arise, the rule need not change. Similarly, if an uncertain rule can be treated as providing an acceptable outcome, the rule need not formally change. The purpose of factual and substantive tricks like these is typically the same: to avoid changing, or appearing to change, the substantive law either in general, or by reducing its ambiguity but still resolving the question in front of the decision-maker under a changed rule. They give scope for the *law in action* to continue or change, without formally changing all of the *law in the books*.[3] It does so by requiring the *law in minds* to pretend or accept that something ambiguous or erroneous is correct.[4] The most interesting effect of such tricks is to maintain not just some rule of substantive law, but an existing intellectual structure, while in fact achieving legal change.

One of the most famous descriptions of an unreal statement of law is the 'legal fiction'. That is perhaps most famously known, at least to Anglophone lawyers, from Henry Maine's *Ancient Law*;[5] he called it one of the three main instrumentalities of legal change. Fictions, along with 'equity' and 'legislation', were said to be necessary to prevent settled systems of law or legal practices from stagnating. For Maine, legal fictions signified 'any assumption which conceals, or affects to conceal, the fact that a rule of law has undergone alteration, its letter remaining unchanged, its operation being modified'.[6] Maine's discussion began in Roman law, but continued through to a few more contemporaneous examples. Other definitions have been more or less pithy.[7] 'Legal fiction' has a vast range of definitions, and centuries of intellectual baggage. It seems better to avoid relying on it, while still being able to draw on the material developed on fictions. Fictions have most commonly been described as covering legal concepts, such as the fiction of 'justice' or 'equity', or facts. And the temptation is that any doctrinal legal rule is expressed at the factual end of the spectrum. Rather than being actively criticised, a technique like this need only be tolerated rather than accepted as correct. Debate and criticism can be present within the legal system, but do not change the effect of the rule.[8] A spectrum of approval can be seen in the cognate legal fictions, from Blackstone and Maine, who praised their utility, to Bentham and to a

---

3 See e.g. R. Pound, 'Law in Books and Law in Action' (1910) 44 *American Law Review* 12; W. Ewald, 'The Jurisprudential Approach to Comparative Law: A Field Guide to "Rats"' (1998) 46 *The American Journal of Comparative Law* 701, 704.

4 H.S. Maine, *Ancient Law*, Dent 1861, 16: 'They satisfy the desire for improvement, which is not quite wanting, at the same time that they do not offend the superstitious disrelish for change which is always present ... To revile them as merely fraudulent is to betray ignorance of their peculiar office in the historical development of the law ... Now legal fictions are the greatest of obstacles to symmetrical classification'.

5 Maine, n. 4.

6 Ibid., 16.

7 Cf. 'consciously counterfactual proposition'—Petroski, said of legal fictions, which might be put as 'consciously counterfactual or ambiguous statement of law': K. Petroski, 'Legal Fictions and the Limits of Legal Language' (2013) 9 *International Journal of Law in Context* 485, 486. Cf. also M. Del Mar, 'Legal Fictions and Legal Change' (2013) 9 *International Journal of Law in Context* 442, 442, noting again of legal fictions, 'any suspension of one or more of the required operative facts leading to the imposition of an associated normative consequence, whether this suspension is introduced because of (1) the absence of proof of some previously required fact; or (2) the presence of proof to the contrary', seen as a process of experimentation where courts communicate with each other about making a particular change more explicit.

8 For a similar use, see L. Harmon, 'Falling Off the Vine: Legal Fictions and the Doctrine of Substituted Judgment' (1990) 100 *Yale Law Journal* 1, esp. 3.

lesser extent Austin, who poured scorn on them as based in ignorance.[9] In some cases, authors who had previously criticised them came later to value them, such as Roscoe Pound.[10]

Of course, factual contexts will be closely connected to legal ones, as legal fictions themselves demonstrate: a legal fiction is attractive as a means to change the facts because you are unwilling or unable to change the law. So, the malleability of fact and law are closely connected. Some examples show that it is not always easy to decide what has been fudged.

One example turns on a vague and counter-intuitive legal concept: an English court in 1969 held it was a 'continuing act' to park a car on a person's foot without knowing, but then to remain in the car once you realise, and thus the fault and act were contemporaneous.[11] This trick would permit a conviction without explaining the doctrinal mechanism required to do so. It seems to layer over a well-known if somewhat complex concept, an 'act', characteristics which were not meaningfully described, or proven, at trial. It blurs from a factual problem, appreciable application of force when the *mens rea* is present, to a legal problem: what satisfies as an act for the purposes of the *actus reus*.

Similarly, English law has perpetuated uncertainty in the make-up of some of its offences, not just its general principles. For example, in England it has been unclear for at least 150 years whether the absence of the complainant's consent is something that must be proven against the defendant in prosecution for battery. The alternative might be true, that the complainant's consent is a defence that the defendant needs to raise and substantiate. Case law and commentary support both positions, but the majority position in the courts seems to be that consent is a defence to a charge, to be raised by the defendant before the prosecution have to disprove it.[12] In practice, only a low level of evidence from the defendant needs to be shown to then require the prosecutor to prove there was no consent. Such evidence is normally obvious, and not self-incriminating, so is easily raised. There has been little pressure on the substantive legal position to become clearer, since in practice its ambiguity rarely disrupts adjudication.

---

9 Ibid., 3–11.
10 R. Pound, 'Spurious Interpretation' (1907) 7 *Columbia Law Review* 379; cf. R. Pound, *Interpretations of Legal History*, Macmillan 1923.
11 *Fagan v MPC* [1969] 1 QB 439.
12 'It is a manifest contradiction in terms to say that the defendant assaulted the plaintiff by his permission': *Christopherson v Bare* (1848) 11 QB 473, 477 (Lord Denman CJ). Glanville Williams said that it is 'inherent in the conception of assault and battery that the victim does not consent': G. Williams, 'Consent and Public Policy' [1962] *Crim. LR* 74, 75; see also the view of P. Murphy, 'Flogging live complainants and dead horses: we may no longer need to be in bondage to *Brown*' [2011] *Crim. LR* 758, 759 cf. the leading decision of *R v Brown* [1994] 1 AC 212.

Factual uncertainty is not the present focus, but a few interesting examples will be noted. One is jury equity/jury nullification decisions,[13] particularly those under the 'Bloody Code'.[14] Larceny of property worth more than 39 shillings was a capital offence, whereas at that value or below it was punishable by transportation. A surprising number of persons convicted of theft were found by the jury to have stolen 39 shillings' worth of goods, despite the allegation concerning property worth more. A more modern example is where appeal courts assert that the evidence clearly demonstrates that the jury must have found fact X, even though, in applying a rule which has since been overturned, the jury were not asked to decide on X.[15] This formulation avoids having to grant an appeal, and might support claims that the relevant recent change in the law was not unacceptably wide in effect.

The parallels between factual and legal uncertainty, and legal actors' responses to them, reveal insights into legal reasoning. The places where legal actors tolerate, openly or without realising, ambiguity of legal rules might better inform how those rules actually work, when understood against the factual uncertainty they have to apply to. The question becomes how far the law can be both stable and flexible without becoming too unreal. The unreality seems to be more accepted in factual instances. There, it seems to be accepted that some gaps in evidence might be overcome by legal power leaps expressed in specific forms. The two examples this chapter will explore are presumptions and deeming provisions.

10.2 Presumptions

One of the most enduring ways to resolve ambiguity in legal rules within the criminal law has been the presumption. The law's approach to an object is given a starting point separate to whose burden it is to show whether the object is present or not. The law starts from the proposition that X is the case. It has been argued that this is different to a 'fiction', though it is not entirely clear that difference holds, or if it holds, that it is worth drawing.[16] The formulation of a proposition of X normally permits the presumption to be rebutted, and a standard for that rebuttal might be set. A modern example can be seen in the non-consensual sexual offences. Under the Sexual Offences Act 2003, rape (sec. 1) and other offences require that the complainant not consent and

---

13 See e.g. Alldridge, n. 2, 369–70.
14 E.g. J. Hostettler and R. Braby, *Sir William Garrow: His Life, Times and Fight for Justice*, Waterside Press 2010, xvii.
15 *R v Johnson* [2016] EWCA Crim. 1613; *R v Grant-Murray and Henry; R v McGill, Hewitt and Hewitt* [2017] EWCA Crim. 1228.
16 Cf. Del Mar, 'Legal Fictions and Legal Change', n. 7, 442–43, saying that presumptions are stances on a particular fact, while legal fictions do not entail any such stance. This distinction might not normally be worth drawing, since the effect is the same where the presumption is irrebuttable.

the defendant not have a reasonable belief in consent. Section 75 of the Act sets out that if certain circumstances apply, and the defendant knows they apply, there is a presumption that the complainant did not consent, and the defendant did not reasonably believe the complainant consented. Section 76 goes further, and in two circumstances the absence of any consent or reasonable belief in it is irrebuttably presumed. Instead of simply stating that the complainant cannot consent in those circumstances, the law will not accept evidence to the contrary. On its face it accepts that there might in fact have been consent, but states that that consent is not receivable by the court.

The use of factual presumptions is mirrored in presumptions about the law. Sometimes fact and law are simply blurred: for example, a person might be presumed 'innocent until proven guilty'. That was, in its modern form of requiring the prosecution to prove all elements relevant to the crime, relatively recent.[17] It also remains unachieved, to the extent that English law has extensive strict liability. By reducing the number of physical components of an offence that there must be proof of fault about, the value of the claim of innocence until proven guilty is curtailed.[18] The best estimate suggests that roughly half of the offences triable in the Crown Court feature strict liability, with perhaps half of those having a due diligence defence (and about 5% of the offences feature negligence).[19] There are, nonetheless, frequent statements that the presumption of an offence needing *mens rea* is important, as discussed below. Indeed, that issue, how the presumptions the law engaged in were about *law* or blurring fact and law, not just about fact, is what we turn to next.

Criminal lawyers from the early 1800s typically used guiding principles, often expressed as presumptions, rather than hard rules, to express fault doctrines. Two presumptions in particular are relevant: that *mens rea* was needed; and that a person intended the natural and probable consequences of his or her act. Over the course of the following century and a half, both presumptions were watered down, and, eventually, the natural and probable consequences presumption was removed. The changes in both are part of the wider shift of fault being specified and its forms redistributed to match newly sharpened offences to a degree not seen before in the criminal law.[20]

The first presumption was that *mens rea* is required for an offence, unless Parliament used very clear words to show that fault was not needed for that offence. The need for *mens rea* has been said to have ancient origins, some

---

17   *Woolmington v DPP* [1935] AC 462.
18   Similarly, the growth in inchoate offences in England, where the normally conceived harm of the offence need not happen for there to be liability, as well as in complicity (liability for the crimes of others) and other areas of law, reduce the significance of the 'presumption' of innocence.
19   A. Ashworth and M. Blake, 'The Presumption of Innocence in English Criminal Law' [1996] *Crim. LR* 306, esp. 308–9.
20   See generally K.J.M. Smith, *Lawyers, Legislators and Theorists: Developments in English Criminal Jurisprudence, 1800–1957*, Clarendon Press 1998, ch. 4.

taking it as far back as religious origins of sin.[21] However, the two earliest firm statements of the need for something culpable were the maxims: *actus non facit reum nisi mens sit rea* (a person is not a criminal by an act unless it was also done with a guilty mind) and *in criminalibus sufficit generalis militia intentionis cum facto paris gradus* (in criminal acts it is sufficient that there be a general evil intent with an act of corresponding degree). One of the earliest appearances of the first of these phrases was in Coke's *Institutes* in 1644.[22] Coke applied it only to high treason and larceny, but it soon spread from there. The second played a more minor role on the surface. It required only 'general evil intent', and an act of sufficient severity, even if, for instance, the ultimate victim was not the intended one.[23] The maxim was not commonly referred to in cases, but the idea of fault being somewhat elastic, a sufficiency of fault and at least some relevant act, does play out in court decisions. One early example is *Agnes Gore's case*,[24] where a wife's use of a poison failed to kill her husband, and the supplying apothecary, to prove his work, stirred the potion properly, drank it, and died. The defendant wife was held liable for the murder of the apothecary. The maxim therefore has some links with what later became known as general malice,[25] or transferred malice. Transferred malice initially meant the same process of death had to occur as intended; it was later widened to causing death to a different person than intended, regardless of the means.[26] There were other cases where the maxim appeared, but it is not clear it was accepted as a wider statement of the law to be applied in all crimes or with much precision on what *mens rea* actually was.[27]

At least initially, there was no precision on what *mens rea* would look like and it served as a proxy for moral wrongdoing, 'evil intent' with a sufficient act.[28] It was effectively judged according to an objective test, where the court would decide whether facts displayed evil intent, and thus *mens rea*. It varied

21 Especially St Augustine; see e.g. F. Pollock and F. Maitland, *The History of English Law before the Time of Edward I*, vol. 2, 2nd ed., CUP 1898, 475 n. 102. Cf. *Leges Henrici Primi* (1118), c. 88, para. 6, on no-fault killing requiring compensation.
22 E. Coke, *The Third Part of the Institutes of the Laws of England*, Lee and Pakeman 1644, 6, 107.
23 F. Bacon, *Elements of the Common Lawes of England*, More 1639, 59–60.
24 (1611) 9 Co. Rep. 81a; see also M. Hale, *Pleas of the Crown*, vol. 1, Sayer et al. 1736, 465–66; Bl. Comm. IV, 201: 'because of the previous felonious intent, which the law transfers from one to the other'.
25 *R v Hunt* (1825) 1 Mood. CC 93, 95–96: a stabbing rush hitting the wrong person, where both the Assize, and the victim, were called Cambridge.
26 J.F. Stephen, *A History of the Criminal Law of England*, vol. 3, Macmillan & Co. 1883, 80, with the text stating he was picking up his Digest, Art. 228(a) (it was actually Art. 223) and the Draft Criminal Code of the Criminal Code Commission, Art. 174(c).
27 *Chune v Piott* (1614) 2 Bulst. 328; *R v Ocullean* (1679) T Raym. 377: words just stated, no explanation; *Lambert and Olliot v Bessey* (1681) T Raym. 421: a civil case asserting the rule in criminal law by comparison; *R v Bigg* (1717) 3 P. Wms. 419, as in *Lambert*. With thanks to Mike Macnair for these references.
28 J.W.C. Turner (ed.), *Russell on Crime*, vol. 1, 10th ed., Stevens 1950, 25–30.

from offence to offence, guided by the precise formulation of the indictments and informations, drawn from common law or statute. On its face, the maxim requires that an act have *mens rea*, or that every crime have some *mens rea* somewhere, in order to be criminal.[29] This did not take us very far in an age where *mens rea* was itself vague. *Mens rea* was expressed predominantly in terms of intent, and *actus reus* only in terms of act. There were only rare references to other physical elements such as consequences or circumstances, or other *mens rea* elements such as 'knowingly'. The last discussions of purpose or motive being relevant to establish liability were in the 1860s.[30]

The presumption of the need for *mens rea* was applied not only to common law crimes, but also to statutory offences. The presumption largely still holds to the present day, but in the late nineteenth century it was narrowed by more easily accepting legislated offences without fault, and proxies were accepted. Implied malice came to be accepted in place of express malice. The idea was known in other areas of law, such as in the case of a civil libel that a banker's notes were not being accepted, even though uttered without ill will.[31] Criminal cases soon mirrored this.[32]

The second presumption was that a person was taken to intend the natural and probable consequences of his actions. It reduced the practical burden of the presumption that *mens rea* was needed.[33]

The presumption began as a rule of evidence, but became so entrenched as to sometimes have the effect of a rule of substantive law.[34] In one of its early judicial formulations, Lord Ellenborough expressed it very widely:

> it was a universal principle that where a man is charged with doing an act, of which the probable consequence would be highly injurious, intention is an inference of law resulting from the doing the act [sic].[35]

Finding out exactly what the defendant had intended or foreseen would have been even more difficult in the nineteenth century than now. A full defence by counsel was permissible from 1836 where the defendant could afford counsel, which was somewhat more likely in the generally more serious cases, namely,

---

29 See generally Pollock/Maitland, n. 21, vol. 2, 468–81; W.S. Holdsworth, *A History of English Law*, vol. 2, Methuen 1927, 50–54.
30 Ended by *R v Hicklin* (1867–1868) LR 3 QB 360.
31 *Bromage v Prosser* (1825) 4 B & C 247, 255 (Bayley J).
32 E.g. *R v Weare* (1840) 4 JP 508.
33 Hale, n. 24, vol. 1, 465; Bl. Comm. IV, 200.
34 Smith, *Lawyers*, n. 20, 49–51, 166–71.
35 *R v Dixon* (1814) 3 M & S 11, 15; see also *R v Sheppard* (1810) R & R 169. In *R v Farrington* (1811) R & R 207 the marginal summary noted (207) 'a man must be supposed to intend the necessary consequences of his own act'. The brief report of the judgment noted (209) 'a party who does an act wilfully, necessarily intends that which must be the consequences of the act'.

felonies.[36] It was only with the Criminal Evidence Act 1898 that a defendant became competent, and, in practice, compellable, to give evidence.

The presumption's decline is hard to pinpoint. At least by 1935, the presumption was less visible, and was probably playing less of a role. The House of Lords decision in *Woolmington v DPP* is well known for its statement that a person was innocent until proven guilty. It achieved this by moving away from the well-established position that, once an unlawful killing was shown, it was the defendant's obligation to show excuse, justification, or that the events happened by accident. Unsurprisingly, it continued the trend of murder cases being the key battleground in fault.[37] A man, armed with a shotgun, visited his estranged wife and after an argument, she died from a gunshot wound. Woolmington claimed it was an accident in the course of his threatening to kill himself, but the trial judge told the jury to convict unless the defendant had persuaded them it had been an accident. The House of Lords allowed the appeal. Murder was no longer an offence capable of being committed without fault.

Most intriguingly, by putting a marker firmly against reverse burdens of proof of fault in general, it may have contributed to the further acceptance of the more extreme route to more easily establishing liability: offences not requiring *mens rea* at all, rather than just reverse burdens of proof of fault.[38]

One of the last clear cases approving the presumption of intending the natural and probable consequences was *R v Steane* in 1947.[39] The presumption was approved in principle, but an exception applied where the acts were done while subject to the power of others. Here, during World War II, pressure from German authorities on the defendant and his family meant his conviction for assisting the enemy through radio broadcasts was quashed. The court flirted with motive in considering what was natural and probable, but ultimately decided not to develop the law in this direction. Instead, it decided the case on the fig leaf of the directions to the jury: that the judge had not made clear that it had been the task of the prosecutor to prove intent beyond reasonable doubt and without that the jury should not convict.[40]

The importance of this on fault standards cannot be underestimated. As K.J.M. Smith put it,

The operation of this leading rule of evidence frequently obscured, if not totally subsumed, positive proof of the substantive culpability requirement in any particular case. So much so that in many nineteenth century

36 See generally, C. Allen, *The Law of Evidence in Victorian England*, CUP 1997, ch. 5; W. Cornish et al. (eds), *OHLE*, vol. XIII, 71–115, esp. 100–7.

37 [1935] AC 462, 472–73, where Swift J had directed the jury in those terms, and thus the appeal succeeded.

38 *Sweet v Parsley* [1970] AC 132, 150 (Lord Reid).

39 [1947] KB 997.

40 Ibid., 1006.

and earlier authorities it is often quite impossible to disentangle the substantive from the evidential.[41]

Into the twentieth century, intention and awareness of risk were replacing the vagueness of malice. The trend was accentuated by some reduction in the use of moral reasoning,[42] the presumption of natural and probable consequences, and wider rules of evidence. In fact, K.J.M. Smith has also argued that the 1898 Act permitting evidence from the defendant on his purpose and foresight did not immediately lead to any marked changes in the judicial approach to the presumption's nature and function,[43] but over time it seems likely to have contributed to a shift in focus towards the factual matrix. Nonetheless, issues of 'natural' and 'probable', and parallel cases using a test of what a reasonable person would have contemplated,[44] continued for nearly three more decades. That had a brief and somewhat undignified life and was formally removed in sec. 8, Criminal Justice Act 1967.

However, intention remains to this day a concept without a definition. Fact-finders are not given a test for intention either.[45] The case law took a variety of turns. It began by allowing juries to take the natural and probable consequences as good evidence which looked a lot like the rule continuing,[46] but ended up without a presumption, and without any guidance for juries.[47] It instead branched a new form of intention, with an unclear relationship with the reasons for criminalising intention. This 'oblique intention' gave the jury space to decide that the defendant foreseeing X as virtually certain, when it was virtually certain, was intention.[48] However, that direction is intended to be given very rarely.[49]

These presumptions have shown the criminal law setting out a default position, whether about what the law in a particular offence was, or about what the meaning of intention is. Regarding the presence of *mens rea*, it is a presumption which continues to this day, but has been stripped of most of its

---

41 Smith, *Lawyers*, n. 20, 166, see generally 162–66.
42 E.g. *R v Wheat and Stocks* [1921] 2 KB 119, where the conviction was therefore easier to obtain, and where the opposite result was achieved compared to *R v Tolson* (1889) 23 QBD 168. It might also happen where judges seek to deny liability, e.g. *R v Middleton* (1873) LR 2 CCR 38, 59 (Bramwell B); *R v Ashwell* (1885) 16 QBD 190, 204–6 (Matthew J) and 220–21 (Field J), rejecting the idea that fraudulent behaviour was enough on its own for a conviction of larceny.
43 Smith, *Lawyers*, n. 20, 288–92.
44 *R v Ward* [1956] 1 QB 351; *R v Vickers* [1957] 2 QB 664; *DPP v Smith* [1961] AC 290.
45 *R v Moloney* [1985] AC 905, 926.
46 Ibid., 929.
47 See e.g. M. Dyson, 'R v Hancock and Shankland (1986)' in P. Handler et al. (eds), *Landmark Cases in Criminal Law*, Hart 2017; *R v Nedrick* [1986] 1 WLR 1025; *R v Walker and Hayles* (1990) 90 Cr. App. R 226.
48 *R v Woollin* [1999] 1 AC 82.
49 Ibid., impliedly approving *R v Nedrick* [1986] 1 WLR 1025, 1028.

meaning. Strict liability offences abound. Vitally, strict liability's dominance has been linked to a very wide definition: at least one physical element of liability does not have a corresponding fault element. This encompasses very many offences, even including murder, which even today does not require a fault element with respect to death.[50] The wide definition also meant that 'constructive liability', where the fault with respect to one level of harm is treated as sufficient for a higher level of harm, was included but began to be seen as a sub-category of strict liability. It is particularly clear that the presumption, though it continues to exist,[51] is in practice easily rebutted by judicial interpretation of Parliamentary wording. The second presumption supplied a functional if incomplete meaning to intention for over a century. Once it was removed, courts accepted that no default position on intention was necessary. The force of the presumption might have been internalised in the behaviour of the finders of fact, or simply felt no longer to be needed.

The outcome for both of the presumptions highlights how English criminal law was itself slow to change. The same outcome was reached, one presumption fell, but it was delayed for decades. The removal of the natural and probable consequences presumption transitioned through rebuttability to the provision of no guidance at all. In its place, we have retained the underlying uncertainty about the content of intention. On the other hand, the presumption of the need for *mens rea* was rebuttable; and it was often rebutted. This ties into what the spectrum of uncertainty is doing, providing a default answer, or a complete one. The more complete the answer, the greater the risk of a disjuncture with reality and, ultimately, its complete rejection as a formal rule. The more complete the answers are, the closer they come to being the next form of technique to deal with the uncertainty spectrum: deeming provisions.

10.3 Deeming provisions

'Deem' is a tricky word in modern English. Its core seems to have remained as a form of judgment, opinion, thought, and the formal processes related to them. But as the *Oxford English Dictionary* makes clear, its origins are bound up with *legal* judgement, adjudication, and the act of sitting in judgement. The OED marks these as obsolete, and modern usage is that 'deem' is most common where the judgement is at least one step removed from reality. A person can deem, without having to state in all honesty that it is a truly held belief. I can deem a black cat to be white. I can deem a dog to be a cat.[52] Linguistically, 'deeming' can blur the focus from the thing being deemed to a space between the person deeming and the object. The person's judgement is

---

50 E.g. *R v Cunningham* [1982] AC 566.
51 *Sweet v Parsley* [1970] AC 132; *B v DPP* [2000] 2 AC 428, esp. 470.
52 'deem, v.', *OED Online*, OUP, June 2022, www.oed.com/dictionary/deem_v?tab=meaning_and_use#7373797 accessed 08.10.2024.

that the dog is a cat. In legal form, the power to deem or the act of deeming, has the result of preventing challenge to that judgment, opinion, or thought. It is even normally free from modifiers, like 'reasonably deem' or 'reasonable grounds for deeming'. Given the archaic nature of the term, and its absence from everyday usage compared to the plain alternatives, it permits untruth through labelling the decision as a deemed one. It asserts a thing to be a matter of a person's judgement, and by default that is even less open to challenge than a statement of fact.[53] Such provisions seem to offend the nature of certainty that legal actors have, in the last century at least, highlighted as necessary for criminal law.[54] They were used sparingly. Where they were used, we can see particular weakness in the arguments used, such that the resort to deeming was considered justified. They clearly differ from the typical, rebuttable, presumptions. Even in the case of an irrebuttable presumption there is something more substantive in a deeming provision. In the example of the Sexual Offences Act 2003 given earlier, in the circumstances specified under sec. 76 it is conclusively presumed that there was no consent and that the defendant did not reasonably believe in consent. A defendant might still try to say, in court and in the wider public world, that there was consent and/or he reasonably believed in it, but it will not be relevant in law. The provision accepts there might be such evidence, and the disjuncture with the facts is acknowledged, just rendered irrelevant in law. To 'deem' there to have been no consent or reasonable belief in it is different. It highlights the power of the decision-maker to decide a question, and typically denies a route to challenge that decision. It is more opaque, it lacks explanation about why the decision was made or what limits there are to it.

10.3.1 *Quasi-criminal*

Reasoning by analogy has a long pedigree and one particular form is especially interesting here: 'quasi' or 'as if' categorisation. In substantive terms, 'quasi' has been well known since Roman times as a way to structure a category of legal abstraction as being close to an established one, but providing enough intellectual distance to permit of differentiation on specific points if that was felt useful. English law used 'as if' less for facts, though it did happen. One interesting example of substantive 'as if'-ing from the nineteenth century is how legal actors sometimes characterised the absence of *mens rea* as making the offence not criminal in some sense. This is the weakest form of deeming being considered here: acknowledging in the terminology that the object was

---

53 J.C. Gray, *The Nature and Sources of the Law*, 2nd ed., Macmillan 1921, 30–37, esp. 32.
54 E.g. the openness created by the House of Lords in its Practice Statement in 1966 to depart from precedent where necessary, but with the note that it would do so, inter alia, bearing in mind 'the especial need for certainty as to the criminal law': [1966] 1 WLR 1234. See also Alldridge, n. 2, 380–82.

only partly criminal, but applying the bulk of criminal rules to it. The deeming through 'as if' is used to plaster over the underlying ambiguity or uncertainty over the nature of the object. It does not purport to solve it, but it permits the established legal order to continue while fitting in a relevant fact.

Towards the end of the nineteenth century, 'quasi-criminal' started to be used to describe something about the prosecution. The term had been used in the early nineteenth century to describe the nature of particular proceedings. It was used in company and bankruptcy law,[55] ecclesiastical law,[56] outlawry,[57] civil debts and forms of imprisonment,[58] summary jurisdiction,[59] and later, actions under the Public Health Act 1875 in relation to whether costs in repairing a highway could be recovered.[60] The characterisation of proceedings was significant. There could be procedural consequences about to which court a matter should go. For example, the cases cited above predated the Judicature Acts 1873–1875 in only giving an appeal jurisdiction in civil matters.[61]

The term was first used in respect of *offences*, rather than *procedure*, towards the end of the nineteenth century: *Lee v Dangar* in 1892 might be the first such case. Counsel for the sheriffs who had taken an unlawful payment referred to the offence as 'quasi criminal', which opposing counsel rejected as a definition; the judges did not refer to it.[62] One of the early judicial discussions references the idea of such proceedings being criminal in form but in fact being 'only a summary mode of enforcing a civil right' developed from Wright J in *Sherras v De Rutzen* in 1895.[63] This quickly became a reference to *quasi-criminal* offences, though with a strong early presence in vicarious and corporate liability cases. The first use was probably *Pearks, Gunston & Tee v Ward*, in 1902, a Sale of Food and Drugs Act 1875 case noting exceptions to the need for *mens rea* for 'quasicriminal offences, as they may be termed'.[64] This was picked up in *Mousell* in 1917,[65] and by Viscount Caldecote CJ in the mid-1940s.[66]

---

55 E.g. *In Re Briton Medical* (1886) 32 Ch. D 503; *In Re Tindall* (1855) 6 De GM & G 741.

56 *Volsey v Noble* (1870) LR 3 PC 357.

57 *Arding v Holmer* (1856) 1 H & N 85.

58 *Greaves v Keene* (1879) 4 Ex. D 73.

59 *AG v Bradlaugh* (1885) 14 QBD 667, 694; *R v Kerswill* [1895] 1 QB 1, about a magistrate's order in respect of an initially unpaid taxi fare.

60 *R v Hutchings* (1881) 6 QBD 300. There is also a strand within Scots law, beyond the scope of this work: *Adam v Allan* (1841) 3 D 1058, 1077 (libel, a 'quasi criminal accusation'); *M'Donald v Gray* (1844) 2 Broun 107.

61 The issue of jurisdiction and its effects is sadly beyond the scope of this work.

62 [1892] 2 QB 337, 342–43. 'Quasi criminal offence' in the context of a 'mixed criminal and civil jurisdiction' was used by counsel in a Scottish case first: *White v Watson, Pellet and Company* (1836) 1 Swin. 344.

63 [1895] 1 QB 918, 922.

64 [1902] 2 KB 1, 11.

65 [1917] 2 KB 836, 843–45. In the same year, D.A. Stroud, *Mens rea or Imputability under the Law of England*, Sweet & Maxwell 1914, 39.

66 *DPP v Kent and Sussex Contractors* [1944] KB 146, 152; *Brentnall & Cleland v LCC* [1945] KB 115.

The term was then used by Lord Reid both in *Warner*, showing that 'moral guilt is not the essence of the offence',[67] and in *Sweet v Parsley*,[68] saying that Parliament has long recognised 'quasi-criminal acts', but that legislation silent as to *mens rea* should be considered carefully in 'a truly criminal offence'.[69] The requirements to be handled by criminal courts, and punished in ways which appear to be criminal punishments by the standards of the times, were being fudged by the label 'quasi-criminal'. Facts which would not otherwise have been criminal, though known perfectly, were made sufficiently criminal to be dealt with by the criminal courts, applying most of criminal law's elements. In fact, the 'quasi' prefix only acted as an explanation for why the normal rules requiring *mens rea* were not applied.

10.3.2 Common purpose liability

Another powerful example of an 'as if' technique applying a legal rule to a set of facts in criminal law is the development of common purpose liability as a mode of participation. Common purpose made participants in a common criminal venture into principals, even if they would otherwise have been accessories. Combined with the wide presumption of intending the natural and probable consequences of your actions, and the rule that a death caused in the course of a felony was murder,[70] this meant that liability could be very wide. Foster, writing in 1762, held that even a bare trespass

> committed in prosecution of some unlawful purpose ... would have amounted to murder in him, and in every person present and joining with him ... For in combination of this kind the mortal stroke, though given by one of the party, is considered in the eye of the law, and of sound reason too, as given by every individual present and abetting. The person actually giving the stroke is no more than the hand or instrument, by which the others strike.[71]

The history of common purpose is elusive, contested, and constrained by limited contemporary discussion. The most likely explanation is that common purpose was a way to avoid four procedural limitations for accessories to misdemeanours: (1) that an accessory could not be tried until a principal had been

---

67 *Warner v MPC* [1969] 2 AC 256, 272.
68 [1970] AC 132, 149.
69 See also *Warner v MPC* [1969] 2 AC 256, 271, 273–74; *Gammon v AG of Hong Kong* [1985] 1 AC 1, 14 (Lord Scarman). See also the earlier Scottish jurisdictional use, e.g. *Inneds v Forbes of Touchon* (1664) Mor. 7415.
70 See e.g. *R v William Appleby* (1943) 28 Cr. App. R 1, 4.
71 M. Foster, *Crown Law*, 3rd ed., E. and R. Brooke 1792. See also *R v Macklin* (1838) 2 Lew. CC 225, 226 (Alderson B).

convicted; (2) an accessory could not be liable for more than the principal;[72] (3) some offences left uncertain whether an accessory could be liable for the full punishment of a principal;[73] and (4) that the evidence of a party to an offence could not be admitted against other parties without corroboration.[74] Since a secondary party might escape justice because of these procedural rules, *Russell on Crime* explained 'to obviate this mischief the judges by degrees adopted a different rule; and at length it became settled law that all those who are present aiding and abetting when a felony is committed are principals in the second degree'.[75] Accordingly, there was no separate form of indictment for common purpose.[76]

The first step in avoiding these procedural limits was to focus on presence. It would have appeared obviously unjust that mere absence at the moment of commission could insulate a planner or encourager from liability for the crime when it happened. And so, by the middle of the sixteenth century, being present and aiding or abetting made the defendant a principal; otherwise, the defendant was an accessory.[77] Such injustice was not, however, enough to challenge the underlying distinction, merely to blur it. It was hardly surprising that 'common purpose' was not referenced originally, or consistently.[78] Cases where parties to a crime did not have it as part of their common purpose were rare since: (1) a person was taken to intend what was natural and probable; (2) a person could not give his or her own evidence about his or her state of mind until 1898;[79] and (3) all complicity asked for was 'felonious intention to be part of the plan' which asks very little of the defendant's purpose.[80] Indeed, *NCB v Gamble* in 1959[81] was one of the first widely reported examples of disinterested assistors, with the few earlier examples also finding indifference to the crime being committed nonetheless sufficient.[82] In due course, the

---

72 Bl. Comm. IV, ch. 3, 4.

73 A defendant could also not be convicted of a misdemeanour, having been indicted for a felony. This is in part because, prior to the Prisoners' Counsel Act 1836, he could have had counsel in a misdemeanour trial, but not in a felony trial.

74 See e.g. S. Prentice (ed.), *Russell on Crime*, 5th ed., vol. 1, Stevens 1877, 600–11. Further limitations on assize jurisdiction also applied.

75 W.O. Russell, *A Treatise on Crimes and Indictable Misdemeanours*, vol. 1, 2nd ed., Butterworth 1826, 21; P.S. Gillies, *The Law of Criminal Complicity*, Ph.D. thesis, 11.05.1981, University of Sydney, 183.

76 The available indictment simply alleged the party was present, and thus a principal in the second degree: *R v Royce* (1767) 4 Burr. Rep. 2073.

77 J.H. Baker, *Introduction to Legal History*, 4th ed., OUP 2002, 525–26; see also K.J.M. Smith, *A Modern Treatise on the Law of Criminal Complicity*, Clarendon Press 1991, 22–23; W. Addington, *An Abridgment of Penal Statutes*, 3rd ed., Whieldon 1786, 1.

78 See e.g. C.S. Kenny, *Outlines of Criminal Law*, CUP 1907, 85–86, whose work makes no mention of 'common purpose' as a separate set of substantive rules.

79 Criminal Evidence Act 1898.

80 J. Chitty, *A practical treatise on the Criminal Law*, vol. 1, 2nd ed., Brooke 1826, 255a, 258.

81 [1959] 1 QB 11, 25.

82 *Benford v Sims* [1898] 2 QB 641; *Cook v Stockwell* (1915) 38 TLR 426.

common purpose came to do more work, so that a contribution made prior to the crime, combined with presence, was sufficient to make the defendant into a principal.[83] In effect, 'aiding and abetting' was no longer required; counselling and procuring within the common purpose was enough.

There was no deeper explanation for common purpose. On the infrequent occasions when any explanation for common purpose was given, courts said (1) the principal's act was 'as if done by the defendant', so simply a fictional attribution; or occasionally also said that (2) the defendant's presence was also deemed a 'terror to [the victim]' (since such offences typically involved violence), so suggesting some level of causation towards the principal's offence.[84] Similarly absent from explanation was the restriction of common purpose to felony: if common purpose had normative content, why was it not used in misdemeanour (or treason) cases? In fact, the very same phrasing of 'act of one is the act of all' was occasionally found in misdemeanour cases, explained not by common purpose but by the procedural rule that 'all are principals in cases of misdemeanour'.[85] In other cases, no explanation was given.[86]

Any substantive effect to common purpose fell away with sec. 1, Criminal Law Act 1967 removing the distinction between felony and misdemeanour. English lawyers were finally discarding procedure as the starting point for avoiding the effect of other legal rules. The Criminal Law Revision Committee, in proposing that effect in a single paragraph,[87] missed all the complications that ended up following.[88] Certainly reported cases and commentary on the rule are much rarer in the twentieth century. In *R v Pridmore* (1910), common purpose was accepted in principle, but not for all crimes 'not improbable to happen' in pursuit of it.[89] That was an instructive case, as the jury had found a common purpose to 'resist arrest at all costs' by how the defendant held a stick, while his partner had a gun.[90] One of the last was *R v Appleby*, which was decided in 1940, again featuring common purpose making all parties to it principals.[91]

---

83 E.H. East, *A Treatise of the Pleas of the Crown*, vol. 1, Strahan 1803, 257; M. Hale, *The History of the Pleas of the Crown*, vol. 1, Nutt and Gosling 1736, 442–43; *Archbold's Pleading and Evidence in Criminal Cases*, 12th ed., Sweet et al. 1853, 766–67; *R v Soares* (1802) R & R 25; *R v Manners* (1837) 7 C & P 801, 802–3.

84 *R v Griffith* (1553) Plow. 97, 98, which went on to say that the act of each was the act of all.

85 *R v Rumble* (1864) 4 F & F 175, 184. See also *R v William Greenwood* (1852) 2 Den. CC 453, 456–57.

86 *Athea's Case* (1834) 2 Lew. CC 191, 192–93.

87 Criminal Law Revision Committee, *Seventh Report: Felonies and Misdemeanours* (Cmnd. 2659), HMSO 1965, [24].

88 Which happened elsewhere as well, e.g. in the effect on the rule that a trespass merges in a felony and so a civil claim was suspended until the felony was prosecuted: M. Dyson, 'The Timing of Tortious and Criminal Actions for the Same Wrong' [2012] *CLJ* 85, esp. 99, 110–12.

89 *R v Pridmore* (1913) 8 Cr. App. R 198, 201.

90 Ibid. See also *R v Short* (1932) 23 Cr. App. R 170.

91 *R v William Appleby* (1943) 28 Cr. App. R 1; see also *Mohan v The Queen* [1967] 2 AC 187.

If we accept the procedural explanation, we can also see why the doctrine was fading away in the twentieth century: the need for it ended as the procedural distinctions fuelling it were removed. It meant that there was no longer a need to deem the conduct to be that of each party to the enterprise. This process really began with the Criminal Law Act 1826,[92] permitting the trial of an accessory before the fact by deeming him a felon, even without the principal being found and convicted. The only remaining distinction was that the accessory could only be punished as an accessory.[93] At first, this would have made no difference since the penalties were normally the same, but statutes began to give defences such as benefit of clergy to some participants but not others.[94] The gap was narrowed by the Criminal Procedure Act 1848, sec. 1 of which treated accessories as if principals not only for trial process,[95] but for punishment as well. In due course, yet another consolidating statute, sec. 1, Accessories and Abettors Act 1861 repeated the 1848 rule.[96] The more familiar provisions in sec. 8, originally only for participants in misdemeanours, were generalised for all indictable offences in 1977.[97] The original deeming provision of substantive equivalence had shifted: now, the procedural difference between accessories and principals was being removed instead.

The foundational writers, Hale, Blackstone, and Foster, were writing about a rule of attribution and there was significant inertia to that rule. It was a rule which merely developed from the fact of presence to add this slight limit of the common purpose. Once that attribution was no longer necessary, the doctrine nonetheless continued to be referred to for a while, in a not uncommon example of lag in the foundations of a rule.[98] That lag is particularly evident in a number of criminal codes drafted by English lawyers in the nineteenth century. They focused on wrongs, not underlying rights,[99] and frequently failed to remove obsolete rules. James Fitzjames Stephen's Draft Code failed to remove

---

92 Section 9; picking up some slight threads from sec. 1, Act for Punishing of Accessories to Felonies 1701 (1 Ann. st. 2, c. 9); sec. 3, Act for Enforcing and Making Perpetual an Act of the Twelfth Year of Her Late Majesty 1717 (4 Geo. I, c. 12); secs 5–7, Act to Continue Several Acts Therein Mentioned 1724 (11 Geo. I, c. 29); sec. 5, Act for the More Effectually Providing for the Punishment of Offences 1803 (43 Geo. III, c. 113).

93 And hence specific provisions on this, e.g. sec. 61, Act for Consolidating and Amending the Laws in England Relative to Larceny 1827 (7 & 8 Geo. IV, c. 29) on larceny; sec. 10, Act for Preventing Malicious Injuries to Persons and Property by Fire 1846 (9 & 10 Vic., c. 25) on malicious injuries by fire or explosive substances.

94 Russell, *A Treatise on Crimes and Indictable Misdemeanours*, n. 75, 25–26.

95 See e.g. *R v Hughes* (1860) Bell CC 242; see later *R v Froggett* [1966] 1 QB 152, 157–58.

96 Including an almost identical sec. 2.

97 While sec. 1, Criminal Law Act 1967 had removed the distinction between felony and misdemeanour, it was not until sec. 65(7), Sch. 12, Criminal Law Act 1977 that the Accessories and Abettors Act 1861 was fully amended.

98 O.W. Holmes, *The Common Law*, Little, Brown, 1881.

99 L. Farmer, 'Reconstructing the English Codification Debate: The Criminal Law Commissioners, 1833–45' (2000) 18 *Law and History Review* 397, 418: the comment is apt for the late nineteenth-century codifications as well.

a variety of obsolete offences, and did not always generalise effectively: he retained separate offences for the theft of wills, post letter bags, post letters, and cattle.[100] In his *Digest of the Criminal Law*, Stephen did have a specific article dealing with common purposes, within his wider treatment of participants.[101] However, he does not explain how it was different to the surrounding articles on principalship or accessoryship and neither describes relevant principles in general, nor gives any explanation for having that separate article. It seems likely it was simply a hangover from when common purpose used to have substantive work to do in deeming accessories into principals. Similar drafts by Edward Dillon Lewis, and the Criminal Code Commissioners, also made clear that the criminal purpose was meant to be the limit of liability. Dillon's makes clear that parties to a common purpose are 'deemed to have committed and be guilty' of all offences with the purpose,[102] which the Commissioners expressed in two separate articles, where D was 'deemed to be equally guilty in respect of any act done by one or more in pursuance of the purpose'.[103] The Commissioners also had a specific provision treating it as murder in each member of a common purpose to commit an unlawful act with violent, tumultuous, or riotous manner against all opposition, where someone died in consequence. They clearly thought the common purpose approach separable from felony-murder, as well as being an example of the duplication common to these codifications.[104]

Modern criminal law tends not to use the same forms of 'deeming', but does on occasion use provisions which have the same effect. The purpose remains to effect change without formally doing so.

One of the most striking examples is in labelling a person as having committed an offence but 'it being sufficient to prove' much less than the label of the offence would suggest. This can be seen in secs 44–47, Serious Crime Act 2007. For example, the offence in sec. 44, of intentionally assisting or encouraging another to commit a crime, appears to label the offender as intending the crime would be committed. The natural meaning of this is that the defendant intended all elements of the other's offence. In fact, sec. 47(2) reduces this, holding that 'it is sufficient to prove that he intended to encourage or assist the doing of an act' only. For all other parts of the offence, other than

---

100 See generally, S.H. Kadish, 'Codifiers of the Criminal Law: Wechsler's Predecessors' (1978) 78 *Columbia Law Review* 1098, 1126.

101 J.F. Stephen, *A Digest of the Criminal Law (Crimes and Punishments)*, 3rd ed., Macmillan 1883, arts. 35–39; art. 38 is on common purpose.

102 E. Dillon Lewis, *A Draft Criminal Code of Law and Procedure*, Kegan 1879, art. 476, extending liability to offences which were necessary or probable consequences of the purpose, or offences which were incited.

103 *Seventh Report of her Majesty's Commissioners on Criminal Law* (Cmnd. 448), HMSO 1843: arts. 16 and 17, and expressly not offences to which they were not privy or assenting.

104 Ibid., art. 54.

the relevant act, one has to turn to sec. 47(5). There one finds that they can in fact be committed with the fault element recklessness, not intention.[105]

A final example is a headline category which then has other items added in which technically do not fit. For example, 'wild creatures, tamed or untamed' are included in the definition of property under the Theft Act 1968, even though they are not the property of a person if untamed.[106]

10.4 Conclusion

Legal actors, at least in England, appear to have found value in presuming, and deeming, their way out of both legal and factual gaps. The spectrum of uncertainty for the decision-maker applies similarly to both forms of gap. Many of the rules discussed have been created by judges or the legislature, though a few examples where lay people have brought their own approaches, such as through jury equity/jury nullification, have been noted. The overarching purpose appears to have been to allow for wider concepts and conceptual structures to be maintained, despite the imprecision or uncertainty about fact or law they contained. It appears to have been one way in which a legal system can change, without changing the form of the law.

> Legal change occurs through filling in gaps between rules in the way that seems most convenient or most just at the time; through twisting existing rules, or rediscovering old ones, to give the impression that a change in the law is no more than the application of the law that was already in place; through reformulating claims into a different conceptual category, normally one less encumbered by restrictive rules; through inventing new rules that get tacked onto the existing ones; through borrowing rules from outside the Common law; through injecting shifting ideas of fairness or justice; and, very occasionally, through adopting wholescale procrustean theoretical frameworks into which the existing law can be squeezed.[107]

It is fascinating, and perhaps surprising, how much ambiguity the criminal law can cope with. Tolerance for ambiguity seems to vary over time, and from location to location, but the system in any case continues.

The spectrum of legal uncertainty legal systems operate on has only two outcomes: liability or no liability. The possible variation extends in other directions, asking for what a defendant might be liable, which crime or civil wrong, and with what remedial response. However, the underlying question

---

105 Parallel changes are made to secs 45–46 by secs 47(3)–(4).

106 Section 4(4), Theft Act 1968, though in practice the force of the inclusion is reduced by preventing a theft unless the animal has been reduced into possession.

107 D.J. Ibbetson, *A Historical Introduction to the Law of Obligations*, OUP 1999, 294.

of liability for a particular offence or civil wrong is binary. It might include subjective and objective components of liability, each engaging with different objects which might be uncertain. Legal systems with adjudicative functions will, normally, have to resolve a dispute brought before a competent authority, and this will normally result in a claim of sufficient certainty in both fact and law. Lawyers have to develop thresholds which satisfy a level of certainty for particular purposes and tasks. For legal uncertainty, the problem is more commonly about an inability to *decide* on the precise legal rule, rather than an inability to *discover* a precise fact. However, that difference does not necessarily mean legal actors have vastly different goals. In both contexts, they have to decide what resources to expend resolving the uncertainty, and, when that limit is reached, they must then decide what resources to dedicate to developing a rule to provide an outcome. That outcome-rule will itself more or less openly acknowledge the underlying uncertainty.

The places where the criminal law has indulged in presumptions and deeming provisions show the places where its law was the least developed, least able to be articulated, and/or most resistant to rational debate. It is notable that just the examples this chapter has been able to explore span the range of the substantive criminal law. The techniques and tricks used to overcome that inability to develop robust law have been similar to those used to overcome inability to find facts for the simple reason that, for criminal lawyers at least, both problems sit on the same spectrum. General principles like fault and the nature of acts, the definition of specific offences, including significant offences such as sexual offences, are covered, just as much as historically all of *mens rea* and particularly intention was. The pervasiveness of the use of these techniques highlights how the English criminal law was sensitive to the difficulties of proving factual matters, and how its substantive law was slower to develop correspondingly powerful counter-pulls in the form of doctrine. That development of doctrine has been gathering pace, particularly in the second half of the twentieth century. However, as the Sexual Offences Act 2003 and the Serious Crime Act 2007 show, the use of substantive legal tricks continues to find purchase in the factually driven criminal law.

11 Known unknowns in Roman law

The second chapter of the *lex Aquilia**

David Ibbetson

A sixth-century Byzantine lawyer, asked if Roman law had any conception of known unknowns, would surely refer the questioner to Book 34.5
of Justinian's Digest, *De Rebus Dubiis*, Of Doubtful Matters. The doubts in
question were not doubts about legal rules or principles; they could not be,
since the emperor had laid down that the Digest should be complete and free
from contradictions. Rather, they were doubts as to the application of law to
facts. If our hypothetical enquirer were to open Digest 34.5, he or she might
doubt whether a classical lawyer asked the same question would have been
quite so easily able to point to an answer. The book is a ragbag of fragments
from different sources: the number of books from which the extracts are taken
is striking. Thirteen separate jurists are represented in the 29 extracts; and only
three works (Paul, 12 *ad Plautium*; Gaius, 1 *Fideicommissorum*; Marcianus, 3
Regularum) merit more than one extract. This on its own suggests that there
was no classical focus on 'doubtful matters', whatever the position might have
been in Justinian's law. A classical lawyer might have felt much the same dismissive way as the late Republican Aquilius Gallus did when asked about the
application of law to uncertain facts: '*Nihil hoc ad ius; ad Ciceronem*'.[1] Much
of what we see in Digest 34.5 is individual jurists' answers to situations of
uncertainty, such as simultaneous or near-simultaneous deaths or situations
of linguistic ambiguity; sometimes they justify their answer by reference to
some abstract value, such as *humanitas* or *reverentia*;[2] but these are simply
hand-waving justifications with no real explanatory force. Perhaps the only
hint in Digest 34.5 that a classical jurist might have been interested in applying
rules of logic to work out what the correct answer to an interpretative issue
was is the extract from Julian's *Liber Singularis de Ambiguitatibus* in Digest

* A word of explanation is in order. A version of this paper was destined for another volume, but
at the last minute it was discovered that Wolfgang Ernst of the University of Oxford had written
a piece for the same volume with a focus on humanist approaches to the second chapter of *lex
Aquilia*. We agreed therefore that his piece would appear in the original volume and that my
piece would find a different home.
1 Cicero, *Topica*, 12.51.
2 For example Digest 34.5.22, 9.2.

DOI: 10.4324/9781003537526-15

34.5.13, a text of considerable complexity.[3] Post-classical and Byzantine law might formulate matters in terms of presumptions,[4] but their doing so merely brought the issues of uncertainty to the fore; and the humanist Cujas opened his commentary on Digest 34.5 by listing some of the principles of interpretation found in Digest 50.17, *De Regulis Juris Antiquis.*[5]

We should probably not be surprised at this. Classical Roman law was characterised by uncertainty. Unless there was a legislated rule or a decision of the emperor, it was only if all jurists agreed that the rule they had identified had determinative force, the same force as legislation. If there was juristic disagreement, the law was indeterminate; the judge in any case was free to follow whichever line he preferred.[6] So it was not just the application of law to facts that was problematic; deciding what the law actually was might be no easier. One might have expected this to have been solved once authoritative imperial pronouncements became widespread; but there was no mechanism for disseminating rescripts (*responsa* were simply given to the parties) so perhaps we should think of these as simple unknowns rather than known unknowns. It was only with the growth of imperial constitutions after about AD 200, and the enactment of the Law of Citations' making certain jurists' opinions authoritative in AD 426, that this endemic unknown-ness began to be remedied.

Medieval scholars of Roman law did not face these difficulties in identifying the law: everything that was in Justinian's *Corpus Iuris* was assumed to be definitive. There were, naturally, problems of interpretation,[7] and different commentators might generalise or expand rules in different ways; but the base line was always the same. The application of law to facts was made more certain by building on the post-classical approach of employing presumptions, and by the sixteenth century these presumptions might be highly detailed: the treatise on presumptions by Menochius, for example, ran to many hundreds of folio pages.[8]

In one context, though, lack of knowledge was insuperable. This was where it was known that some legal provision had existed but there was no information to say what the provision was. In effect, therefore, it was a problem of history rather than a problem of law. A very good case in point was the second

---

3 The difficulties are well brought out in the three-page footnote in *Das Corpus Juris Civilis in's Deutsche übersetzt*, vol. 3, Focke 1831, 579: '*Quanta in eo monumenta horroris et stragis cruenta signa! Quanta quamque altissima Juliani arx est, quamque insuperabilis?*' For an argument that Julian's text can be understood without radical emendations, L. de Ligt, 'A Philologist Reads the Digest: D.35.4.13(14).2-3' (1988) 66 *Tijdschrift voor Rechtsgeschiedenis* 53.
4 G. Donatuti, *Le Praesumptiones Iuris in Diritto Romano*, Tipografia G. Guerra 1930.
5 J. Cujas, *Ad titulum de rebus Dubiis Lib 34*, in *Ad Diversos Titulos Pandectarum*, in *Opera*, vol. 4, Paris 1658, col. 1547.
6 Gaius 1.7; cf. Digest 1.2.2.12.
7 E.g. W. Ernst, *Justinian's Digest 9.2.51 in the Western Legal Canon*, Intersentia 2019.
8 A. Giuliani, 'Civilian Treatises on Presumptions, 1580–1620', in R.H. Helmholz and W.D.H. Sellar, *The Law of Presumptions: Essays in Comparative Legal History*, Duncker & Humblot 2009, 21.

chapter of the *lex Aquilia*, a statute (probably) of the third century BC. Before the discovery of the Veronese palimpsest of the Institutes of Gaius in 1816, all that was known about this chapter was that it had existed—there are abundant references to the third chapter—and that the late-classical jurist Ulpian had said that it had fallen out of use.

The first and third chapters of the *lex* were very well known; the modern reconstruction is largely based on the texts in the Digest:

Si quis servum servam alienum alienamve quadrupedem, quae pecudum numero sit, iniuria occiderit, quanti ea res in eo anno plurimi fuit tanti domino dare damnetur.

If one has wrongfully killed another's male or female slave or his four-footed beast of the class of cattle, he shall be condemned to pay the owner the highest value thereof in that year.[9]

<Ceterarum rerum> si quis alteri damnum faxit, quod usserit fregerit ruperit iniuria, quanti ea res fuit in diebus triginta proximis tantum aes ero dare damnas esto.

In respect of other things/matters, if anyone may cause loss to another, insofar as he shall have burnt, smashed or maimed unlawfully, whatever may be the value of that matter in the thirty days next preceding/following, so much money is he to be condemned to give to the owner.[10]

Before the sixteenth century, lawyers were content to leave it at that. The second chapter (and any other chapters) was simply unknown: there was no evidence whatsoever of the content of the second chapter of the *lex*. Even after the sixteenth century, many writers urged that the wisest course was not to try to penetrate behind the absence of evidence but rather to admit that there were some things about Roman law of which we were simply ignorant.[11] For them, there was little value in speculating where there was no information. But some scholars were unable to resist the challenge.

Perhaps the first attempt to fill the gap in knowledge came with the legal humanists of the sixteenth century. The earliest humanists sidestepped the problem in view of the lack of evidence. Zasius, for example, simply says that it

---

9 Gaius 3.210, accepted with minor variants in M. Crawford (ed.), *Roman Statutes*, Institute of Classical Studies 1996, 725.

10 Ibid., 725, substantially based on Digest 9.2.27.5. I have restored the opening words given by Ulpian but rejected there.

11 E.g. M. Wesenbeck, *In Pandectas Iuris Civilis et Codicis Justinianei Commentarii*, ad D.9.2 no. 8, Basel 1629, 321; A. Vinnius, *Institutionum Imperialium Commentarius ad Inst 4.3.12*, Amsterdam 1703, 688; G. Noodt, *Ad Legem Aquiliam*, in *Opera Omnia*, vol. 1, Leiden 1724, 159.

dealt with some unknown abuse.[12] Jacques Cujas was more inventive. Having accurately stated the effect of chapters one and three, he noted that chapter two had fallen into desuetude, but it seemed to have been about causing loss (*damnum*) without injuring property, by preventing a person making use of some thing.[13] He based this on a story in the *Historia Naturalis* of Pliny the Elder.[14] Pliny recounts the way in which a fisherman used to catch anthias fish by gradually accustoming them to his presence until one fish, more courageous than the rest, would approach his boat. The more timorous fish would follow this lead in a shoal, whereupon the fisherman would conceal a fish-hook in a piece of bait, allowing him to catch one of the shoal. One day, Pliny tells, a dis-affected companion or partner (*socius*) maliciously (*malefica voluntate*) killed the decoy leader fish, but when it was recognised by the original fisherman in the market, he brought an action for the loss (*damni formulam editam*) and recovered compensation for the loss he had suffered. *Damni formula* might of course have referred to an action on the *lex Aquilia*, but it need not have done so. The language is sufficiently vague that it could equally have been a decretal *actio utilis* or *in factum*, or an *actio doli*, or perhaps even an *actio pro socio*. Notwithstanding the ambiguity of Pliny's story, Cujas's explanation was accepted by Gothofredus without demur,[15] it was followed by Mornacius and Zoesius,[16] and still in the eighteenth century was repeated without critical com-ment in de Ferriere's French edition of Justinian's Institutes.[17] Nevertheless the conjecture was highly implausible: there would have been no need for the praetors to supplement the *lex* by granting decretal actions if chapter two had already given a remedy for non-patrimonial loss; the chapter would hardly be said to have fallen into desuetude; and, as with the post-1816 construction of the *lex* based on Gaius, there would remain the problem of explaining why the provision about non-patrimonial loss was placed between the killing of slaves and animals and other physical injuries.

A pupil of Cujas, Claude Chifflet (Chifletius), took a different—and mar-ginally more plausible—line than his master's.[18] For him, chapter two of the *lex* dealt with the corruption of slaves, *servi corruptio*. If chapter one was about

---

12 U. Zasius, *Commentary on D.44.7.34.pr*, in *Opera*, vol. 3, Lyon 1550, reprinted Scientia Verlag 1965, col. 1008, no. 4.

13 *Paratitla in Libros Quinquiginta Digestorum*, ad. D.9.2, in *Cujacii Opera Omnia*, vol. 1, Paris 1658, col. 769.

14 Pliny the Elder, *Historia Naturalis*, Bk 9, 85 (59).

15 *Corpus Iuris Civilis cum Notis Dionysii Gothofredi*, ad D.9.2.27.4, Frankfurt 1663. Compare A. Faber, *Rationalia in Pandectas*, ad D.9.2.27.4, part 2.2, Lyons 1659, 296, citing Cujas but without committing himself: '*Divinare facile est, sed bene divinare difficile est*'.

16 H. Zoesius, *Commentarius ad Digestorum seu Pandectarum Juris Civilis Libros L*, ad D.9.2 no. 3, Cologne 1716, 273.

17 C.-J. de Ferrière, *Les Instituts de l'Empéreur Justinien*, vol. 5, Paris 1719, 320–23. Also by A. Perez, *Institutiones Imperiales, Erotematibus Distinctae*, ad Inst. 4.3, Louvain 1760, 397.

18 *De Secundo Capite Legis Aquiliae*, in E. Otto, *Thesaurus Iuris Romani*, vol. 5, 2nd ed., Trier 1731, col. 873.

causing *damnum* to slaves (he glosses over killing animals) and chapter three included injuring slaves, then chapter two should also have been about causing *damnum* to slaves. He was therefore able to give a conceptual unity to the first three chapters of the *lex* (leaving open the possibility that there were later chapters to which we have no reference). He argued that the chapter would, or might, have fallen into desuetude after the edictal *actio servi corrupti* was introduced: it gave double damages in all cases and not simply against the person who denied liability as in chapters one and three, and—although Chifletius did not argue this directly—the understanding that chapter three applied to cases of *corruptio*[19] would have meant that a remedy was available for non-deliberate acts too, such cases perhaps falling from the start within chapter three. It was easy to draw the parallel with the disappearance of the Twelve Tables remedies for *os fractum* and *membrum ruptum*, which were superseded by the edictal remedy *de iniuriis aestimandis*. Normally a praetorian action had to be brought within the year while an *actio civilis* was perpetual, but the *actio servi corrupti* was perpetual by analogy (he said) with the civil action; but this argument was not well grounded.[20] He had to postulate an interpolation to the beginning of chapter three, suggesting that the compilers had deleted an original reference to corrupted slaves alongside killed slaves and animals. And just as Cujas had done, he strengthened his argument by a literary reference, this time to Plautus' *Poenulus* (c. 200 BC) involving the concealment of a slave. But this was over-interpreted: Plautus' reference is more obviously to theft, *furtum*,[21] and there was no necessity therefore to speculate that the law at this time recognised a pre-edictal remedy for *servi corruptio*.

Chifletius' hypothesis did have a certain attraction, allowing as it did a degree of coherence in the first three chapters of the *lex*. A progression from killed slave to corrupted slave to injured slave made sense. It was followed by Voet, who described it as probable,[22] and by Heineccius, who thought it more likely than Cujas's conjecture,[23] strengthening the argument by pointing to the very close parallels between the edictal clause embodying chapter one of the *lex* and the edict *de servo corrupto*. Nonetheless, if the ordering of the Edict was anything to go by it was not obvious why the *lex Aquilia* and *servi corruptio* should have been dealt with in well-separated clauses.[24]

Another student of Cujas, the German humanist Marquard Freher (Freherus), turned his mind to the question,[25] in good humanist fashion larding his analysis with literary texts as well as legal. He rejected the idea that

19 Digest 9.2.27.13.

20 According to Digest 44.7.35, praetorian actions *ad rem persequendam* were also perpetual.

21 A. Watson, *Roman Private Law around 200 BC*, Edinburgh University Press 1971, 148–49.

22 J. Voet, *Commentarius ad Pandectas*, 9.2 ad 5, The Hague 1731, 538–39.

23 J.G. Heineccius, *Antiquitatum Romanarum Syntagma*, 4.3.9, in *Opera Omnia*, vol. 4, Geneva 1737, 504–5.

24 O. Lenel, *Das Edictum Perpetuum*, 3rd ed., Tauchnitz 1927, 171, 198.

25 *Parergon seu Verisimilium Libri Duo*, 2.3, in Otto, n. 18, vol. 1, col. 907.

the second chapter was concerned with loss without physical damage and the suggestion of Chifletius that it dealt with *servi corruptio*; he also raised, and rejected, the possibility that it dealt with a precursor of the *actio de rebus effusis vel deiectis*. Rather, he conjectured, it covered the case where damage was inflicted by an animal, the classical *actio de pauperie*. Unlike the *actio servi corrupti*, in the Edict the *actio de pauperie* was close to the action on the *lex Aquilia*—both were dealt with by Ulpian, for example, in the eighteenth book of his commentary. Cases of injury caused by animals would not have fallen within the first or third chapter of the *lex*, since an animal could not be said to have acted wrongfully, *iniuria*. There was a degree of plausibility in the ordering of the chapters of the *lex*, supposing that the aggressor animal had killed the other animal, chapter one dealing with the killing of animals (and slaves, of course) by a human wrongdoer while chapter two covered the killing of animals by a non-human. Still, though, there were problems. *Pauperies* had been punished by the Twelve Tables, so it was hard to see why there would have been any necessity to deal with it in the *lex Aquilia*; equally, it would be difficult to understand why it should have been said that the action had fallen into desuetude.

Yet another conjecture was put forward by the Frenchman Jacobus Constantinaeus.[26] With more confidence than the evidence justified,[27] he argued that chapter two of the *lex* had dealt with the liability of the master of a slave who had caused loss with the knowledge of his master. Liability here would not be noxal (as it would have been if the master had not known). The only evidence put forward of this was the juxtaposition of texts in Ulpian 18 *ad Edictum*, reproduced in Digest 9.2. Immediately before his mention of chapter two in Digest 9.2.27.4, Ulpian had been dealing with noxal surrender. In 27.1 he had considered the case of a slave owned in common who had killed another slave owned by one of his masters; in 27.2 he had discussed the case of a commonly owned slave killed by the slave of a third party; and in 27.3 the liability of the owner of a fugitive slave or one who was bona fide serving another. Constantinaeus conjectured that Ulpian had moved from these cases to the case of the master who was privy to the slave's wrong. But the argument was in truth very weak indeed: the reference to chapter two in Digest 9.2.27.4 is much more easily explained as the natural bridge between the treatment of the first chapter of the *lex*, ending at 27.3, and the treatment of the third chapter, beginning at 27.5.

The Dutch judge and scholar Cornelius van Bynkershoek, who was also incidentally the moving force behind the publication of Everard Otto's humanist *Thesaurus Iuris Romani*, which had contained the pieces of Chifletius, Freherus, and Constantinaeus, entered the fray. He criticised the suggestions of both Cujas and Chifletius, suggesting instead that the second chapter of

---

26 *Subtilium Enodationum seu Elucidationum Libri Duo*, 1.6, in Otto, n. 18, vol. 4, col. 492.
27 '*Nullus in posterum ignoret, quid secunda legis Aquiliae parte statutum fuerit*'.

the *lex* had introduced the *actio de effusis vel deiectis*, the quasi-delictual action where something was poured or thrown from a building. Freherus had earlier rejected this possibility, but Bynkershoek made no reference to this. His argument was thoroughly unconvincing. In Digest 9.2.31 Paul had held that a pruner killing a slave by lopping the branch of a tree and throwing it, or letting it fall, onto a passing slave, would be liable on the *lex Aquilia*; Paul had cited Mucius for this, and whichever Mucius—either Publius or his son Quintus—was meant it was someone active before Labeo, who had commented on the edictal action. Therefore, the reference might be to a pre-edictal liability for throwing. But Digest 9.2.31 was a wholly orthodox case of Aquilian liability for fault (*culpa*), wholly unlike the strict liability of the occupier of a building under the *actio de effusis vel deiectis*. Secondly, he cited Digest 9.3.5.4, a text on the edictal action. Here Ulpian refers to Labeo's opinion that, where an occupier of a building had been held liable on the *lex Aquilia* when his guest or someone else had thrown something out of the building, an action should lie against the thrower for an indemnity. Unlike Digest 9.2.31, Aquilian liability here would not have been quite so orthodox. The easiest solution, suggested already by a scholium on the Basilica and made concrete by Cujas,[28] was to emend the reference to the Aquilian action to 'this' action, in context the edictal remedy. Bynkershoek saw no reason to emend the text, supposing that old commentaries dealing with throwing or pouring had referred to the *lex Aquilia* and it was a reminiscence of this liability that was being picked up by Labeo. All this, though, is over-ingenious. It would give the *lex Aquilia* an odd structure: killing slaves and animals in chapter one; some indeterminate liability for things being thrown in chapter two; and other physical injury (possibly limited to slaves and animals) in chapter three. A conservative reading of Digest 9.3.5.4 is not impossible: an occupier might be liable under the *lex Aquilia* (or perhaps a decretal action) if he had been at fault in his selection of a guest or lodger (his so-called *culpa in contrahendo*), but the suggested emendation of the text, expunging the reference to the *lex Aquilia*, is altogether more likely, avoiding as it does the inelegant and unexpected intrusion of the *lex Aquilia* into a lengthy passage of uninterrupted Ulpian dealing with the *actio de effusis vel deiectis*.

By the eighteenth century all this speculative enthusiasm which characterised the early humanist scholarship had died down, though it had not wholly died out.[29] Perhaps typical was the Neapolitan J.P. Cyrillus.[30] He went through the various theories of Cujas, Chifletius, Bynkershoek, and Constantinaeus and the criticisms which had been levelled at each of them, finishing with a

28 Sch. ad Bas. 60.5.4; Cujas, *Notae ad Inst.* 4.5.1, in *Opera*, n. 13, vol. 1, col. 246.
29 W. Ernst, *Caput Secundum Legis Aquiliae in the History of Roman Law Scholarship*, in H. de Jong (ed.), *Secundum Doctores*, VU University Press 2023, 17, 23–24.
30 J.P. Cyrillus, *Ad Librum Quartum Institutionum Civilium Commentarius*, Naples 1738, 25–26.

measured scepticism: *Omnia incerta*. Perhaps better, he wrote, was the opinion of Wesenbeck that one should not shy away from admitting ignorance where so much was unknown.

A further feature of early modern thinking about the *lex Aquilia* needs to be noted. According to some writers, the author of the *lex Aquilia* was Cicero's friend C. Aquilius Gallus, who had been Tribune of the Plebs in the first century BC. This is stated as a simple fact by Ulrich Zasius in the first half of the sixteenth century and by the German Joachim Mynsinger in the latter part of the century;[31] it was repeated without qualification by the Italian Gian Vincento Gravina in the short biography of Aquilius Gallus in his *Origines Iuris Civilis*, though in his treatment of the *lex Aquilia* he does say that the attribution has not been satisfactorily proved.[32] Already by this time the Dutch antiquarian Stephanus Vindius Pighius had pointed to the impossibility of this in the light of the fact that Brutus and Quintus Mucius Scaevola had commented on the *lex*; he conjectured that the author was L. Aquilius Gallus, who had been Tribune of the Plebs in AUC 672 (81 BC).[33] More influential on legal scholars was Gerard Noodt, who, though noting that it was a commonly held opinion that Aquilius Gallus was the law's author, said that this was impossible since it was known that the earlier jurists Brutus and Quintus Mucius had commented on the *lex*.[34] Later authors tended to follow this, sometimes citing Pighius or Noodt;[35] nonetheless, that it was still worth saying that C. Aquilius Gallus was not the author suggests that the misidentification was perhaps still present in the popular imagination.[36]

All of the approaches from the sixteenth to the eighteenth century to the second chapter of the *lex Aquilia* have one thing in common. They were pure guesses which seemed more or less likely to their authors, and which were expressed with varying degrees of confidence. It was only the association with C. Aquilius Gallus that could be shown to be wrong.

The discovery and edition of the Veronese palimpsest of Gaius' Institutes in 1816 pointed to a very different content for chapter two of the *lex*:

> *Capite secundo <adversus> adstipulatorem qui pecuniam in fraudem stipulatoris acceptum fecerit, quanti ea res est, tanti actio constituitur.*

---

31 Zasius, n. 12, ad D.9.2, 208; J. Mynsinger von Frundeck, *Apotelesma*, Helmstadt 1598, 480.
32 G.V. Gravina, *Origines Iuris Civilis*, Venice 1758, 44–45, 346.
33 S.V. Pighius, *Annales*, vol. 2, Antwerp 1615, 330–31.
34 G. Noodt, n. 11, 137.
35 E.g. A. Agustin, *De Nominibus Propriis tou Pandektou Florentini*, in Otto, n. 18, vol. 1, col. 350n. (not in Agustin's original text); Cyrillus, n. 30, 21; Heineccius, n. 23, ad Inst. 4.3 no. 4; R.-J. Pothier, *Pandectae Justinianae*, Paris 1818, 312n.
36 Astonishingly, the sixth edition of *Black's Law Dictionary*, West Publishing 1990, *sub verb* Lex Aquilia, states without qualification that the *lex* was passed in AUC 672. Later editions have expunged the error.

The second chapter provides, against an adstipulator who has released the debtor, in fraud of his principal, an action for the amount in question.[37]

This was—unsurprisingly—soon accepted as the true explanation,[38] though it was not easy to explain the link between causing property damage and fraudulently releasing a debt. Gaius had offered an explanation of this:

> *Qua et ipsa parte legis damni nomine actionem introduci manifestum est, sed id cavere non fuit necessarium, cum actio mandati ad eam rem sufficeret, nisi quod ea lege adversus infitiantem in duplum agitur.*

This part of the statute, like the rest, obviously introduces an action for loss, but the provision was unnecessary as the action of mandate would meet the case, except that the statutory action is for double against a defendant who denies liability.[39]

Scholars who were not content either simply to reproduce Gaius' explanation or to examine the nature of *adstipulatio* tried to find a context in which the fraudulent release by an adstipulator (a co-promisee added probably for the purpose of enforcing liability) might have been a problem in need of a remedy long before a general remedy for causing loss by fraud was invented;[40] a near-impossible task. And the approximation of the release of a debt to corporeal damage to property necessitated the adoption of a theory of the nature of incorporeal property—or, what amounts to the same thing, regarding a debt as property that could be destroyed[41]—at a relatively early date in the Republic.[42] But even if one could swallow the need for a remedy in this particular situation and accept the existence of a rather sophisticated notion of property, it was very hard to explain the position of chapter two between the first and third chapters. Was there any convincing explanation of an ordering of the *lex* which began with the killing of slaves and animals, proceeded to the fraudulent release of a debt by an adstipulator, then reverted to other forms of

---

37 Gaius 3.215 (I follow the translation of F. de Zulueta, *The Institutes of Gaius*, Clarendon Press 1946).

38 See, for example, C.G. Haubold, *Iuris Romani Privati Historico-Dogmaticarum Lineamenta*, Hinrichs 1826, 408; A. Schweppe, *Römische Rechtsgeschichte*, vol. 2, Vandenhoeck und Ruprecht 1832, 599; J.G. Heineccius, *Syntagma Antiquitatum Romanarum*, C.G. Haubold and C.F. Mühlenbruch (eds), H.L. Brönner 1841, 618–20. On the reception of the Gaius text, see C. Vano, *Der Gaius der Historischen Rechtsschule*, Vittorio Klostermann 2008.

39 Gaius 3.216 (translation of de Zulueta, slightly amended).

40 See especially P. Birks, 'Wrongful Loss by Co-Promisee' (1994) 22 *Index* 181.

41 G. Grosso 'La Distinzione fra "Res Corporales" e "Res Incorporales" e il Secondo Capitulo della Lex Aquilia' in A. Guarino and L. Labruna (eds), *Synteleia Arangio Ruiz*, Jovene 1964, 791; C.A. Cannata, 'Considerazioni sul Testo e la Portata Originaria del Secondo Capo della Lex Aquilia' (1994) 22 *Index* 151.

42 On these approaches, see Ernst, n. 29, 26–34.

property damage?[43] What were possibly the opening words of chapter three—
ceterarum rerum, in respect of other matters or things—were problematic,
appearing to follow on directly from chapter one, but this could be explained
by seeing them as an explanatory addition, perhaps after the first and third
chapters were incorporated into the praetors' Edict in the late Republic.[44] But
this did nothing to solve the structural problem. For Daube, the explanation
was that the *lex Aquilia* was a *lex satura*, containing unrelated provisions, with
chapters one and two being enacted first and chapter three added later;[45] but if
chapter three was indeed a later addition, some reason was needed to explain
why it was added to an earlier *lex* rather than enacted independently, and
Daube's explanation of this, based on apparently analogous examples from
early law codes, has been cogently rejected.[46] Nor could his argument be sal-
vaged by suggesting that all three chapters were enacted together as a *lex
satura*; the problem would then arise as to why the second chapter was placed
between the first and third rather than putting the first and third together, as
would have been more logical, adding the second (and perhaps other provisions too) after this.[47] The argument of Pringsheim,[48] seeing several layers in
the text of the *lex* as we have it, is no better: even if one were to accept that
these layers could be discerned, the theory could hardly explain why the gradual creation of a *lex* dealing with property damage should incorporate a very
disparate provision relating to the fraudulent release of debts. Westbrook's
suggested solution[49] does not convince either. For him, the three chapters are
ordered as they are to reflect the chronology of the assessment of damages:
the past year for chapter one, the next 30 days for chapter three, and presumptively the time of the commission of the wrong for chapter two. However,
ordering in terms of the time by reference to which damages fall to be assessed
is not directly analogous to ordering in terms of seriousness of wrongdoing
and its associated penalty, as in Twelve Tables 8.2–8.4 (*membrum ruptum*,
os fractum, other *iniuria*), nor is there an easy parallel to be drawn with the

---

43 Scholars have disagreed over the focus of the third chapter. It may have dealt with any other
property damage, total destruction of things other than slaves and four-footed grazing animals, or just injury to these. We do not need to enter into that controversy here.

44 D. Ibbetson, 'The Dating of the Lex Aquilia' in A. Burrows et al. (eds), *Judge and Jurist:
Essays in Memory of Lord Rodger of Earlsferry*, OUP 2013, 167.

45 D. Daube 'On the Third Chapter of the Lex Aquilia' (1936) 52 *LQR* 253, 266–68.

46 R. Westbrook, 'The Coherence of the Lex Aquilia' (1995) 42 *Revue Internationale des Droits
de l'Antiquité* 437.

47 The problem is solved by D. Pugsley, *The Roman Law of Property and Obligations*, Juta 1972,
68–71, reinterpreting the text as dealing with the killing of a slave by a seller who had made a
stipulatory promise to deliver, fitting this with an interpretation of chapter one as dealing with
credit sale. But this involves too radical a reinterpretation.

48 F. Pringsheim, 'The Origin of the "Lex Aquilia"', in *Droits de l'Antiquité et Sociologie
Juridique: Mélanges Henri Lévy-Bruhl*, Sirey 1959, 233. As the author himself states at the
start of his paper, his theory fails to solve many of the problems associated with the *lex Aquilia*.

49 Westbrook, n. 46.

Ancient Near Eastern codes cited by Westbrook. We come down once again to the problem of a *lex satura* in which two closely related provisions are separated by a seemingly unrelated one.

Most recently, Wolfgang Ernst has put forward a theory that deals with all of the problems.[50] His argument is detailed and a full examination of it is beyond the scope of this paper, but a brief outline is in order. Like others before him—he refers in particular to Beinart—he relates the enactment of the *lex* to the plebeian secession of 287 BC, providing in chapter one a form of *manus injectio* against a person who had killed a slave or *pecus* in the civil unrest associated with the secession. This, he argues, was only possible because the assessment of the loss, the highest value in the previous year, was a sum certain (*certa pecunia*). The assessment of the value of other forms of damage, as provided in chapter three, would not give a certain sum, so the procedure of chapter one was inapplicable there. As part of this theory, he argues that *lis crescens*, generally associated with *manus injectio*, probably only applied to claims under chapter one. Chapter two, for him, was related specifically to the procedure introduced in the first chapter: the *adstipulatio* envisaged was specifically a praetorian *stipulatio* made in the context of litigation, the adstipulator having an essentially representative function in the *legis actio* procedure equivalent to that of a procurator under the formulary system. If this is right, it provides an explanation of the positioning of chapter two immediately after chapter one; in so far as it refers to a very specific sort of *adstipulatio* it is easier to provide an explanation for it in plebeians' concerns that they might be defrauded by their (presumptively patrician) representatives; and its desuetude was a natural consequence of the disappearance of the procedure *per legis actionem*.

Ernst's thesis is powerful, but in order to justify the positioning of chapter two after chapter one and before chapter three it requires that the procedural frameworks of the outer two chapters were very different. This may not be easy to accept: the suggestion that *lis crescens* only applied to chapter one goes against the more natural reading of the Institutes of Gaius and the Sentences of Paul,[51] for example, and the suggestion that a claim for damages under chapter one was a claim for a fixed sum (with no need for any process of assessment) is problematic.

For upward of two centuries scholars have been grappling to understand the second chapter of the *lex Aquilia* on its own terms, in its relationship to the *lex* as a whole and in its positioning between chapter one and chapter three. If it was no longer a 'known unknown' it was certainly a 'known not-understood'.

---

50 W. Ernst, 'The Politics of the Lex Aquilia' (2022) 90 *Tijdschrift voor Rechtsgeschiedenis* 315.
51 Gaius 4.9; Pauli Sententiae 1.19.1.

Might it have been that Gaius' text is not reporting accurately the content of chapter two?[52]

We cannot simply assume that Gaius was straightforwardly reproducing the known text of chapter two of the *lex*. He may, of course, have been, and there is a heavy burden on any historian who wants to set aside the only evidence we have for something. But there is at least some reason for doubt. He was referring to a *lex* passed at least three centuries before his time, and much modern scholarship would place it four centuries earlier. The first question, therefore, is whether he would have had access to an epigraphic copy of the *lex*. It is known that enacted *leges* were to be deposited in the treasury, the *aerarium*, but already two centuries before Gaius Cicero was complaining about the lack of organisation here and the losses it had suffered.[53] The archive surely survived in some form into the empire, but there is little evidence that its contents were consulted.[54] Generally speaking, jurists seem not to have relied upon any archival texts,[55] and there is no good reason to suppose that Gaius was atypical: the linguistic variants between the text of the first chapter of the *lex Aquilia* given by him in Gaius 3.210 and the damages clause quoted at Gaius 3.214[56] perhaps suggest that he was not slavishly following an original text (although we cannot definitively rule out simple paraphrase or a scribal error).[57]

A second indication that Gaius was not following any archival copy of the *lex* is his opening statement of the effect of chapter three: *Capite tertio de omni cetero damno cavetur*.[58] Since he later (at Gaius 3.219) restricts the scope of the *lex* to cases where *damnum* is caused by direct bodily contact, it was simply not the case that chapter three had dealt with all other *damnum*. It is more likely that he is here summarising the opening words of chapter three as reported by Ulpian in Digest 9.2.27.5: *ceterarum rerum*.[59] A residuary clause in this form would have made perfect sense in the Edict, where chapter three followed straight on from chapter one, but it would have made little sense in the original statute, where chapter two was interposed between chapters one and three—or, at least, it would have made little sense there if Gaius had correctly reported the purport of chapter two.[60]

---

52 I owe it to the shades of Tony Honoré to say that when I raised what follows with him many years ago he was totally unconvinced.

53 Crawford, n. 9, 9, 23; Cicero, *De Legibus*, 3.20.46.

54 Crawford, n. 9, 33.

55 Ibid., 33.

56 '*quanti ea res in eo anno plurimi fuit*' (Gaius 3.210); '*quanti in eo anno plurimi eas res fuerit*' (Gaius 3.214).

57 The same conclusion is reached in H.L.W. Nelson and U. Manthe, *Gai Institutiones III 182-225*, Duncker & Humblot 2007, 221.

58 Gaius 3.217.

59 See n. 10.

60 The language is defended by A.M. Honoré, 'Linguistic and Social Context of the Lex Aquilia' (1972) 7 *Irish Jurist (New Series)* 138.

As well, it looks as if Gaius himself was unsure of his ground in describing chapter two as dealing with the fraudulent release of a debt by an adstipula-tor. At Gaius 3.216 he linked chapter two to the rest of the *lex* (or at least to chapter one) by saying that it obviously deals with *damnum*, which we may safely translate as loss: *Qua et ipsa parte legis damni nomine actionem introduci manifestum est.*[61] But, whatever else we may say about it, it is not at all obvi-ous. Dare we suggest, that like many a teacher today presented with a difficult step in an argument, Gaius took refuge behind saying that something was just obvious, getting his audience to accept a step in an argument without spend-ing time or energy testing the reasoning behind it?

A further curiosity of Gaius' treatment of chapter two is his statement in Gaius 3.216 that the enactment was unnecessary since the situation he has described would in any event have been covered by the *actio mandati*, except in so far as in the *actio mandati* there would have been no *lis crescens*, whereas in the supposed Aquilian action there (supposedly) would have been. But we know that Gaius was a historically minded jurist,[62] and, unless he had some positive reason to suppose that the *actio mandati* already existed at the time that the *lex Aquilia* was passed, the most obvious historical assumption was that the *lex* had been passed earlier and had fallen into desuetude for some rea-son after the introduction of the *actio mandati*. He expresses no such doubts about the *lex Publilia*, which also featured *lis crescens* and was superseded by the *actio mandati*.[63] Why ever assume that it was redundant from the start? Might Gaius himself have believed that the *lex Aquilia* was the work of C. Aquilius Gallus around the middle of the first century BC?

That Gaius was a historically minded jurist does not mean that his historical statements were always transparently accurate (assuming always that the text which has come down to us has not been corrupted). His statement that the Twelve Tables forbade the *usucapio* of stolen property, with no mention of the later *lex Atinia*, is problematic since the *lex* as quoted by Aulus Gellius seems to have covered the same ground as Gaius describes the effect of the Twelve Tables.[64] No less problematic is his statement that the *actio furti concepti* gave threefold damages where stolen goods were found on another man's land at the same time as saying that the Twelve Tables specified that the person on whose property stolen goods were found after a ritual search was to be liable as a *fur manifestus*, to a fourfold penalty therefore.[65]

Perhaps the strongest argument for the accuracy of Gaius' description of chapter two of the *lex* is its sheer implausibility. The early modern lawyers who

61 W. Studemund, *Gaii Institutionum Commentarii Quatuor Codicis Veronensis Denuo Collati Apographum Confecit*, Hirzl 1874, 278, emending the nonsensical '*introducimus factum*'.
62 Digest 1.2.pr; see F. Schulz, *History of Roman Legal Science*, Clarendon Press 1953, 134, 187; J. Macqueron, 'Storia del Diritto e Arcaismo in Gaio' in *Gaio nel Suo Tempo*, Jovene 1966, 76.
63 Gaius 4.22.
64 Gaius 2.45; Gellius, *Noctes Atticae*, 17.7.1; cf. Digest 41.3.4.6 (Paul).
65 Gaius 3.191, 192.

speculated on its contents had good reasons for their opinions, whether those were based on textual connections with the *lex* or filling in gaps between the first and third chapters. By contrast, there was no visible textual link between the fraudulent release of a debt and the cases of physical injury and damage covered by the other chapters; and even Gaius himself might have been feeling hard pressed to explain why his version of chapter two fitted into the scheme of the *lex*.

There may, however, be a way through this thicket. If we could suppose that there might have been a tradition associating C. Aquilius Gallus with the *lex Aquilia*, as there clearly was in the early modern period, two known features of Gallus' work resonate with Gaius' description of chapter two of the *lex*. First was his concern with *dolus*: he is regarded as having introduced both the general *exceptio doli* and the *actio doli*. Second was the *stipulatio Aquiliana*, a form of novatory *stipulatio* in which existing liabilities were released and replaced by a single stipulatory promise.[66] Neither of these features relates directly to the fraudulent release of a debt by an adstipulator, of course, but after the time of Gaius in the so-called vulgar law of the Western Empire there was a clearly confused association between the *stipulatio Aquiliana* and a '*lex Aquilia*' (probably best seen here as an Aquilian clause rather than the Aquilian law).[67] Moreover, the *lex Aquilia* itself had drifted far from its original function giving compensation for property damage, becoming the general basis of *lis crescens* applicable in a variety of situations.[68] While it would be a bad mistake to read back sixth-century evidence into the second century, an association between the *lex Aquilia* and C. Aquilius Gallus would provide some explanation of Gaius' possible misunderstandings of the date and content of the *lex*.

We should not dismiss Gaius' explanation of the second chapter of the *lex Aquilia* as a fanciful invention on his part: he was hardly in the business of making up stories. However, he may have been retailing a tradition already current in his time and proffering some defence of it which might—just—satisfy his audience of its veracity.

This may be—and very probably is—all wrong. It may not—and almost certainly does not—matter. Whether the second chapter of the *lex Aquilia*, which had no lasting impact on Roman law, remains a 'known unknown' or a 'known not-understood', or has become a 'now-known-and-understood', is hardly of interest to anybody except a handful of specialists in early Roman law. This would have been equally true of the humanists' conjectures discussed above. Despite the learning and ingenuity demonstrated by these scholars, their suggestions led them nowhere; their interest was purely antiquarian. That said, the continuing inconsequence of the legal-historical question contrasts markedly

---

66 F. Sturm, *Stipulatio Aquiliana*, Beck 1972.
67 E. Levy, *Weströmisches Vulgarrecht: Das Obligationenrecht*, Böhlaus Nachfolger 1956, 134–35.
68 Ibid., 331–35.

and valuably with Roman law's post-classical and medieval shift towards near-definitive answers to known-unknown questions of fact and interpretation, by the wide use of presumptions, and its shift towards definitive answers to questions of law by treating juristic texts as authoritative and giving binding force to imperial constitutions.

Part 5

Conclusions

12 Known unknowns

Tracing a map

Andrew J. Bell and Joanna McCunn

12.1 Introduction

'Known unknowns', intractable factual uncertainties,[1] are, as shown across this volume, a persistent and endemic problem for legal systems. They can engage wherever we find potential disjuncture between the factual data required to apply a legal rule and that which can be produced by the law's fact-generating mechanisms. It is therefore vital to understand more broadly the problems generated by such uncertainty and the solutions that might be crafted to resolve it. Inter alia, there is great potential for inconsistency and incoherence across the law at these extremes of the law's view of its knowledge. Insofar as fundamental elements and principles of the legal system are engaged by knowledge and facts, and can profoundly affect the results of litigation and the operation of the justice system, the threat raised by such failings is significant. Yet the threat is also underappreciated.

We now draw on the data from the preceding chapters to confront the broader threat of intractable uncertainty. This final chapter considers general trends and themes emerging across the diverse areas of legal material considered, understood against the methodological and substantive background outlined in Chapter 1, and draws conclusions and insights on our broader target. It has three parts.

First, we return to the core questions posed at the outset, which engaged with the scope of each uncertainty problem, the solutions used to resolve it, and the policies and aims in play. We offer an overview of the major features that emerge from our contributors' analyses (Section 12.2). This paints a broader initial picture of how uncertainty presents and is understood and confronted.

Next, we identify important general themes and recurrent points of engagement and interest which emerge across the various areas, eras, and jurisdictions represented (Section 12.3). These demonstrate wider contextual factors and issues that characterise, define, and restrain uncertainty in its operation, and

---

1 A.J. Bell and J. McCunn, 'Known unknowns: uncharted waters', this volume, 1.2.1.

DOI: 10.4324/9781003537526-17

are apt to inform and mould our confrontations with it. In isolating over-arching ideas, we cannot be comprehensive, given the materials' richness, but we consider particularly significant touchstones. There is much else for other, future work to glean from the materials.

Finally, from these findings we extract a summary framework to help analyse, and provide guidance for those approaching, problems of intractable factual uncertainty (Section 12.4). This includes future instances of re-engagement with recognised problems, like those analysed here, or, equally, interactions with novel manifestations of uncertainty. Intractable uncertainty scenarios are highly varied and fact-sensitive, and there is inevitably no single 'correct' or 'best' response. But with the fuller insights gained through our study, we can offer a practical view on important elements for interrogating the problem and making decisions to tailor a response that remains consistent with the legal system's wider commitments. This novel guidance can enrich the future development of the law and help smooth the often-rocky path to fair and appropriate solutions in the face of the intractable.

12.2 Scope and solutions in overview

12.2.1 *The scope of uncertainty problems*

12.2.1.1 *Core and periphery*

First, we consider the role that uncertainty plays in each of the problem areas examined. We have seen that uncertainty problems may be conceptualised in numerous ways, but all of our uncertainties evidence some form of irreducible core that grounds their status as intractable problems. This might involve the inherent ambiguity of language or impenetrability of mind;[2] metaphysical mysteries about 'life';[3] other physical mysteries, like the nature of simultaneity;[4] or engagement with future or hypothetical events.[5]

In some areas, uncertainty also itself consistently represents, and is recognised as, the core of the relevant problem scenario. For example, there has been much explicit discussion of the mysteries of childbirth[6] and the difficulties of

---

2 J. McCunn, 'Contractual interpretation and *ad hominem* rules of construction', this volume; B. Douglas and L. Maniscalco, 'Mixing and unmixing intangible assets', this volume.

3 G. Seabourne, '"In the beginning": dealing with "unknowns" at the start of life', this volume; C. McGrath, 'The subtle conclusion: epistemic uncertainty and law at the end of life', this volume.

4 A.J. Bell, '*Commorientes*: deaths, disasters, disappearances', this volume.

5 K. Oliphant, 'Causal uncertainty in tort law: the special case of mesothelioma', this volume; S. Schnobel and J. Skillen, 'Known unknowns: loss of a chance and intractable connections', this volume; D. Messner-Kreuzbauer, 'Quantifying or avoiding the unknown? Damages for future lost earnings in tortious personal injury cases', this volume.

6 Seabourne, n. 3.

accounting for the loss of a chance.[7] Likewise, the law can hardly avoid discussion of future loss of earnings.[8] 'Scientific uncertainty' is the explicitly recognised core of the mesothelioma causal problem,[9] and causation problems are often 'shrouded in' or 'fraught with mystery'.[10] This is not universally true, however; contrasting examples include the nature of uncertainty about contractual meaning, which is rarely explicitly addressed.[11] Likewise, the allocation of payments from mixed funds may centre more or less on factual uncertainty with changes in the conceptualisation of the problem (i.e. whether it lies in intention).[12] Uncertainty can move in or out of a central role in understanding a problem scenario; its presence within the factual matrix is often, not invariably, an obvious focus of discussions.

Around some irreducible core, which may not be the law's core focus, we can find the emergence, if not expressly the recognition, of multiple *levels* of uncertainty. However, in describing these we cannot rely on blunt divisions between the known and unknown, or knowable and unknowable (or 'epistemic' and 'evidential' uncertainty[13]).[14] Given the infinite variability of many uncertainty-generating problems—including the endless variety of contractual language;[15] the many modes for mixing and unmixing assets;[16] and manifestations of injury and death in infinitely varied lives[17]—there will be a blurring of boundaries. Approaches taken to future pecuniary losses starkly demonstrate the existence of uncertainty along a spectrum, with a corresponding range of responses available as uncertainty increases. Tracing the boundaries of each solution can be controversial and difficult within that spectrum.[18]

These different levels of uncertainty are also more readily identified in some areas or times than others. General uncertainties about birth[19] and death[20] have been recognised for centuries, but only more recently have these problems been dissected and levels of more and less intractable uncertainty drawn

7 Schnobel/Skillen, n. 5—though this might hide a different, underlying (causal) uncertainty problem.
8 Messner-Kreuzbauer, n. 5.
9 Oliphant, n. 5, 5.1.5.
10 *Hotson v East Berkshire Area Health Authority* [1987] AC 750, 782 and *Kitchen v Royal Air Force* [1958] 1 WLR 563, 576; see Oliphant, n. 5, 5.3.1.2 and Schnobel/Skillen, n. 5, 6.1.1.
11 McCunn, n. 2, 8.2.1.
12 Douglas/Maniscalco, n. 2, 9.4.
13 Bell/McCunn, n. 1, 1.2.1.
14 While the law may draw clear lines between what is and is not knowable, these may be impossible to maintain in practice—e.g. the assertion that the occurrence of past facts is provable, that of future events not: Schnobel/Skillen, n. 5, 6.2.
15 McCunn, n. 2.
16 Douglas/Maniscalco, n. 2.
17 Bell, n. 4; McGrath, n. 3; Oliphant, n. 5; Schnobel/Skillen, n. 5; Messner-Kreuzbauer, n. 5.
18 Messner-Kreuzbauer, n. 5, 7.3.
19 Seabourne, n. 3, 2.1.
20 McGrath, n. 3, 4.1; Bell, n. 4, 3.1.

out. In contrast, the glossators were keen to finely slice uncertainties about contractual meaning, but this approach is now criticised as artificial and overly complex.[21] Just as 'uncertainty' can fall in or out of the law's central focus within a problem, so can its nature be more or less intently investigated, its scope expanded or contracted, depending on usage and external influences and conditions.

Given these changes in the centrality, extent, and level of uncertainty, the initial question of when a 'special' intractable problem is recognised as requiring separate treatment beyond ordinary evidential rules becomes only more significant. We have encountered several triggers for recognition. Some factual questions are recognised as special because they engage inherent normative concerns, requiring difficult choices from the outset, as with identifying 'death' or a 'loss'.[22] Others involve facts for which adducing evidence is considered impossible, leading to an inevitable misfire of the burden of proof. Unless the justificatory basis of that burden can extend to forcing someone to prove the impossible, the fundamental unfairness of this can require an alternative approach.[23] Take mesothelioma: where the precise aetiology of the disease is unknown, the ordinary burden-of-proof solution is rejected for producing answers 'deeply offensive to instinctive notions' of justice.[24]

Beyond these situations, there is a further region of looser dissatisfaction with the results achievable under orthodox rules, where meeting the burden of proof is not impossible, but felt to be especially, unsatisfactorily 'onerous'/'burdensome'.[25] As noted, instances of the same problem may be more or less unknown and unknowable, and a policy decision must be made as to the level of difficulty, understood via the sense of dissatisfaction experienced,[26] that justifies any particular departure from the ordinary burden of proof in its particular context. Near-identical scenarios may fall either side of the line between 'epistemic' and 'evidential' uncertainty; some cases do not fall clearly into either camp; and the line may move over time.[27] For example, alternative causation problems may be affected by 'scientific' or merely 'evidential' uncertainty, and may move between categories as scientific knowledge improves.[28] Similarly, some *commorientes* cases (e.g. aerial bombings) cannot be resolved by any conceivable evidence; some must involve a mere lack of

21 McCunn, n. 2, 8.2.1.
22 McGrath, n. 3, 4.2; Messner-Kreuzbauer, n. 5, 7.2. See further below, 12.3.3.1.
23 Cf. e.g. H. Reece, 'Losses of Chances in the Law' (1996) 59 *MLR* 188, 204: a claimant should not bear the risk of 'uncertainty in the world'.
24 Oliphant, n. 5, 5.3.2.
25 Schnobel/Skillen, n. 5, 6.1.2.
26 As is clear from the sections below, dissatisfaction will be a question of the overall effect of a rule in its particular context of multiple tensions, not a perfect parallel of scientific difficulty in proof.
27 Bell, n. 4, 3.2.2.
28 Oliphant, n. 5, 5.2. Cf. *Gregg v Scott* [2005] 2 AC 176, [79].

evidence (including many foundational calamity scenarios); and some might be either.[29] Any concretely framed rules or articulations of the problem for the law are likely to cross these thresholds. Engaging an expansive rule will salvage unsatisfying cases but sweep up others; limiting expansion will fail to meet all dissatisfaction.

Once recognised, defining the ambit of an uncertainty problem can be difficult. Some problems, like determining whether someone is dead, or pregnant, are essentially fixed in extent, but may be more or less significant in different kinds of dispute. Other problems might initially appear to be niche, fixed concerns, but ultimately have expandable and nebulous boundaries, so that the scope of the facts that generate the uncertainty becomes surprisingly wide. Basic fairness and justice, in the sense of treating like uncertainties alike, may encourage us to expand the problem's scope without obvious limits. For example, '*commorientes* problems' might mean simple common calamities, but it is soon hard to distinguish these satisfactorily from a far wider array of situations.[30] Something similar might apply to mesothelioma-related causation rules in England, with questionable boundaries based on the number of operative agents or substantial similarity of their operation.[31]

We must also be cautious here, as the language of a particular kind of factual uncertainty might persist despite the contours of the problem having shifted significantly. For example, the same terminology has clothed '*contra proferentem*' rules for millennia, despite their changing conceptual content,[32] while the terminology of 'simultaneous deaths' and '*commorientes*' persists even where this does not match the breadth of current rules.[33]

12.2.1.2 Incidence

Closely related to the scope identified for a particular problem is the incidence of that problem: the frequency and mode of its emergence. Trace the problem more widely, it becomes a larger problem that will be seen more often, in a wider variety of cases. But the frequency with which uncertainty problems arise can also be affected more directly by other, external pressures, like technological and socio-economic change. Existing problems may appear more or less often with the emergence of new technology, as when mass transit and modern weaponry produced more *commorientes* and disappearance cases,[34] industrial development increased toxic harms,[35] and medically

---

29 Bell, n. 4, 3.2.2.
30 Ibid, 3.2.1. France is there unusually resistant to expanding the conception of the problem.
31 Oliphant, n. 5, 5.3.3.
32 McCunn, n. 2, 8.1.
33 Bell, n. 4, 3.2.1. Per Maine, a purpose of legal fictions is to conceal change in the operation of a legal rule: M. Dyson, 'A spectrum of uncertainty', this volume, 10.1.
34 Bell, n. 4, 3.1.
35 Oliphant, n. 5, 5.1.

assisted ventilation allowed for suspended states that could be designated as life or death.[36] Equally, improved scientific investigation can expand what factual data can be produced, as with modern paternity testing.[37] This will lower uncertainty's incidence.

Technology can also create problems by presenting us with new decisions to make, or forcing us to reconsider otherwise settled or sidelined concerns. When may pregnancies be terminated, if developing abortion and prenatal technologies place changing pressures on the presence of 'life'?[38] When can organs be transplanted, if new technology allows this as soon as 'death' occurs?[39] What role will existing principles of interpretation play in smart contracts?[40] Science may develop enough to raise a problem, but not to resolve it, as with our limited knowledge of mesothelioma's aetiology.[41] New forms of interaction and investigation, then, can strain at the same core problems with growing or flagging strength as technology shifts; new challenges emerge, and the old see temporary, or even final, release.

Uncertainties may also arise or be litigated more frequently with increasing complexity in societies and their economies: for example, with the growing use of intangible assets[42] and standard-form contracts;[43] the increased complexity of industry and mobility of workers;[44] or the greater number of variables (including income, lifestyle, and tax) to be considered when calculating compensation for lasting personal injuries.[45] Even a basic uptick in general economic activity, or in active but inexperienced participants, could drive the effect. For disputes to come to law, though, parties must be willing and able to litigate, with sufficient resources to do so and no better options for resolving their dispute.[46] The expansive effect thus has limits.

Socio-economic changes may also reduce the importance of facts plagued by uncertainty, and so ease pressure to produce those facts or litigate over them, as with disputes over parentage or triggered by capital punishment, where those matters have now lost significance.[47] However, we again see flux: social trends can make problems more acute, as where increasingly multi-cultural

---

36 McGrath, n. 3, 4.2.2. Medical improvements also complicate damages assessments, if claimants survive to suffer harms longer, rather than dying: Messner-Kreuzbauer, n. 5, 7.3.2.3.3.
37 Seabourne, n. 3, 2.1.
38 Ibid., 3.2.
39 McGrath, n. 3, 4.2.2.
40 McCunn, n. 2, 8.1.
41 Oliphant, n. 5, 5.1.1.
42 Douglas/Maniscalco, n. 2, 9.1.
43 McCunn, n. 2, 8.3.2.
44 Oliphant, n. 5, 5.1.2.
45 Messner-Kreuzbauer, n. 5, 7.3.1.3.1, 7.3.2.3.1.
46 Bell, n. 4, 3.1.
47 On both, Seabourne, n. 3, 2.4.

and multi-faith societies face the need to account respectfully for a greater variety of perspectives on death.[48]

We see, then, that uncertainties change in significance and emerge with fluctuating frequency within and outwith the law; drivers include various socio-economic and scientific-technological pressures. New or re-vitalised uncertainty problems can emerge, or quiescent issues become more pressing. Legal structures, built for these problems, must have room to flex with such changes.

12.2.1.3 *Legal setting*

The contours of the legal system itself can also affect how and when uncertainty problems arise and are understood, beyond the basic conflict with the burden of proof. We noted in Chapter 1 that evidential rules, including rules on permissible evidence and the standard of proof (alongside the burden of it), will shape the factual uncertainties that arise in different systems,[49] and that whether a question is seen as factual or legal may differ across jurisdictions.[50]

We have also now seen that conceptions of uncertainty problems are affected by substantive legal rules and (controversial) normative conceptions.[51] The structure of a legal doctrine may obscure, reveal, or affect the conceptualisation of, a factual uncertainty,[52] whilst under-articulated normative ideas may delimit understandings of the problem.[53] Identifying a factual uncertainty may also depend upon the existence of a particular form of remedy.[54] The very existence of a solution can bring 'issues of uncertainty to the fore'[55]—though some solutions, such as delegating decision-making to a jury, simply re-bury the problem.[56]

Such issues of setting will impact each legal system's path to interaction with an intractable uncertainty problem and its initial preferences when crafting a solution.[57] For example, in a number of instances, continental European systems have arrived earlier than their common-law counterparts at an extensive discussion of problems qua matters of law, and have also more often invoked

---

48 McGrath, n. 3, 4.3.7-4.3.8.
49 Bell/McCunn, n. 1, 1.2.3.1. Other relevant procedural rules include limitation periods: cf. Oliphant, n. 5, 5.1.2.
50 Bell/McCunn, n. 1, 1.2.1.1; McCunn, n. 2, 8.2.3, 8.3.2. See also below, 12.3.3.1.
51 See below, 12.3.3.1.
52 Schnobel/Skillen, n. 5, 6.3.2.1.
53 E.g. English lawyers' refusal to conceptualise chances in personal injury as comparable to injuries: ibid., 1.2.
54 Douglas/Maniscalco, n. 2, 9.1. Cf. Schnobel/Skillen, n. 5, n. 89.
55 D. Ibbetson, 'Known unknowns in Roman Law: the second chapter of the *lex Aquilia*', this volume, p. 260.
56 Bell/McCunn, n. 1, 1.2.3.1.
57 Cf. J. Bell, 'Path Dependence and Legal Development' (2012–13) 87 *Tulane Law Review* 787.

presumptive solutions. This can be attributed, at least partly, to features like the early development of an extensive theory of presumptions and continental conceptions of evidence on the one hand, and the prevalence of the English jury burying factual discussions on the other.[58]

Finally, it is important to note that the identification and exploration of an intractable uncertainty problem has frequently encouraged lawyers to look at other systems; this has influenced discussions and understandings. As examples: in England, the '*commorientes* problem' was first identified as such by drawing on civilian work,[59] whilst continental writers referred across to other codes.[60] English writers borrowed the idea of interpretive rules of last resort from the *ius commune*,[61] whilst versions of the *contra proferentem* rule were later spread by European and international instruments.[62] Comparative work is also influential in confronting modern causal problems with toxic torts,[63] and France's early and broad approval of recovery for loss of a chance has at least inspired discussion elsewhere.[64]

We see in these instances that comparative analysis has been used to apprehend that a special problem is generated or to 'fortify'[65] an existing sense that a difficult problem does exist and requires a distinct approach. This is roughly the limit, though; rarely are *solutions* directly adopted. Departing from ordinary proof and formulating a special problem and rule requires a solid basis. Where this rests on a general argument from injustice or vague or weak policy imperatives, comparative material offers reassurance:[66] the special problem is a true one.

In sum, there are complex interactions between the scope of an intractable uncertainty problem, the rate of its incidence, and the legal and historical setting in which it emerges. Each of these can help define the problem and whether and how it is seen at any particular place and moment, as well as the eventual terms of any solution produced. Full engagement with such a problem means investigating these contextual features.

---

58 E.g. Bell, n. 4, 3.1. This differs for uncertainty problems that emerge in more modern times, backed by more universal scientific ideas: e.g. McGrath, n. 3.
59 Bell, n. 4, 3.1.
60 E.g. ibid., 3.1, 3.2.
61 McCunn, n. 2, 8.2.1.
62 Ibid.
63 Oliphant, n. 5, 5.3.2.
64 See J.-S. Borghetti, 'France' in B. Winiger et al. (eds), *Digest of European Tort Law, Vol. 2: Essential Cases on Damage*, de Gruyter 2011, 26/6 nos. 3, 10; see Martens and Zimmermann, 'Germany' in ibid., 26/2 no. 3 with references for comparatively inspired German reform proposals. Cf. Schnobel/Skillen, n. 5, 6.3.1.
65 Oliphant, n. 5, 5.3.2.
66 See below, 12.3.5.2.

12.2.2 Solutions

12.2.2.1 Form

As noted, the ordinary burden of proof determines the default, general answer for instances of 'uncertainty'.[67] Where systems have chosen to institute special solutions to intractable problems, these have generally involved four main forms. The kinds of solution available in any given system will, again, depend on broader features of the legal setting.[68]

The most popular option is to create a presumption, fiction, or 'deeming' rule, establishing a factual basis to facilitate the operation of a relevant, existing legal rule that is to some extent independent of that basis's truth in the world. This option has been used by a large number of systems to resolve disputes about, for example, *commorientes*,[69] paternity,[70] the meaning of contracts,[71] and withdrawals from mixed funds.[72] Some of these survive periods of more general antithesis to fictional ideas,[73] and many presumptions are remarkably long-lived, having ultimately Roman roots.[74] The ancient authority of the Roman jurists might provide a counterweight where the difficult epistemological position requires an obvious departure from truth.[75] Indeed, where modern law has no Roman rule to adopt, straightforward presumptions may be conspicuous by their relative absence.[76]

A second option is to delay decision-making, postponing the issue until, or hoping that, the evidential problem resolves itself. Some unknown facts will become knowable with sufficient time, though this may not be foreseeable. Examples include uncertainties around pregnancy[77] and the assessment of damages.[78] In other cases, a 'wait and see' approach is unhelpful, either because no new facts will likely emerge (as with contractual interpretation disputes) or because waiting will create new problems (as with certain cases on the determination of death).[79]

A third option sees the law avoiding uncertainty problems (to some degree) by sidestepping the questions that raise them. Legal rules may be framed to

---

67 Bell/McCunn, n. 1, 1.2.3.1; above, 12.2.1.1.
68 E.g. unlike other systems, English law has no standard mechanism to reverse the burden of proof: Oliphant, n. 5, 5.3.1.1.
69 Bell, n. 4, 3.3.2.
70 Seabourne, n. 3, 2.3.3.
71 McCunn, n. 2, 8.3.1.
72 Douglas/Maniscalco, n. 2, 9.3.1.
73 On critiques of legal fictions, see Dyson, n. 33, 10.1.
74 Bell, n. 4, 3.3.2; McCunn, n. 2, 8.1; Douglas/Maniscalco, n. 2, 9.3.1.1.
75 On 'truth'/factual accuracy, see below, 12.3.1.1.
76 Consider e.g. Messner-Kreuzbauer, n. 5.
77 Seabourne, n. 3, 2.3.
78 Messner-Kreuzbauer, n. 5, 7.3.1.2.2, 7.3.2.2.1.
79 For the latter, McGrath, n. 3, 4.2.2. On the relevance of timing, see below, 12.3.4.1.

bypass uncertain facts from the outset,[80] or criteria may be formulated to function as a diversionary proxy for the real, uncertain factual interest.[81] Legal rules may embrace the uncertainty of the facts, but only to trigger a doctrinally exceptional solution, crafting those replacement structures so as not to engage that uncertainty directly.[82] In extremis, the law may even abandon questions that are too difficult to resolve.[83]

The final option is to delegate the case or some of its elements to a decision-maker other than the court, or to engage new fact-finders external to it. Resolutions of many uncertainty problems were long hidden in English juries' inscrutable verdicts, for example;[84] the parties might even be required to resolve the dispute themselves.[85] Alternatively, resort might be had to expert authorities[86] or new forms of data.[87]

One option not often taken is a form of compromise or split-decision solution. We see few attempts at this, save in very niche areas or unusual scenarios. Perhaps the most significant example for English lawyers is proportional liability under the very (and arbitrarily) limited 'material contribution to risk' test for causation as developed at common law.[88] This was adopted despite the rejection of, for example, proportional liability for loss of a chance in personal injury.[89]

Notably, the most radical, uncommon solutions to uncertainty problems appear to be implemented when the problem is very limited and easily confined. They include drawing lots to determine the sequence of twin births;[90] the court's power to appoint a new trustee in certain English *commorientes* cases;[91] and shared or chosen paternity in *turbatio sanguinis* cases.[92] Alongside discomfort over the substantive legitimacy or credibility of these rules, floodgates concerns might discourage more frequent attempts at radical solutions.[93]

---

80 Seabourne, n. 3, 2.3.4.
81 Ibid., 2.3.2 (baby's cry heard); Bell, n. 4, 3.2.2 (time of entry into water); McGrath, n. 3, 4.2 (death certification).
82 Oliphant, n. 5, 5.1.5.
83 Messner-Kreuzbauer, n. 5, 7.3.1.3.3, 7.3.2.3.3.
84 Bell, n. 4, 3.1; Messner-Kreuzbauer, n. 5, 7.1; Schnobel/Skillen, n. 5, 6.1.1.
85 Bell, n. 4, 3.3.3.
86 Seabourne, n. 3, 2.3.1; Bell, n. 4, 3.2.2.
87 Consider actuarial data: Messner-Kreuzbauer, n. 5, 7.3.1.3.1, 7.3.1.3.2, 7.3.2.3.2; statistical and epidemiological data: e.g. *Sienkiewicz v Greif (UK) Ltd* [2011] 2 AC 229, [72]–[106] (use rejected).
88 *Barker v Corus (UK) plc* [2006] 2 AC 572; see Oliphant, n. 5, 5.3.3.
89 Schnobel/Skillen, n. 5, 6.2.1.
90 Bell, n. 4, 3.3.2.1.
91 Ibid., 3.3.3.
92 Seabourne, n. 3, 2.3.3.
93 Where e.g. English law hits a more radical approach to causation, judicial language is notably cautious, and the rule's boundaries hotly contested: Oliphant, n. 5, 5.3.1; 5.3.3.

12.2.2.2 Content

Turning from the form of solutions to the factors driving their substantive content, we start with a pivotal notion: factual truth. Concern with factual accuracy varies significantly across and within our subject areas. Neat, simple solutions to uncertainty problems may be accepted in some eras and systems, but rejected in others for a lack of factual plausibility and apparent arbitrariness.[94]

Other solutions may be accepted though they are understood to be poor at identifying the truth, perhaps because they serve other purposes.[95] Corresponding policy ideas are frequently brought to bear in justifying particular solutions. Sometimes, the policy cited is simply that disputes should be resolved with certainty and finality, and so the creation of any rule, or a particularly clear or simple rule, is beneficial.[96] Clarity and certainty are constant, cardinal values. Other policies are invoked to support creating a specific rule. These include protecting weaker parties or victims of wrongdoing;[97] penalising those at fault or responsible for creating the uncertainty;[98] or ensuring that expected arrangements or intentions are implemented.[99]

We must also remember that these justifications may be imposed on chosen rules retrospectively, after some more-or-less arbitrary choice is made and a need later emerges for a respectable explanatory basis to maintain it. They may also represent wider aims for which the uncertainty can be conveniently leveraged. A feedback loop might then develop, whereby the policy goals served by a solution later influence re-constructions of the problem that it purports to solve.[100]

Over time, particular solutions may evolve or be replaced. Better arguments or new policy concerns can emerge to displace weaker rules, or a different solution might be adopted from elsewhere.[101] As noted, however, the latter happens rarely, perhaps because of the general pervasive weakness of reasons in the realm of the intractable.[102] Weak justifications might suffice to ensure the bare survival of an existing rule, but nothing more, like extend the rule's sphere of application, or greatly influence other systems, short of some

---

94 E.g. Bell, n. 4, 3.3.1; Douglas/Maniscalco, n. 2, 9.3.1. See below, 12.3.1.1.

95 E.g. McCunn, n. 2, 8.3.2.

96 Bell, n. 4, 3.3.2.1–3.3.2.2; McCunn, n. 2, 8.3.2; Douglas/Maniscalco, n. 2, 9.3.1.

97 McCunn, n. 2, 8.3.2; Douglas/Maniscalco, n. 2, 9.3.1.2; 9.3.4.1; Oliphant, n. 5, 5.1.3; 5.3.2; Bell, n. 4, 3.3.2.3; Schnobel/Skillen, n. 5, 6.3.1, 6.3.2.

98 McCunn, n. 2, 8.3.2; Douglas/Maniscalco, n. 2, 9.3.4.1; Seabourne, n. 3, 2.3; Oliphant, n. 5, 5.3.2; Schnobel/Skillen, n. 5, 6.3.1.1.1, 6.3.1.2; and Borghetti, n. 64, 26/6 nos. 10–11.

99 Bell, n. 4, 3.2.1, 3.3.2.3; Seabourne, n. 3, 2.3; McCunn, n. 2, 8.3.2; Douglas/Maniscalco, n. 2, 9.3. See below, 12.3.1.2.

100 E.g. McCunn, n. 2, 8.3.2; Bell, n. 4, 3.2.1.

101 McCunn, n. 2, 8.3.2.

102 Above, 12.2.1.3.

further impetus emerging.[103] Local context is highly significant when framing a concrete response to uncertainty, and any given solution may be defensible through easy criticism of the other weak options.[104]

In summary, solutions crafted for intractable uncertainty problems are very varied—more so than would be expected from examining any instance in isolation—and may change significantly over time. They are sensitive to changes in their particular factual, legal, and historical context. Nevertheless, some obvious general preferences emerge, and it is noteworthy that these generally involve no very radical novel solution where the problem is not niche or somewhat artificially constrained. Clear, simple presumptive answers securing certain resolution are consistently popular approaches.

12.3 Themes and influences

Having examined the key features that emerge across our chapters, sketching the general state of affairs as we can now understand it, we may further explore the themes and influences revealed. These include the relevance of factual plausibility and wider policy concerns in defining and resolving uncertainty problems; the possibility of avoiding a problem or decisive solution; the interweaving of factual and legal/normative questions about uncertainty problems; the relevance of chronologies; and the use and status of other sources and systems of knowledge.

12.3.1 Competing imperatives

12.3.1.1 The weight of accurate truth

As demonstrated, factual uncertainty may be more or less central to the framing of an uncertainty problem; a concern with the facts may similarly be more or less central to a solution.[105] For example, theoretically neat solutions to *commorientes* problems have been accepted in some eras and systems, but rejected in others due to scepticism over their plausibility.[106] Such (as it were) untruthful rules might be 'tolerated' rather than fully accepted.[107] The more central factual truth is to the understanding of the problem, though, the more central we may expect it to be in solutions.

---

103 A rationale may be *just* convincing *enough* to keep the ball rolling a while longer: e.g. 'weak' justifications for the *contra proferentem* rule could ensure its survival until re-engaged for consumer protection purposes: McCunn, n. 2, 8.3.2; factually unconvincing continental *commorientes* presumptions little influenced England, but a later native sense of need emerged in the twentieth century: Bell, n. 4, 3.3.1, 3.3.2.2–3.3.

104 Cf. below, 12.3.5.2.

105 Above, 12.2.1.1, 12.2.2.2.

106 Bell, n. 4, 3.3.1.

107 Dyson, n. 33, 10.1.

Sometimes, systems display a kind of 'factual puritanism': they focus squarely on finding the correct factual answer and flatly reject other solutions or compromises. This might characterise courts' treatment of *commorientes* problems in nineteenth-century England, for instance.[108] We may also see increased interest in factual truth when a new and seemingly more accurate solution[109] or more detailed investigative method[110] presents itself; for example, due to scientific progress.[111] Elsewhere and in other periods, there is less concern with finally achieving a factually accurate outcome; even a factually improbable or impossible outcome can seem acceptable, as with the presumption of simultaneous deaths, now standard for *commorientes* in many systems.[112] Sometimes, as with 'deeming' rules, the fictionality of a solution is acknowledged openly.[113]

The demand for factual accuracy can wax and wane, then, but there are particular pressures that reinforce the ordinary, baseline level of demand. Features of a case that might be relevant here include the extent to which core personal and social interests are at stake. For example, the law must obviously reach accurate conclusions on matters of life and death.[114] Taking a less extreme example, the law has highly developed tools for assessing losses in relation to physical integrity and earning capacity, even where the complexity and difficulty of that assessment is explicitly recognised.[115] *Commorientes* rules determine receipt of a gain, in contrast to the protection of vital interests in a personal injury damages context; it seems unsurprising that there is less interest in an intricate, fact-sensitive spectrum of answers in that sort of claim.[116] As regards social importance, there may have been a greater desire for factually accurate outcomes in paternity cases amongst the richest (and poorest) families, where questions of inheritance held the most significance.[117]

The law might also especially favour factually accurate decisions where it is thought to risk committing a serious moral transgression, such as permitting

---

108 Bell, n. 4, 3.3.1. Cf. the German courts' 'uncertainty-averse' approach to the assessment of lost earnings: Messner-Kreuzbauer, n. 5, 7.3.2.1.
109 Seabourne, n. 3, 2.3.1–2.3.2.
110 McGrath, n. 3, 4.3.3.
111 See below, 12.3.5.1.
112 Bell, n. 4, 3.3.2.2.
113 Dyson, n. 33, 10.3; see e.g. Oliphant, n. 5, 5.1.3.
114 McGrath, n. 3, 4.3.6.
115 Messner-Kreuzbauer, n. 5, 7.4.3.
116 Compare Messner-Kreuzbauer, n. 5, with Bell, n. 4.
117 Seabourne, n. 3, 2.3.3. Cf. Sir Geoffrey Vos' suggestion that small-claims parties prefer 'swift cost-free resolution' over 'robust and dependable' outcomes, larger disputes requiring 'objectively correct solutions': G. Vos, 'The Future for Dispute Resolution: Horizon Scanning' (Brian Neill Lecture 2022) <https://www.judiciary.uk/wp-content/uploads/2022/03/MR-to-SCL-Sir-Brain-Neill-Lecture-2022-The-Future-for-Dispute-Resolution-Horizon-Scannings-.pdf> accessed 17.08.2023.

a bigamous marriage or executing a pregnant felon.[118] However, moral codes differ, and we see only limited evidence of the law accounting *individual* moral choices.[119] Where determination of death is concerned, for instance, legal systems have generally preferred to follow the claims of medical science, and the appeal of its secular empiricism, rather than seeking to incorporate plural ethical or religious views.[120]

The (changing) scope and complexity of the relevant uncertainty problem or its solution are themselves important pressure factors that come to bear on the call for factual accuracy.

We have seen that uncertainty problems vary in scope; some are also more complex than others, either because they involve difficult concepts (e.g. uncertainty about meaning), or because they can be factually intricate (e.g. mixed-fund cases). The same is true of potential solutions, and complexity might bite at both levels for the same problem matrix. For example, *commorientes* rules can be conceptually difficult (interrogating concepts like 'simultaneity') or factually intricate (balancing complex succession arrangements, involved death scenarios, and multiple parties) and various solutions adopted historically have entailed these elements too.[121] Where a problem scenario expands too far, or becomes too intricate, we might expect reduced interest in factually accurate solutions, which would be more cumbersome or complex to achieve. There may eventually be resort to a single or simplified rule to cut the Gordian knot. Alternatively, there might be an attempt to disaggregate the problem, severing different scenarios.[122] With *commorientes*, for example, the problem's perceived scope has tended to expand, but solutions have then simplified and generalised.[123] Meanwhile, though *ad hominem* rules of construction have separately targeted different features of contractual relationships, they have each engaged simple heuristics.[124]

Similarly, when problems become conceptually too complex, the law's preferred answer may become practically unworkable. For example, early common-law treatises suggested that pre-birth killing constituted homicide, but it was not treated as such in practice because of the difficulty of determining foetal life.[125] Likewise, although the scalar nature of death may be culturally

---

118 English rules on a waiting period before presuming death originated in the Bigamy Act 1603 (1 Jac. 1, c. 11). On pregnant felons, see Seabourne, n. 3, 2.3.

119 McGrath, n. 3, 4.3.1. More homogenous contexts might be different, if e.g. a dominant religion supplies moral content. Cf. Seabourne, n. 3, 2.3.

120 McGrath, n. 3, 4.3.1; though the system might respect individual sensibilities by waiting to enforce this: ibid., 4.3.7. On the significance of *waiting*, see below 12.3.4.1.

121 Bell, n. 4, 3.3.2.

122 For the latter, see e.g. ibid., 3.2.1.

123 Ibid., n. 4, 3.4. See also Douglas/Maniscalco, n. 2, 9.4, arguing that current English law on mixtures of intangible assets is incoherent and requires simplification.

124 McCunn, n. 2, 8.3.1—albeit focus on consumer problems has recently produced significant simplification across the field.

125 Seabourne, n. 3, 2.3.

acknowledged, the law prefers the ease of determining binary states;[126] the difficulty of identifying contracting parties' subjective intentions throws the law back on objectively ascertained intentions;[127] and although tort laws may be committed in principle to full compensation, they may abandon attempts to assess losses that are too difficult to evaluate.[128] Definitive answers can be more desirable than truthful ones.[129]

In many instances, therefore, a 'good-enough' solution is the order of the day in regard to truth. We see another example with financial interests, in the case of withdrawals from mixed funds; the *Restatement (Third) of Restitution and Unjust Enrichment* prefers a 'rough, practical compromise' to detailed investigations of parties' intentions.[130] Single, simplified rules may hold intuitive appeal, even if their operation is increasingly arbitrary.[131] This appeal may suffice to see a rule into force if, as above, stronger social, moral, and personal concerns do not intervene.

As factual accuracy becomes less central to the problem, this goes hand in hand with policy imperatives moving in from the periphery. More complex or malleable problems leave greater scope, and create greater imperatives, for external policy to intrude. We must remain alive to the possibilities for the boundaries we set to expand more-or-less deliberately; and equally to the consequences, including shifting policy imperatives, should that happen.

12.3.1.2 The weight of wider policy concerns and goods

Given the difficulties of defining, delimiting, and resolving intractable factual uncertainties, with true accuracy unachievable, it is unsurprising that policy concerns and general considerations of fairness or justice carry significant weight and are often invoked to fortify or justify particular approaches to such problems. Where factual truth wanes in significance, other ways of looking at the problem can be preferred. Rules may be re-directed from factually reconstructing events plagued by uncertainty to addressing broader concerns. For example, *ad hominem* rules of contractual interpretation are rarely framed as solutions to an uncertainty problem, and are often re-purposed to achieve other goals.[132]

As suggested, decreasing interest in factually accurate solutions may be the cause or result of infiltration by policy reasoning. A solution instituted to deal with limited cases of true unknowability may see mission creep and suffusion

---

126 McGrath, n. 3, 4.2.1.
127 McCunn, n. 2, 8.3.2.
128 Messner-Kreuzbauer, n. 5, 7.3.1.3.3, 7.3.2.3.3.
129 McGrath, n. 3, 4.2.1. Cf. Schnobel/Skillen, n. 5, 6.2.3.
130 Douglas/Maniscalco, n. 2, 9.3.4.1.
131 E.g. the 'first-in, first-out' rule for withdrawals from mixed funds (ibid., 9.3.1), or presuming an elder *commoriens* died first (Bell, n. 4, 3.3.2.3).
132 McCunn, n. 2, 8.3.2: especially consumer protection.

with policy ideas, and, as discussed, this perhaps especially where the under-lying uncertainty problem itself has an ill-defined ambit. Once approved, a policy-driven solution can take on a life of its own. The rule's scope may expand and contract as the importance of the relevant *policies*, rather than the incidence or relevance of the *uncertainty*, changes. Ultimately, a particular policy aim might consume the original reason for the rule entirely. This might be temporary, though, so that, where the policy concern is later resolved by other means, the rules are re-focused on the real uncertainty question. We see this pattern of development especially clearly with *ad hominem* rules of construction.[133] In short, policy's influence is fluctuating and can operate in different directions. Its effect is highly context-dependent.

Factual uncertainty may fall by the wayside completely as a basis for the rules framed, taking concern for a factually accurate solution with it. For example, 'third-generation' *commorientes* rules apply even where an order of deaths is perfectly clear.[134] Here, a rule born initially of uncertainty proves its policy value beyond the scope of that problem, leading to a focus on short-lived sur-vivorship more generally.[135] Similarly, the English 'first-in, first-out' rule for withdrawals from mixed funds applies where parties' intentions are uncertain, but also where there is a policy reason for refusing to implement ascertainable intentions.[136] Such rules may therefore function both as presumptions and as legal fictions.[137] While their policy holds, their relationship to truth is not nec-essarily constant across instances of the problem's emergence.

Where they do *not* feature as a particularly potent force, policy concerns may be engaged only as convenient fig-leaves, 'hand-waving justifications with no real explanatory force'.[138] Lawyers strongly resist the idea that their chosen solution is wholly arbitrary, and generally insist that a rationale can be offered for it, however weak that may be.[139] Sometimes, different commentators even offer wholly contradictory rationales for exactly the same rule.[140] Our 'human instinct to keep things in an apparent state of intellectual tidiness'[141] impels us to identify some rationality behind the existing law, even if that is only an *ex post facto* justification with little persuasive force. We must be alert to whether

---

133 Ibid., 8.4.
134 Bell, n. 4, 3.2.1. Similarly, the 'four seas' rule might legitimise children regardless of com-mon sense: Seabourne, n. 3, 2.3.3.
135 Cf. also Bell, n. 4, 3.2.1 (Nagel's proposals). Contrast loss of a chance reasoning, though, rejected in England because of its potential to affect cases currently resolved by the burden of proof: Schnobel/Skillen, n. 5, 6.2.3.
136 Douglas/Maniscalco, n. 2, 9.3.1.2.
137 See Bell/McCunn, n. 1, 1.2.3.2.
138 Ibbetson, n. 55, p. 259.
139 Cf. also attempts to find a coherent explanation for the *lex Aquilia*'s structure: ibid.
140 McCunn, n. 2, 8.2.2, contrasting Savigny and Blackstone.
141 Douglas/Maniscalco, n. 2, 9.3.1.1.

policy is serving as a fig-leaf or doing real intellectual work, ideally avoiding the former but acknowledging the latter.

Since uncertainty problems arise across the law, almost any kind of policy concern may be relevant to their resolution. Many important policy aims are formal and procedural, simply concerned with resolving disputes per se, efficiently, or with *ex ante* clarity.[142] When determining death, for instance, the law is concerned with providing a simple framework and clear, binary answers to offer swift closure for parties.[143] These values may be invoked to justify imposing a particularly clear/simple rule, in order to allow the efficient resolution of disputes and avoid unedifying litigation.[144] It has also been recognised that leaving disputes unresolved may distress parties, and even create a risk of exploitation.[145] Clarity and certainty are pivotal and stand among the concerns with the widest impact across our example areas; they reflect the broader, pragmatic imperatives of the legal system in its social context.

Meanwhile, other policies seek a particular substantive result; perhaps one that rights a wrong[146] or protects a weak or innocent party.[147] With mesothelioma claims, for example, legal systems have been motivated to provide a remedy for injured claimants.[148] Such policy choices may be anchored into a jurisdiction's broader normative commitments.[149] Rules might help to discourage future misbehaviour,[150] or redress wider social or legal problems.[151] Others aim to ensure social stability, perhaps by securing the transfer of property through expected lines of succession, or otherwise preserving parties' intended arrangements.[152]

Some policy concerns are less universal and more specific to particular areas of private law or interactions: for example, certain public, distributive concerns will inevitably be engaged in healthcare contexts,[153] where we also see an emerging concern with patient autonomy.[154] Similarly, concerns to uphold the certainty of contracts will affect courts' approaches to contractual

---

142 See references in n. 96.
143 McGrath, n. 3, 4.2.1. There may be attempts in practice to mitigate the more distressing consequences of this approach: ibid., 4.3.7; and see below, 12.3.2.2.
144 Bell, n. 4, 3.3.2.2; Douglas/Maniscalco, n. 2, 9.3.1.1, 9.3.1.2.
145 Messner-Kreuzbauer, n. 5, 7.3.2.2.2.
146 E.g. Oliphant, n. 5, 5.3.2; Bell, n. 4, 3.3.2.3 (slayer rule); Messner-Kreuzbauer, n. 5, 7.1, 7.3.2.1.
147 E.g. McCunn, n. 2, 8.3.2; Seabourne, n. 3, 2.3; Douglas/Maniscalco, n. 2, 3.1.2; Schnobel/Skillen, n. 5, 6.3.2.
148 Oliphant, n. 5, 5.3.1.
149 Schnobel/Skillen, n. 5, 6.3 (liberty); Messner-Kreuzbauer, n. 5, 7.3.2.1 (full compensation).
150 McCunn, n. 2, 8.3.2; Oliphant, n. 5, 5.3.2.
151 McCunn, n. 2, 8.3.2.
152 Ibid; Bell, n. 4, 3.2.1, 3.3.2.3; Seabourne, n. 3, 2.3; Douglas/Maniscalco, n. 2, 9.3.
153 McGrath, n. 3, 4.2.2.
154 Schnobel/Skillen, n. 5, 6.3.2.2.

interpretation.[155] To affect the resolution of an uncertainty problem, any policy concern must be both relevant to the facts of the dispute and strong enough to command respect and influence. It must at least bear weight alongside the unsatisfied demand for factual accuracy, potentially even to the extent of displacing that concern.

Finally, the willingness to recognise policy as underpinning the solutions offered for uncertainty problems may differ by jurisdiction. US law, for instance, perhaps influenced by legal realist thought, seems to have an unusually strong preference for policy reasoning in instances we have seen, preferring to conceptualise rules as straightforward interventions by the court, rather than outworkings of the parties' intentions.[156] Arguably, if the law is surrendering some or all of its interest in truth, it should at least be transparent about its reasoning to retain public confidence. The fig-leaf form in which some concerns are deployed is naturally most problematic here.

12.3.1.3 Summary

Thus, the scope of, and solutions to, an uncertainty problem reflect an intricate systemic to-and-fro engaging, inter alia, the centrality of factual uncertainty to our underlying sense of the problem at hand; our level of concern for the factual accuracy of a result; the importance of both the parties' interests and other (wider, systemic) goals that a solution may achieve; and the practical likelihood and significance of achieving a 'correct' outcome. As further goals intrude, or difficulties appear, factual accuracy (or fact-finding at all) might become a less significant concern. In short, the framing and resolution of an intractable uncertainty problem depend on how interested we are in the uncertainty itself, and on what any resolution is likely to achieve.

Any solution must usually have *some* degree of factual plausibility. The greater the risk of a disjuncture between rule and reality, the more likely the rule is ultimately rejected.[157] If the facts, or understandings of them, change, a rule must be reconsidered or it will become increasingly arbitrary. Nevertheless, an arbitrary rule or implausible answer can be accepted, even thrive, if it achieves another useful goal and on the basis of other preoccupations. Where a rule is criticised for its lack of accuracy, this may in fact be a sign that it is (now) failing to fulfil another purpose. A dubious presumption, for example, can only be tolerated if it brings other benefits, or as long as it is not pressed too far.[158]

---

155 J. Morgan, *Contract Law Minimalism: A Formalist Restatement of Commercial Contract Law*, CUP 2013, 228–31.
156 McCunn, n. 2, 8.3.2, Douglas/Maniscalco, n. 2, 9.3.1.3, 9.3.4.1.
157 Dyson, n. 33, 10.2.
158 See e.g. Douglas/Maniscalco, n. 2, 9.3.1.2.

12.3.2 Avoidance and compromise

12.3.2.1 Avoidance by doctrinal and procedural rules

All our uncertainty problems are by definition to some degree intractable.[159] However, their intractable cores can, to differing extents, be avoided, whether by the legal system, the parties, or the intervention of another mechanism. Legal, social, and economic developments will contribute to determining what, if any, frameworks of avoidance are possible/acceptable in practice. The law may avoid making a decision by seeking compromise between the parties. Parties who are deemed responsible for the problem's arising, meanwhile, may be penalised for failing to avoid it, or doctrinal rules calibrated to encourage their future avoidance.

The law may hardly avoid some issues, such as assessing a loss's value, except insofar as it can disengage generally from the problem by declining to recognise or compensate certain losses at all.[160] For example, the law may refuse to compensate losses that are too difficult to assess, such as the income that a seriously injured young child could have earned in 'lost years'.[161] A careful balance must be struck, though, as there are sometimes compelling reasons *not* to avoid the issue. For example, some questions about the presence of life could be avoided by banning post-mortem organ transplantation, but this would abandon the good achievable through donation.[162] Issues surrounding the uncertainty of language could be avoided by rendering all uncertain contracts void, but that outcome may be undesirable.[163] Indeed, England's 'lost-years' damages rule is controversial because of its perceived unfairness.[164] Questions of damages may be particularly difficult to abandon, as refusing to compensate a loss might undermine prior liability determinations. Avoidability is thus, like other factors, a feature that cuts both ways, exerting pressure inconsistently across scenarios.

More nuanced forms of avoidance involve engaging the uncertainty of the facts as a trigger for an extraordinary solution, but with replacement structures crafted not to engage that uncertainty directly. For example, 'scientific uncertainty' is a key feature of mesothelioma cases. This uncertainty can explicitly trigger an extraordinary rule, which does not itself resolve the uncertainty, instead bending the focus of causation: from unprovable causation of damage to provable causation of the risk of that damage.[165] This contrasts with

---

159 Above, 12.2.1.1.
160 Messner-Kreuzbauer, n. 5, 7.3.1.3.3, 7.3.2.3.3. Cf. McGrath, n. 3, 4.2.
161 Messner-Kreuzbauer, n. 5, 7.4.2.
162 McGrath, n. 3, 4.2.2.
163 McCunn, n. 2, 8.2.1.
164 Messner-Kreuzbauer, n. 5, 7.3.1.3.3.
165 Oliphant, n. 5, 5.3.1.3.

solutions that do engage the uncertainty, such as a presumption of causation or reversal of the burden of its proof.[166]

There again, the law can sidestep uncertainty from the outset, as, for example, where abortion legislation is drafted to avoid requiring proof of pregnancy.[167] Because such strategies rely on an abstract legislative framing and are not case-sensitive, they are likely more effective where there is less variation or complexity in the underlying facts. In particular, there may otherwise be a danger of chasing one's own statutory tail. Where *commorientes* statutes use longer survivorship periods, for example, they avoid most 'simultaneous' death problems, but can still leave open uncertainty at the new temporal boundary.[168]

This kind of avoidance may happen more-or-less openly. In the modern mesothelioma example, open engagement with uncertainty is a hallmark.[169] But the law may find it convenient to avoid focusing on the factual reconstruction of the events plagued by uncertainty, and direct its attention instead to broader policy. For example, when dealing with problems around the meaning of ambiguous contracts, courts have often preferred to frame their discussion in terms of protecting weaker parties and avoid questions of uncertainty altogether.[170] Whilst practically expedient and bringing important policy reasoning to the fore, this does obscure uncertainty and proof issues, bringing the usual risks of intransparency.

A further alternative is for the law to 'avoid' an issue within its trial procedures, delegating the matter to an alternative decision-maker or decision-mechanism, for instance. In medieval Europe, for example, the mysteries of conception and childbirth were seen as matters for God alone, and judicial duels and ordeals were used to elicit divine judgment on disputes involving them.[171] In modern English law, legal determinations of death are outsourced to medical science, with the law declining to provide any answers of its own.[172] A decision might also be delegated to chance, or the parties themselves.[173] These procedural approaches hide, delegate, or disaggregate the reasoning behind any answer, while allowing the law to proceed otherwise as usual.

---

166 Ibid., 5.3.1.1.
167 Seabourne, n. 3, 2.3.4. Cf. Chau and Herring's proposal to sidestep the problem of determining death: McGrath, n. 3, 4.3.4. Strategically, parties may seek to avoid a determination of one issue by contesting another: ibid., 4.3.7.
168 Bell, n. 4, 3.2.1, citing e.g. sec. 11, Succession (Scotland) Act 2016.
169 Oliphant, n. 5, 5.1.5.
170 McCunn, n. 2, 8.2.1.
171 Seabourne, n. 3, 2.3.
172 McGrath, n. 3, 4.3.5.
173 Bell, n. 4, 3.3.2.1, 3.3.3.

12.3.2.2 *Avoidance by compromise solutions*

The law may also 'avoid' decisions in the sense of abandoning its ordinary quest for all-or-nothing outcomes by instituting 'compromise' solutions to uncertainty problems.

Perhaps surprisingly, we see relatively little interest in these, even where some argue that they produce fairer, more intuitive results in cases of intractable uncertainty. In the common-law context, for example, Jaconelli observes that, where a judge finds the evidence on each side equally compelling, it is arbitrary to hand down a decisive verdict for either party.[174] This will look different in jurisdictions where 'more-likely-than-not' is not the standard of proof's tipping point. But the same basic idea applies, in terms of the definitiveness of all-or-nothing results and genuine tension over the crossing of a firm proof threshold, even where that tipping point sits to one side (or is reframed as e.g. judicial conviction). The issue is perhaps reflected in continued use in the civilian tradition of *non liquet* to describe scenarios of present concern: the problem is genuinely insoluble to the judicial figure.[175]

The lack of interest in compromises is all the more notable where we see an uncertainty problem conceptualised in terms of a common loss or calamity, where one of multiple innocent parties must be chosen to bear a loss, or where a boon must be granted amongst equally deserving parties.[176] For withdrawals from mixed funds, for example, it has been said that 'there is no reason in law or justice why' a loss should not be borne equally.[177]

Compromise, 'split-the-difference' solutions do have clear disadvantages, including producing certainly 'erroneous' outcomes[178] and perverse incentives for litigants.[179] The law may also be dissuaded by floodgates concerns. For example, recognising liability for loss of a chance threatens to increase litigation and undermine binary systems of proof more generally.[180] In other cases, identifying a good compromise between the parties' interests demands significant imagination. Sometimes, the willingness to do so is simply lacking; 'winner-takes-all' is often well entrenched in the legal mindset.[181]

---

174 J. Jaconelli, 'Solomonic Justice and the Common Law' (1992) 12 *OJLS* 480, 485.

175 See Bell/McCunn, n. 1, 1.2.3.3.

176 See e.g. Bell, n. 4, 3.3.3; Douglas/Maniscalco, n. 2, 9.3.1.3; cf. *Ingram v Little* [1961] 1 QB 31, 73–74.

177 Douglas/Maniscalco, n. 2, 9.3.1.3.

178 Jaconelli, n. 174; J.E. Coons, 'Approaches to Court-Imposed Compromise–the Uses of Doubt and Reason' (1963–64) 58 *Northwestern University Law Review* 750, 757.

179 Coons, n. 178, 760–61.

180 *Gregg v Scott*, n. 28; cf. Schnobel/Skillen, n. 5, 6.2.

181 Jaconelli, n. 174, 480; cf. e.g. E.L. Nell, *Wahrscheinlichkeitsurteile in juristischen Entscheidungen*, Duncker & Humblot 1983, 15, questioning reliance on 'quasi-certainty' achieved through definitive operation of the burden of proof over the certainties of probability analyses, and noting the minimal account of probability in legal discussions.

Compromise solutions have, however, been mooted, if rarely adopted, across many of our problem areas. They have been tentatively embraced in some of them. Loss-of-a-chance or risk-based approaches are one example. Notably, the most daring solutions are usually confined to narrow fields with close-drawn boundaries, such as mesothelioma claims in tort, with greater conservatism in loss-of-a-chance claims more generally.[182]

In jurisdictions where loss-of-a-chance recovery is made available, key limiters are placed on the loss notion still, securing a sufficiently 'certain' loss;[183] a 'real' and 'present' loss (valued by probabilities) can be required, existing in the loss of a 'concrete and effective' opportunity to achieve a result, 'open to independent evaluation in legal and financial terms'.[184] We again see the importance of normative decisions here, with two distinct views on what can count as 'loss' (what a lost chance really represents), with perhaps corresponding differences on the appropriateness and limits of a compromise, proportional-recovery solution. Seeing a defined limit is pivotal to opening the field up with a more expansive loss concept.[185]

Elsewhere, though, there is relatively little enthusiasm for compromise.[186] Compromise solutions are rarely encountered in matters of life and death, for example: while death may be a gradual process, legal conceptions of death are generally binary.[187] There may be attempts to mediate the consequences of a declaration of death in order to accommodate different purposes and values, but even these are seen to risk uncertainty and intransparency[188]—dangerous here, where legal clarity is so vital.[189]

Similarly, solutions involving explicit proportional division or sharing have only been adopted in very limited instances of *commorientes* problems.[190] Here it is important to consider the effect of solutions that find/presume simultaneous death, however: this is a popular option and does produce a 'split' result, insofar as no party takes all of the assets involved (albeit total assets are not divided); it also occurs in defiance of factual probability, as true simultaneity of death is at least extraordinarily unlikely.[191] The answer thus tends in the same direction of compromise.

---

182   Oliphant, n. 5, 5.3.3; Schnobel/Skillen, n. 5, 6.2.
183   E.g. Borghetti, n. 64, 26/6.
184   N. Coggiola et al., 'Italy' in Winiger et al., n. 64, 26/9 nos. 10, 12.
185   Schnobel/Skillen, n. 5, 6.3.1.2.
186   E.g. in contractual interpretation disputes, for example, there is no appetite for identifying meanings that balance both parties' interests: McCunn, n. 2, 8.3.2.
187   McGrath, n. 3, 4.3.4. Although a person may 'die' whilst their organs remain 'alive': ibid., n. 12.
188   Ibid., 4.3.7.
189   Ibid., 4.2.1.
190   Bell, n. 4, 3.3.3.
191   Ibid., 3.3.2.2.

In relation to damages assessments, meanwhile, statutory caps could be seen as a compromise position, insofar as they allow a claimant compensation for at least some of their loss, whilst the defendant is not burdened too heavily by demands for full compensation.[192] Indeed, where a defendant may be over-burdened, they may themselves be able to recover within a wider framework, allowing the claimant to receive full compensation, but not all ultimately at the individual defendant's expense.[193]

The law, then, has some options available for compromising disputes over intractable uncertainties, but these are more often indirect and not readily expanded. Others may be provided at a systemic level, as where the defence of contributory negligence nuances liability determinations.[194] It may be, how-ever, that compromise solutions are better secured outside the law or litiga-tion. Parties may be encouraged to reach a settlement by the courts,[195] or the general state of the law,[196] or may simply be keen to make private arrange-ments where acceptable compromise (or intuitive fairness) is not on the formal legal menu.[197]

12.3.2.3 Avoidance by the parties

The question of 'avoidability' can also arise at the level of the parties' own prior behaviour. As well as avoiding a legal problem *ex post*, by declining to bring it to law and finding negotiated/extra-legal solutions, parties can avoid problems *ex ante*. For example, (especially experienced) contracting parties can better clarify their meaning at formation; similarly, parties can keep their assets separate or make the attribution of any disposition from a mixed fund clear. Parties may be encouraged thus to avoid uncertainty problems by wider systemic mechanisms: for instance, solicitors or notaries may be required to warn parties of potential issues; well-drafted standard-form contracts and wills may circumvent them.

Where such avoidance strategies are possible at the outset, we might expect more responsibility- or fault-based solutions, with perhaps less concern over factual accuracy and limited interest in compromised results. The law may deter difficult behaviour by reacting strongly here as a form of control. In

---

192 Messner-Kreuzbauer, n. 5, 7.4.2.

193 Oliphant, n. 5, 5.3.4.

194 Ibid., 5.1.5.

195 Bell, n. 4, 3.3.3.

196 Dissatisfaction with litigation outcomes or prospects in factual uncertainty cases can encour-age parties to settle or establish redress schemes, securing legal recourse through bargaining on the back of the claim framework: see e.g. J.C.P. Goldberg and B.C. Zipursky, *Recognizing Wrongs*, Harvard University Press 2020, 281–89; R. Wakeford et al., 'A review of probability of causation and its use in a compensation scheme for nuclear industry workers in the United Kingdom' (1998) 74 *Health Physics* 1.

197 Seabourne, n. 3, 2.3.

particular, presumptions may serve to penalise a party whose actions/decisions created the situation of uncertainty; perhaps especially where a powerful party would exploit it to their advantage. *Ad hominem* rules of construction, for example, have often been justified on the basis that the *proferens* was responsible for creating the ambiguity or even did so in bad faith.[198] In the case of mixed funds, English law applies different rules where a wrongdoer created the uncertainty problem by mixing another's assets with their own.[199] Presuming a child's legitimacy has also been explained on the basis that a cuckold was responsible for failing to control his wife.[200]

In toxic tort litigation, meanwhile, defendants can share a responsibility for creating the uncertainty problem, insofar as each is a proven wrongdoer only possibly causative of the harm.[201] Other ideas of responsibility and fault may engage here, perhaps concerning whether a party has certainly committed a wrong or is well placed to bear the resultant burden. Fault seems only to be relevant as a reason to tip the balance in favour of a claimant, however; there is no sensitive investigation of the defendant's degree of fault, and this is not necessarily linked to the extent of the risk they created.[202]

In contrast, ideas of responsibility and fault are likely to play a smaller role when the uncertainty problem has a triangular structure: two parties dispute an uncertainty that fundamentally relates to an independent third party. For example, potential heirs dispute a sequence of deaths, or a widower and heir dispute the birth of live, legitimate issue.[203] Here, we might expect more interest in policy concerns that centre on protecting the third-party interests, and less interest in 'responsibility'. While the problem could have been avoided, for example, by better estate planning,[204] such a failure cannot be attributed to the eventual litigants. Only exceptionally will fault or responsibility break through here.[205]

Finally, the institution of any specific rule for resolving uncertainty problems may itself encourage parties to avoid the problem arising: a general nudging or channelling function. For example, *commorientes* rules raise awareness of problems around coincident deaths, encouraging testators (at least when advised) to account for the problem through mechanisms like survivorship clauses.[206] Similarly, the existence of default rules of construction, like *contra proferentem*, should encourage (experienced) parties to clarify the meaning

---

198 McCunn, n. 2, 8.3.2.
199 Douglas/Maniscalco, n. 2, 9.2.1.
200 Seabourne, n. 3, 2.3.
201 Oliphant, n. 5, 5.3.2.
202 Oliphant, n. 5, 5.1.3. Cf. fault in contractual interpretation cases: McCunn, n. 2, 8.3.2.
203 Bell, n. 4; Seabourne, n. 3, 2.2. We could also envisage cases where contracting parties dispute the meaning of a contract made to benefit a third party.
204 Bell, n. 4, 3.3.4.
205 See e.g. (still somewhat tangentially) death sequencing and the slayer rule: ibid., 3.3.2.3.
206 Ibid., 3.3.4.

of their contracts at the outset.[207] Here, the precise result mandated is much less important than the rule's mere existence, and problems are avoided at a systemic level.[208]

12.3.3 *The interactions of fact and law*

12.3.3.1 *Fact and law distinguished?*

We have already noted the difficulty of distinguishing satisfactorily between fact and law.[209] Our exploration of intractable uncertainty problems has further demonstrated the close interweaving of questions of law and fact. It is sometimes difficult to identify whether an issue is one of fact or law at all, especially, for example, when our concern is with the intentions of the parties. It is impossible to ascertain another's intentions directly, and the issue is compounded when the intentions are those of multiple parties. It is often questionable whether a presumption about the parties' intentions really aims to identify factual intentions, or is merely a legal rule imposing an otherwise appealing solution in the absence of facts (perhaps under the useful guise of factual investigation).[210] Like others we have seen, this may not be an either-or question: the same rule can sometimes plausibly engage factual intentions, and sometimes be fictional.

In the same way, identifying death might entail an initial legal definitional question, or it might present for the law as a question of fact.[211] If the latter, normative issues will still need addressing elsewhere; perhaps buried within the medical conceptions used to supply the fact-answer.[212] Medical science cannot answer normative questions surrounding death, but medical *practitioners* can, as they do in England. The law sloughs off these questions by treating the issue as one of fact, creating useful ambiguity as to where the normative answers emerge. The normative authority of law and empirical authority of medical science secure the socially accepted, practically necessary outcome in tandem, but its exact sources are obscured.[213]

Whether or not the law provides its own definitions, it can still be difficult to disentangle factual and normative questions. Some normative decisions must be made before we can begin to discover the facts of a dispute.[214] For

---

207 McCunn, n. 2, 8.3.2.
208 There is another crossover here between mechanisms for dealing with factual and legal uncertainty (cf. Dyson, n. 33, 10.1): parties' practical avoidance may inhibit legal clarification/development.
209 Bell/McCunn, n. 1, 1.2.1.1; 1.2.1.3.
210 McCunn, n. 2, 2.3, 3.2; Douglas/Maniscalco, n. 2, 9.3.1.2, 9.3.4.1.
211 McGrath, n. 3, 4.1.
212 Ibid., 4.3.4.–4.3.5, 4.3.8.
213 Ibid., 4.3.4.
214 Cf. J.A. Jolowicz, 'Factfinding: a comparative perspective' in D.L. Carey Miller and P.R. Beaumont (eds), *The Option of Litigating in Europe*, UK National Committee of Comparative Law 1993, 136.

example, in order to identify the presence of new life, we must first decide what counts as life;[215] to identify a death, what counts as dying;[216] and to value a loss, what counts as loss.[217] However, as Milsom observed, we must discover some facts before we can begin to make normative decisions: law and fact are not 'so separate that either can be seen as the fixed background to an examination of the other'.[218] Thus, we have seen that (unlike continental traditions) English law did not set clear rules for dealing with *commorientes* or the valuation of damages while these matters were 'locked' in the jury room;[219] and few legal systems developed rules on identifying death before medical technology disaggregated cerebral, respiratory, and cardiovascular activity.[220]

We must therefore be prepared to spot intractable uncertainty problems emerging from shifts in the wider legal context, and understand how laws and facts are affecting one another. Traditional dichotomies, between fact and law or the scope of a problem and its solution, are under particular pressure here, and may begin to break down as we tweak the equation to find a satisfying outcome.

12.3.3.2 Scope and solutions interwoven

Thus, in order to define an uncertainty problem, we must also engage with a tangled web of fact and law in terms of the interwoven elements of scope and solution. The ways in which we think or speak about a problem influence its solution, and vice versa. Again, we see that this may produce a feedback loop, whereby understandings of and solutions to a problem are continually renegotiated in the light of one another.

Accordingly, frequently occurring fact patterns will tend to set initial understandings of a problem, as with 'common danger' *commorientes* cases;[221] these then direct our subsequent expectations about the nature and boundaries of that problem and appropriate solutions. On the other hand, the legal rule instituted to deal with an uncertainty problem may also come to influence understandings of the problem itself.[222] It may become desirable for policy reasons to expand the ambit of a problem and its solution. Or, if the same

---

215 Seabourne, n. 3, 2.1.
216 McGrath, n. 3, 4.1.
217 Messner-Kreuzbauer, n. 5, 7.2.
218 S.F.C. Milsom, 'Law and Fact in Legal Development' (1967) 17 *Toronto Law Journal* 1, 1.
219 Bell, n. 4, 3.1; Messner-Kreuzbauer, n. 5, 7.1. See Milsom, n. 218, 11.
220 McGrath, n. 3, 4.3.3. Jewish law is an unusual example: see I. Offer-Stark, 'When halakhah, science, technology, and ethics converge' in H. Fox and T. Meacham (eds), *Jewish Law Association Studies XXVIII*, Lieberman 2020.
221 Bell, n. 4, 3.2.1.
222 See above, 12.2.2.2.

policy does not obtain across the board, the problem and solutions may be sliced up accordingly.[223]

Lawyers' attachment to, or dissatisfaction with, an available legal solution may also influence their rhetoric about the underlying uncertainty problem. Levels of factual uncertainty can be played up or down to invoke a convenient presumption or avoid its undesirable application. Emphasising doubt about the possible length of a pregnancy, for example, could extend application of the (convenient) presumption of legitimacy, while slim evidence might be allowed to rebut an (undesirable) presumption of infanticide.[224] Reframing tort problems alternatively as matters of damage or causation may equally play on preferences as to tolerated uncertainty and outlets for preferred outcomes.[225]

We may also see variations in the levels of factual uncertainty needed to trigger a special solution—playing at the boundaries of the problem's emergence.[226] For example, mid-twentieth-century English courts were prepared to apply the *contra proferentem* rule to any contract that was not 'perfectly clear', and German courts likewise to contracts that were not really ambiguous, significantly expanding the rule's scope.[227] Similarly, English courts have sometimes appeared to suggest that any uncertainty at all in a *commorientes* case can engage a statutory presumption, while New Zealand openly institutes a stricter standard of proof.[228] Emphasising the extent of factual uncertainty bolsters arguments for departing from the ordinary burden-of-proof solution.[229] Thus, the facts may be reframed to suit our view of the law.

12.3.3.3 A web of tensions

Fact and law can blend, then, and scope and solutions interplay within those elements. This must also be combined with the interplay discussed earlier between different notions of what is ultimately most desirable in each particular context: principally, securing factual accuracy or particular policy goods.[230]

Above, it became clear that a solution to an uncertainty problem becomes more or less desirable depending on its compatibility with both the likely truth of the facts and the law's wider values and policy goals. We can now add that the calculation involves an additional variable: legal and normative issues as to scope are blended with the factual and policy decisions embedded in solutions

---

223 As with *ad hominem* rules of construction: McCunn, n. 2, 8.3.1.
224 Seabourne, n. 3, 2.3.3.
225 Consider Oliphant, n. 5, 5.3.1; Schnobel/Skillen, n. 5, 6.4.
226 See above, 12.2.1.1.
227 McCunn, n. 2, 8.2.1.
228 Bell, n. 4, 3.3.1; sec. 3, Simultaneous Deaths Act 1958 (New Zealand). In determining death, English courts reject a stricter standard of proof, but apply the civil standard with 'anxious scrutiny': McGrath, n. 3, 4.3.6.
229 See e.g. Jaconelli, n. 174, 491.
230 Above, 12.3.1.

to create a complex system of interrelated and unstable options. There is no simple progression from identifying a problem to instituting a solution, or from fact to law;[231] instead, fact and law, scope and solution, and the various desiderata for the outcome are all in flux. In the context of loss-of-a-chance claims, for example, the courts are capable of manipulating a variety of legal doctrines to ensure their desired outcomes are achieved.[232] Creative thinking opens up such options, allowing parties to argue for a remoulding of the legal concepts.[233] If acceptable and efficacious, the law may acquiesce.

Our response to uncertainty, then, is susceptible to change, in step with new understandings of the problem and its context, whilst any shifts will have a concomitant effect on other elements within the system. Rapid changes may lead to increased uncertainty across both factual and legal questions. Factual uncertainty may also be compounded by (factual or legal) uncertainty as to the present or past content of rules themselves. These issues all interact, as the law grapples with a total level of uncertainty across all questions.[234] If the law will only tolerate a certain level of overall uncertainty,[235] clearer legal rules will likely be preferred as fact patterns become more difficult to manage. We might also see greater levels of change, experimentation, or novelty in legal rules created where the factual issues are more straightforward or contained.

Factual uncertainties are closely interwoven with legal and normative ones. An issue cannot always be isolated; rather, we must be open to considering it as part of a wider web or system of response, incorporating normative and wider systemic strands.

12.3.4 The importance of time and timing

12.3.4.1 Self-resolving problems

Delaying a decision is one option sometimes engaged when facing an intractable factual uncertainty.[236] For example, a claimant may have to wait to bring their claim until a certain kind of harm (not merely a risk) manifests.[237] Some uncertainty problems have no critical temporal dimension, as where the passage of time usually has no significant effect on decisions about contractual meaning. Likewise, unless unexpected new evidence emerges, knowledge

---

231 *Pace* e.g. T.M. Shadwell (ed.), *The Posthumous Works of Charles Fearne*, Butterworth 1797, 61–62 ('If laws, therefore, were made for facts...'); see Bell/McCunn, n. 1, 1.1. Cf. also Milsom, n. 218.
232 Schnobel/Skillen, n. 5, 6.4.
233 Ibid., 6.3.2.
234 Dyson, n. 33, 10.4.
235 Ibid.
236 See above, 12.2.2.1.
237 Schnobel/Skillen, n. 5, 6.1.2.

and the knowability of entirely past facts are unlikely to change with time.[238] However, several uncertainties do have, and are perhaps characterised by, critical temporal dimensions. Some are time-responsive in the sense that they naturally resolve themselves with sufficient time: for example, it will become clear whether a person is pregnant[239] or has died.[240]

Sometimes, though, waiting is not an acceptable option; there is a pressing need to make a time-sensitive decision. This can be true, for example, when deciding on the presence of life for abortion or organ-transplantation purposes.[241] Waiting may also cause distress. For instance, the passage of time certainly reveals whether a person has died, but awaiting bodily putrefaction would be upsetting for all involved, and the delay entailed could have serious legal consequences.[242]

A compromise solution can allow the law to wait for a limited period, before a backstop rule engages. For example, the law will generally wait for some specified time before presuming the death of a missing person.[243] The waiting period allows for the possibility of further information emerging, but here also itself serves to strengthen the evidence of death, given the time elapsed without news—making this a perfect candidate for the delaying tactic.

A particularly interesting example is the assessment of damages for lost earnings. Here, the law must grapple both with uncertainty involving the future (which may resolve with time) and uncertainty about counter-factual events (which will not).[244] Generally, English courts prefer to fight through both kinds of uncertainty, awarding once-and-for-all lump sums to claimants.[245] In contrast, and at least as a matter of doctrine, Germanic systems' rules as standard wait out at least some uncertainty as to the future.[246]

Therefore, a careful balance needs striking, if the law decides to 'wait and see', in view of features that, like so many others in this area, can cut two ways. The need for certainty, closure, or efficient administration of justice may recommend speedy decisions. Parties may also wish to be freed from ongoing relationships with each other,[247] or from the difficulties that can be caused

---

238 A possibility that cannot be completely discounted; consider DNA testing and historic crimes.
239 Seabourne, n. 3, 2.3—save some later intervention (such as the potentially pregnant person's disappearance) preventing further insight. Doubtful paternity might also, aside modern testing, become more certain over time, if e.g. a fully grown child unmistakeably resembles its father.
240 McGrath, n. 3, 4.1.
241 Ibid., 4.2.2.
242 Ibid., 4.2.1.
243 On which, cf. Bell, n. 4, 3.2.1.
244 Messner-Kreuzbauer, n. 5, 7.2.
245 Ibid., 7.3.1.2.1; though cf. ibid., 7.3.1.2.2 on e.g. periodical payments as a limited alternative.
246 Ibid., 7.3.2.2.1.
247 Ibid., 7.3.2.2.2.

when their rights are held in suspense.[248] The Germanic experience of personal injury claims for future lost earnings suggests that, in practice, these considerations are valued highly by parties, if not always so highly by doctrine.[249]

On the other hand, confronting uncertainty requires us to expend intellectual and practical resources;[250] delay may be more economically efficient, especially if this does not worsen the parties' situation. The results of an over-hasty resolution may also prove to be inaccurate, with serious implications for parties, or as discussed above produce intolerable moral transgressions.[251] Similarly, a needy claimant may be left significantly under-compensated by less accurate early damages assessment,[252] or a person presumed dead may return to find their assets dissipated.[253] The drive for quick decisions may thus trigger outcomes that are, in hindsight, patently unjust.

12.3.4.2 Inertia, entrenchment, and mutability

The chronology of an individual case, then, will affect its resolution. The chronology of the law's systemic development is also significant. Fact and law again intertwine,[254] as a resolution depends upon the dispute's place on both a factual and a legal timeline.

Some solutions to uncertainty problems are remarkably enduring, especially where continued reliance on a Romanist presumption long discourages any fundamental re-think.[255] Nevertheless, significant change can and does occur. In some instances, this is prompted by a sudden or impending threat,[256] or a longstanding concern may finally be addressed when general reform arrives.[257] The development of organ transplantation, for instance, further heightened pressures on death determination, and regulating the new medical procedures served as a vehicle and opportunity for change.[258] Elsewhere, the law may only gradually get to grips with a new social problem and existing tools that can address it, as when courts began to deploy *ad hominem* rules of construction to rebalance exploitative standard-form contracts.[259]

The law may react differently depending on the speed and urgency of change and calls for answers in disputes. For example, the need to determine

---

248 Seabourne, n. 3, 2.3.
249 Messner-Kreuzbauer, n. 5, 7.3.2.2.1.
250 Dyson, n. 33, 10.4.
251 Above, 12.3.1.1.
252 Messner-Kreuzbauer, n. 5, 7.4.1.
253 McGrath, n. 3, 4.1; the concern applies equally in disappearance cases, cf. Bell, n. 4, 3.2.1.
254 Cf. above, 12.3.3.
255 See references in n. 74.
256 As with Germany's 1939 *commorientes*/disappearances reforms: Bell, n. 4, 3.2.1.
257 As when a *commorientes* provision was introduced within the 1925 overhaul of English property law: ibid., 3.1.
258 McGrath, n. 3, 4.2.2.
259 McCunn, n. 2, 8.2.2.

death is a longstanding problem familiar to the law, albeit requiring swift resolutions in individual cases. The law's approach could therefore develop gradually, with occasional acceleration prompted by specific new problems, as just discussed.[260] The need to determine the causation of mesothelioma, by contrast, was a problem with a long latency period, which suddenly inundated the law in the later twentieth century. Struggling to address a newly urgent problem, courts may make more pragmatic, arguably less principled, decisions that may later be regretted.[261]

The mode of any development introduced will affect the speed of change and the future mutability of the new rules. Case law might allow a gradual evolution, within the confines of 'casuistic path-dependence',[262] and legislative intervention might provide an opportunity for more democratic input.[263] Some legislation only plugs urgent gaps in the law;[264] however, codification or broad law-reform work may offer an opportunity for a principled overhaul within an entire field,[265] while international collaboration may influence domestic reforms.[266] A new statute or code may freeze the law in place, however, minimising future judicial development; albeit it may also encourage parties to test a new rule's boundaries.[267] It remains true regardless that if parties regularly succeed in avoiding a problem *ex ante*, the relevant law will not develop further.[268]

In terms of longevity, the long institution of a rule will not alone necessarily hinder the development of the law; the stability of its framing may conceal changes to its practical implementation.[269] Even where, for example, an ancient Roman presumption has dominated, we may see changes to its precise focus, boundaries, or nuances over time in line with the developmental pressures we have been discussing, as with the many incarnations of *contra proferentem*.[270] Some rules are more mutable than others, though: for instance, the use of imprecise criteria may facilitate longer-term change, by allowing continued resort to contemporary science without freezing it in place.[271] While imprecise rules may increase *legal* uncertainty, this does not always cause immediate

---

260 McGrath, n. 3, 4.3.5.
261 As by some of the English judiciary: Oliphant, n. 5, 5.4.
262 McGrath, n. 3, 4.3.8.
263 Ibid., 4.3.8.
264 E.g. Oliphant, n. 5, 5.1.5, 5.3.4.
265 E.g. McGrath, n. 3, 4.3.2.
266 Ibid., 4.3.3.
267 Consider the rush of English *commorientes* cases preceding statutory intervention: Bell, n. 4, 3.1; little such litigation now arises, after a few mid-century cases on the statute.
268 Cf. above, 12.3.2.3.
269 Maine ascribed a fictional quality to all such rules: see Dyson, n. 33, 10.1. Cf. L. Shmilovits, *Legal Fictions in Private Law*, CUP 2022, 189–93.
270 McCunn, n. 2, 8.3.1.
271 Seabourne, n. 3, 2.3.2; McGrath, n. 3, 4.3.8. Though using imprecise criteria may lead to anxiety about potential exploitation: ibid., 4.3.4.

practical problems[272] and can be accepted, at least unless the overall combination of factual and legal uncertainty proves intolerable.[273] Longevity is a product of mutability in individual elements of the solution (fact and law), but mutability cannot exceed the system's, or its users', tolerance level.

Change may come with scientific progress, too, of course; uncertainty problems may be resolved as new ways to find answers emerge. Consider, for example, the development of reliable pregnancy and paternity tests. Social and legal changes may also render problems moot, though: abolishing capital punishment and the declining significance of legitimate birth had already reduced the importance of uncertainties about pregnancy and paternity when these options emerged.[274] Likewise, where asbestos has been banned, problematic litigation on the causation of mesothelioma will decline[275]—perhaps before the scientific uncertainty is fully resolved. A form of 'wait-and-see' response, then, may operate beyond any individual parties or dispute, with longer-term, system-level consequences.

Absent any such external impetus, a rule might still change if better (contemporary) arguments emerge from within the law.[276] However, there may also be reason to resist such changes. The stability of a rule itself has value insofar as it provides clarity and certainty; especially in areas so lacking against these aims, this may justify inertia, even with an unpopular rule.[277] As we have seen, any change is also likely to have a ripple effect, with perhaps unintended consequences.[278] In the context of mesothelioma claims, for instance, the English courts' departure from ordinary principle has given rise to knock-on legal problems, characterised by some as 'a sort of juridical version of chaos theory'.[279] The value of stability should therefore be accorded due weight whenever new policy ideas are brought into the balance. As we have noted, desiring *ex ante* clarity is a prime constant across the instances we have examined.[280]

12.3.5 Science and knowledge

12.3.5.1 Knowledge of the world

We have seen that our understandings of and responses to uncertainty problems are profoundly mutable, sometimes blurring, bending, or breaking under

---

272 Dyson, n. 33, 10.1, 10.2.
273 See above, 12.3.3.3.
274 Seabourne, n. 3, 2.4.
275 Oliphant, n. 5, 5.1.1.
276 Above, 12.2.2.2.
277 The 'principle of inertia' demands stable rules be maintained unless there is sufficient reason for change: cf. F. Picinali, 'The Presumption of Innocence: A Deflationary Account' (2021) 84 *MLR* 708.
278 Above, 12.3.3.3.
279 Schnobel/Skillen, n. 5, n. 80.
280 Above, 12.3.1.2.

external pressure. As noted, one defining stimulus for such change, generally and over centuries, is the pressure exerted by extra-legal knowledge systems. In particular, scientific advances may change our understanding of a problem, raise entirely new questions, or vary the frequency or complexity of existing issues.[281] New knowledge might also change our appreciation of available solutions. Simple presumptions and proxies may suffice to resolve most uncertainty problems in a pre-modern society,[282] but as science and technology advance, factual accuracy frequently becomes more attainable, and perhaps therefore more appealing. The law's solutions must adapt to respond to such investigative refinements.

While new knowledge may offer new solutions or refine one that already exists, however, this depends on the law's willingness to involve an external knowledge system in its decision-making processes. Sometimes, the law clearly is keen to divest itself of uncertainty problems, as where issues around childbirth were identified as concerning 'secrets of women'.[283] The law may here more extensively engage expert fact-finders to resolve the uncertainty by better, more knowledgeable or skilled, approximation to truth. Women could thus be used as information sources for pregnancy and childbirth, even though their involvement in legal fact-finding was usually heavily restricted; later, medical professionals became acknowledged as authorities on pregnancy instead.[284] Equally, as medical science developed, the law for a time ceded ground to experts to interpret evidence for sequencing deaths.[285] Meanwhile, today, at least English law is wholly dependent upon medical science for its definition of death, seeking not to make any proper normative or factual determination, but only reflect medical experts' conclusions.[286]

New sources of data may likewise be invoked to assist. In the context of damages assessment, for example, actuarial data has been integrated into accounts of future lost earnings, and courts have even resorted to using national average earnings data for an injured child with no set career path.[287]

The law must tread a careful line here. If it will provide an authoritative guide and check on parties' behaviour, it cannot simply replicate those parties' views; yet, to retain credibility, it cannot wholly disregard them.[288] The difficulty is particularly acute where, as with medical science, there is both widespread deference to and distrust of a particular body of knowledge.[289]

281 Above, 12.2.1.2.
282 Ibbetson, n. 55, pp. 272–73.
283 Seabourne, n. 3, text to n. 3. Cf. Bell, n. 4, 3.2.2 (matters 'for science, not law').
284 Seabourne, n. 3, 2.3.1.
285 Bell, n. 4, 3.2.2.
286 McGrath, n. 3, 4.3.5.
287 Messner-Kreuzbauer, n. 5, 7.3.1.3.1.
288 McGrath, n. 3, 4.3.1.
289 Ibid., 4.2.2.

Where the law itself defers to that knowledge system, its role may be limited to providing procedural reassurance without substantive control.[290]

The law may thus become attached to, even dependent upon, external knowledge sources.[291] Perhaps related to such dependence, it is striking how often the law and lawyers have resorted to pseudo-scientific methods where no better source of knowledge is available. Efforts to offer insight on *commorientes* cases have seen discussion of the asphyxiation of guinea pigs, and the buoyancy of breasts.[292] Pseudo-science may even persist in the legal arena long after being widely discredited. The 'lung-float' test for live births was doubted by 1750, for example, but saw use by US courts into the twenty-first century.[293] There is a risk here of law's solutions losing what relatively weak credibility they have (derived from truth-approximation or policy input[294]) if the approach to external knowledge systems is insufficiently discerning.

Elsewhere, correspondingly, we see suspicion or rejection of external knowledge systems. Absent outright rejection, suspicion may manifest as the law's seeking to control external experts, instructing them on how to conduct their investigations. Medieval law offered advice to juries of matrons, for example, but as respect for medical experts grew in this context, the choice of evidence was left to professional discretion.[295] Epidemiological evidence has been at the forefront of discussions about the causation of mesothelioma. However, such evidence has been carefully confined to limited issues that it is apt to prove, resisting a temptation to expand its influence.[296] The law has preferred its own (internally controllable) conceptual or procedural solutions here.[297] Similarly, for *commorientes* cases, numerous legal writers expressed scepticism about scientific evidence and its limited usefulness in resolving cases, even as the authors of medico-legal texts confidently pushed their wares.[298] *Commorientes* rules likewise now tend to impose presumptions, or play with the burden or standard of proof, reducing the room for scientific input to prove decisive.[299]

This approach is consistent with a view of experts as (merely) better approximators of truth in the arena of intractable uncertainty. In our scenarios, we cannot hope by pushing the usual boundaries of expert involvement or data acceptance to render the relevant fact properly 'known'. Relevant wider

---

290 Ibid., 4.3.2, 4.3.4.
291 Ibid., 4.3.7. Similarly, emphasis on 'scientific uncertainty' around the causation of mesothelioma privileges a scientific framework: Oliphant, n. 5, 5.1.5.
292 Bell, n. 4, 3.2.2.
293 Seabourne, n. 3, 2.3.2.
294 See above, 12.3.1.3.
295 Seabourne, n. 3, 2.3.2.
296 See e.g. *Sienkiewicz*, n. 87. Extra-legal compensation schemes may willingly rely more on epidemiological evidence; see e.g. Wakeford et al., n. 196, 5.
297 Oliphant, n. 5, 5.3.1, including e.g. burden-of-proof changes and new 'increase-in-risk' causal tests.
298 Bell, n. 4, 3.2.2.
299 Ibid., 3.3.1–3.3.2.

knowledge frameworks simply frame a narrower field for the unknown and so better approximate truth. It always remains open to law to reject any such system or its answer as no better: it may be still too inadequate,[300] or stray too far from the law's principal question,[301] or take too much of the legal system's role.[302]

Indeed, we may find legal actors over-emphasising the uncertainty of evidence to encourage resort to a preferred, default legal rule. Thus, judges have been accused of playing up documentary ambiguities to invoke their favoured *contra proferentem* rule.[303] Likewise, in one English *commorientes* case, even uncontradicted medical evidence could not dislodge the law's default answer.[304] Lawyers may grow attached to their presumptions, or at least prefer them to over-confident experts. Again, feedback loops can emerge here: an initial choice to include or exclude certain kinds of knowledge risks ossifying over time, overshadowing potential alternatives.[305]

Sometimes science simply cannot help us, because the nature of the dispute is not amenable to empirical work. While it may be able to provide relevant facts (for example, as to the quickening of a foetus,[306] or the cessation of brain-stem function[307]), it cannot determine their social, political, or moral significance.[308] Scientific inconclusiveness may perhaps facilitate moral controversy, but increasing knowledge will not always resolve it. Indeed, as noted, an uncertainty problem may even become socially insignificant before scientifically resolvable.[309] Broader social developments can be as important as increasing knowledge or technological prowess. Again, if we seek to overcome intractable uncertainty problems, we may do better to look beyond the law, finding helpful consensus outwith its mechanisms.

The law, then, may engage with external knowledge structures where it faces an intractable uncertainty problem. Legal knowledge may be independent and definitive for its particular adjudicative purpose, but it is also porous, even parasitic: it can and does engage answers from other disciplines where it can credibly and usefully turn them to the same purpose of resolving a particular dispute.

---

300 Cf. pseudo-scientific methods: references in nn. 292 and 293.

301 Cf. the limited relevance of statistical evidence as proving only general causation. See e.g. *Hotson v East Berkshire Health Authority* [1987] 2 WLR 287, 303; *Gregg v Scott*, n. 28, [193]: Schnobel/Skillen, n. 5, 6.2.3.

302 Cf. McGrath, n. 3, 4.3.2. Per McGrath, law may seem 'diminished' if it outsources too much: ibid., 4.4.4.

303 McCunn, n. 2, 8.2.1.

304 Bell, n. 4, 3.3.1.

305 With inertia's attendant costs/benefits: cf. above, 12.3.4.2.

306 Seabourne, n. 3, 2.3.2.

307 McGrath, n. 3, 4.2.2.

308 Seabourne, n. 3, 2.4.

309 See e.g. paternity: above, 12.3.4.2.

To draw from outside its own knowledge system in this sense, though, the law must express preferences between other value systems on offer: for example, prioritising medical over religious conceptions of death.[310] To be acceptable, these further sources of knowledge must sufficiently accord (or not obviously conflict) with the values of the legal system itself, but also with wider social values.[311] The widespread lay acceptance of medical control over death, for example, has enabled the law to accord medical science greater authority there.[312] This re-engages the question of the credibility of answers chosen in a context where there is only a weak, if any, hope of securing a factually true answer. If the law does not answer on its (defensible) policy positions, it may yet answer by absorbing other, themselves credible and respected, bodies or holders of knowledge. As above, the normative and empirical interplay here, substantively and institutionally, is important.[313]

More generally, we may also find societies becoming more or less tolerant of factual uncertainty over time. As our knowledge of the world increases, any persisting uncertainties may seem more unsettling[314]—ships lost untraced might prompt greater unease now than in past millennia. We may relatedly have greater resort to other investigative mechanisms available, beyond possible private litigation, to investigate the truth of past events. The answers provided by such inquiries, however, may not always be admitted during fact-finding in litigation if the latter does follow. In *Ommaney v Stilwell*, for instance, the court seemed reluctant fully to use evidence collected by Dr Rae on the Franklin expedition's fate.[315] In other cases, evidence provided to another form of inquiry will be simply inadmissible.[316] Where knowledge exists publicly beyond the field of 'legal' knowledge produced by private-law litigation,[317] this (and its perhaps broader base of fact-finding material) may satisfy society's need. Any compromised understanding at trial will then matter less, generating less pressure for definitive legal answers to intractable factual concerns: wider truth-finding might de-fang the law's limitations and private litigation's struggle to impose legal consequences.

---

310 McGrath, n. 3, 4.3.7.
311 Ibid., 4.3.1.
312 Ibid., 4.3.3.
313 Above, 3.3.1.
314 Uncertainty also causes stress: see A.O. de Berker et al., 'Computations of uncertainty mediate acute stress responses in humans' (2016) *Nature Communications* 7.
315 Bell, n. 4, 3.3.1.
316 E.g. in criminal law, *R v Soldier A & Soldier C* [2021] NICC 3.
317 Beyond the 'virtual facts' recognised through the litigation, perhaps; cf. G. Samuel, *An Introduction to Comparative Law Theory and Method*, Hart 2014, 9.VI.

12.3.5.2 Knowledge of the law

On a different level, we should note the use of another kind of knowledge that might be engaged to help resolve uncertainty problems. This is knowledge of other legal systems, or other parts of the same system. Lawyers may look to these areas, which may differ significantly in outlook, to help understand and conceptualise intractable uncertainty problems, and identify potential solutions.

Sometimes, our uncertainty problems have been compared or combined with other, similar problems that the law faces. For example, 'doubtful matters' were jumbled together in the Digest.[318] More recently, systems have more and less closely associated *commorientes* and disappearance cases.[319] However, such comparisons appear surprisingly rare.[320] As noted, problems of intractable factual uncertainty are usually seen as niche concerns of their own fields.[321] Thus, *commorientes* have not been further aligned with other, comparably structured sequencing issues in modern law.[322] Similarly, *ad hominem* rules of construction resolve uncertainties about the meaning of contracts, but may be deemed inappropriate to apply to wills or statutes,[323] the issues, contexts, and policy concerns being quite different.

We have also seen lawyers look to other jurisdictions for knowledge about uncertainty problems and potential solutions,[324] as when English treatise-writers adopted, more or less openly, continental scholarship on contractual interpretation.[325] Similarly, English writers, lawyers, and legislators relatively extensively canvassed (though ultimately rejected) continental approaches to *commorientes*.[326] When confronting the causation problem in *Fairchild*, the House of Lords reviewed a range of jurisdictions' approaches to the issue,[327] while the US President's Commission examined global legal systems' approaches to determining death.[328] In neither of those cases, notably, did the review decisively indicate a result then accepted—only general ideas (like the injustice of an orthodox outcome, or the importance of brain function), requiring further choice to be exercised within the home system.

318 Ibbetson, n. 55, p. 259.
319 Bell, n. 4, 3.2.1.
320 Comparable cases might also serve as counterfactuals—e.g. the transplantation hypothetical in *Re A* [1992] 3 Med. LR 303: McGrath, n. 3, 4.3.5.
321 Bell/McCunn, n. 1, 1.2.2.
322 Bell, n. 4, 3.2.3.
323 McCunn, n. 2, 8.2.2.
324 Above, 12.2.1.3.
325 McCunn, n. 2, 8.2.1; cf. Bell, n. 4, 3.2.1.
326 Bell, n. 4, 3.1.
327 Oliphant, n. 5, 5.3.2.
328 McGrath, n. 3, 4.3.2.

As discussed above, then, even where systems have identified the same problem, there may be considerable divergence in solutions.[329] Attempts to challenge a solution on the basis of divergence from common practice elsewhere seem likely to fail.[330] Some systems have reached similar results through deliberate borrowing[331] or convergent evolution,[332] but even systems that began with similar (perhaps Romanist) rules may later move in quite different directions.[333] Similar rules may also be justified on very different bases,[334] or agree generally whilst engaging different practical methods for assessing whether their tests are met.[335] This stresses the significance of local context in framing a concrete response (along the various lines discussed in this chapter) alongside also the value of engaging in the wider reviews involved (to reinforce a sense of the problem and broaden perspectives).

Finally, Ibbetson's chapter reminds us that factual investigation may also be required to determine the content of laws,[336] and, as Dyson observes, there is a limit to the resources available to expend on such problems.[337] Lawyers might be especially willing to devote their attention to these valuable investigations when their uncertainty problem is seen as particularly unusual or intractable,[338] or when circumstances make at least some comparative data collection apparently simple.[339] While exploring other understandings of or solutions to uncertainty problems can be beneficial, it does also bring costs of its own. Simplifying those exercises by understanding the broader uncertainty problem within particular contexts only further shows its value here.

12.3.5.3 Summary

Intractable uncertainty problems, then, change over time, alongside the development of knowledge and technology. Scientific advances may offer solutions to these problems, but can also increase problems; cannot fully resolve difficult

---

329 Above, 12.2.2.

330 McGrath, n. 3, 4.3.6.

331 E.g. *ad hominem* construction rules were frequently Roman-/canon-law imports: McCunn, n. 2, 8.1.

332 E.g. English and Germanic systems both tend towards lump-sum compensation payments in practice, although their doctrinal positions differ: Messner-Kreuzbauer, n. 5, 7.3.1.2, 7.3.2.2.

333 McCunn, n. 2, 8.3.1.

334 Douglas/Maniscalco, n. 2, 9.3.4.1.

335 McGrath, n. 3, 4.3.3.

336 Ibbetson, n. 55.

337 Dyson, n. 33, 10.4.

338 E.g. Oliphant, n. 5, 5.3.1.

339 Though simplicity may be illusory; thus, Kahn-Freund, writing in England, was unaware of Germany's 1939 *commorientes* reforms: O. Kahn-Freund, [Note] (1942) 6 *MLR* 89, 90; assuming stability/inertia may be especially understandable in the intractable uncertainty context, of course: see above, 12.3.4.2.

social and moral questions; and may be rejected by the law for other internal reasons. Chosen solutions may need reviewing and reforming over time as shifts occur. Meanwhile, we can benefit from knowledge about other areas of law and legal systems, even if perhaps only to increase our awareness of the problem and its potential solutions and avoid the trap of imagining a problem is niche and unique.

12.4 An uncertainty toolkit

12.4.1 Form and purpose

This ends our account of critical features and themes in the intractable uncertainty problems analysed. We turn to the use that may be made of this. We have noted the risk of uncritical path-dependence for legal systems addressing 'known unknowns',[340] and hoped that, by exploring uncertainties alongside one another, in their comparative, historical contexts, we can foster fuller, more explicit discussions of uncertainty's many facets.

To that end, we conclude with an 'interrogative toolkit': a framework of questions for issues that have been identified as relevant when framing and resolving a problem of intractable factual uncertainty. This 'toolkit' should facilitate more expansive engagement with the problem, and dissuade us from viewing uncertainty problems only as specific, isolated, and niche concerns, instead re-focusing our attention on the broader underlying choices and imperatives involved.

As indicated,[341] we do not claim that there is any single 'best' solution to any particular problem of intractable uncertainty, let alone intractable uncertainty generally. Proper solutions may and do differ significantly across areas of law, jurisdictions, and time periods. Furthermore, a range of policies and principles need weighing when choosing a response to a particular problem, and these cannot be exhaustively identified or pre-balanced in the abstract.

It is important to read the toolkit alongside the rest of this volume. Firstly, it does not indicate *a priori* where uncertainty problems are to be found. It is not a treasure map to uncertainty's emergence; only a guide for processing an uncertainty problem. We hope, though, that the analyses of particular areas in this book help in considering where other 'known unknowns' may exist in the law, especially where these are currently obscured. Secondly, the toolkit must necessarily be framed in abstract and general terms; concrete application will turn on the particular problem in its particular legal, socio-economic, technological, and temporal context. The chapters in this volume demonstrate how the different problems that we have been able to consider each actually sit within their own contexts.

---

340 Bell/McCunn, n. 1, 1.1.
341 Above, 12.1; Bell/McCunn, n. 1, 1.3.1.1.

In relation to uncertainty problems and their scope, the framework aims to open up the theme of uncertainty and ensure a fuller account of the problem at hand, facilitating proper control of it and appreciation of its implications. As for solutions, it aims to give indications of the range of options available and prompt reflection on the factors influencing which to choose.

12.4.2 Interrogative toolkit

12.4.2.1 Scope

- **Core**: Does the problem have an intractable or irreducible core? Can the field of enquiry be limited to this? At least initially, this may be a more secure approach. The scope of the problem may appropriately flex with the solution and justificatory bases; such flexibility may indeed be necessary to secure and stabilise the rule. The core idea may drift away from uncertainty (especially under the influence of particular solutions or policy goals), but its complete obscuring should be avoided.
- **Levels of uncertainty**: Does the problem cover multiple levels of uncertainty, presenting in more or less unknowable forms across different fact patterns? The kinds and levels of uncertainty involved should be identified as clearly as possible. It may be necessary to pull these apart to frame fitting solutions or better understand a need for an overarching approach (where e.g. the levels of uncertainty are too blurred at the edges to be cleanly, non-arbitrarily separated).
- **Boundaries**: Can the boundaries of the problem be clearly defined in terms of both the fact patterns in which it emerges and the nature of the legal-doctrinal problem that the uncertainty produces? A problem should not be left unbounded, or arbitrarily bounded, if this is avoidable, and regard should be had to the potential routes for expansion and contraction in the scope of the field. The choice of where a boundary is ultimately set must be carefully related to the solution chosen, in light of the purposes pursued; this requires appreciation of how the scope of the problem can be manipulated.
- **Interaction**: Does the scope of the problem depend upon its interaction with (other) legal rules? Does it depend upon the availability of scientific knowledge? It should be noted if these are likely to shift over time, and room should be made for flexibility.
- **Factual or legal/normative**: Is the problem really one of squarely factual, or else legal, uncertainty, or a mix of both? Is there a legal or normative question that needs answering before the factual uncertainty can be resolved, or that could be reconsidered in order to shed fresh light on the construction of the facts? (Re-)defining core concepts can help to simplify the factual enquiry and should be considered, but transparency should be sought on how the various enquiries are bounded and dealt with.

- **Social significance**: What is the social significance of the problem? If it engages particularly important social, moral, or personal interests, these should be identified and consideration given to whether any mechanisms can account for them. Preference usually remains with the internal reasons of the legal system, or empirical-scientific authority, but these preferences should be made explicit.
- **Recognition in other systems**: Do other legal systems recognise the problem? Are there lessons that can be learnt from their understanding of its scope and limits, including the fundamental question of whether an unorthodox, special treatment is justified? If other systems do not experience the question as an intractable factual uncertainty problem, why and how is that so? Consider e.g. conceptual divergences in understanding and normative or procedural re-directions of the problem; consider then whether comparable conceptualisations could be adopted.
- **Analogues**: Is the problem analogous, substantively or structurally, to others faced by the law? Could a corresponding, or overarching/linked, framing (and solution) be crafted to increase overall coherence? This will be tied to the overall scope of the problem identified and any limit that can be placed on it, but also requires an appraisal of the social, scientific, and other policy imperatives engaged.
- **Complexity**: Having regard to the previous questions, does the problem prove to be particularly complex or intricate in its overall structure or manifestations? If so, consider whether it would be valuable to disaggregate into more discrete scenarios to ensure that any solutions will be manageable. Once disaggregated, it may be possible to render some elements with more certainty and so reduce instances of the problem or the weight of demands for accuracy or conceptual integrity. (This can only be assessed by referring to particular available solutions and their reasoning.)

12.4.2.2 Solutions

- **Burden of proof**: Does the ordinary burden of proof produce a generally satisfying outcome? Any departure will ideally require the clear articulation of its justification, though this is less often achieved in practice. The ordinary procedural framework will need to be respected generally, unless a clear basis for departure is identified.
- **Reformulation**: Can the issue be reformulated to avoid the uncertainty question entirely, without causing fresh difficulties? Or to bring into play related policy aims, and so exploit the advantages of the opportunity to create a new rule?
- **Timeliness**: Is it particularly desirable to resolve cases quickly and with certainty in this precise context? Systemically, is the problem in urgent need of resolution, or can it wait for a more general, theoretically grounded reform? In the former contexts, more weight can be credited to clear

and simple presumptive rules and, correspondingly, less to strict factual accuracy.

- **Self-resolving problems**: Can the problem be expected to resolve itself, or further relevant factual information come to light, in the reasonably proximate future? Where this is at least conceivable, are there any mechanisms available to hold the dispute in abeyance for a period or create interim answers? Delays will need to be limited and their prospects for successfully attenuating the uncertainty problem balanced against associated costs.
- **Factual accuracy**: How important is it in this particular context to at least seek a factually accurate solution? The factual plausibility of a solution is usually an important consideration, but varies in significance across contexts. Regard should be had, for example, to the personal, social, and moral interests that are at stake, as well as to the likelihood of achieving factual accuracy in practice. If factual accuracy is desirable but not easily achievable, it should be considered whether there are any proxies that might offer a defensible approximation of it.
- **Other bodies of knowledge**: Are there bodies of expertise and knowledge whose conceptual structures could be absorbed to relieve the pressure on the legal fact-finding mechanisms? This might include special reliance on fact-finders beyond the law's ordinary mechanisms, or even complete disengagement from the problem in favour of an extra-legal resolution. Widely accepted lay authorities can prove valuable to the law, but an entirely separate decision-making framework is unlikely to be satisfactory in the modern context.
- **Policy imperatives**: What other policy imperatives impinge upon the case (e.g. is one of the parties at a particular disadvantage to the other)? Consider whether any of the possible solutions can also serve these policy goals (in lieu of/alongside securing factual truth).
- **Fault**: Was the uncertainty, or its manifestation as a problem in litigation, positively caused by a party to the dispute? Equally, could the problem have been avoided (perhaps at a later stage) by one or both of the disputants? Was either at fault in this regard? If so, the problem might be conceived in terms of that fault element (and thus a responsibility-based rule considered). If the uncertainty problem was caused by a third party, this will generally not be a helpful approach.
- **Compromise**: Is there an obvious way for the law to find a compromise position between the parties' interests, such as a sharing of disputed value? This will likely carry intuitive appeal and produce reasonably satisfying, even if factually clearly inaccurate, results. If compromise is not possible, consider whether it would be better for the law to disengage from the problem and encourage or make space for an extra-legal resolution (in light of the level of accuracy achievable and whether any strong policy imperatives apply).
- **Complexity**: Is a proposed solution particularly complex or intricate in terms of its elements or variations? If so, this tends to lend weight to a more simplified approach, even in the face of substantive compromises, and

the consequent promotion of greater efficiency and certainty. Consider also whether the conceptualisation of the problem area can be altered to ensure that the law in the area is sufficiently certain and simple, securing an overall level of complexity that is manageable in practice.

- **Publicity**: Will the identification of the problem or the creation of a rule raise awareness of the issue and help future parties account for it without the need for dispute (regardless of the particular content of the rule that might be imposed)? This can itself be given weight in determining whether a new solution is required and its form.
- **Solutions in other systems**: If other legal systems recognise the problem, would it be appropriate to adopt a similar solution? Simple transfers are unpromising, but comparative engagement can at least broaden the sense of potential solutions conceivable. If integrating insights from other systems, inter alia the conceptualisation of the problem, its doctrinal and procedural context, and the forces supporting its solution must be considered. Any solution's justificatory basis may be relatively weak, but this may be tolerated as a feature of intractable uncertainty solutions generally; it should not be dismissed for being weak without reference to its context and to alternatives.

12.4.3 Final remarks

This completes our review of the salient features of the problems investigated across the study, and our formulation of an interrogative framework to help guide future engagements with these sorts of uncertainty problems within the law. The picture is complex, with many case-sensitive variables. The analysis has, though, been able for the first time to bring together these disparate substantive areas explicitly as manifestations of the broader problem of uncertainty. We have revealed a first mapping of this overlooked problem field and identified clear trends and imperatives. Nevertheless: 'tho' much is taken, much abides', and further work, in relation to particular intractable uncertainty problems or uncertainty generally, may now produce more integrated and coherent reasoning by reference to a wider picture.

Index

abortion 29, 34, 282, 305
absence provisions, *Code Civil* 51–52
abstract annuities 177
Accessories and Abettors Act 1861 255
accessories to misdemeanors, avoiding 252–253
Act to Prevent the Muthering of Bastard Childre 1623 36–37
actio civilis 263
actio de effusis vel deiectis/actio de rebus effusis vel deiectis 264–265
actio de pauperie 264
actio doli 262, 272
actio furti concepti 271
actio pro socio 262
actio servi corrupti 263
actio utilis 262
actus non facit reum nisi mens sit rea 245
actus reus 242, 246
ad hominem rules of construction 185, 195–198, 204–205, 290–292, 300, 306; historical overview of 185–187; justifications 198–204; kinds of contracts 191–194; kinds of uncertainty 187–191
additional causation 112
adjudication 240
Administration of Estates Act 1925 67
adstipulatio 267, 269
adulterine bastardisation 39
AGB-Gesetz 193, 202
Agnes Gore's case 245
aiding and abetting 254
Airedale NHS Trust v Bland 90–91
Allgemeines Landrecht (ALR) 65
Allied Maples Group v Simmons & Simmons 131
ALR *see Allgemeines Landrecht*
alternative causation 113–114
ambiguity 240–241

ambiguous contracts 199
animals, as cause of injury 264
annuities, awarding damages 171–172
apportionment 119–120
Aquilian liability 265
arbitrariness 287
artificial life support 84, 88
'as if' 250–251
asbestos 103–105, 137, 308; *Barker v Corus* 107, 109–110; but for test 112–113; Compensation Act 2006 109–110; *Fairchild v Glenhaven Funeral Services* 106–108; and the law 105–106; Mesothelioma Act 2014 111–112; self-exposure 125; *Sienkiewicz v Greif* 110–111; *see also* mesothelioma
asbestosis 104
assessing damages 158–159; *see also* damages
assessment criteria for life 32–35
assessment of losses 162–163, 180–182; Germany 174–178
Australia: loss of chance 142; unmixing intangible assets 216
Austria: abstract annuities 173, 177; ad hominem rules of construction 196; *commorientes* 64; deaths 49; flexible periodic payments 174; kinds of contracts 193; loss of earnings 169–178; mathematical precision in awarding damages 176
Austrian ABGB 188, 191
Austrian ZPO 174, 176–177
avoidance: by compromise solutions 297–299; by doctrinal and procedural rules 295–296; by the parties 299–301
avoiding: occurrence of doubt 41; procedural limits 253; uncertainty problem 285–286

awarding damages 158–159;
see also damages
awards, rules for 179–180; see also
compensation

balance of justice 121
balance of probabilities 118, 133, 170
bank accounts 229; mixing 210
*Barker v Corus*07–110, 126, 139–140
Barlow Clowes International v Vaughan
219–220
Barts Health NHS Trust v Dance 91–92,
96–97
bastardising children 38
bastardy 29, 42
Bavarian BGB 196
Belgium, loss of chances 142–144
beneficiary's rights 216, 225
BGB 98; BGB¹⁹⁰⁰ 51; German BGB 188,
196, 198
BGH 7, 51
biological parentage 25–26
birth 286; concealment of 36–37
*Blamire v. South Cumbria Health
Authority* 167, 176
Bloody Code 243
bon pere de famille 143
boundaries between legal and factual
uncertainties 5–6
Bracton 30, 32
brain death 83, 85, 89, 92, 96; see also death
breach of trust 223
British Transport Commission v Gourley
153–154, 163
Broughton v Randall 55–56
Brown v Adams 213–214
burden of proof 3n6, 116, 317;
commorientes 59–64; reversal of
114–117
but for causation 150
but for test 112–113, 138
Bynkershoek, Cornelius van 264–265

California: reversal of the burden of
proof 115; *Rutherford v Owens-Illinois
Inc* 119
Canada: loss of chances 142; reversal of
the burden of proof 115
cancer, asbestos 104; see also
mesothelioma
capital punishment 41
causal expansion, loss of chance 137–141
causal uncertainty 103; asbestos 103–
105; but for test 112–113; damages

for loss of chance 117–119; *Fairchild
v Glenhaven Funeral Services* 103,
106–108, 120–123, 126; *Gregg v
Scott* 123; liability for contribution
to risk 119–120; mitigating cost on
employers and insurers 123–125;
reversal of the burden of proof 114–
117; uncertain alternative causation
113–114; *Wilsher v Essex Area Health
Authority* 122
cessation of brain functions 83–84
ceterarum rerum 268, 270–271
"chance, of value 147–149
Chaplin v Hicks 29–130
Chifflet, Claude 262–264
childbed deaths 55
Chinese Tort Liability Law of 2010 115
Cicero 270–271
civil law jurisdictions: confusion of
money 231–232; dissipations by fund-
holder 232; mixed funds 232; tracing
232–234; unmixing intangible assets
229–231
Clarke v Maltby 166
Clayton's case 212–214, 217–218
Code Civil 64, 188, 192, 198; *absence*
provisions 51–52
Code of Deontology 146
Codex Theresianus 196
coma, irreversible 83
commercial fairness 206
common calamity 49–50, 53, 71
common danger 48; *commorientes* 302–303
common purpose liability 252–257
commorientes 2, 17, 44, 280–281, 284–
285, 288–290, 292, 300, 302–303,
310, 313–314; comparable questions
58–59; factual scenarios 47–54;
historical overview of 45–47; litigation
45–46; medical evidence 311; ordinary
burden of proof 59–64; presumed
sequences 67–70; presumptive bases
64–70; rules 8; science and 310; sharing
and reallocating 70–72; survivorship
periods 296; uncertainty 54–58
comparative method 16–17
compensable loss 170
compensation 153–154; full
compensation 170; lump-sum awards
171–172
Compensation Act 2006 109–110
complexity, interrogative toolkit
318–319
compromise 297–299, 318
concealment of birth 36–37

confusio 230
confusion of money, unmixing intangible assets 231–232
consensual mixtures 206, 209–212, 223–224; and intentions 221–223
consent 242
consignation 231
Constantinaeus, Jacobus 264
Constitutio Criminalis Carolina 35
constructive liability 249
consumer contracts 193
consumer protection rules 185, 202; *see also* ad hominem rules of construction
continuing acts 242
contra creditorem 196
contra proferentem rule 187–190, 192–194, 196–197, 200–203, 281, 284, 300, 303, 307, 311
contra venditorem rule 200
contracts 295; ad hominem rules of construction *see* ad hominem rules of construction; ambiguous contracts 199; kinds of uncertainty 191–194; loss of chances 129
contractual interpretation 313; intractable uncertainty 194–195; kinds of contracts 191–194; kinds of uncertainty 187–191
convicted felons, pregnancy 30, 32
Cook v Cook 159–160
Couch, Edward 60
Couch, James 60–61
counterfactual uncertainty 157
Courts Act 2003 160
Criminal Evidence Act 1898 247
Criminal Justice Act 1967 248
criminal law 240
Criminal Law Act 1826 255
Criminal Law Act 1967 254
Criminal Procedure Act 1848 255
Croke v Wiseman 164, 168
Cujas, Jacques 262
culpability 206, 209
cumulative causation 112
cycle of life 83
Cyrillus, J.P. 265

Damages (Variation of Periodical Payments) Order 2005 160
damages: compromise 295, 299; *Fairchild v Glenhaven Funeral Services* 140; negligence 136; *see also* loss of earnings
damages for loss of chance 117–119, 133–137
damni formula 262
damnum 263, 270
Davies v Taylor 134
de iniuriis aestimandis 263
de servo corrupto 263
de ventre inspiciendo procedure 32
death 74–75, 96, 282, 289–290, 301, 302; *Airedale NHS Trust v Bland* 90–91; *Barts Health NHS Trust v Dance* 91–92, 97; baseline in English law 87–91; *Bradshaw v Toulmin* 70; *Broughton v Randall* 55–56; cessation of brain functions 83–84; determining 290–291, 306–307; drowning 55; extra-legal frameworks 79–81; framing legal resolutions 85–87; *General Stanwix's Case* 62; importance for law 76–78; of infants 35–36; instantaneous death 56–57; justifying law's choices 97–99; legal definitions 92–94; *Manchester University NHS Foundation Trust v Namiq* 94–95; *Mason v Mason* 62; multiple deaths in one disaster 47–49; neurological turn 82–85; *Ommaney v Stilwell* 60; plurality and mitigation in England 95–97; plurality of legal response 81–82; presumption of 51; *Re: A (A Child)* 91–92, 95–96; *Re A* 89, 97; *Re Bate* 61; *Re Beure* 61; *Re Potter* 88; *In re Pringle* 57; role of medical progress 78–79; sequence 44; short-lasting survivors 53–54; *Sillick v Booth* 68; simultaneous death 56–57, 61; somatic death 75–76; uncertainty 54–58; *Wing v Angrave* 62; *see also* brain death; *commorientes*
death by neurological criteria (DNC) 88
debts: fraudulent release of 272; property damage 267
decision-making rules 15–16
Declaration of the Rights of Man 1789 143
declaration of trust 222–223
deeming provisions 249–250, 257; common purpose liability 252–257; quasi-criminal 250–252
delay decision-making 285, 304–305
delegation of choice of criteria to experts, life 32–35
Diffuse Mesothelioma Payment Scheme (DMPS) 111

Digest of Justinian: Digest 34.5 259–260; Justinianic compilations 13
disappearances 51
DMPS *see* Diffuse Mesothelioma Payment Scheme
DNC *see* death by neurological criteria
dolus 272
double-hanging 55
doubt, avoiding 41
drowning 55
duty of care 131, 149–151

earning capacity 158, 176
ECC Directive on Unfair Contract Terms 1993 193, 202
economic loss, loss of chances 131–132
Edict Against the Concealment of Pregnancy 1556 (France) 35
entrenchment 306–308
environmental exposure 125
epidemiological evidence 310
epistemic uncertainty 280
Ernst, Wolfgang 269
estimation of damages, Germany 174
evidential rules 11–13
evidential uncertainty 280
evil intent 245
ex post uncertainty 8–9
exceptio doli 272
Executors Act 1830 71
external knowledge systems 310–312
extra-legal frameworks, death 79–81

fact-finders 248, 309
fact-finding/expertise, life 31–32
facts 1, 239n1; and law 301–304
factual accuracy 287, 289–291, 318
factual causation 115, 128, 142, 146–147, 151
factual plausibility 287–288
factual presumptions 244
factual puritanism 289
factual truth 291
factual uncertainty 5–6, 240, 243, 288, 304
fair compensation 167
Fairchild v Glenhaven Funeral Services 103, 106–108, 111, 119–121, 126; compensation 124; exceptions 137–141; field of application 121–123
fault 143, 245, 247, 300, 318
favor debitoris 196
Festellungsklage 9

fictions 241–242; responding to uncertainty 13–15
fiduciaries 224
fiduciary acts 207, 213–215; *see also* unmixing intangible assets
fiduciary principle 225
fiduciary relationships 224, 225
FIFO *see* first-in, first-out basis
Financial Services Compensation Scheme 124
first-in, first-out basis (FIFO) 212–213, 292; innocent accidental mixtures 217–221
flexible payments of damages 159–160
flexible periodic payments: Austria 174; awarding damages 171; Germany 174
foetus/infant 26–27; concealment of birth 36–37; death of 35–36; determining life 290; legitimacy 37–40; *pater est* presumption 40; pre-birth killing 29; succession 28; uncertainty problem 27–28; viability 34–35; *see also* abortion
Foskett v McKeown 216
France: ad hominem rules of construction 197; *Code Civil* 192, 198; *commorientes* 47, 49–50; contracts 196; disappearances 51–52; Edict Against the Concealment of Pregnancy 1556 35; loss of chances 142–145; presumed sequences, death 67–70; Public Health Code 146
free proof 11–12
Freher, Marquard 263–264
freie Beweiswürdigung 11–12
full compensation 170
fund-holders, dissipations by 232

Gaius 270–271
Gallus, C. Aquilius 259, 266, 272
general malice 245
General Stanwix's Case 62
German ZPO 174
Germany: ad hominem rules of construction 196; annuities 171–172; assessment of losses 174–178; burden of proof 62–63, 116; common calamity 53; *commorientes* 47–48, 64; *contra proferentem* rule 192–193; loss of earnings 169–178; simultaneous-death rule 54; social security system 170
Gissing v Gissing 220

good faith 173
good-enough solution 291
Gravina, Gian Vincento 266
Gregg v Scott 117–118, 123, 132, 135–136, 138, 141, 148

Hales v Petit 58
Harvard Criteria, death 83
heirs, claim for earnings 178
Heneghan v Manchester Dry Docks 121–122
Hickman v Peacey 62
homicide, pre-birth killing 29; *see also* abortion
honesty, presumption of 215, 224
Hotson v East Berkshire Health Authority 117–118, 135, 138
human reproduction 26–27
Human Tissue Act 2004 95
Hunter v Moss 222, 224
hydrostatic test 35

IEG v Zurich see International Energy Group v Zurich Insurance
ILGS *see* index-linked government stocks
illegitimacy 26–27
impotence 39
in criminalibus sufficit generalis militia intentionis cum facto paris gradus 245
incidence of uncertainty 10, 281–283
index-linked government stocks (ILGS) 165
Indian Penal Code 1860 37
inertia 306–308
infanticide 37, 303
infants: concealment of birth 36–37; death of 35–36; *see also* foetus/infant
Inheritance Tax Act 1984 67
injury caused by animals 264
instantaneous death 56–57
intangible assets 207–208; *see also* unmixing intangible assets
intention 206–207, 209, 248; consensual mixtures 221–223; presumed intentions 220, 225; unmixing intangible assets 223–224, 227–229
International Energy Group v Zurich Insurance 126, 138, 140
interpretation questions 6; *see also* ad hominem rules of construction
interrogative toolkit 315–319
intime conviction 11–12
intra vires 225

intractable uncertainty 1, 186, 301; contractual interpretation 187–191, 194–195; intractable uncertainty problem 2–3; objective uncertainty 6–8
intractable uncertainty problem 2–3
investment, lump-sum awards 165
Iqbal v Whipps Cross University Hospital NHS Trust 169
Ireland, burden of proof 61–62
Italy: *contra proferentem* rule 203; mixed funds 231
ius commune 196, 284

joint bank accounts 210, 221–222
Judicature Acts 1873–1875 251
jury equity/jury nullification 243
jury trials 12
justifications 287–288; ad hominem rules of construction 198–204

Kitchen v Royal Air Force 130
knowledge: of the law 313–314; new knowledge 309; other bodies of knowledge 318; and science 308–315

Laferriere v Lawson 142, 148n89
land, line of descent 29–30
Langford v Hebran 162, 166
larceny 243
law: and facts 301–304; knowledge of 313–314
Law Reform (Succession) Act 1995 52
Lee v Dangar 251
legal actors 240, 257
legal change 257, 308
legal fiction 241–242
legal reasoning 243
legal uncertainty 239, 257–258, 307
legis actio 269
legitimacy of foetus/infant 26–27, 29; *pater est* presumption 40
lex Aquilia 261–262, 264–272
lex Publilia 271
lex satura 269
liability 124–125; Aquilian liability 265; common purpose liability 252–257; constructive liability 249; for contribution to risk 119–120; loss of chances 139; of master of slaves 264; strict liability offences 249
Liber sextus 199

life 26–29, 282, 289, 302; abortion 34;
    assessment criteria 32–35; avoiding
    occurrence of doubt 41; delegation
    of choice of criteria to experts 32–35;
    fact-finding/expertise 31–32; live birth
    33; presumptions 35–41; reproductive
    technology 42; uncertainty problem
    27–28
line of descent, land 29–30
lis crescens 269
litigation, *commorientes* 45–46
live birth 29, 33; *see also* birth; life
longevity of rules 307
loss of chance 128–129, 133–135, 145–
    147, 304; adverse effect on personal
    injury claimants 141; in Belgium
    142–144; 'chance' as something of
    value 147–149; duty of care 149–151;
    economic loss 131–132; *Fairchild v
    Glenhaven Funeral Services* 137–141;
    in France 142–145; historical overview
    of 129–132; medical negligence
    actions 135–137
loss of earnings 153–154, 156–158,
    167; assessment of losses 180–182;
    Austria 169–178; England 158–169;
    Germany 169–178; historical overview
    of 154–156; rules for awards 179–180
lost years, claim for earnings 178
Lowe v Guise 181
lump-sum awards 157, 179; Germany
    171–173; investment of 165; and
    rigidity 172–173
lung-float test 35, 310

Mallet v McMonagle 134, 162, 168, 180
*Manchester University NHS Foundation
    Trust v Namiq* 94–95
manus injectio 269
Mason v Mason 62
mathematical precision, in awarding
    damages 175–177
McGhee v National Coal Board 121
medical experts 31–33
medical negligence 119; loss of chance
    135–137
medical progress, role in determining
    death 78–79
medical science 301, 309
membrum ruptum 263
mens rea 242, 244–246, 249
mesothelioma 104–105, 107–108, 137,
    280, 282; *Barker v Corus* 107–108;

causation 307; Mesothelioma Act
    2014 111–112
misdemeanours 252–253, 255
missing persons 51
mixed bank accounts 218
mixed funds 279; dissipations by the
    fund holder 232; priority claims
    231–232; *see also* unmixing intangible
    assets
mixed substitutions 208–209
mixtures: innocent accidental mixtures
    209–221; first-in, first-out basis
    (FIFO) 217–221; innocent mixing
    206
moral reasoning 248
*Mousell Bros v London & North Western
    Railway* 251
multiple deaths in one disaster 47–49
murder 247, 252; death of infants 37
mutability 306–308

National Institute for the Deaf (NID)
    218–219
natural law 191
natural loss 177
NCB v Gamble 253
negligence 130–131; damages 136; duty
    of care 149–151; medical negligence
    135–137
neurological turn, death 82–85
non liquet 4, 7, 16, 297
non-consensual sexual offences 243–244
Noodt, Gerard 266
normative (legal) uncertainty *see* legal
    uncertainty
normative authority of law 301
normative loss 177

objective factual uncertainty 6–8
oblique intention 248
Ommaney v Stilwell 60, 312
organ transplantation 78–79, 84, 89, 97,
    305–306
os fractum 263
overlapping causation 112–113

Palliser v Fate (In Liquidation) 133
pari passu approach 219, 226–227
partial proofs 13
parties, avoidance 299–301
pater est presumption 40
paternity 25–26, 28–29, 40–41, 282,
    286, 308

path-dependence casuistic 307
patrimonies, separation of 230–231
pauper settlement cases 38
Pearks, Gunston & Tee v Ward 251
peerage, succession 38–39
Pennell v Deffell 213–214
periodical payment order (PPO) 161
periodical payments of damages 159–160
Perry v Raley's Solicitors 132
personal injury 282; *see also* loss of
    earnings
Pickett v British Rail Engineering 168
Pighius, Stephanus Vindius 266
Pliny the Elder 262
plurality of legal response in death 81–82
policy concerns and goods 291–294
policy imperatives 318
Poor Law, Elizabethan 36
PPO *see* periodical payment order
pre-birth killing 29
precautionary principle 9
predictive uncertainty 156
pre-empted causation 112
pregnancy 26–27, 308; of convicted
    felons 30, 32; *de ventre inspiciendo*
    procedure 32; fact-finding/expertise 31
preponderance of probabilities *see*
    balance of probabilities
presumed intentions 220, 225
presumed sequences, *commorientes*
    67–70
presumption of death 51, 60
presumption of honesty 215, 224
presumptions 243–249, 257, 285;
    commorientes 64–70; factual
    presumptions 244; life 35–41;
    responding to uncertainty 13–15
Primeau v Granfield 216
Pringle, In re 57
Pringsheim, Fritz 268
priority claims into mixed funds
    231–232
probabilistic assessment 175
procedural limits, avoiding 253
proferens 192, 196–197
proof of causation 113–114
proof of sequence 51
proof, standards of 11–12
property: damage 268, debts 267;
    mixing 210; rights, traceable assets
    233
proportional liability 120
provisional damage awards 160

Prussia, *Allgemeines Landrecht* (ALR)
    65, 188, 191
pseudo-science 310
Public Health Act 1875 251
publicity, interrogative toolkit 319

quasi-criminal 250–252

R v Appleby 254
R v Pridmore 254
R v Steane 247
R3RUE *see Restatement (Third) of
    Restitution and Unjust Enrichment*
Rapson v Cubitt 155–156
rateable approach 218
Re A 89, 97
Re: A (A Child) 95–96
Re Bate 61
Re Beare 61
Re Bishop 221
Re Diplock 216–219, 221, 224, 227,
    229
Re Hallett's Estate 214–217, 224
Re Oatway 216, 224
Re Phéne's Trusts 50
Re Potter 88
Re Sutherland 216
*Re Walter J Schmidt & Co., Ex parte
    Feuerbach* 220
regulatory solutions 8–9
Reichsgericht 193, 200, 202
reproductive technology 42
responding to uncertainty: decision-
    making rules 15–16; evidential rules
    11–13; presumptions and fictions
    13–15
Restatement (Second) of Torts 115
*Restatement (Third) of Restitution
    and Unjust Enrichment* (R3RUE)
    226–229
Restatement (Third) of Torts 115
resuscitation 83
reversal of the burden of proof, causal
    uncertainty 114–117
right of separation 230
right to trace 230
rolling charge distribution method 219
Roman law 11, 18, 27, 31, 113, 186–
    187, 241, 260; ad hominem rules of
    construction 196, 199; contracts 191;
    presumed sequences, death 67–70; *see
    also lex Aquila*

Rothwell v Chemical & Insulating Co.
  136, 147
Royal Sailors' Orphan Girls' School and
  Home 219
Rutherford v Owens-Illinois Inc 119

Sale of Food and Drugs Act 1875 251
'same event' *see* common calamity
Satterthwaite v Powell 67
Saxon BGB (1863) 188, 196
science, and knowledge 308–315
scientific inconclusiveness 311
scientific uncertainty 25, 279
self-resolving uncertainty problems
  304–306, 318
Senior Courts Act 1981 160
sequester 231
servi corruptio 263–264
Sexual Offences Act 2003 243–244, 250
sexual offences, non-consensual 243–244
Shalson v Russo 216
sharing, *Bradshaw v Toulmin* 70
Sherras v De Rutzen 251
Sienkiewicz v Greif 110–111, 126
Sillick v Booth 68
simultaneity 56–57; presumptions of
  66–67
simultaneous death 56–57, 61
simultaneous-death rule, Germany 54
Sinclair v Brougham 216
slaves 262–265
Smith v Manchester Corporation 167,
  176, 181–182
social security system, Germany 170
somatic death 75–76
Spain: dissipations by fund-holder 232;
  mixed funds 231–232; tracing 233
split-the-difference solutions 297
Spring v Guardian Assurance 131
stability of rules 308
standard form contracts 200–201
standards of commercial practice 209
standards of proof 11–12
start of life, presumptions 35–41;
  see also life
stipulatio 272
stolen property 271
strict liability offences 249
subordination 216, 223–224
Succession (Scotland) Act 2016 52
succession 28; peerages 38–39
survivorship: short-lasting survivors
  53–54; survivorship periods 296
Sweet v Parsley 252

Sydney Declaration 84

Tabet v Gett 142
technology 282
tiebreaker rules 187–188, 190–191
timeliness 317–318
Totham v King's College Hospital 169
tracing fictions 228
transferred malice 245
Trigger Litigation 140
trust, declaration of 222–223
Trustee Act 1925 71
truth, weight of accurate truth 288–291
turbatio sanguinis 40, 286
Turner v Jacob 216
Twelve Tables 271
'two-hunter' causal scenario 12–13

UDDA *see* Uniform Determination of
  Death Act
ultra vires 225
uncertainty problem 278–281; incidence
  of uncertainty 281–283; legal setting
  283–284
Unfair Contract Terms Act 1977 201
Uniform Determination of Death Act
  (UDDA) 81, 84, 86–87; unmixing
  intangible assets 226–234
Uniform Simultaneous Deaths Act
  (USDA) 1993 52, 81
United States: *Restatement (Second)*
  of Torts 115; *Restatement (Third) of*
  Torts 115; Uniform Simultaneous
  Deaths Act (USDA) 1993 52, 81
unmixing intangible assets 206–212; civil
  law jurisdictions 229–231; *Clayton's*
  case 212–214; consensual mixtures
  221–223; dissipations by fund-holder
  232; historical overview of 207–208;
  innocent and wrongful mixtures
  212–221; overarching principles of
  223–226; *Pennell v Deffell* 214; *Re*
  Hallett's Estate 214–215; rules for
  tracing through commingled funds
  228; tracing 232–234
usus modernus 187

VerschG 51, 53
viability of newborns 28, 34–35

wait and see 305, 308
War Stock 219
Warner v MPC 252
Wells v Wells 164

Westbrook, Raymond 268–269
White v Shortall 222, 225
Willson v Ministry of Defence 160
Wilsher v Essex Area Health Authority 122
Wing v Angrave 50, 62
winner-takes-all 297
women: death of infants 35–36; fact-finding/expertise 31; sexual behaviour 36; who married quickly then had a child 40–41
Woolmington v DPP 247
Wright v Sarmuda 67
wrongful mixing 206, 209–221

Zasius, Ulrich 261–262, 266

www.ingramcontent.com/pod-product-compliance
Ingram Content Group UK Ltd.
Pitfield, Milton Keynes, MK11 3LW, UK
UKHW020001211224
452763UK00002B/21